BECKETT'S POLITICAL IM

Beckett's Political Imagination charts unexplored territory: it investigates how Beckett's bilingual texts reimagine political history, and documents the conflicts and controversies through which Beckett's political consciousness and affirmations were mediated. The book offers a startling account of Beckett's work, tracing the many political causes that framed his writing, commitments, collaborations and friendships, from the Scottsboro Boys to the Black Panthers, from Irish communism to Spanish republicanism to Algerian nationalism, and from campaigns against Irish and British censorship to anti-apartheid and international human rights movements. Emilie Morin reveals a very different writer, whose career and work were shaped by a unique exposure to international politics, an unconventional perspective on political action and secretive political engagements. The book will benefit students, researchers and readers who want to think about literary history in different ways and are interested in Beckett's enduring appeal and influence.

EMILIE MORIN is Senior Lecturer in the Department of English and Related Literature at the University of York. She works on modern literature, theatre history and forms of political writing. She has published widely on the work of Samuel Beckett, including a monograph entitled *Samuel Beckett and the Problem of Irishness* (2009), and has co-edited *Theatre and Ghosts: Materiality, Performance and Modernity* (2014) and *Theatre and Human Rights after 1945: Things Unspeakable* (2015).

BECKETT'S POLITICAL IMAGINATION

EMILIE MORIN

University of York

CAMBRIDGE
UNIVERSITY PRESS

University Printing House, Cambridge CB2 8BS, United Kingdom

One Liberty Plaza, 20th Floor, New York, NY 10006, USA

477 Williamstown Road, Port Melbourne, VIC 3207, Australia

314–321, 3rd Floor, Plot 3, Splendor Forum, Jasola District Centre, New Delhi – 110025, India

79 Anson Road, #06–04/06, Singapore 079906

Cambridge University Press is part of the University of Cambridge.

It furthers the University's mission by disseminating knowledge in the pursuit of education, learning and research at the highest international levels of excellence.

www.cambridge.org
Information on this title: www.cambridge.org/9781108417990
DOI: 10.1017/9781108284011

First published 2017
First paperback edition 2018

Printed and bound in Great Britain by Clays Ltd, Elcograf S.p.A.

A catalogue record for this publication is available from the British Library.

Library of Congress Cataloging-in-Publication data
Names: Morin, Emilie, 1978– author.
Title: Beckett's political imagination / Emilie Morin.
Description: New York : Cambridge University Press, 2017. | Includes bibliographical references and index.
Identifiers: LCCN 2017020175 | ISBN 9781108417990 (hardback)
Subjects: LCSH: Beckett, Samuel, 1906–1989 – Knowledge – Politics. | Beckett, Samuel, 1906–1989 – Criticism and interpretation. | BISAC: LITERARY CRITICISM / European / English, Irish, Scottish, Welsh.
Classification: LCC PR6003.E282 Z78163 2017 | DDC 823/.912–dc23 LC record available at https://lccn.loc.gov/2017020175

ISBN 978-1-108-41799-0 Hardback
ISBN 978-1-108-40620-8 Paperback

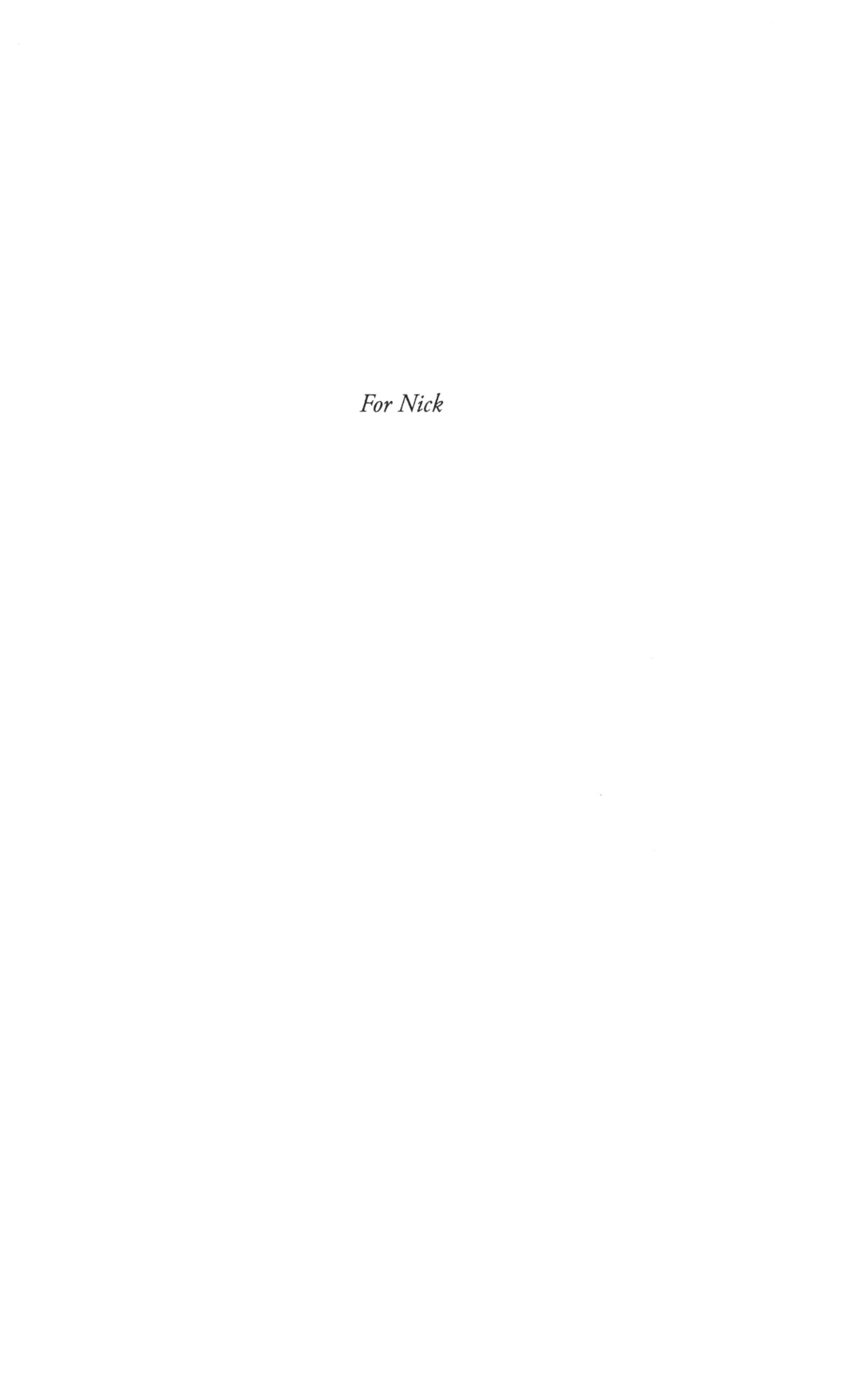

For Nick

Contents

Acknowledgements

As I write these lines, a decade has elapsed since I began researching a book on Beckett and politics. The research support offered by the Department of English and Related Literature at the University of York enabled me to write the actual monograph, and the book-in-progress was nurtured by years of conversations with friends, students and colleagues. Thanks are due to Derek Attridge and Hugh Haughton, for their support and generosity; to Michelle Kelly, for her input and responses to chapter drafts; to Lauren Arrington, Aisling Carlin, Victoria Coulson, David Dwan, Jason Edwards, Mary Fairclough, Helen Fulton, Kevin Killeen, Catherine Laws, Mary Luckhurst, Emma Major, Michael McAteer, Jon Mee, Linne Mooney, Bryan Radley, Lawrence Rainey, Reena Sastri, Freya Sierhuis, Helen Smith, Elizabeth Tyler, Claire Westall and Michael White, for research conversations about major and minor book matters; to Boriana Alexandrova, for enriching discussions and for the index; and to Megan Girdwood, Timothy Lawrence, Julia Mason, Jay James May, Alexander Price and Nick Wolterman, for stimulating dialogues. My appreciative thanks to Marthe Gautier and Tommy Murtagh, for kindly agreeing to speak to me about Samuel and Suzanne Beckett; to David Barnett, Emmanuel Blanchard, Raphaëlle Branche, Salem Chaker, Monique Courty-Garnier, Marie Cosnay, Masin Ferkal, Jim House, Daniel Lee and Renata Morresi, for their readiness to reply to research queries and their generosity; to Mark Nixon, for judicious advice and archival expertise; to Deirdre Bair, Maurice Harmon, James Knowlson and John Pilling, for helpful responses to Beckett-related questions; to Jean-Michel Rabaté and Seán Kennedy, for their close reading of the manuscript as external peer-reviewers; and to Elizabeth Barry, Peter Boxall, Alan Warren Friedman, Julian Garforth, Jonathan Heron, Patrick Lonergan, Ulrika Maude, Rónán McDonald, James McNaughton and the late Rosemary Pountney, for thought-provoking discussions about Beckett. Many thanks also to Amélie and Olivier Cahn, Dominique and Bernadette

Coco, Paul Cooney, Lisa Foran and Nilantha McPartland, Orlaith Fitzpatrick, Willow Coyle and Helen McClements, for their hospitality. It has been a pleasure to work with Ray Ryan at Cambridge University Press, and I thank him for his support and extraordinary dedication. I began assembling materials for this book after my doctorate at Queen's University Belfast; the research ethos of friends and mentors in the School of English at Queen's and at University College Dublin has remained a source of inspiration. Ultimately, none of this would have been possible without the support of my parents and siblings, Anne, Jean, Jean-Baptiste and Loïse, and the support of the Melia family. I also owe more than I can express to Nicholas Melia, for years of intellectual nourishment, responses to chapter drafts and so much more. This book is dedicated to him, with all my gratitude for making so much else possible.

The research for this book was conducted in many archives and research libraries including the BBC Written Archives, Caversham; the Beckett International Foundation, University of Reading; the British Library; the Harry Ransom Humanities Research Center, University of Texas at Austin; Oxford's Taylor Institution Library; Trinity College Dublin; the National Library of Ireland; the Bibliothèque Polonaise, Paris; the Bibliothèque Sainte-Geneviève, Paris; and the Institut Mémoires de l'Edition Contemporaine, Caen, where I was able to consult the Beckett collection by kind permission of Edward Beckett and Irène Lindon. Thanks are also due to the Andrew W. Mellon Foundation, for the fellowship that enabled me to work on Ransom Center collections in 2012; to Elizabeth L. Garver at the Ransom Center, for supplying the cover image; to Lisa Eveson, Olivia Else, Margaret Dillon, Lisa Hopwood, Elaine Hickes and Keith Webster at the University of York library; Justine Sundaram at the Burns Library, Boston College; Jane Maxwell at Trinity College Dublin; Monica Thapar and Louise North at the BBC Written Archives; and York's F. R. Leavis Fund, for covering research and indexing costs.

An early version of the subsection entitled 'Inquests and Investigations' in Chapter 3 was published as 'Beckett's Inquests: *Malone Dies* and the Mysteries of the State', in *Revisiting Molloy, Malone meurt/Malone Dies and L'Innommable/The Unnamable*, ed. David Tucker, Mark Nixon and Dirk Van Hulle, spec. issue, *Samuel Beckett Today/Aujourd'hui* 26 (2014): 137–50.

I thank the Dedalus Press, acting for the Devlin Estate, for kind permission to cite from Denis Devlin's unpublished correspondence, held at the Ransom Center; Indiana University Press, for allowing me to cite from Octavio Paz's *Anthology of Mexican Poetry*, translated by Samuel Beckett (Indiana University Press, 1958); Fondo de Cultura Económica, for allowing me to cite from the poems of Alfonso Reyes; Association Guy Lévis Mano, for permission to cite from Guy Lévis Mano's translations in Octavio Paz's *Anthologie de la poésie mexicaine* (© Association GLM).

Notes and Abbreviations

Unless otherwise indicated in the footnotes, all translations from non-English sources are by the author.

Samuel Beckett is designated as SB in the footnotes.

BR/RB:	*Beckett Remembering/Remembering Beckett*, ed. James and Elizabeth Knowlson (New York: Arcade Publishing, 2006)
CDW:	Samuel Beckett, *The Complete Dramatic Works* [1986] (London: Faber, 2006)
Chronology:	John Pilling, *A Samuel Beckett Chronology* (Basingstoke: Palgrave Macmillan, 2006)
DF:	James Knowlson, *Damned to Fame: The Life of Samuel Beckett* (London: Bloomsbury, 1996)
DFMW:	Samuel Beckett, *Dream of Fair to Middling Women*, ed. Eoin O'Brien and Edith Fournier (London: Calder, 1992)
D:	Samuel Beckett, *Disjecta: Miscellaneous Writings and a Dramatic Fragment*, ed. Ruby Cohn (London: Calder, 1983)
IT:	*Irish Times*
JoBS:	*Journal of Beckett Studies*
JORF:	*Journal officiel de la République française*
LM:	Anthony Cronin, *Samuel Beckett: The Last Modernist* [1996] (London: Flamingo, 1997)
LSB1:	*The Letters of Samuel Beckett, vol. 1: 1929–1940*, ed. Martha Dow Fehsenfeld and Lois More Overbeck (Cambridge: Cambridge University Press, 2009)
LSB2:	*The Letters of Samuel Beckett, vol. 2: 1941–1956*, ed. George Craig, Martha Dow Fehsenfeld, Dan Gunn and Lois More Overbeck (Cambridge: Cambridge University Press, 2011)

LSB3: *The Letters of Samuel Beckett, vol. 3: 1957–1965*, ed. George Craig, Martha Dow Fehsenfeld, Dan Gunn and Lois More Overbeck (Cambridge: Cambridge University Press, 2014)

LSB4: *The Letters of Samuel Beckett, vol. 4: 1966–1989*, ed. George Craig, Martha Dow Fehsenfeld, Dan Gunn and Lois More Overbeck (Cambridge: Cambridge University Press, 2016)

MPTK: Samuel Beckett, *More Pricks than Kicks* [1934] (London: Calder, 1993)

NABS: *No Author Better Served: The Correspondence of Samuel Beckett and Alan Schneider*, ed. Maurice Harmon (Cambridge, MA: Harvard University Press, 1998)

NYT: *New York Times*

SB: Deirdre Bair, *Samuel Beckett: A Biography* (London: Jonathan Cape, 1978)

SBTA: *Samuel Beckett Today/Aujourd'hui*

Trilogy: Samuel Beckett, *Molloy, Malone Dies, The Unnamable* [1959] (London: Calder, 1994)

Introduction

There is, seemingly, little to say about Beckett's politics. Many interviews and memoirs portray a writer peculiarly unqualified for political activity, ill-at-ease with mundane realities and more comfortable with philosophical abstraction. Some have celebrated his apparent detachment from the political world: notably, on the occasion of Beckett's seventieth birthday, Emil Cioran paid tribute to a figure living 'parallel to time', gifted with the ability of making others 'understand history as a dimension man could have dispensed with'.[1]

Such established consensus, however, flies in the face of abundant evidence to the contrary. Beckett's texts, with their numerous portrayals of violence, torture, dispossession, internment and subjugation, harbour a real political immediacy, while his notebooks, manuscripts and correspondence reveal a fine and astute observer of political symbols, attuned to the long history of political myths in the Irish Free State, Nazi Germany and France in the aftermath of the Second World War and during the Algerian War of Independence. The literary cultures in which he worked were intensely politicised, and there is little in his translations, his collaborations, the publishing and dissemination of his texts that does not carry a political charge. For the editors who represented his professional position and interests – Jérôme Lindon, Barney Rosset and John Calder – publishing came with distinctive responsibilities to defend civil liberties and freedom of expression. Their catalogues bring Beckett's texts into proximity with important turning points in political thought: the Editions de Minuit situate Beckett in the same cultural and material spheres as Leon Trotsky, Herbert Marcuse, Nelson Mandela, Henri Lefebvre or Gilles Deleuze, while Grove Press boasts works by Roger Casement, Franz Fanon, Malcolm X and Che Guevara alongside Beckett's slim volumes.

[1] Emil Cioran, 'Quelques rencontres', in *L'Herne: Samuel Beckett*, ed. Tom Bishop and Raymond Federman (Paris: L'Herne, 1976), 46.

Naturally, there are many ways of apprehending the political currency of Beckett's texts within the national and global contexts in which they were written, read and performed. In the past decade, numerous studies have explored the intricacy and multiplicity of Beckett's historical experiences, emphasising the enduring capacity of the writing to speak to circumstances marked by war, suffering and oppression. Yet the obstacles to understanding the work's political tenor have often seemed insurmountable: to discuss Beckett's relation to politics is to confront, all too often, a series of impediments to political reflection and political action. Some assumptions – that Beckett did not give interviews, had little political sentiment, was not interested in current affairs and did not sign petitions – have left a tenacious legacy, and have been compounded by a long-standing tendency to interpret the texts as expressions of a tortured psyche.

The purpose of this book is neither to assess the grounds upon which Beckett may be considered a political writer, nor to reflect on the politics of non-naturalistic forms. Beckett, who worked in different languages, cultural industries and artistic media at the same time, tends to test many of the pieties surrounding available categories of political writing – categories which are historically and culturally specific to such a degree that they often obfuscate the tensions that have commonly arisen between political activity and creative work, even for writers commonly considered as politically engaged and revolutionary. Rather, my aim is to reinscribe Beckett and his work into their political milieux. This task involves documenting the political coordinates of Beckett's bilingual *oeuvre*, and its tangential reimagining of the political histories of Ireland, France and Europe through satire, displacement, elision, substitution and imaginative appropriation. To reinscribe Beckett's career into its political milieu is also to negotiate the relation between the domain of political activity and a sphere of citizenship which, in Beckett's case, remains a mutating concept involving the inherited, the elected and the imagined. The conjunctions and disjunctions between Beckett's literary and political work are equally important, and this book pays heed to the tensions that frequently developed between Beckett's work as essayist, translator and public figure and the demands of writing, and foregrounds his shifting positions as observer and participant in diverse forms of political activism developing in France, Great Britain and Europe after the interwar years. Beckett was far more than a sardonic observer of political folly; he endorsed numerous international petitions in which the defence of freedom of speech for artists, publishers and intellectuals acted as a response to specific political urgencies, more than a simple matter of liberal principle. His contributions to petitions are scrutinised and contextualised here for the first time. Three different periods are brought together: the 1930s, during which Beckett's identities as writer, translator and critic were formed; the great artistic turning point known as the 'siege in the room' between 1946 and 1948,[2] which came with different political demands and urgencies; and the period between 1958 and 1962, marked by other kinds of political activism and a new reflection on literary and dramatic forms.

Chapter 1, 'False Starts: The "Material of Experience" and the Writing of History', considers Beckett's frustrated efforts as a historical writer and political essayist, tracing his shifting perspective on the fortunes of the Irish Left and his responses to the debates that shaped the accession of Fianna Fáil to power, the rise of the Blueshirts and the dynamics of anti-communist sentiment in the Irish Free State during the 1930s. During periods of time spent in Dublin, London, Paris and Germany, Beckett wrote politically inflected parodies inspired from eighteenth-century traditions of life writing and pamphleteering, making various attempts to integrate historical subject matter into his work, albeit with mixed results: some of these texts were abandoned or remained unpublished for decades, in keeping with his wishes. This chapter investigates the distinctive ways in which this body of work ventriloquises competing idioms in Irish political culture, interrogating the narratives of political exclusion and disaffection that are commonly deployed in discussions of Beckett's early writing. The cultures through which his political education was mediated at Trinity College Dublin and the Ecole Normale Supérieure in Paris, his friendships and literary partnerships, and his plans to travel to Moscow and experiences in Nazi Germany are central to my discussion.

Chapter 2, 'Another War Entirely: Internationalist Politics and the Labour of Translation', explores the ways in which Beckett's political interests impacted on his translation practices, showing that his numerous translations of texts by other writers offer a fruitful terrain for charting his responses to broader mutations within anti-colonial politics and the internationalist Left. The peculiarities of Beckett's practice as 'jobbing' translator are known through the work of Sinéad Mooney, who has demonstrated that these activities are inseparable from the thematic preoccupations and the form of his self-translated texts.[3] My chapter considers how the work of translation, for Beckett, was inscribed in a wider reflection on the history of empire, colonialism, social injustice and segregation, conducted not

[2] On the origin of 'siege in the room', see *SB*, 346, 687 n1.

[3] Sinéad Mooney, *A Tongue Not Mine: Beckett and Translation* (Oxford: Oxford University Press, 2011), 27–34, 119–47.

only by others but also by himself as translator. Of particular importance are his contributions to *Negro: Anthology Made by Nancy Cunard, 1931–1933* (1934), an endeavour that owed much to anti-segregationist campaigns and international organisations such as the League Against Imperialism and Colonial Oppression, and Octavio Paz's *Anthology of Mexican Poetry* (1958), a work commissioned by UNESCO and indexed to rising Cold War tensions. My discussion addresses the circumstances in which these anthologies were compiled and published, the dialogues that shaped Beckett's engagement with their internationalist remit, and his shifting relation to the politicised literary cultures of Surrealism.

The Second World War did not instigate Beckett's political consciousness: this was forged through other means, notably translation. However, the war's aftermath granted him a new political identity, shaped by his connections to the new literature of the French Resistance. The subsequent chapters turn to Beckett's internationalist politics after 1945, charting the evolution of his political thinking through his struggles with historical writing and testimony. Chapter 3, 'Aftermaths: The "Siege in the Room" and the Politics of Testimony', considers how Beckett's novellas and novel trilogy render the thorny and unresolved legacies of French collaborationism, while charting their relation to literary debates about the remit of historical testimony dominated by the voices of non-Jewish survivors. 'Suite', *Mercier et Camier*, *Eleutheria*, *Molloy* and *Malone meurt* or *Malone Dies* are of particular significance to this chapter, as texts that reflect on the principles of testimony as well as the conventions of detective fiction.

Beckett's conflicted relation to the reimagining of Nazi occupation in post-war France bears upon the subjects that he addressed in the 1950s and 1960s, and upon the dramatic and prose texts he wrote during the Algerian war (1954–1962). My final chapter, 'Turning Points: Torture, Dissent and the Algerian War of Independence', focuses on the Algerian war and its impact on political activity, in Paris in particular, examining the connections between Beckett's representations of torture and guerrilla war, and wider debates about decolonisation, historical repetition and political legitimacy, which found expressions across the catalogue of the Editions de Minuit and other politically informed publications. The cultures of dissent that crystallised in France around Lindon and others ignited a profound change in Beckett's view of his own remit as a writer, and his work bears many traces of his attempts to imagine new historical transparencies, appropriate to shifting political circumstances. Looking at the fraught political contexts in which Beckett worked further illuminates his internationalist politics, revealing how, under genuine duress, the challenges to political activism become greater than commonly acknowledged. Offering a new context for understanding *Catastrophe*, commonly perceived as Beckett's only direct political gesture, the conclusion documents his responses to political debates about censorship, freedom of expression and human rights tied to the cultural politics of the Cold War, discussing the many petitions that he endorsed during the 1970s and 1980s and the work's continued political significance.

Politics and the Making of Beckettian Myths

Since the 1950s, much attention has been paid to the structural ambiguity of Beckett's writing – more precisely, to the capacity of the Beckettian sentence to interrogate the conditions of its own possibility, and its intimacy with omission, elision and unspeakability. Maurice Blanchot was the first to scrutinise the tension between the obligation to speak and the impossibility of continuing to speak central to so many of Beckett's texts: his celebrated essay on *L'Innommable* read the novel according to its own narrative terms, since familiar literary and theoretical models failed to account for its apparent placelessness and remoteness.[4] Following the novel's opening salvos, 'Where now? Who now?', Blanchot presented as Beckett's principal design the creation of a narrative voice divorced from recognisable political and historical parameters. A decade later, the same line acquired a different weight in notes that Theodor Adorno compiled on the novel's German counterpart: for Adorno, Beckett was engaged in a critique of solipsistic writing indebted to dialectical materialism, which also harboured a reflection on utopia complicit with the work of Ernst Bloch.[5] From Adorno's perspective, the historicity of Beckett's work revolved around its resistance to clear-cut referents, and its apophatic and euphemistic mode conveyed a proximity to horror, war and genocide. Such reflections are part of a wider endeavour to rethink the critical value of pessimism: for Adorno as for other theorists of the Frankfurt School, pessimism was the only philosophical route available in order to interrogate contemporary irrationality.[6] As political critique, however, Beckett's work had clear limitations: for Adorno, the very idea of Beckett 'as a key political witness' was 'ridiculous'.[7] Following

[4] Maurice Blanchot, 'Où maintenant? Qui maintenant?', *La Nouvelle Nouvelle Revue Française* 10 (1953): 678–86.

[5] Theodor W. Adorno, *Notes sur Beckett*, trans. Christophe David (Caen: Nous, 2008), 41.

[6] See Theodor W. Adorno and Max Horkheimer, *Towards a New Manifesto*, trans. Rodney Livingstone (London: Verso, 2011).

[7] Theodor W. Adorno, 'Trying to Understand *Endgame*', trans. Michael T. Jones, *New German Critique* 26 (1982): 125.

his study of *Endgame*, however, Adorno reconfigured the terms of the equation, reaching striking conclusions about the demise of consensual political forms, and presenting Beckett and Kafka as the only writers able to gesture towards a new political art that 'explode[s]' the strictures of socialist realism, Sartrean commitment and Brechtian technique.[8]

Many subsequent commentaries have made Beckett an attractive philosophical subject by virtue of his capacity to portray destruction and suffering. Seldom, however, have the philosophical and the political been perceived as Beckettian concerns of equal measure. Notable exceptions include Alain Badiou's reflection on Beckett's 'political tenacity' and the recent work of Slavoj Žižek, who returns to Beckett's celebrated variations on failing and going on when discussing the legacy of communism, utopian political thought and other 'lost causes'.[9] For Žižek, Beckettian aphorisms on the inevitability of failure can offer an imaginative way back to utopian thought, and resonate with the challenges that Che Guevara and Mao Zedong faced when articulating their own political visions and doubts.

As these disparate reflections reveal, the kind of political event to which Beckett's work responds tends to evade neat associations, largely because his career was shaped by circumstances in which the domain of the political was frequently boundless, and the dichotomies between political and aesthetic reflection frequently obscure. Jacques Rancière's work sheds light on this problem: in an essay taking issue with Hannah Arendt's and Giorgio Agamben's definitions of the political sphere of human rights, Rancière excavates a different realm of political activity, and re-examines the traditional oppositions between the private individual and the public citizen. The political subject, for Rancière, is the subject who can 'put to test the power of political names, their extension and comprehension', and who has the 'capacity for staging [. . .] scenes of dissensus' (or 'putting two worlds in one and the same world').[10] Politics is apprehended accordingly, as the border between the sphere of citizenship – or political life – and the sphere of private life on the one hand, and, on the other, as the 'activity that brings [that border] back into question'. Similar tensions underlie the argument developed in this book, not least because the problem of where the personal ends and the political begins shaped so many aspects of Beckett's life and artistic endeavour.

[8] Theodor W. Adorno, 'Commitment', trans. Francis McDonagh, *New Left Review* I, 87–8 (1974): 86, 89.

[9] Alain Badiou, *On Beckett*, ed. Nina Power and Alberto Toscano (Manchester: Clinamen, 2003), 31; Slavoj Žižek, *In Defence of Lost Causes* (London: Verso, 2008), 7, 178, 200, 351, 423.

[10] Jacques Rancière, 'Who Is the Subject of the Rights of Man?', *South Atlantic Quarterly* 103, no. 2&3 (2004): 304, 303.

Over the course of the historical period addressed here, the field of political thought has been ceaselessly redefined, in debates frequently underscored by anxieties concerning the workings of democracy, totalitarianism, the birth and death of political utopias, and the possibility of an end point to the political. Claude Lefort, notably, has defined the political as the dynamic that circumscribes and institutes politics in the social sphere, and is 'revealed, not in what we call political activity, but in the double movement whereby the mode of institution of society appears and is obscured'. More specifically, the political appears 'in the sense that the process whereby society is ordered and unified across its divisions becomes visible. It is obscured in the sense that the locus of politics (the locus in which parties compete and in which a general agency of power takes shape and is reproduced) becomes defined as particular, while the principle which generates the overall configuration is concealed'.[11] Pierre Bourdieu has offered similar definitions of the duality of the political field, stressing its capacity to function 'both as a field of forces and as a field of struggles aimed at transforming the relation of forces which confers to this field its structure at any given moment'.[12] For Bourdieu, politics is an elusive force, both known and unknown, stamped by a 'blinding familiarity' that precludes a genuine understanding of the political world.[13]

Conceptualisations of politics as a totality that functions dialectically and involves shifting patterns of legibility are particularly pertinent to the diverse European moments to which Beckett's work of displacement and translation is sutured. Indeed, the literary worlds in which his political sensibility was articulated remained shaped by intractable tensions around the visibility of political activity and the legibility of political transformations. This multiplicity and simultaneity pose serious challenges to scholarly enquiry, and have pushed discussions of politics to the margins of Beckett studies. One moment is frequently invoked: Beckett's decision to join the French Resistance in September 1941, widely considered as the logical outcome of a political experience garnered in 1936 and 1937, during a formative journey through Nazi Germany. Ultimately, however, little is known about the political mechanisms that shaped Beckett's familiarity with the idioms of fascism, communism, Stalinism or the conservative Right. Since the turn of the millenium, publications clearly signposted as explorations of the political Beckett have focused on other terrains,

[11] Claude Lefort, *Democracy and Political Theory*, trans. David Macey (Cambridge: Polity, 1988), 11.

[12] Pierre Bourdieu, *Language and Symbolic Power*, ed. John B. Thompson, trans. Gino Raymond and Matthew Adamson (Cambridge: Polity, 1991), 171.

[13] Pierre Bourdieu, *Propos sur le champ politique* (Lyon: Presses Universitaires de Lyon, 2000), 72–3.

dominated by the prevalent sense that the work's political dimensions revolve primarily around its Irishness. Beckett's fractured relation to his privileged social class, his perspective on Irish Free State politics, and the tensions contained within the work between neutrality and engagement have been prioritised in these debates.[14] Variously, Peter Boxall and Leslie Hill have discussed the fundamental problems inherent in outlining Beckett's political coordinates, pointing to the considerable difficulties posed by the bilinguality of the work, which forbids the construction of a stable political and historical referent to which critical readings can then be indexed.[15] Beckett's fiction, Boxall remarks, 'has stood at a very peculiar, oblique angle to the cultures that have produced it', and inhabits 'a different history altogether, a history that cannot easily be slotted between 1929 and 1989'.[16]

In the realm of theatre, Beckett's work has also acquired its own peculiar temporality, not least because his plays have remained stubbornly embedded in politicised areas of performance practice. His legacy is strewn with paradoxes: Suzan-Lori Parks, for example, has described Beckett as someone who had an innate understanding of social and political marginalisation, on the grounds that he 'just seems so black to [her]'.[17] It is largely through the performance history of *Waiting for Godot* and *Endgame* in situations of political hardship and oppression that Beckett's name has migrated into debates about the nature of political writing. Notably, in partitioned Germany and beyond the Iron Curtain, during the 1950s and thereafter, his early plays were commonly perceived as having a stark, yet somewhat imprecise, political dimension.[18] These developments grate with

[14] See Peter Boxall, ed., *Beckett/Aesthetics/Politics*, spec. section, *SBTA* 9 (2000); Alan Warren Friedman, ed., 'Introduction', in *Beckett in Black and Red: The Translations for Nancy Cunard's Negro (1934)* (Lexington: University Press of Kentucky, 2000), i–xl; David Weisberg, *Chronicles of Disorder: Samuel Beckett and the Cultural Politics of the Modern Novel* (Albany: SUNY Press, 2000); Henry Sussman and Christopher Devenney, eds., *Engagement and Indifference: Beckett and the Political* (Albany: SUNY Press, 2001); Terry Eagleton, 'Political Beckett?', *New Left Review* 40 (2006): 67–74; my own *Samuel Beckett and the Problem of Irishness* (Basingstoke: Palgrave Macmillan, 2009); James McNaughton, 'The Politics of Aftermath: Beckett, Modernism, and the Free State', in *Beckett and Ireland*, ed. Seán Kennedy (Cambridge: Cambridge University Press, 2010), 56–77; McNaughton, 'Samuel Beckett's "Echo's Bones": Politics and Entailment in the Irish Free State', *Modern Fiction Studies* 60, no. 2 (2014): 320–44.

[15] Peter Boxall, 'Samuel Beckett: Towards a Political Reading', *Irish Studies Review* 10, no. 2 (2002): 159–70; Leslie Hill, '"Up the Republic!": Beckett, Writing, Politics', *MLN* 112, no. 5 (1997): 909–28.

[16] Peter Boxall, *Since Beckett: Contemporary Writing in the Wake of Modernism* (London: Continuum, 2009), 3–4.

[17] Cited in Andrea Stevens, 'A Playwright Who Likes to Bang Words Together', *NYT*, 6 March 1994, 5.

[18] Wilhelm Füger, 'The First Berlin *Godot*: Beckett's Debut on the German Stage', *SBTA* 11 (2001): 57–63; Werner Huber, 'Godot, Gorba, and Glasnost: Beckett in East Germany', *SBTA* 2 (1993): 49–58;

available models of political theatre, which tend to focus on the practices pioneered by Brecht, and foreground the unrelenting pessimism of Beckett's drama and its emphasis on absence and silence, commonly perceived as obstacles to political traction. It is fair to say that Beckett has remained a moving target in theorisations of political theatre – particularly in British contexts, where debates about the idea of political writing pose interesting questions about the continued pre-eminence of social realism. For writers such as Dennis Potter, John Arden and Edward Bond, the idea of Beckett as a political playwright was anathema, and the ruthless critiques of his work that they issued at various points from the 1960s to the 1980s were also critiques of its dissociation from naturalism. Elsewhere, numerous actors and directors have celebrated Beckett's distinctive take on hope and despair, and the capacity of his plays to give rise to transformative political allegories – in this respect, the work of the San Quentin Drama Workshop, whose work Beckett supported over the years, has proved immensely important. Some performances of *Waiting for Godot* – in particular, the bilingual Hebrew-Arabic production directed by Ilan Ronen in Haifa in 1984 and Susan Sontag's 1993 production in Sarajevo – have been celebrated for their capacity to generate political metaphors appropriate to times of great international tension.[19] Such politicised interpretations emerge from a longer history of acting and directing: for Roger Blin, Beckett's first director, *En attendant Godot* always had a political remit, and all other aspects of the work stemmed from that political origin.[20] Ironically, one of the first to publicly acknowledge the political power of Beckett's early plays was Jean-Paul Sartre: at a conference in Bonn in 1966, he celebrated Genet, Ionesco, Adamov and Beckett as the vanguard of a new political theatre that questioned the insufficiencies of theatre itself, rather than life's absurdity.[21] This idea was firmly at odds with Sartre's previous pronouncements on the theatre of the absurd. The position of Ernst Fischer, the Communist veteran, shifted further still; after denouncing the 'macabre idiocy' of *Endgame*,

Octavian Saiu, 'Samuel Beckett behind the Iron Curtain: The Reception in Eastern Europe', in *The International Reception of Samuel Beckett*, ed. Mark Nixon and Matthew Feldman (London: Continuum, 2009), 251–71; David Bradby, *Beckett: Waiting for Godot* (Cambridge: Cambridge University Press, 2001), 162–4.

[19] Lois Oppenheim, 'Playing with Beckett's Plays: On Sontag in Sarajevo and Other Directorial Infidelities', *JoBS* 4, no. 2 (1995): 35–46; Ilan Ronen, '*Waiting for Godot* as Political Theater', in *Directing Beckett*, ed. Lois Oppenheim (Ann Arbor: University of Michigan Press, 1994), 239–49; Shifra Schonmann, 'Between Text and Counter-Text: Theatre in Search of Political Meaning', *Contemporary Theatre Review* 3, no. 2 (1995): 171–80.

[20] Roger Blin, *Souvenirs et propos recueillis par Lynda Bellity Peskine* (Paris: Gallimard, 1986), 87.

[21] 'Jean-Paul Sartre: "Genet, Ionesco, Beckett, Adamov, etc. forment le théâtre critique"', *Le Figaro Littéraire*, 26 January 1967, 2.

he revised his opinion, forcefully arguing that the play deals with exactly the same problem as Aleksandr Solzhenitsyn's *One Day in the Life of Ivan Denisovich*: unfreedom.[22] Ernst Bloch concurred.[23]

The sense that Beckett, as a playwright, was also a political figure has sometimes given rise to unlikely exchanges; for example, when Harold Hayes, editor of *Esquire*, invited him to cover the 1968 American Democratic Convention in Chicago alongside Eugène Ionesco and Jean Genet.[24] Beckett and Ionesco declined; Genet, Terry Southern, William Burroughs and the war journalist John Sack penned striking reports of this legendary convention, marked by escalating protests against the Vietnam War. Such side-stepping was not unusual, yet many other anecdotes attest to Beckett's confrontations with the day-to-day demands of politics. Ultimately, however, very little is known about the histories and ideologies through which Beckett's connections with political theatre were formed. Rather, in theatre studies, much emphasis has been placed on *Catastrophe* and *What Where*, commonly described as political but in a non-specific sense. In that strand of the discussion, which is indexed to the end of the Cold War and the dissolution of the Soviet bloc, 'political' tends to mean conventionally liberal, and Beckett's political identity is defined in accordance with a seemingly uprooted politics of free speech and empathy, carrying the promise of a new Western-dominated polity in which the artist's voice can act as a political force in its own right. The common emphasis on Beckett's capacity to ventriloquise contemporary liberal values has had some unfortunate side-effects, and has obscured the rich traditions of political thought that feed his work, and the longer historical span to which it responds. In fact, Beckett's relation to post-1970s liberal values only constitutes a small part of a much more difficult equation.

When reflecting on the challenges raised by Beckett's writing, scholars have tended to be somewhat more partial to the questions outlined by Blanchot than to those discussed by Adorno, and have generally avoided the granular and meandering narratives of the political. Indeed, Pascale Casanova has argued that, especially in France, Blanchot's configuration of the Beckettian voice has remained 'the sole authorized commentary', helping to 'fabricate a tailor-made Beckett, hero of "pure" criticism', who

[22] Ernst Fischer, 'Das Problem der Wirklichkeit in der modernen Kunst', *Sinn und Form* 10, no. 3 (1958): 476; Fischer, *Art against Ideology*, trans. Anna Bostock (London: Allen Lane, Penguin Press, 1969), 15.

[23] Ernst Bloch, 'Kulturkommunist ohne Parteizierat: Zu Ernst Fischers 70. Geburtstag', *Die Zeit*, 4 July 1969, *Zeit Online*, www.zeit.de/1969/27/kulturkommunist-ohne-parteizierat.

[24] *SB*, 599; *LSB4*, 121–3; Edmund White, *Genet* (London: Picador, 1993), 581–92.

lacked 'a history, a past, an inheritance or a project'.[25] This process of severance can be traced through portrayals of Beckett as figurehead of the new 'alittérature' and the literature of 'unrevolt' in the 1950s.[26] Blanchot's reading of a Beckettian prose driven by a voice that comes from nowhere, as a challenge to hermeneutics and narration, continues to shape Beckett's critical reception and to inform arguments celebrating his anti-historical spirit and philosophical achievements. This consensus around a Heideggerian Beckett is, nevertheless, in need of some reconsideration in the wake of other reappraisals of Blanchot's politics and controversies around Heidegger's legacy.[27] In the last two decades, numerous studies have put influential interpretations of modern intellectual history to the test, demanding a better integration of political questions into examinations of theoretical and literary writing. These developments have implications for Beckett scholarship, where Beckett's relation to history has been carefully scrutinised since the publication of James Knowlson's biography. The Beckett that has emerged from this reappraisal is a courageous yet mysterious figure, unafraid of the spectral silences and absences inherent in historical narratives. The version of Beckett presented in this book is indebted to the tradition of historicisation furthered by Andrew Gibson and Lois Gordon, who have documented the cultural circumstances in which Beckett turned to writing and rose to fame, and to the work of Elizabeth Barry, Patrick Bixby, Matthew Feldman, Seán Kennedy, Rónán McDonald, James McNaughton, Sinéad Mooney, Mark Nixon and John Pilling, to name some of the many scholars who have explored the diverse European histories shaping Beckett's career and his texts. Nonetheless, there are major differences between this large field driven by diverse historicisation methods and the far smaller body of scholarship strictly focused on the political Beckett. Reflecting on the work's political currency raises important questions about the relation between the author's creative imagination and the published work, the remit of personal persuasions and their modes of expression, the circumstances of the work's reception in different languages

[25] Pascale Casanova, *Samuel Beckett: Anatomy of a Literary Revolution*, trans. Gregory Elliott (London: Verso, 2006), 11.

[26] Claude Mauriac, *L'Alittérature contemporaine* (Paris: Albin Michel, 1958); Raymond Giraud, 'Unrevolt among the Unwriters in France Today', *Yale French Studies* 24 (1959): 11–17.

[27] Examples of such analyses in fields adjacent to French literary studies and Beckett studies include Pierre Bourdieu, *The Political Ontology of Martin Heidegger*, trans. Peter Collier (Cambridge: Polity, 1991); Emmanuel Faye, *Heidegger, L'Introduction du Nazisme dans la philosophie: Autour des séminaires inédits de 1933–1935* (Paris: Albin Michel, 2005) (see also the controversies that surrounded the book); Christophe Bident, *Maurice Blanchot: Partenaire invisible* (Seyssel: Champ Vallon, 1998); Michel Surya, ed., *Les politiques de Maurice Blanchot, 1930–1993*, spec. issue, *Lignes* 43 (2014).

and literary cultures – and, last but not least, the politics of accepted historical narratives utilised as part of the process of contextualisation. These are problems of great magnitude, to which Peter Boxall has been particularly sensitive.[28]

Ultimately, defining a Beckettian politics has remained a perilous exercise, not least because different diagnoses of his political sympathies have been advanced over time. In 1978, Deirdre Bair portrayed Beckett as a hermit who was 'consistent in his apolitical behaviour', for whom politics was 'anathema', and who 'walked away from any conversation that veered into politics'.[29] In 1996, Knowlson presented a very different author, whose perspective was 'basically left-wing and anti-establishment'; his biography described Beckett's opposition to Nazism, apartheid and all forms of censorship, and his immense generosity towards friends in need.[30] In a later essay, Knowlson identified political commitments that were often driven by chance and personal acquaintance, concluding that Beckett's political activism 'operated mainly at a private and individual level'.[31] Likewise, W. J. McCormack has asserted that Beckett's politics consisted of occasional activation and de-activation of political conscience as circumstances shifted; Alan Warren Friedman and Jackie Blackman have argued that Beckett was impervious to partisan politics, but remained driven by an unfailing loyalty to his friends and a deep concern about suffering.[32] Such models of political activity ascribe to Beckett an erratic tendency to act as mouthpiece for beliefs and struggles that are not his own, an incapacity to engage with political problems as part of a more systematic and principled investigation, and a residual naivety.

This book charts different ideological and political affiliations, through Beckett's eagerness to reclaim the dregs of historical narrative as his material, his fascination for a broad spectrum of radical politics, and a work of translation conducted in the shadows of international campaigns. The Easter Rising, Irish independence and partition, the Nazi occupation of France and Vichy's National Revolution, the threats of a *coup d'état* during the Algerian war, the partition of Germany and Berlin, and the Iron

[28] Peter Boxall, *Samuel Beckett: Waiting for Godot/Endgame; A Reader's Guide to Essential Criticism* (Cambridge: Icon Books, 2000), 137–8; 'Introduction to *Beckett/Aesthetics/Politics*', *SBTA* 9 (2000): 207.

[29] *SB*, 308, 133. [30] *DF*, 641.

[31] James Knowlson, 'A Portrait of Beckett', in *Images of Beckett*, by Knowlson and John Haynes (Cambridge: Cambridge University Press, 2003), 35.

[32] W. J. McCormack, 'Samuel Beckett and the *Negro Anthology*', *Hermathena* (1992): 74; Friedman, 'Introduction', *Beckett in Black and Red*, xxv; Jackie Blackman, 'Post-War Beckett: Resistance, Commitment or Communist Krap?', in *Beckett and Ethics*, ed. Russell Smith (London: Continuum, 2008), 68.

Curtain were not political abstractions for Beckett, but material realities that shaped his youth and later career in the worlds of translation, theatre and television. Few writers of his generation witnessed as many revolutions and counter-revolutions, and as many wars concealed under the pretence of peace. Exposure to danger and upheaval clearly stimulated his imagination: he began to think about a play on the life of Samuel Johnson in December 1936, while in Nazi Germany, and worked on *Human Wishes* during the 'phoney war' that preceded the partition and Nazi occupation of France; he wrote *Watt* during wartime periods marked by great uncertainty, and began translating *Murphy* with Alfred Péron in the midst of Resistance activities involving the synthesis, duplication and translation of military intelligence. His responses are never devoid of complexity, particularly when he affirmed a distance from conventional models of politicisation. When Richard Stern asked him, in 1977, whether he 'was [. . .] ever political', Beckett reportedly answered, 'No, but I joined the Resistance'.[33] The connotations of this 'but' as well as other slippery questions surrounding this pivotal period are explored in this book; my aim is to work beyond the accepted narrative concerning Beckett's political maturation, by tracing the subtle continuities between his writing and the political worlds in which his career unfolded.

To read Beckett's texts through political history raises fascinating questions about the cultural referent within which their political currency can be apprehended, and about the political idioms and symbols that the work engages through its bilinguality and internationalism. Asking these questions of his texts can, in turn, make close reading and contextualisation rather uncomfortable tasks. To read Beckett's tales of dispossession, starvation, slow death and torture in relation to French political history is also to place them in dialogue with accounts of anti-colonial conflicts whose memorialisation entertains an ambivalent relation to the Holocaust and French collaboration with Nazism. This is an issue specific to post-war literary cultures that is long familiar in the field of memory studies: Michael Rothberg, in particular, has drawn attention to the dangers of seeking to prioritise one historical narrative over others, and his warning is pertinent to Beckett's work as well as other forms of transnational writing.[34] In Irish studies, Terry Eagleton, Jim Hansen, Declan Kiberd, David Lloyd, Mark

[33] Cited in Richard Stern, *One Person and Another: On Writers and Writing* (Dallas, TX: Baskerville Publishers, 1993), 43.

[34] Michael Rothberg, *Multidirectional Memory: Remembering the Holocaust in the Age of Decolonization* (Stanford: Stanford University Press, 2009).

Quigley, Julieann Ulin and others have inscribed the discussion of Beckett's historicity in a clearer critical context, yet the political aspects of Beckett's writing continue to pose difficult questions: there are intractable tensions between, on the one hand, his overdetermined position within a conservative and urban Protestant upper-middle class, and, on the other, his elusive role in francophone and diasporic literary cultures shaped by global movements of decolonisation. Such relation to the political world brings to mind the concept of 'cleft habitus' coined by Bourdieu in order to qualify a work permeated by compromise, distance and ambivalence towards inherited social alliances.[35] There is another considerable rift, between the France and the Europe Beckett got to know before 1938 as an affluent and leisurely traveller, and the political realities he faced in wartime and post-war France, as part of an everyday life marked by a progressive 'impoverishment' that was stylistic as well as economic.[36]

In French contexts, Beckett's trajectory does not intersect with established narratives of political engagement either. Intellectual historians have often privileged generational patterns, following the model sketched out by Karl Mannheim, for whom political engagement was firmly circumscribed by social class, generational consciousness and singular periods of action specific to each generation: Jean-François Sirinelli and Pascal Ory, for example, have documented the ways in which generations of French writers articulated and refined their political stance in the contexts of the Popular Front, the Second World War and the Algerian war.[37] Beckett worked within different and often less established political spheres, and his distaste for post-war Gaullism and distance from the French Communist Party offer a stark contrast to the positions taken by his contemporaries (he nevertheless continued to refer to the French Communist Party knowingly, as 'le parti' or 'le Parti', like its adherents).[38] His identity as an Irish exile keen to proclaim his persistent failure was also a political identity, deployed as a foil to the assimilationist drive shaping French literary production and the politics of 'francophonie'. As carrier of a 'green Eire passport', as he called it, he had no voting rights and was obliged to renew his residence permit periodically; he is said to have queued up at

[35] Pierre Bourdieu, *Esquisse pour une auto-analyse* (Paris: Raisons d'Agir, 2004), 127–8; Bourdieu, *Manet: Une révolution symbolique, Cours au Collège de France (1998–2000)*, ed. Pascale Casanova et al. (Paris: Raisons d'Agir and Seuil, 2013), 84–5.

[36] Or 'appauvrissement'; see Ludovic Janvier, *Samuel Beckett par lui-même* (Paris: Seuil, 1969), 18.

[37] Jean-François Sirinelli and Pascal Ory, *Les intellectuels en France: De l'affaire Dreyfus à nos jours* (Paris: Armand Colin, 1992); Karl Mannheim, 'The Problem of Generations', in *Essays on the Sociology of Knowledge*, ed. Paul Kecskemeti (London: Routledge and Kegan Paul, 1952), 276–320.

[38] *LSB1*, 668; *LSB2*, 203–4.

the immigration services without seeking to be exempted from common requirements.[39] This figure waiting patiently in the corridors of the *préfecture de police* in Paris seems a world away from the celebrated writer published by the Editions de Minuit, connected to influential and politicised circles. Lindon's catalogue, dedicated to history, psychoanalysis and the social sciences as well as literature, redefined many intellectual parameters after 1960: notably, the series 'Arguments' (created by Kostas Axelos in 1960), 'Le Sens Commun' (edited by Bourdieu from 1964 onwards) and 'Critique' (founded by Jean Piel in 1967) contributed to the emergence of radically new developments in literary and political theory, critical sociology and psychoanalysis. On a broader political level, the editorial strategy of the Editions de Minuit played an important role during the Algerian war and, at later points, in response to international campaigns against apartheid and the Israel-Palestine conflict. Crucially, Lindon always perceived Beckett's work as his stepping stone. At various points, he ascribed the very existence of his publishing house to the day he first read the manuscript of *Molloy*, concluding: 'Nothing happened prior to that and everything that happened afterwards follows from that'.[40]

Rarely have the French, Irish and global political coordinates of Beckett's writing collided. The numerous press articles covering his Nobel award, for example, mostly revolved around nationality (French or Irish?) and belonging (anglophone or francophone?).[41] More interesting, still, is the manner in which, at the time of the hunger strikes in Northern Ireland, his work was momentarily integrated into a precise political landscape after the deaths of Bobby Sands and Francis Hughes. In 1981, in the French newspaper *Libération*, Gérard Mordillat emphasised the parallel between the acute distress of Beckett's characters and the situation of the republican hunger strikers, deploring that, since 1969, Beckett's every book 'has been stamped as "metaphysical" and crumbles under the weight of superlatives', just as the Nobel prizewinner himself has been transformed into 'a kind of haughty, unapproachable hermit [. . .] working within the realm of the sublime'. Mordillat presented this transformation as a 'remarkable [. . .] conjuring trick', arguing that, 'if we try to throw Beckett into current affairs, we discover in his texts a concrete, immediate reality and a direct political power'.[42]

39 Cited in Harold Hobson, ed., 'Samuel Beckett: Dramatist of the Year', in *Theatre Annual 1* (London: Calder, 1956), 153; Pierre Assouline, 'Enquête sur un écrivain secret', *Lire* 127 (1986): 31.

40 Anne Simonin, *Les Editions de Minuit, 1942–1955: Le devoir d'insoumission* (Paris: IMEC, 2008), 297.

41 See John Harrington, *The Irish Beckett* (Syracuse, NY: Syracuse University Press, 1991), 1–3.

42 Gérard Mordillat, 'L'Irlande: La littérature, la religion et l'hygiène', *Libération*, 15 May 1981, 25.

Ultimately, Beckett's work has been persistently perceived as a challenge to established categories of political writing precisely because his texts reimagine political history in ways that are idiosyncratic, juxtapose the factual and the symbolic, and play with allegory and historical anachronism. On the surface, there is little about his destitute characters that might suggest an aspiration to political theorising or political action. And yet they partially function as political metonymies: the political order to which they belong, sketched in the shadows and recesses of the texts, materialises precisely as they struggle through ruins, mud, deserted landscapes, empty rooms and other residues of a historical horror escaping categorisation. On a broader scale, the work presents a proliferation of narratives created and destroyed by political circumstance, but the formal and semantic role conferred to translation often renders the historical attachments of individual texts as ambiguous, divided and often coded. Didacticism was never part of Beckett's arsenal: upon this issue he remained militant and often belligerent. Yet many texts, notebooks and letters reveal a lengthy reflection on the workings of political history, polemical writing about literature and censorship, and a defence of coherent political values voiced as writer, translator and public figure.

Petitions and Political Action

The beginnings of Beckett's petition-signing coincide with his first attempts to write: from the early 1930s onwards, he endorsed a diverse range of petitions and appeals, always in his specific capacity as writer, and contributed to important reflections on international solidarity and social justice. This domain of political activity was not simply driven by the law of networks, but intersected with broader and more elusive political communities. Beckett's name features on significant political documents, from the Scottsboro appeal issued by Nancy Cunard in 1931 to the international petition denouncing the 1989 fatwa against Salman Rushdie. There were many in-between, inscribed within specific political traditions and moments. Beckett's denomination on these petitions changes: he is designated as an Irish citizen, a French writer, a British playwright or a Nobel prizewinner. Clearly, the Nobel Prize gave him a new sense of political legitimacy, regardless of his feelings about the award: his name features, for example, on a petition issued in December 1969 to General Ovando Candía, President of Bolivia, which called for clemency for the writer and political thinker Régis Debray, convicted for assisting Che Guevara in an attempted *coup d'état*, and serving a prison sentence in

Bolivia.[43] The petition was a sequel to other appeals issued after news of Debray's arrest in 1967, and it garnered broad international support like its predecessors: figures as varied as Luis Buñuel, Aimé Césaire, Charlie Chaplin, Herbert Marcuse, Alberto Moravia, Pablo Picasso, Igor Stravinsky and Giuseppe Ungaretti signed it. Ironically, many of the appeals that Beckett endorsed were published in large-circulation newspapers, but his contributions rarely attracted attention, so unlikely a signatory did he appear. Beckett, for his part, remained immensely secretive about the petitions and causes that he supported, and mostly perceived these matters as entirely separated from the business of writing. Yet he retained a genuine interest in the mechanics of public protest and held in great esteem those among his acquaintances who decided to take to the streets, such as Fernando Arrabal and Kay Boyle; occasionally, he expressed a wish that things had turned out otherwise. To Lawrence Harvey, he explained in the early 1960s that, although there was 'no revolt at all' in his work, he was 'revolted but not revolting'.[44] In 1974, he wistfully confided to Boyle – whose commitment to picket lines, protest marches and direct political action sometimes worried him – that he would have been a better person and a better artist if he had been more like her.[45] A few years later, he talked to Stern about the inefficacy of contemporary politicians in the face of suffering and pain, and explained that he was 'ashamed' and that he had 'wasted his life': he had 'dealt with nothing but words'.[46]

Many among Beckett's contemporaries in France shared his reluctance to speak publicly about politics, and emphasised the necessary separation between their roles as citizens and as intellectuals – particularly sociologists and philosophers who, like many writers, found themselves under pressure to speak to their epoch and offer to it a faithful reflection of itself. These debates have unfolded primarily in relation to, and within, the history of the French Left, finding influential articulations in Bourdieu's approach to political engagement. For Bourdieu, the writer-intellectual since Emile Zola has traditionally intervened in the political world 'with the authority and the competence that come with belonging to the autonomous world of art, philosophy or science'.[47] This model – as is the case with later

[43] 'Chaplin et Stravinsky s'associent à une démarche en faveur de M. Régis Debray', *Le Monde*, 13 December 1969, 24; 'World Figures Plead for Régis Debray', *Times*, 11 December 1969, 8; Jean-François Sirinelli, *Intellectuels et passions françaises: Manifestes et pétitions au XXème siècle* (Paris: Fayard, 1990), 226–9.

[44] *BR/RB*, 137.

[45] SB to Boyle, 22 February 1974, Beckett Collection, Harry Ransom Humanities Research Center, University of Texas at Austin (hereafter HRHRC).

[46] Stern, *One Person*, 39, 44.

[47] Bourdieu, *Propos*, 105.

models of politicisation – cannot accommodate the elusive realities born out of the Cold War. Nor can the 'total intellectual', under pressure to harness all capacities – as writer, philosopher, thinker and political prophet – for every campaign, since this model was specific to Sartre and the moment of its invention.[48] This line of reasoning leads Bourdieu to argue that the connections and disjunctions between intellectual thought and political action are at the very core of politics, and to explain why the public role of writers has become so controversial. These are issues to which Bourdieu returned during the 1990s, emphasising that the antinomies between autonomy and engagement, separation and collaboration no longer existed, since all of these facets could be equally conflictual and critical.[49] He frequently reiterated his belief that intellectuals have no choice but to negotiate the intractable ambiguities that come with working outside of the political field, while having access to certain truths about the social and political world.[50] In other circumstances, Francis Jeanson also asserted his right to speak about politics only in a professional capacity, when the context made it appropriate for him to do so. Jeanson's work as philosopher, essayist and political activist had a significant political reach in the 1950s and 1960s; in the 1990s, he explained that he had chosen to stay silent after a long period of activism in support of Algerian independence because he believed that he had already played the role he had to play.[51]

These reflections accord with the views of Michel Foucault, who coined the term 'specific intellectual' to describe the new and more modest model of punctual action that emerged over the course of the twentieth century, in France in particular. This concept was also an attempt to account for the abyss separating contemporaneous models of political activity from those ignited by the Dreyfus affair. In 1972, in conversation with Deleuze, Foucault evoked the embarrassment that arises when attempting to identify forms of activism appropriate to the present moment, noting here, as he had done elsewhere, the obstacles posed by the continuing ignorance of that which constitutes political power, who exercises it and how.[52] Subsequently, Foucault explained that the political work of the specific intellectual did not take place at the level of the universal or the exemplary, but in precise areas of public life which have become familiar through professional or personal circumstances. This shift, he suggested, has generated

48 Pierre Bourdieu, *The Rules of Art: Genesis and Structure of the Literary Field*, trans. Susan Emanuel (Stanford: Stanford University Press, 1996), 209–10.

49 Bourdieu, *Propos*, 105.

50 Ibid., 68.

51 Francis Jeanson to Bernard Rapp, Caractères, Antenne 2, 22 November 1991, Institut National de l'Audiovisuel online archive, www.ina.fr/.

52 Michel Foucault, *Dits et écrits, vol. 2: 1970–1975* (Paris: Gallimard, 1994), 312.

a new class of political activists and intellectuals with a more concrete and immediate understanding of the modalities of political struggle.[53]

Foucault's analysis chimes with the stance taken by Beckett, whose political interventions were always extremely specific, contained within his professional milieux, and informed by artistic and intellectual affinities. The warnings issued by Bourdieu and Jeanson are also relevant to Beckett's approach to public life and the dilemmas he faced: at various points, he signalled his disengagement from the model demanding that the intellectual speak about anything in any circumstance. His oft-cited statements about ignorance, inability and despair are also indications of his lucidity concerning the modest capacity of literature for social and political intervention. When he said to Gabriel d'Aubarède in 1961, 'I'm no intellectual. All I am is feeling', he was also speaking to a specific context, and about his remove from the model offered by Sartre, whose voice dominated the debates about the Algerian war and decolonisation.[54] A few years later, when he was asked why he had joined the French Resistance, he resorted to the same idiom of impulse and inevitability: he said, 'almost apologetically', that he 'simply couldn't stand [by] with [his] arms folded'.[55]

The sense that action mattered far more than words continued to inform Beckett's dialogue with the kind of politics that makes and unmakes laws and governments, and his activities often subverted common attachments to nationality, place and language: for political purposes, he was remarkably willing to reimagine the sphere of citizenship to which he belonged. He supported campaigns for civil liberties led by British Labour MPs and writers in the United Kingdom, and maintained an involvement in Irish political life long after his departure: in 1961, he agreed to support Owen Sheehy Skeffington's campaign for reelection to the Irish Seanad to pursue a liberal programme; in 1981, he allowed Tommy Murtagh of Trinity College Dublin to include him among those supporting his candidacy for the 15th Seanad election.[56] In France, Beckett contributed to punctual and focused forms of political campaigning around the arts world and the book

[53] Foucault, *Dits et écrits, vol. 3: 1976–1979* (Paris: Gallimard, 1994), 109–10.

[54] Cited in *Samuel Beckett: The Critical Heritage*, ed. Lawrence Graver and Raymond Federman (Abingdon: Routledge, 1979), 217. The original has a different tinge: 'Je ne suis pas un intellectuel. Je ne suis que sensibilité'. Gabriel d'Aubarède, 'En Attendant . . . Beckett', *Les nouvelles littéraires* 1746, 16 February 1961, 7.

[55] Cited in Alec Reid, *All I Can Manage, More than I Could: An Approach to the Plays of Samuel Beckett* (New York: Grove, 1968), 14.

[56] See Andrée Sheehy Skeffington, *Skeff: The Life of Owen Sheehy Skeffington 1909–1970* (Dublin: Lilliput, 1991), 208. Warm thanks to Tommy Murtagh for discussing this moment with me in the summer of 2009, and for explaining that his request was mediated by Con Leventhal. The correspondence is held at Trinity College Dublin (TCD MS 9038).

trade. In 1977, alongside Bourdieu, Deleuze, Roland Barthes, Alain Robbe-Grillet, Philippe Sollers and others, he adhered to the Association pour le Prix Unique, a lobbying group formed by Lindon to campaign for the regulation of book prices and stronger state support for book sales, small publishers and independent bookshops.[57] In 1986, he endorsed an appeal to vote for the Socialist Party in forthcoming French parliamentary elections, as part of a large international group of artists and intellectuals including Anthony Burgess, Francis Ford Coppola, Marguerite Duras, Graham Greene, Félix Guattari, Gabriel García Márquez, Issey Miyake, Léopold Sédar Senghor, William Styron, Elizabeth Taylor, Vercors, Andrzej Wajda and Elie Wiesel. The appeal, addressed to the French nation, celebrated the Socialist Party's cultural achievements, paying homage to the manner in which President François Mitterrand and Minister of Culture Jack Lang had bolstered the international prestige of French culture.[58] This moment marked the continuation of political dynamics established at the beginning of Mitterrand's presidency: his first mandate ushered a new golden age for writers living in France, and Beckett suddenly found himself 'overwhelmed' with requests from Lang and the Elysée Palace.[59] On that occasion in 1986, Beckett's signature attracted much attention and was greeted with the comment that 'the man who never signs' had finally capitulated.[60] Other press reports asserted that his close friends were bewildered, shocked and sceptical, since it was well known that Beckett never stepped forward to defend ideas, although he had publicly supported artists such as Fernando Arrabal and Václav Havel.[61] Of course, Beckett did defend ideas – more often and more fiercely than most, and sometimes at great personal cost. He participated in other prominent campaigns and occasionally took a stance on the action of foreign governments. The only political party to which he ever made a donation, in the form of a manuscript for auction, was the African National Congress,[62] a party indissociable from campaigns for labour rights and human rights, and allied to international Communist

57 This campaign eventually came to fruition in 1981, with the 'Lang Law' enforcing a fixed price on books, set by publishers. Anne Simonin, 'L'édition littéraire', in *L'édition française depuis 1945*, ed. Pascal Fouché (Paris: Electre-Editions du Cercle de la Librairie, 1998), 77–8.

58 'Appel des créateurs', *Le Monde*, 2–3 March 1986, 5.

59 Anne Atik, *How It Was: A Memoir of Samuel Beckett* (London: Faber, 2001), 107.

60 Gilles Anquetil, 'Jack Lang plébiscité', *Nouvel Observateur*, 28 February–6 March 1986, 39; Jean-Michel Thénard, 'Au secours, Lang s'en va', *Libération*, 25 February 1986.

61 Assouline, 'Enquête sur un écrivain secret', 28; A.G., 'Samuel Beckett: Pourvu que ça dure', *Libération*, 25 February 1986, 11.

62 SB to Henry Wenning, 8 December 1967, cited in Sharon Bangert, *The Samuel Beckett Collection, Washington University Libraries, St Louis, Missouri: A Guide* (St Louis: Washington University Libraries, 1986), 10.

groups and organisations. The moment at which Beckett made this donation in the late 1960s was distinctive: armed struggle, with weapons and training largely provided by the Soviet Union, remained the ANC's main strategy; the South African Terrorism Act had become law a few months previously; and the ANC, with most of its leaders in jail, exiled or banned from political activity, was in deep crisis.[63] By that point Beckett was also known for his support to British and Irish strands of the international anti-apartheid movement.

He continued to contribute to political campaigns affiliated to the European Left throughout the 1970s and 1980s. He made clandestine donations, for example, to the Polish Solidarity movement when it was still a conglomerate of trade unions: the translator and editor Antoni Libera recalls how, after the military *coup d'état* and the proclamation of a 'state of war' in 1981, Beckett offered his support and asked for his Polish royalties to be donated to Solidarność.[64] The funds were redistributed to families of arrested trade unionists and dissenters.[65] This gesture was aligned with other work undertaken after the strikes and repression of 1976 – for example, by the Comité de Solidarité avec les Travailleurs Polonais, a committee hosted in Paris by *Cahiers du Cinéma* and supported by Sartre, Simone de Beauvoir, Laurent Schwartz, Pierre Vidal-Naquet and others, which raised funds for Polish workers sanctioned for their involvement with the opposition.[66] In the early 1980s, numerous calls were issued across the socialist and liberal Left in France and beyond, to denounce human rights violations in Poland, the growth of poverty, and political repression across the Eastern bloc more broadly. Beckett's name features among French signatories to an international petition issued in 1981 denouncing Jaruzelski's proclamation of martial law and the detention of political dissenters, and calling for Polish prisons and internment camps to be placed under the control of human rights organisations and the United Nations.[67] Other signatories included Bourdieu, Deleuze, Duras, Foucault, Lindon, Robbe-Grillet, Pierre Boulez, Peter Brook, Patrice Chéreau, Jacques Derrida, Jacques Le Goff, Emmanuel Le Roy Ladurie and Claude Simon, many of whom rallied around similar petitions thereafter.

[63] See Francis Meli, *South Africa Belongs to Us: A History of the ANC* (London: James Currey, 1989), 145–70; Anthea Jeffery, *People's War: New Light on the Struggle for South Africa* (Johannesburg: Jonathan Ball, 2009), 4–9.

[64] John O'Mahony, 'Beckett Comes Home', *Plays International* 7, no. 6 (1992): 26. Libera's specific account contrasts with the non-specific instructions Beckett issued to Faber & Faber; see *LSB4*, 586.

[65] Knowlson, 'A Portrait of Beckett', 33.

[66] 'Pas de dégel', *Nouvel Observateur*, 30 May 1977, 44.

[67] 'Appel des intellectuels européens pour la Pologne', *Libération*, 30 December 1981, 36.

Precisely when Beckett's political voice became clearly audible, his image as a withdrawn, silent writer was consolidated. In 1981, for his seventy-fifth birthday, *Libération* published a blank page to mark the publication of *Mal vu mal dit* – a homage that Beckett greeted with delight.[68] In 1988, he was assigned to a peculiar pantheon of 'Great Silent Men', alongside Louis Althusser, Balthus, Leos Carax, Blanchot and the long-serving editor of *Le Monde*, Hubert Beuve-Méry, all praised for their capacity to influence the future rather than the present.[69] These tributes accord with the consensus nurtured by friends and acquaintances. Cioran was not the only one to assume that Beckett lived irremediably outside of time and had nothing valuable to say on political matters: other friends spoke authoritatively and sometimes adamantly of Beckett's assumed disaffection. As early as 1969, Bettina Jonic, then Calder's wife, described Beckett as a non-signer who had only ever supported one petition – against the poor regulation of French slaughterhouses.[70] Calder also emphasised Beckett's remove from political culture at large, associating his assumed silence with a sense that 'with his Irish passport, he was only really a guest in France'.[71] Barbara Bray – Beckett's lover, who defined herself as 'a bolshie' – contended that he had no interest whatsoever in politics, arguing that the petitions for freedom of expression that he had signed had been engineered by her (clearly, she knew little about his political activities).[72] Some close collaborators have invoked the old precept according to which the politically motivated eye fundamentally misapprehends the pure work: David Warrilow has warned against political interpretations of the plays, on the grounds that everything Beckett ever undertook was driven by the same non-political 'regard for the sanctity of human life'. In his view, Beckett had 'an unshakeable respect for the human being and cared deeply about artists being allowed to do what they must do', but remained fundamentally indifferent to politics: 'We never spoke about politics, ever'.[73] Such declarations are important precisely because they accord with a widespread reluctance to acknowledge the work's political coordinates, and the insights it can offer into a transnational history marked by important mutations within Western liberal values and murderous colonial and civil wars.

[68] Jean-Pierre Thibaudat, 'Le silence à pleine tête' and the adjacent page, *Libération*, 18 November 1981, 22–3; Mathieu Lindon, *Jours de* Libération (Paris: POL, 2015), 38–9.
[69] Gilles Hertzog, 'Top 30: Les grands silencieux', *Globe* 24, January 1988, 45.
[70] Pendennis, 'Backpage', *Observer*, 12 October 1969, 44.
[71] John Calder, 'Samuel Beckett: A Personal Memoir', Naxos Audiobooks podcast, www.naxosaudiobooks.com/531912.htm, last accessed 17 March 2015.
[72] Marek Kędzierski, 'Barbara Bray: In her Own Words', *Modernism/Modernity* 18, no. 4 (2011): 896.
[73] Cited in Nick Curtis, 'Beckett Remembered', *Plays & Players* 436, March 1990, 25.

The trajectory traced in this book is marked by tensions, problems and assumptions concerning the visibility and invisibility of Beckett's political gestures. If the label 'apolitical' has remained so persistently affixed to him, it is also because his trajectory from obscurity to fame involves so many displacements and postponements that it cannot be easily shoehorned into familiar narratives of political literacy, activism and disenchantment. His relation to politics contravenes the developmental narratives that might, for example, have been crafted for Sartre, who began as a libertarian philosopher and became a political activist spanning the international Left, or for Blanchot, who supported far-right monarchist movements before becoming an advocate of the international Left, Algerian self-determination and the social movements of 1968. Beckett's allegiances did not shift nearly as radically: from the early 1930s onwards, he steadfastly supported the same causes – freedom of expression and movement – and struggles against censorship and political oppression. He responded to and frequently participated in campaigns for individual liberties that absorbed the energies of artists, philosophers and editors around him. Throughout his life, he remained preoccupied by questions arising from the relations between artist and state, and between writing, justice and the law, voicing his concerns in ways that remained consistent with the liberal political cultures in which he worked, and with forms of activism historically afforded to Irish, British and French writers and intellectuals. There are clear patterns to his activism: he took action when he discerned threats to intellectual and artistic work and to free thought. On this front, it is important to note that, although he had many confidantes and female collaborators (his wife Suzanne had strong leftist opinions), his gestures of support remained in keeping with the conventions and dynamics of the professional networks in which he operated, and almost exclusively benefited male artists and intellectuals with credentials that matched his own. All too often, the campaigns for freedom of speech and human rights to which he contributed unfolded without raising other political issues, and it is clear that labour rights, feminism and women's rights were not among his political priorities; in fact, his tendency to only side publicly with white men was noticed in the French press in the 1980s.[74]

Censorship remained an issue guaranteed to attract his attention, particularly when Irish, British and American writers known to him were affected. In the 1960s, for example, he supported Calder's campaign against British censorship through various means. He wrote a statement of

[74] A.G., 'Samuel Beckett: Pourvu que ça dure', 11.

support, to be read in court, praising Henry Miller's *Tropic of Cancer* when Calder feared prosecution.[75] He co-signed a letter (with Al Alvarez, Christine Brooke-Rose and Kingsley Amis) in the *Guardian* that celebrated the international significance of Burroughs's *The Naked Lunch* and opposed legal action against Calder and Boyars.[76] In 1967, he became one of the major figures involved in the Free Art Legal Fund set up by Calder and Boyars to cover legal costs incurred in the trial against Hubert Selby Jr's *Last Exit to Brooklyn*. Subsequently, he sponsored the Defence of Literature and the Arts Society, a pressure group chaired by British Labour MPs and political activists that grew out of these fundraising events, with the specific aims of safeguarding freedom of expression in the United Kingdom and raising funds for artists affected by censorship.[77]

In French contexts, the picture is less clear, as Beckett's name does not appear in high-profile petitions dealing with censorship. One representative example is the petition published by Lindon in *Le Monde* in 1970 to denounce the sanctions taken against Pierre Guyotat's Sadean novel *Eden, Eden, Eden* (shortly after its publication by the Editions de Minuit, the novel was struck by a partial ban: its sale to minors was forbidden, as were all forms of publicity and public exposition). Beckett did not endorse the text, although he frequently followed Lindon on other political fronts. The petition is a veritable who's who of 1970s francophone culture: it attracted hundreds of signatures, from Blin to Duras, from Derrida to Deleuze, from Kateb Yacine to Delphine Seyrig.[78] Generally, the appeals that Beckett supported in response to public controversies in France were more clearly articulated as protests against state interference and had a more precise international remit. In 1968, for example, he added his name to a long list of writers, actors and filmmakers protesting against the dismissal of Henri Langlois, the celebrated Director of the Cinémathèque Française, by André Malraux and his Ministry of Cultural Affairs.[79] Hundreds of signatories supported the campaign led by Jean-Luc Godard, Jean Renoir, Alain Resnais, Jacques Rivette and François Truffaut to defend Langlois's vision and achievements. The protest became a rehearsal ground for revolutionary cultural campaigns after May 1968. Later still, in the wake of the 1986 appeal celebrating Mitterrand's achievements, Beckett signed documents that were critical of French cultural policies: in 1987, for example,

[75] *LSB3*, 667. [76] 'Letters to the Editor', *Guardian*, 7 January 1965, 8.

[77] John Calder, *Pursuit: Uncensored Memoirs* (London: Calder, 2001), 318–19; Geoffrey Moorhouse, 'Appeal for Funds to Defend *Last Exit to Brooklyn*', *Guardian*, 11 November 1967, 10.

[78] Pierre Guyotat, *Littérature interdite* (Paris: Gallimard, 1972), 187–218.

[79] 'Protestations', *Cahiers du Cinéma* 199, March 1968, 45–6; *Cahiers du Cinéma* 200–1, April-May 1968, 62–71.

he endorsed a petition protesting against Michel Polac's dismissal from the television channel TF1 and the suppression of his polemical talk-show. The text denounced a 'new attack upon cultural life, so often invoked and so rarely represented on television', and lamented the emergence of 'a television devoid of books, writers and impertinence'.[80] Deleuze, Lindon, Philippe Djian and Françoise Sagan also lent their support. The following year, Beckett added his signature to those of sixty-three artists and intellectuals supporting Giorgio Strehler's plea asking Mitterrand to grant permanent status to the Théâtre de l'Europe, an institution linked to the Socialist Party's electoral victory. Strehler's statement denounced the 'hypocritical politics' threatening the theatre that he had managed since its inception in 1983.[81] Other signatories included Rafael Alberti, Ingmar Bergman, Willy Brandt, Peter Brook, Federico Fellini, John Gielgud, Heiner Müller, Tom Stoppard and Peter Ustinov. These snapshots illustrate particularly clearly Beckett's ties to international networks of artists, politicians and intellectuals that are rarely integrated into national narratives of political activity.

What is known of his reading habits further testifies to his fascination regarding the day-to-day stuff of politics. He was faithful to French left-leaning newspapers, and both he and his wife stated that they had little regard for *Le Figaro* – the newspaper of the conservative Right – and did not read it unless they had no other option.[82] In the 1940s, he read *Combat* and sometimes *Franc-Tireur*, which began as underground Resistance publications.[83] Thereafter, some sources point to his penchant for *L'Humanité*, the newspaper of the French Communist Party, which has also spoken to the broader Left, and *Le Monde*, which has often moved left of centre.[84] There is evidence that he read *Libération* assiduously in the 1980s; the newspaper, founded in the 1970s by Sartre and others, represented the non-communist Left and was distinguished by an attention to international politics, literature and culture.[85] Many memoirs and interviews – permitted and unauthorised – attest to Beckett's keen interest in the political press. Unfortunately, the nervousness that many of his interlocutors display towards political subjects has led to important details being

80 'Des éditeurs, des écrivains, des libraires pour Michel Polac', *Le Monde*, 2 October 1987, 19; Angela Moorjani, '*En attendant Godot* on Michel Polac's *Entrée des Auteurs*', *SBTA* 7 (1997): 48.

81 Odile Quirot, 'L'avenir du Théâtre de l'Europe', *Le Monde*, 16 April 1988; 'Théâtre: L'avenir du Théâtre de l'Europe', *Le Monde*, 23 April 1988; Brigitte Salino, 'Vingt ans d'une Europe à inventer', *Le Monde*, 26 April 2006, 2.

82 *LSB2*, 242–4; *LSB4*, 481.

83 *LSB2*, 83.

84 Knowlson, 'A Portrait of Beckett', 13; Mel Gussow, 'An Intimate Look at Beckett the Man', *NYT*, 31 December 1989, 3; Assouline, 'Enquête sur un écrivain secret', 29.

85 Mel Gussow, *Conversations with and about Beckett* (New York: Grove, 1996), 60; *DF*, 701; Lindon, *Jours*, 36–41.

anonymised or cut, while conversations about politics are often rendered as insignificant or irrelevant asides among seemingly more valuable reflections about metaphysics and aesthetics.

It is nonetheless clear that Beckett cultivated a detailed knowledge of international political culture, and could initiate discussion about matters as varied as the pressures of McCarthyism, the overthrow of the Shah of Iran, the blood shed in the Iran-Iraq War, Spanish politics prior to the death of Franco, the Sabra and Shatila massacres, the parallels between English and Soviet imperialism in Ireland and in Poland, or IRA strategy in the mid-1980s (his verdict: 'Get the British out of Ireland').[86] His correspondence with Alan Schneider is punctuated by reflections on the Algerian War of Independence, the Watergate scandal and the Vietnam War; Schneider, following common historical parallels, described the last as a '*malaise extraordinaire*, akin to your Algeria times', and as another moment when resistance lay beyond the remit of organised protest.[87] Anne Atik's memoir relates Beckett's eagerness to talk about diverse matters including Israeli military provision, Solidarność and the politics of student movements in France.[88] Clearly, Mitterrand's election to the French Presidency was for Beckett a profound event and a source of joy. When it was announced that the new government would include ministers from the French Communist Party, Avigdor Arikha expressed concern that Mitterrand might 'succumb to communist pressure', and Beckett replied: 'What will a few communists do? [. . .] Anyway, the communist intellectuals are all against Georges Marchais. He's no good'.[89] Like many of Beckett's pronouncements, the conversation has a political referent: it echoes questions asked during the early 1970s about Marchais, a long-standing figurehead of the French Communist Party who was accused of having volunteered during the Second World War for the labour draft in Germany (the Service du Travail Obligatoire or STO).[90] Other accounts have portrayed Beckett as 'knowledgeable and up-to-date' on the political situation in South Africa in 1988, and have described the relish with which he talked about Idi Amin Dada's career and about the 'diamonds affair' – one of the great financial

86 Gussow, *Conversations*, 52, 110; Daniel Rondeau, *Tanger et autres Marocs* (Paris: Nil Editions, 1997), 89; Stern, *One Person*, 47; Charles Juliet, *Conversations with Samuel Beckett and Bram van Velde*, trans. Janey Tucker (Leiden: Academic Press Leiden, 1995), 159–60; André Bernold, *L'Amitié de Beckett* (Paris: Hermann, 1992), 81; O'Mahony, 'Beckett Comes Home', 26.

87 *NABS*, 268; see also David L. Schalk, *War and the Ivory Tower: Algeria and Vietnam* (Lincoln: University of Nebraska Press, 2005).

88 Atik, *How It Was*, 91, 118, 15, 114, 122.

89 Alba Arikha, *Major/Minor: A Memoir* (London: Quartet, 2011), 125.

90 See, notably, Auguste Lecoeur, *La stratégie du mensonge: Du Kremlin à Georges Marchais* (Paris: Ramsay, 1980).

scandals of the 'Françafrique' involving Bokassa I, Emperor of the Central African Republic, and Valéry Giscard d'Estaing.[91] In conversations, he quoted François Mitterrand to describe religious fanaticism as a form of idiocy, and discussed the styles of delivery honed by Margaret Thatcher and Ronald Reagan, confessing that he 'disliked' Thatcher's voice 'but was interested in Reagan as a communicator' – a comment recalling Reagan's transition from Hollywood to politics.[92] He was amused by the artistic pretensions of Giscard d'Estaing, 'our literary president', and unimpressed by his approach to foreign affairs.[93] At the end of his life, he continued to pay close attention to international political developments. 'I could only walk along the Gaza Strip today', he would say when feeling too weak to venture beyond the small garden of his retirement home, traversed by a strip of green matting.[94] He greeted the fall of the Berlin Wall and the concurrent tide of political and economic reform with great worry and agitation, deploring that 'ça va trop vite' [it's all going too fast].[95] Many would agree. The subject of this book is not simply Beckett's political sensibility, but the political imagination that continued to shape the work, no matter how precarious or unsteady the author's position might be.

[91] Kenneth S. Brecher, 'Samuel Beckett: Private in Public', *NYT*, 12 June 1988, 18; *BR/RB*, 216.
[92] Juliet, *Conversations*, 159; Gussow, *Conversations*, 44.
[93] Stern, *One Person*, 39, 45. [94] *DF*, 701. [95] *LM*, 591.

CHAPTER I

False Starts
The 'Material of Experience' and the Writing of History

'[T]he material of experience is not the material of expression and I think the distress you feel, as a writer, comes from a tendency on your part to assimilate the two'.[1] On these terms, in 1960, Beckett recommended a change of direction to the Israeli poet Matti Megged, a new acquaintance who appears to have sought his guidance. By that point, Megged had written little, and his work included historical studies of Ha-Shomer, the Jewish self-defence association of Palestine, and the Palmach, the elite branch of the Haganah.[2] To Megged, Beckett remarked that the vital difference between the 'material of experience' and the 'material of expression' was not simply a stylistic and aesthetic matter, but a working method honed from many years spent running into the same intractable problems of representation. Recalling Proust's 'campaign against naturalism', he explained that the only artistic path he was able to follow after 1945 was a 'failure to express', once he realised that 'there is nothing more exciting for the writer, or richer in unexploited expressive possibilities'. The argument that Beckett develops carries oblique reference to world politics: what is designated as the 'material of experience' applies specifically to the relation between political experience and writing. Acknowledging such connections offers new perspectives on the concept of failure that Beckett articulated on other occasions, and the forms of elision, encoding and magnifying through which political history itself is recorded in his writing.

The formative period that preceded this realisation – the 1930s, during which Beckett, by his own admission, laboured in a state of ignorance on the aggregate of experience – generated texts peculiarly resistant to completion and publication, which also displayed a keen interest in the formation

[1] *LSB3*, 377.

[2] Matti Megged and Yoram Kaniuk, *Ha-Gedud Ha-shishi Mesaper* [The Sixth Brigade Reports] (Tel-Aviv, 1948); Yitzhak Ben-Zvi, Israel Shochat, Matti Megged and Yochanan Twersky, eds., *Sefer Ha-Shomer* [The Book of Ha-Shomer] (Tel Aviv: Dvir, 1957); Zerubavel Gilead and Matti Megged, eds., *Sefer ha-Palmah* [The Book of the Palmach, 1953] (Buenos Aires: Editorial 'Undzer Vort', 1959).

of national narratives around war and imperial conquest in the long history of France, Germany, Great Britain and Ireland. The literary cultures in which he worked as poet, critic and translator were in no sense insulated from broader political dynamics; *The Dublin Magazine*, for which he was briefly considered for the post of editor in 1936, was one of many literary reviews refracting ideological tensions around Irish and European nationalisms and the rise of authoritarian regimes. For his part, Beckett frequently turned to the past in order to reflect upon contemporary forms of political fervour, using anecdotes and phrases gleaned from historical surveys and memoirs as imaginative triggers. *Dream of Fair to Middling Women*, for example, began with assiduous work on military history and the life of Napoleon Bonaparte, and subsequently encompassed satires of the ideological tensions fermenting in the Irish Free State and across Europe.[3] A precise political topography remains at the heart of the short stories he developed in parallel for *More Pricks than Kicks*, a book noted for its satirical content upon publication (for the *Irish Times*, satire was Beckett's 'strongest point').[4] There are further traces of his enduring concern for the broad span of political history in critical essays, notes on Irish history, myth and the cattle trade compiled for the discarded satire known as 'Trueborn Jackeen', and notes on Samuel Johnson gathered for *Human Wishes*.

This was a period during which Beckett remained alert to the political fragility of his own social class, and occasionally perceived himself as a suitable subject for life writing due to an enduring sense of estrangement: while in Nazi Germany, he reflected on the imperative to 'find something rueful for im Dritten Reich', pondering a possible 'Journal of a Melancholic' that was soon relegated to the scrapheap, like other attempts to write directly about history.[5] Although his fascination for international politics is evident in early texts and discarded notes, it remains difficult to imagine him as a writer aspiring to take a stance on political ideologies or programmes during this period. Clearly, his interest in the mechanics of political rhetoric ran deep, but his understanding of what the conjoined historical developments might entail fluctuated greatly. He read widely and indiscriminately: readings upon his return from Germany included pamphlets such as Louis-Ferdinand Céline's *Mea Culpa* and *Bagatelle pour un massacre*,[6] steeped in Hitlerian and anti-Semitic rhetoric, as well as Fritz Mauthner's *Beiträge zu einer Kritik der Sprache*, a work that interrogates the philosophies

[3] John Pilling, *Beckett's Dream Notebook* (Reading: Beckett International Foundation, 1999).
[4] 'New Novels', *IT*, 23 June 1934, 5.
[5] Mark Nixon, *Samuel Beckett's German Diaries, 1936–1937* (London: Continuum, 2011), 121.
[6] John Pilling, 'Dates and Difficulties in Beckett's *Whoroscope* Notebook', *JoBS* 13, no. 2 (2004): 39–48.

underlying myths of Germanic sovereignty and Aryanism, and bears the traces of Mauthner's deep reflection on ethnic nationalism and anti-Semitism.[7] To understand why the idea of domesticating the 'material of experience' proved so uncertain and yet remained so enticing, it is necessary to look not simply at the work, but at the many unrealised aspirations that fill this period, and at Beckett's political education, friendships and literary associations.

Political Affiliations and Literary Partnerships in Beckett's Dublin

For Beckett, friendships were frequently synonymous with literary partnerships, and the dialogues he sustained with Irish writers and artists during the 1920s and 1930s offer precious insight into his own political education and positioning. Much is known of his close friendships with Thomas MacGreevy and Con Leventhal, and of his formative exchanges with Denis Devlin and Brian Coffey. In Dublin, their shared interest in Surrealism came across as somewhat iconoclastic, and was affirmed in a context antagonistic to the continental avant-garde in which Surrealist poetry was, at best, perceived as a nonsensical endeavour with a limited future.[8] Leslie Daiken, for example, presented Beckett and his modernist acolytes as disciples of a distant Surrealism hostile to Irish politics (or, in his terms, as members of a 'cultured studentry' who have merely 'fostered pessimism').[9] His anthology *Good-bye, Twilight: Songs of the Struggle in Ireland*, published in 1936 with illustrations by Harry Kernoff, firmly dissociated their poetry from Irish political verse, as part of a manoeuvre that sheds light on broader perceptions of Surrealism in Dublin. However, such consensus was unrepresentative of the political concerns displayed by Beckett and his friends: all of them had distinctive commitments and credentials. MacGreevy was a liberal republican knowledgeable about national politics, seemingly enamoured by Eamon de Valera.[10] Few of his letters to Beckett have survived, but his correspondence with others such as Ernie O'Malley is peppered with anecdotes about international politics, recalling Beckett's own

[7] See my 'Samuel Beckett, the Wordless Song and the Pitfalls of Memorialisation', *Irish Studies Review* 19, no. 2 (2011): 187–95; Jacques le Rider, *Fritz Mauthner: Une biographie intellectuelle* (Paris: Editions Bartillat, 2012).

[8] M. C., 'In Search of Surrealism', *IT*, 13 June 1936, 7; M. C., 'More About Surealism', *IT*, 20 June 1936, 7.

[9] Leslie H. Daiken, ed., 'Introduction', in *Good-bye, Twilight: Songs of the Struggle in Ireland* (London: Lawrence and Wishart, 1936), xii.

[10] See Susan Schreibman, ed., *The Work and Life of Thomas MacGreevy: A Critical Reappraisal* (London: Bloomsbury, 2013).

missives.[11] Devlin had a long and successful career as diplomat, which began in the Irish Department of External Affairs, took him to the League of Nations in Geneva in 1935, and then to Mussolini's Italy; after 1939, he held a series of high-ranking posts at the Consulate General in New York and the Irish Legation in Washington, and his last post was Irish Ambassador to Italy.[12] Leventhal was an active Zionist, who spent a year in Palestine after the First World War; he was a member of Chaim Weizmann's Zionist Commission, and worked for the *Palestine Weekly* and the London *Zionist Review*.[13] During the 1930s, he was deeply committed to the creation of a Jewish state, and there are traces of his involvement in Dublin Zionist groups.[14] Less is known about Coffey's political persuasions, but through his Surrealist translations it is possible to trace associations with anti-fascist campaigns: in 1937, for example, he contributed a translation to *Solidarité*, a pamphlet conceived to raise funds for Spanish republican forces.[15] Beckett himself, as author and translator, was associated with the continental Left in a broad sense: a review published in the *Irish Times* in 1936 presented him as a major contributor to Eugene Jolas's *transition*, the review of the artistic Left that was once 'uncompromisingly left-wing'.[16]

Beyond this closed circle, Beckett frequented artists, writers and intellectuals affiliated with the Irish Left, notably Owen Sheehy Skeffington, Leslie Daiken, Peadar O'Donnell, Charlie Gilmore, Harry Kernoff and Liam O'Flaherty (he is said to have avoided Kernoff and O'Flaherty at times, but appears to have spent more time in their company than avoiding them). Sheehy Skeffington and Daiken – once Beckett's students at Trinity College Dublin – shared strong political convictions. Daiken briefly edited *Irish Front*, the newspaper of the London Republican Congress, and edited revolutionary poetry.[17] His relations with Beckett were friendlier than his *Good-bye, Twilight* might suggest (in many ways Daiken's account of Irish poetic modernism reads as a response to 'Recent Irish Poetry', where Beckett had noted that Daiken wrote verse 'when his politics let

[11] See *The Thomas MacGreevy Archive* and *The Correspondence of Ernie O'Malley and Thomas MacGreevy*, www.macgreevy.org/collections/omalley/index.html.

[12] See Alex Davis, *A Broken Line: Denis Devlin and Irish Poetic Modernism* (Dublin: University College Dublin Press, 2000).

[13] See Eoin O'Brien, ed., *A. J. Leventhal, 1896–1979: Dublin Scholar, Wit and Man of Letters* (Dublin: Con Leventhal Scholarship Committee, 1984), 19.

[14] 'National Home for Jews', *IT*, 3 June 1937, 4; Eileen O'Brien, 'Israel: A Nation Built on Work and Idealism', *IT*, 26 February 1968, 12; 'Mr Sokolow in Dublin', *IT*, 18 May 1933, 5.

[15] Paul Eluard, *Œuvres Complètes*, vol. 1 (Paris: Gallimard, 1968), 841, 1530–1.

[16] '*Transition*: A Very Modern Magazine', *IT*, 25 July 1936, 7.

[17] Emmet O'Connor, *Reds and the Green: Ireland, Russia and the Communist International, 1919–43* (Dublin: University College Dublin Press, 2004), 217; *LM*, 215.

him').[18] Sheehy Skeffington, who followed in Beckett's footsteps as *lecteur* at the Ecole Normale Supérieure and as lecturer at Trinity, joined the Irish Labour Party in 1934 in response to the rise of the Irish Blueshirts and parallel events in France, and wrote occasionally for newspapers of the Left. He subscribed for a while to the *Irish Workers' Voice*, the newspaper of the Communist Party of Ireland, and joined the League Against Imperialism, which had a strong following in Dublin.[19] In 1935 and thereafter, he supported the Marxist Republican Congress led by Frank Ryan, Peadar O'Donnell and George Gilmore, and spoke at anti-fascist demonstrations. Over time, he became someone that the Communist Party of Ireland (founded in June 1933, after the dissolution of a prior organisation in 1924) wished to include in its ranks in order to assist with the formation of a new popular front.[20]

Around the time of his trip to Germany, Beckett sought out new friends among Irish republicans and socialists, and became close to Peadar O'Donnell and Charlie Gilmore. There are many anecdotes about the roles played by O'Donnell and Gilmore, individually and as part of a larger group, in Irish socialist republicanism during the 1920s and 1930s. In June 1933, for example, a march organised by the Communist Party of Ireland to commemorate James Connolly's work and urge party members to disclose their Communist affiliations was stewarded by fifty IRA men led by O'Donnell and Gilmore.[21] Charlie Gilmore and his brothers Harry and George had a long record of involvement with the IRA in South Dublin, while O'Donell quickly grew into a leading voice of the radical Left; he was, at different points, a prominent figure in the IRA and in the Marxist republican organisation Saor Éire, a founder of the Republican Congress, an active member of the League Against Imperialism and a 'fellow traveller' of the Moscow-led Communist Party.[22] He was a committed political thinker too, intent on linking Irish republicanism to the historical struggle against capitalism, often against great odds and at a high personal cost. He was reportedly attacked by a large crowd at a Republican Congress debate on the formation of an Irish anti-fascist front on College Green in April 1936; 'Go back to Moscow with your social justice' was, allegedly, the cry

[18] *D*, 75.

[19] Sheehy Skeffington, *Skeff*, 38–9, 72–4, 77; Margaret Ward, *Hanna Sheehy Skeffington: A Life* (Cork: Attic Press, 1997), 316; Kate O'Malley, *Ireland, India and Empire: Indo-Irish Radical Connections, 1919–1964* (Manchester: Manchester University Press, 2008), 31–52. His parents were Francis Sheehy Skeffington, the Irish suffragist and pacifist campaigner, and Hanna Sheehy Skeffington, the women's rights campaigner.

[20] O'Connor, *Reds and the Green*, 221. [21] Ibid., 190.

[22] Donal Ó Drisceoil, *Peadar O'Donnell* (Cork: Cork University Press, 2001), 1–3.

that put a halt to his speech when an angry crowd launched an attack on the speakers.[23]

On several occasions in 1936 and 1937, Beckett visited O'Donnell at home in Upper Drumcondra, and went to parties at Charlie Gilmore's house in County Wicklow.[24] These, it seems, were easy and comfortable friendships, and Beckett clearly enjoyed being in the company of O'Donnell and Gilmore. In August 1936, somewhat enigmatically, he recalled a Peadar O'Donnell consumed by his own sense of moral rectitude.[25] His letters describe Gilmore as 'sehr simpatisch [*sic*], a gipsy, on the dole', and detail attempts to help him while he was 'looking for a job as a fireman'.[26] During the same period, Beckett became friends with Ernie O'Malley, another illustrious figure in Irish political republicanism, whose memoir, *On Another Man's Wound*, appeared in 1936. O'Malley greatly admired Beckett, and esteem was reciprocal: Beckett introduced O'Malley to his much-loved aunt Cissie Sinclair in 1937, dedicated a copy of *Proust* to him when he returned to Dublin in 1946, and they continued to meet in Paris in the 1950s.[27]

Liam O'Flaherty is also mentioned in biographies as someone who frequented the same Dublin pubs as Beckett. Anecdotes do not stretch further, but during the 1930s Beckett and O'Flaherty had much in common, including the experience of seeing their work banned by the Irish Censorship Board, an interest in visiting Russia (O'Flaherty travelled there in 1930), an eagerness to speak against Irish censorship (O'Flaherty published an incendiary essay in 1932 denouncing the 'tyranny of the Irish Church' and the 'culture of dung', a verdict that anticipates Beckett's 'Recent Irish Poetry'),[28] and an aspiration to work with film (O'Flaherty later wrote scripts for Hollywood films and in other contexts). O'Flaherty, alongside Seán O'Casey, is named first among the censored Irish writers mentioned in Beckett's essay 'Censorship in the Saorstat', in a list that seems

23 Sheehy Skeffington, *Skeff*, 77; R. M. Douglas, *Architects of the Resurrection: Ailtirí na hAiséirghe and the Fascist 'New Order' in Ireland* (Manchester: Manchester University Press, 2009), 29–30.

24 *LM*, 239, 261; *LSB1*, 547.

25 SB to MacGreevy, 7 August 1936, TCD MS 10402/104, Trinity College Dublin.

26 *LSB1*, 351, 570.

27 *Broken Landscapes: Selected Letters of Ernie O'Malley 1924–1957*, ed. Cormac K. H. O'Malley and Nicholas Allen (Dublin: Lilliput Press, 2011), 360; Richard English, *Ernie O'Malley: IRA Intellectual* (Oxford: Oxford University Press, 1998), 69; Carlton Lake, *No Symbols Where None Intended: A Catalogue of Books, Manuscripts and Other Material Relating to Samuel Beckett in the Collections of the Humanities Research Center* (Austin: Humanities Research Center, University of Texas at Austin, 1984), 15; *LSB1*, 490; *Chronology*, 126.

28 Julia Carson, ed., *Banned in Ireland: Censorship and the Irish Writer* (London: Routledge, 1990), 139–41.

ordered by degree of perceived politicisation. O'Flaherty had been one of the most visible advocates of communism in the Irish Free State; Emmet O'Connor offers a vivid portrayal of him, during the 1920s, as 'a familiar figure haranguing crowds outside Liberty Hall' and selling the *Workers' Republic*, which he edited, at Nelson's Pillar.[29] Harry Kernoff, whom Beckett also knew through his pub and theatre rounds, was a painter with an interest in stage design; he was involved in a society close to the Communist Party of Ireland, the Irish Friends of Soviet Russia, whose committee consisted mainly of republicans, and he also visited Russia in 1930.[30]

Other acquaintances from Beckett's youth had ties to Irish republican organisations: Vera Esposito, the sister of his Italian language tutor, with whom he spent much time during his trip to Florence in 1927, was a former IRA member driven out of Ireland due to her political activities during the Irish Civil War, while her brother Mario, who became Beckett's holiday companion, was a former Sinn Féin agent.[31] These friendships contrast sharply with the kind of literary mentor that Beckett found in James Joyce, whose taste for ill-judged provocation when it came to politics was well known among common acquaintances.[32] Beckett later wondered about Joyce's political blindness and indifference, describing him as someone capable of taking action, yet ultimately remaining '[b]eyond it all' at a time when taking sides mattered.[33] His verdict was without appeal: Joyce 'never rebelled, he was detached, he accepted everything. For him, *there was absolutely no difference between a bomb falling and a leaf falling*'.[34] Jack Yeats – whom Beckett described as 'very Republican', 'exclusively Republic', and as a keen Irish speaker – and Nancy Cunard played a far more important role in shaping his political education.[35]

Beckett's many friendships with committed republicans, socialists and anti-colonialists certainly grate with dominant narratives of Irish republicanism, which emphasise the estrangement of Irish Protestants and the polarisation of public life according to religious parameters. Richard English, notably, argues that Irish republicanism, with its emphasis on Catholicism, Gaelicism and separatism, was 'distinctly unappealing' to most Protestants, and that republicans across the spectrum, including the left fringe, had a poor understanding of Irish unionism.[36] Clearly, there

[29] O'Connor, *Reds and the Green*, 51, 58–60. [30] Ibid., 150. [31] *DF*, 72–3; *BR/RB*, 24–5.
[32] See Morris Beja, 'Political Perspectives on Joyce's Work', in *Joyce & Paris 1902 . . . 1920–1940 . . . 1975*, ed. Jacques Aubert and Maria Jolas (Paris: CNRS, 1979), 115–17.
[33] *LSB4*, 67.
[34] Cited in Emil Cioran, 'Encounters with Beckett', *Samuel Beckett: The Critical Heritage*, 378.
[35] *BR/RB*, 58.
[36] Richard English, *Radicals and the Republic: Socialist Republicanism in the Irish Free State, 1925–1937* (Oxford: Clarendon Press, 1994), 256.

was no place for republicanism of whatever hue at Cooldrinagh, the family home in Foxrock. The ideology of unionism permeates accounts of Beckett's early years, and shaped everything from his aspirations ('play cricket for Ireland') to his childhood readings and belongings (which included a magazine entitled *Union Jack* and a handkerchief with a Union Jack motif).[37] His education took place in long-standing and militant bastions of Irish unionism. This was family tradition: his cousins attended a school at which 'God Save the King' was sung with windows open, 'so that the IRA would know exactly where [the institution] stood'.[38]

Much has been said about Beckett's youth as a time of profound psychological unrest and estrangement, and his biographers report that after trips to Italy and France his sartorial and social habits shifted. These shifts also suggest a new perception of his own social and political identity. His father wore a bowler hat, smoked a pipe and frequented the Kildare Street Club and the Royal Irish Automobile Club; Beckett became known for wearing a beret, the insignia of the working man and the bohemian artist, and took to drinking beer in pubs and smoking Woodbine cigarettes.[39] His letters evoke terrible bouts of frustration: a letter from November 1930 to MacGreevy, for example, relates his 'tired abstract anger' and 'inarticulate passive opposition'.[40] There are many traces of his increasing irritation towards inherited political allegiances: Knowlson's biography describes an evening in 1936 that Beckett partially spent 'throw[ing] rocks at England' from the Dublin coast, with friends who were unlikely to join in.[41] This is only one of many anecdotes showing the relish with which Beckett sought to subvert the common conventions of political propriety. Georges Belmont, likewise, recounts a party organised around late 1930 by Barbara Greg, daughter of the Protestant Archbishop of Dublin, at which Beckett took the Archbishop's round hat, turned it into a kind of Napoleonic bicorne hat, and proceeded to a remarkable imitation of Mussolini's speeches, shouting in a mixture of real and invented Italian, as though there was an innate proximity between the Church of Ireland, Napoleon's Empire and Italian fascism.[42] It is certain that Beckett's education at Trinity made him poorly equipped to understand the long span of political history, although the subjects he studied – French, Provençal and Italian – were intimately implicated in broader international tensions. The reading lists published in the *Dublin University Calendar* reveal syllabi dominated by an avoidance

[37] Andrew Gibson, *Samuel Beckett* (London: Reaktion, 2009), 26; *SB*, 21. [38] *DF*, 27.

[39] *SB*, 55, 115; *DF*, 11; *LM*, 150; 'Trinity College Notes', *IT*, 5 July 1930, 6; 'An Irishman's Diary', *IT*, 28 July 1945, 3.

[40] *LSB1*, 55. [41] *DF*, 228.

[42] Georges Belmont, *Souvenirs d'outre-monde: Histoire d'une naissance* (Paris: Calmann-Lévy, 2001), 302.

of social and political debate; in any case, the institution at large had frequently been at war with wider trends in Irish political life (a lone Union Jack defiantly flew over one of the main gates until 1935; at the other end, at the West Front, an Irish tricolour was added in 1922 by way of concession, as well as a college flag in the middle of campus).[43] Until meeting Jack Yeats and Nancy Cunard, Beckett remained short of mentors in political history: everything he learned, he learned alone.

Networks and Political Cultures at Trinity College Dublin and the Ecole Normale Supérieure

The institutional context in which Beckett learned French and Italian at Trinity was tense; the two figures who played an important role in his education, Thomas Rudmose-Brown and Walter Starkie, did not get along, due to a political incompatibility that transformed their professional relationship into a 'guerilla war'.[44] Rudmose-Brown portrayed himself as 'neither Fascist nor Communist, Imperialist nor Socialist', and saw Beckett as his disciple; a 'great enemy of imperialism, patriotism and all the Churches'.[45] He was proud of Beckett's proficiency in Old Occitan and Modern Provençal, and through his teaching Beckett acquired some knowledge of the Félibrige (the notes Beckett later took for Ethna McCarthy suggest that he was more interested in the movement's separatist politics than its literature, however).[46] Rudmose-Brown's writings on French literature display no taste for political history, and the incendiary letters he sent to the editor of the *Irish Times* denouncing the Catholic Church and Irish nationalism at large testify to a limited understanding of ideology and anarchism. Starkie, who taught Beckett Italian, had clearer affiliations: he was a prominent supporter of Italian fascism, an occasional anti-Semite and a vocal detractor of 'Bolshevistic talk' and 'Bolshevistic propaganda'.[47] Like W. B. Yeats, he was deeply interested in Croce's and Gentile's idealism and Mussolini's education reforms.[48] These

[43] R. B. McDowell, *Trinity College Dublin 1592–1952: An Academic History* (Cambridge: Cambridge University Press, 1982), 433–4.

[44] Ibid., 458.

[45] *DF*, 50–1; Roger Little, 'Beckett's Mentor, Rudmose-Brown: Sketch for a Portrait', *Irish University Review* 14, no. 1 (1984): 34–41.

[46] *LSB1*, 525; 'TCD MS 10971/4: Frédéric Mistral and the Félibrige Poets', *Notes Diverse Holo*, ed. Everett Frost and Jane Maxwell, *SBTA* 16 (2006): 133–6.

[47] Jacqueline Hurtley, *Walter Starkie: A Biography* (Dublin: Four Courts, 2013), 200, 190.

[48] Clair Wills, *That Neutral Island: A Cultural History of Ireland during the Second World War* (London: Faber, 2007), 347–8; 'Dublin and the Provinces', *IT*, 19 March 1827, 8; 'Secondary Teachers: Modern Ideas Wanted', *IT*, 20 April 1927, 4.

interests were well known in Dublin, where Starkie held prominent roles, acting as educational advisor for Cumann na nGaedheal and as Secretary of Yeats's Academy of Letters. He was also an international advocate of Italian fascism and, in 1927, became General Secretary to the Centre International d'Etudes sur le Fascisme, an international organisation based in Lausanne led by a select group of aristocrats, parliamentarians, ministers and professors, whose role mainly consisted in disseminating propaganda for Mussolini.[49] What makes Starkie's fascination for fascism distinctive is that it endured, while many of his contemporaries became less enthusiastic about Mussolini's regime after the invasion of Ethiopia. Even in 1940, the *Irish Times* described Starkie as someone who counted Mussolini and Franco among his friends, but did not support the Berlin-Rome axis.[50] Starkie's work as propagandist appears to have been much valued during the 1930s: in 1935, he went to Ethiopia as guest of Mussolini's military forces, and his 1938 autobiography, which recalls meetings with Mussolini, Gentile and Edmondo Rossoni, was partially funded by Mussolini's government.[51]

At the Ecole Normale Supérieure, the elite institution at which he taught in 1928–1929 and 1929–1930, Beckett was confronted with another generational model of political activity and different political codes. He was no longer a student, and while he seems to have been relatively isolated on Rue d'Ulm, he nonetheless sustained strong friendships with Alfred Péron, Jean Beaufret and Georges Pelorson (later Georges Belmont). The friendship with Beaufret does not seem to have continued beyond these early years, but Péron and Pelorson became steadfast friends and collaborators. Much is known about the influence of these friendships on Beckett's literary and philosophical tastes, but little has been said about the wider political context shaping these encounters. Circumstances are important, not least because the political culture of the ENS underwent several mutations between the wars, while remaining dominated by radical political orientations. These changes are recorded in Paul Nizan's *La conspiration*, based on Nizan's time at the ENS, which he left two years before Beckett's arrival; this semi-autobiographical novel relates the attempt of students who have an insufficient understanding of political action to form a revolutionary group in order to steal secret military documents for the

[49] Thomas P. Linehan, *British Fascism, 1918–39: Parties, Ideology and Culture* (Manchester: Manchester University Press, 2000), 128; Hurtley, *Starkie*, 146–7; Michael A. Ledeen, *Universal Fascism: The Theory and Practice of the Fascist International, 1928–1936* (New York: Howard Fertig, 1972), 86–90.

[50] 'Trinity College Notes', *IT*, 13 January 1940, 9.

[51] Walter Starkie, *The Waveless Plain: An Italian Autobiography* (London: John Murray, 1938), 405.

Communist Party.[52] Throughout momentous times, the institution continued to foster a spirit of camaraderie capable of enduring despite fierce political differences, as Pim Den Boer has shown, and remained known for its *esprit de corps*.[53] This cultural question is important for understanding how Beckett's subsequent career, friendships and expressed solidarities relate to the two years he spent there: the ENS had strong alumni networks, and, in difficult times, these affiliations helped Beckett to secure work – for example, at UNESCO, where *normaliens* held prominent roles.

Beckett joined the ENS at a turning point in its history: the period between 1928 and 1930, as Diane Rubenstein has shown, saw brutal shifts in the political enthusiasms nurtured at the institution. Many of the pupils who enrolled between 1922 and 1927 went on to illustrious political careers on the French Left, or subsequently became renowned for their activities within the cultures of the Left: notable figures include Pierre Brossolette, Jean Cavaillès, Maurice Merleau-Ponty, Sartre and Nizan (Beckett was particularly alert to the circumstances surrounding Nizan's departure from the Communist Party in the wake of the 1939 German-Soviet Pact).[54] In contrast, ENS cohorts from 1927 to 1929 featured an increasing number of right-leaning intellectuals, some of whom later occupied prominent positions in the Vichy regime and its culture. The 1928 class is a good example of this shift.[55] It included militants of the Left such as Simone Weil and Beaufret, as well as Jacques Soustelle, the later Gaullist deputy and Governor General of Algeria. It also included Pelorson – Beckett's pupil and soon close friend – and some important voices in the history of the French Far Right: Maurice Bardèche, Robert Brasillach and Jacques Talagrand. The last is better known under his penname, Thierry Maulnier, as a staunch supporter of Maurras and Action Française, recognised in the pre-war years for his strident anti-Semitism. At the ENS, Pelorson shared a room with Talagrand, and Bardèche and Brasillach occupied the next room.[56]

Pelorson's politics prior to the war make for a peculiar mixture, and reveal his interest in the rhetoric of revolution developing within both the Communist Left and the Fascist Right. He has been described as someone

[52] Paul Nizan, *La conspiration* (Paris: Gallimard, 1938), 30, 57–8.

[53] Pim Den Boer, *History as a Profession: The Study of History in France, 1818–1914* (Princeton: Princeton University Press, 1998), 187.

[54] *LSB1*, 668.

[55] Diane Rubenstein, *What's Left?: The Ecole Normale Supérieure and the Right* (Madison: University of Wisconsin Press, 1990), 31, 37.

[56] Belmont, *Souvenirs*, 130–2; Etienne de Montety, *Thierry Maulnier*, revised ed. (Paris: Perrin, 2013); Vincent Giroud, 'Transition to Vichy: The Case of Georges Pelorson', *Modernism/modernity* 7, no. 2 (2000): 223.

who was impregnated by the ideas of the revolutionary Left from a young age – as an anarchist, an anti-militarist ideologue, a Communist sympathiser and an admirer of Lenin and Trotsky.[57] His enthusiasm for fascism, however, became apparent on several fronts in the late 1930s; in his autobiography, Eugene Jolas recalls that Pelorson wrote plays 'with a fascist tendency' and read them to Beckett and others in and around 1938.[58] In letters that year, Beckett described Pelorson's latest achievements as 'very dull', and his work for the review *Volontés* as edging towards something 'considerably more ignominious'.[59] Beckett was aware of the literary activities driving this strand of the Far Right in the late 1930s: he owned, for example, a worn copy of Maulnier's *Introduction à la poésie française*,[60] which upon its publication in 1939 sold well, but caused controversy due to its ideological stance and exclusion of Victor Hugo and other political voices. André Gide, in particular, objected to Maulnier's 'partisan ferocities'.[61]

Pelorson's career within the Far Right and the Vichy regime was literary as well as political, and owed much to contacts formed prior to the war and during his studies at the ENS. At the time of the Spanish Civil War, for example, he became close to Lucien Combelle, later known as a prominent collaborationist, anti-Semite, anti-communist and anti-republican.[62] Historians have also drawn attention to Pelorson's friendships with members of the far-right organisation Ordre Nouveau, and to his contributions to the literary section of Jeune France, the cultural body created by Vichy, as part of ventures also supported by Maurice Girodias, the later publisher of *Watt* and *Molloy*.[63] It was Pelorson who introduced Blanchot to Jeune France in 1941, in the hope that Blanchot would take up the role he had formerly held within the organisation.[64] It has been argued that it is precisely by virtue of his familiarity with the vocabularies of the revolutionary Left and the Fascist Right that Pelorson was appointed to high-ranking posts in the Vichy administration; he had the kind of political knowledge that made propaganda work for Pétain's National Revolution unassailable.[65]

Beaufret's and Péron's political persuasions took them down different paths. Beaufret's work as a philosopher, teacher and Heidegger scholar has

[57] Limore Yagil, 'Les équipes nationales: 1942–1944', *Guerres mondiales et conflits contemporains* 184 (1996): 96–7.

[58] *LSB1*, 616 n9, 620. [59] *LSB1*, 620, 627.

[60] Dirk Van Hulle and Mark Nixon, *Samuel Beckett's Library* (Cambridge: Cambridge University Press, 2013), 75, 278.

[61] André Gide, 'Interviews imaginaires: Outrelouanges, injustes critiques', *Le Figaro*, 29 November 1941, 3.

[62] Pierre Assouline, *Le fleuve Combelle* (Paris: Calmann-Lévy, 1997), 152, 139–40.

[63] Giroud, 'Transition to Vichy', 234. [64] Bident, *Maurice Blanchot*, 127 n1, 158–60.

[65] Yagil, 'Les équipes nationales', 97.

been widely discussed, but he also had a strong political identity, and is reported to have been particularly vocal about his support for the Far Left in the late 1940s.[66] In 1933, Beckett prophetically wrote to MacGreevy that he would 'love to see Beaufret en militaire, looking something between the drummer and the mascot'; in the 1990s, Vidal-Naquet remembered Beaufret as an early member of the Resistance who, in the context of his wartime teaching of philosophy in Grenoble, had trained his students in how to use a machine-gun.[67] Among Beckett's many friends, Péron stands out, as a figure whom Beckett held in great esteem and affection. They met when Péron started his teaching term as the exchange *lecteur* at Trinity in September 1926.[68] At the ENS, Péron was highly regarded by everyone (he belonged to the illustrious cohort admitted in 1924), and he knew Nizan and Sartre, with whom he once shared a study, particularly well (Sartre was briefly engaged to one of his cousins).[69] Politically, Péron remained a steadfast socialist; he joined the SFIO – the Section Française de l'Internationale Ouvrière, precursor to the French Socialist Party – in 1925, alongside others at the ENS.[70] His political enthusiasms are documented: in a letter to de Beauvoir from 1938, in a somewhat mocking tone, Sartre described Péron returning from a 14 July march and wearing on his lapel a label celebrating republican Spain and the French Popular Front.[71]

The spoof Beckett conceived with Pelorson when the latter was teaching French at Trinity – *Le Kid*, written for Trinity's staff and students and performed at Dublin's Peacock Theatre in early 1931 – owed much to traditions established at the ENS: the spoof play was one of the channels through which Sartre, Péron and others had manifested their opposition to French militarism in a boisterous fashion, at the time of the *revue annuelle*, an annual performance by students. The 1927 *revue* caused scandal; it featured anti-militaristic songs, evidently authored by Georges Canguilhem, Péron and others from their cohort.[72] Beckett and Pelorson's text has not survived

[66] Pierre Vidal-Naquet, *Mémoires, vol. 1: La brisure et l'attente, 1930–1955* (Paris: Seuil, 1995), 217. On Beaufret's negationism and support of Heidegger's politics, see Faye, *Heidegger, L'Introduction du Nazisme dans la philosophie*, 501–4; Dominique Janicaud, *Heidegger en France, vol. 2: Entretiens* (Paris: Albin Michel, 2001).

[67] *LSB1*, 153; Vidal-Naquet, *Mémoires, vol. 1*, 217.

[68] *Chronology*, 13.

[69] Annie Cohen-Solal, *Sartre: A Life*, trans. Anna Cancogni (London: Heinemann, 1987), 64, 72–3; Isabelle Grell, *Les chemins de la liberté de Sartre: Genèse et écriture (1938–1952)* (Bern: Peter Lang, 2005), 15.

[70] Jean-François Sirinelli, *Génération intellectuelle: Khâgneux et normaliens dans l'entre-deux guerres* (Paris: Quadrige and PUF, 1994), 587; Georges Lefranc, *Visages du mouvement ouvrier français* (Paris: PUF, 1982), 65.

[71] Jean-Paul Sartre, *Lettres au Castor et à quelques autres, 1926–1939*, ed. Simone de Beauvoir (Paris: Gallimard, 1983), 183.

[72] Jean-François Sirinelli, *Deux intellectuels dans le siècle, Sartre et Aron* (Paris: Arthème Fayard, 1995), 83–5.

and accounts of the performance are scarce, yet it is clear that *Le Kid* owed as much to this precedent as to Corneille and Chaplin.[73] The costumes were taken from Pelorson's production of Jean Giraudoux's *Siegfried* – a play about an amnesiac First World War soldier who, through a strange twist of fate, finds himself torn between his new life in Germany and his French past. Pelorson, like Talagrand, held the play and its author in great esteem.[74] For *Le Kid*, Beckett and Pelorson put materials from this previous production to inventive use: Pelorson was dressed as a German general and wore a First World War uniform with a spiked helmet; his performance involved leaping into the auditorium and chasing balloons with a sabre. Beckett wore modern dress and lifted his bowler hat 'each time the king was mentioned'.[75] His salute would have come with a discernible political charge: George V, titular commander-in-chief of the British army, had retained a political status in the Irish Free State, and the Anglo-Irish Treaty required all members of Parliament to take an oath of allegiance to the King and State. The removal of the oath was a prominent feature in de Valera's party policy in 1931 and thereafter, and it influenced the outcome of the 1932 General Election in his favour.[76] Little is known of *Le Kid*, but it is clear that it was conceived as a politically oriented satire, which summoned troublesome historical spectres through its flirtation with familiar political symbols invoking a belligerent Germany, the trenches and the English Crown. As such, the performance responded not simply to the tradition of experimental performance at the Peacock Theatre, but to controversial questions arising from Irish involvement in the First World War under the British flag, and the conditions in which Irish independence was secured. It does not seem that these echoes were handled particularly gracefully. Yet Beckett was born and bred of these political tensions and knew many war veterans, such as his uncle Howard Beckett, whom the family had 'more or less pushed' or 'blackmailed' into 'join[ing] up' (to borrow his words),[77] MacGreevy, who had fought at Ypres and the Somme, and Alan Duncan, who had served in the British army in the same areas and had been gassed.

It is important to consider the political cultures that shaped Beckett's artistic tastes during this formative period: other moments widely recognised as turning points – notably, his trip to Germany between September 1936 and April 1937 – take on a different dimension when considered

[73] See *DF*, 122, 124; Belmont, *Souvenirs*, 299.
[74] Belmont, *Souvenirs*, 208; de Montety, *Maulnier*, 56–7. Happily, Giraudoux's later political affiliations under the Vichy regime coincided with theirs.
[75] Dougald McMillan and Martha Fehsenfeld, *Beckett in the Theatre* (London: Calder, 1988), 20–1.
[76] 'Mr de Valera Outlines his Party's Policy', *IT*, 28 October 1931, 7.
[77] *DF*, 9.

against the political tensions that shaped his education and artistic awakening. By this point, he was no longer a privileged witness; Hitler's regime had long been at the centre of a global and carefully orchestrated spectacle, as part of a process accelerated by the 1936 Olympic Games in Berlin. Visiting Berlin was fashionable, still; this was a trend that Irmgard Keun gently caricatured, in a novel from 1937, as the 'study tour of Germany' undertaken by young Englishmen eager to see 'the change in the German nation'.[78] The road to Germany was well-travelled in the intellectual milieu with which Beckett was familiar: the ENS alumni who had preceded him included Beaufret, Sartre, Raymond Aron, Maurice de Gandillac and René Maheu. In Dublin, Beckett's journey had other precedents: Flann O'Brien, for example, travelled to Germany in late 1933, and this trip, clearly a turning point for him, has been shrouded in secrecy. Another Dubliner visited Germany the same year as Beckett: R. M. Smyllie, editor of the *Irish Times* and initiator of the 'Irishman's Diary', who published under the pseudonym Nichevo, in November 1936, a series of detailed articles on Hitler's policies, rearmament, censorship and espionage.[79] Beckett's own journey was undertaken in the wake of many visits to Kassel to see the love of his youth, his cousin Peggy Sinclair, and Nixon has shown that Beckett had many personal and artistic reasons for wanting to spend more time in Germany in the wake of her death. Over the course of six months, he filled several notebooks with painstakingly detailed accounts of his activities and conversations; his German Diaries are known through Knowlson's biography, Nixon's scholarship and the work of contextualisation undertaken by McNaughton and Erika Tophoven.

It is important to consider the distinctive context in which Beckett made plans in the first place. He resolved to undertake this trip to Germany after abandoning a very different project, to which he was deeply dedicated: moving to Moscow to study cinematography with Sergei Eisenstein. Eisenstein was then renowned for his mastery of the historical documentary, and for his allegorical portrayals of struggles around labour and the control of agricultural and industrial production. Beckett never received a reply to his letter of application, and it seems unlikely that Eisenstein ever received it. Undefeated, he began to make plans to study with Vsevolod Pudovkin instead, writing a long letter, which also remained unanswered, about the virtues of the naturalistic silent film to Pudovkin.[80]

[78] Irmgard Keun, *After Midnight*, trans. Anthea Bell (New York: Melville House, 2011), 108.

[79] The first and last articles in the series are Nichevo, 'Germany under Adolf Hitler: First Impressions of Bavaria's Beauties', *IT*, 2 November 1936, 4; 'Germany under Adolf Hitler: Preparing for the Next Great War', *IT*, 17 November 1936, 4.

[80] *SB*, 204–5.

Moscow: Another Journey

When Beckett applied for admission to the All-Union State Institute of Cinematography in March 1936, he made clear that he was ready to live in Moscow for 'a year at least'.[81] The institute, founded fifteen years previously as a platform for political education and agit-prop work, was firmly established as the heart of political and historical filmmaking, and Beckett would have been aware of this fact. His interest in Soviet film began long before, and there are many traces of his absorption in Russian literature and Soviet politics in his lectures at Trinity College Dublin, critical essays and correspondence.[82] Alan Schneider, born at the time of the Russian Revolution to a Russian-speaking Jewish family in Kharkov, had vivid memories of a Beckett keen to hear anecdotes from his youth during their first meeting in Paris.[83] Beckett later attempted to learn Russian alone, describing it to Schneider in 1962 as 'a useful tongue and an impossible one'.[84] Throughout the 1930s, he was most attentive to artists whose relation to Soviet Communism was under strain or put them in some professional difficulty: foremost among them, Eisenstein, as well as Andrey Bely and O'Casey, who also saw their careers affected by their political stance.

During the 1930s, Beckett's Moscow plan ran counter to the dominant current. Opportunities to watch recent Soviet films were few and far between: British tax levies were high, making such films inaccessible in Dublin. Censorship also played a role: Eisenstein's *Battleship Potemkin* was banned in Britain until 1929, and Soviet films using montage were deemed propagandist.[85] *The General Line*, a film that Beckett clearly appreciated, was also perceived as subversive; in some contexts, it denoted political dissent, as when Cunard organised a private screening of the film in London in 1933 to raise funds for the Scottsboro case.[86] In Dublin, efforts were regularly made to show Soviet films, with mixed results. In February 1930, for example, plans were formed to launch a Dublin film society that would

[81] *LSB1*, 317.

[82] See my *Samuel Beckett and the Problem of Irishness*, 31–2; Brigitte Le Juez, *Beckett before Beckett: Samuel Beckett's Lectures on French Literature*, trans. Ros Schwartz (London: Souvenir Press, 2009).

[83] Alan Schneider, *Entrances: An American Director's Journey* (New York: Viking, 1986), 224.

[84] *NABS*, 117.

[85] Sarah Street, *British National Cinema*, 2nd ed. (Abingdon: Routledge, 2009), 195; Ian Christie, 'Censorship, Culture, and Cod Pieces', in *Eisenstein at 100: A Reconsideration*, ed. Al LaValley and Barry P. Scherr (New Brunswick, NJ: Rutgers University Press, 1991), 110, 118 n6.

[86] Hugh Ford, 'Introduction', in *Negro: An Anthology*, by Nancy Cunard, abridged ed. by Hugh Ford (New York: Continuum, 2002), xxii. When Beckett wrote to Ussher about the film, *The General Line* had not yet been shown in Dublin (W. B. Yeats made plans to see it in London). See R. F. Foster, *W. B. Yeats: A Life, vol. 2: The Arch-Poet* (Oxford: Oxford University Press, 2003), 393.

show foreign films, organise lectures, run a film library and give Dublin audiences an opportunity to discover the work of German and Russian directors such as Eisenstein, Pudovkin and Pabst (all of whom were banned in Germany).[87] The launch, announced for the following month, was to consist of a showing of *Battleship Potemkin*, but the Society was unable to cover the tax duties and these plans were soon abandoned. In July that year, Dublin's Sackville Cinema showed Pudovkin's *The End of St Petersburg*, and in October and November *Storm Over Asia*, a film presenting the imagined British occupation of Mongolia.[88] Eventually, in mid-February 1936, the Dublin Little Theatre Guild organised a semi-private screening of *Battleship Potemkin*, at a time that coincides with Beckett's discussions about Eisenstein with friends.[89] The film had become the focus of heightened anxiety, and its importation by the Irish Film Society by means of a private licence caused uproar in Dublin, with *The Irish Catholic* newspaper condemning its showing as the work of a Communist cell.[90]

These disputes probably added to the appeal of Eisenstein and Pudovkin for Beckett, and shed light on the ostentatiousness with which their films are invoked in *Dream of Fair to Middling Women* and the short stories that derived from it. In a fulsome letter that reappears in *More Pricks than Kicks*, the Smeraldina tries to convert Belacqua to Soviet cinema, praising Pudovkin's *Storm Over Asia* and *The Living Corpse*, a film in which Pudovkin acted.[91] Echoing her prompt, Belacqua recalls *Battleship Potemkine* with some fondness in 'Echo's Bones', evoking '[t]hat pram I found most moving'.[92] For Beckett, working with film was to remain a dream until *Film*, but even this singular experiment was connected to his early interest in the camera work pioneered in Soviet cinema: *Film*'s cinematographer was Boris Kaufman, brother of Dziga Vertov and Mikhail Kaufman, who had a long and distinguished career working on documentaries and with Jean Vigo, and a lesser-known trajectory of exile shaped by the Cold War.[93]

[87] 'Dublin Film Society', *IT*, 13 February 1930, 6; 'The Battleship Potemkin', *IT*, 21 February 1936, 4; 'A Dublin Film Society: Why It Was Abandoned', *IT*, 13 November 1930, 4; Jean-Michel Palmier, *Weimar in Exile: The Antifascist Emigration in Europe and America*, trans. David Fernbach (London: Verso, 2006), 25.

[88] 'Public Amusements', *IT*, 28 July 1930, 6; 'Dublin Theatres and Cinemas', *IT*, 27 October 1930, 4.

[89] 'Film Notes', *IT*, 25 February 1936, 4.

[90] 'Little Theatre Guild', *IT*, 18 February 1936, 4; Anthony Slide, *The Cinema and Ireland* (Jefferson, NC: McFarland, 1988), 16; Wills, *That Neutral Island*, 303.

[91] *The Living Corpse* doesn't seem to have been shown in Dublin; however, it was shown in London in 1929, and Pudovkin was hosted by the Film Society in London that year.

[92] SB, *Echo's Bones*, ed. Mark Nixon (London: Faber, 2014), 29.

[93] Michael North, *Machine-Age Comedy* (Oxford: Oxford University Press, 2009), 146–8; Erik Barnouw, *Media Lost and Found* (New York: Fordham University Press, 2001), 163–9.

Moving to Moscow was a dream that Beckett began to nurture at the start of 1936, as his correspondence suggests. In letters to McGreevy, he professed his commitment to film editing and montage, describing his attempts to obtain advice on technique and equipment, and relating his new acquaintance with texts by and about Eisenstein, Arnheim and Pudovkin.[94] He borrowed these publications as well as issues of *Close-Up* from Niall Montgomery, the son of the Irish film censor James Montgomery (which goes some way towards explaining why the Montgomery home was so well furnished in rare publications about Soviet filmmaking). He read far and wide about cinematic technique: his correspondence suggests that he found Pudovkin's lectures rather underwhelming, even though the practical issues tackled address topics about which he professed curiosity (Pudovkin discusses the differences between stage acting and film acting, the work of Meyerhold, the changes ushered by film technologies, and the challenges of casting non-professional actors).[95]

Eisenstein's visual aesthetic had a lasting influence on Beckett; however, little is known about the context of his application to Eisenstein, and taking this context into account gives a rather different sense of Beckett's intent. Connections to Moscow were, of course, politically significant, particularly in the Irish Free State, where the very word 'Moscow' evoked Communism as readily as Rome evoked the Catholic Church. Individuals and societies associated with Russian and Soviet cultures, perceived as motors of republican socialist revolt facilitating the rise of a leftist front, were subject to close public scrutiny.[96] In 1930, in the context of the land annuities campaign, O'Donnell was accused by the *Irish Rosary* magazine of having studied the 'technique of revolution' in Moscow, an accusation that stuck for some time.[97] A scheme to facilitate trips to Moscow had been in place since 1929, when the Moscow Comintern decided to pursue alternative means to encourage support for Communism in Ireland; young Irish cadres were taken in as students at the Lenin School in Moscow, while the Comintern worked on forging links with the IRA through cultural organisations and intermediaries such as O'Donnell.[98] These opportunities were closely regimented, and Emmet O'Connor observes that 'a combination of Soviet secrecy, mistrust of anti-Soviet propaganda, and defensiveness [...] obscured the grim realities of famine, poverty and terror' in Stalin's Russia,

94 *LSB1*, 311.

95 *LSB1*, 324; V.I. Pudovkin, *Film Acting: A Course of Lectures Delivered at the State Institute of Cinematography, Moscow*, trans. Ivor Montagu (London: George Newnes, 1935).

96 English, *Radicals and the Republic*, 140–1.

97 Ibid., 111; Sheehy Skeffington, *Skeff*, 77.

98 Ó Drisceoil, *Peadar O'Donnell*, 50–1, 57.

even among well-informed Irish Communists and students of the Lenin School.[99]

All things considered, any form of educational or professional training in Moscow in 1936 would have been difficult to undertake for someone who, like Beckett, was making ad-hoc plans and had no knowledge of Russian. Beyond the restricted opportunities offered by the Communist Party of Ireland, trips undertaken by students of the Lenin School and members of the Friends of Soviet Russia, there was little traffic from Dublin to Moscow during the 1920s and 1930s. Yet several of Beckett's acquaintances knew Russia well, and this probably made Moscow appear within reach. George Reavey, Beckett's first literary agent, had lived there until 1919, and the Russian-born Paul Léon until 1918 (Léon remained a staunch anti-communist, like his wife Lucie Noel, born in Moscow). Others still went to Moscow in search of political certainty: O'Flaherty travelled to Russia in 1930, and published a disillusioned account of his journey the following year.[100] Cunard spent a month in Moscow in August 1935, where she met some American contributors to her *Negro* anthology.[101] O'Flaherty and Cunard wore their politics on their sleeves; as for Reavey, it is clear that he had no sympathy for Soviet Communism or Marxism. In 1938, Beckett characterised Reavey as someone who worked to further his own 'metaphysico-political' line, a claim that describes Reavey's politics effectively.[102] Samuel Putnam was also sensitive to the peculiarity of Reavey's literary politics, praising his ability to take Surrealism 'with no bad after-effect', or without yielding to the Surrealist interest in radical politics.[103] Yet Reavey knew how to respond to the interest in Soviet culture prevalent across the Left; the numerous projects that he initiated include a volume published by Wishart & Co., the publisher of the British Communist Party and the British Left, entitled *Soviet Literature: An Anthology* (1933). The book, edited by Reavey and Marc Slonim, mapped literary developments after the Russian Revolution, but conveyed a clear desire to dissociate literature from politics: as the French newspaper *L'Humanité* emphasised, the anthology did not display any sympathy for Marxist analyses, and the absence of a political dimension acted as a political statement in itself.[104]

[99] O'Connor, *Reds and the Green*, 168.
[100] Anne Chisholm, *Nancy Cunard: A Biography* (New York: Knopf, 1979), 230–1.
[101] Liam O'Flaherty, *I Went to Russia* (London: Jonathan Cape, 1931).
[102] *LSB1*, 621.
[103] Samuel Putnam, 'Foreword to a Sunken Continent', in *Faust's Metamorphoses*, by George Reavey (Fontenay-aux-Roses: New Review, 1932), 8.
[104] René Garmy, 'Les livres', *L'Humanité*, 9 September 1935, 4.

The letters Beckett wrote in 1936 make clear that he was serious about moving to the Soviet Union. He explained to MacGreevy in March that being accepted to the 'Moscow State Institute of Cinematography' did not ultimately matter, and that he would 'probably go soon whether or no'.[105] His tone suggests that he felt under pressure to justify his choice as an aesthetic pursuit divorced from ideological consideration: 'What I would learn under a person like Pudovkin is how to handle a camera, the higher trucs of the editing bench, & so on, of which I know as little as of quantity surveying. The most liberal government imaginable, in effect & disposition, would not make me a bit wiser in that respect'.[106] His portrayal of Soviet Russia as anti-liberal is certainly a mild rendering of a political situation that had long been presented rather differently around him. As early as 1921, Slonim had denounced Bolshevism as a carefully organised dictatorship in *Le Bolchévisme vu par un Russe*, which offered a detailed account of Soviet political structures, the use of propaganda, and the persecution of dissidents and socialists.[107] The 1930s saw many other accounts of these problems; Gide's *Retour de l'URSS*, published in November 1936, was a formative book for many, including in Dublin, where it attracted attention from figures as varied as Owen Sheehy Skeffington and W. B. Yeats.[108] In this book, Gide stated that he had been mistaken to proclaim his unconditional support of Soviet Communism; he lamented the grip of propaganda on public opinion, qualifying Stalin's USSR and Hitler's Germany as the two countries in which thought is least free and the people most fearful.[109] Other voices were more confused: two years later, Herbert Read also denounced Stalinism in *Poetry and Anarchism*, but without giving it a name, and outlined direct analogies between Anglo-American liberalism, Soviet Communism and German National Socialism in order to support his embrace of a non-specific anarchism.[110]

The plans that Beckett nurtured in the early months of 1936 continued to cast a shadow over his journey across Germany. In January 1937, from Berlin, he wrote to Mary Manning Howe that Daiken had sought to secure him 'a place [. . .] at the Court of Eisenstein in Moscow through his friend Malraux's brother', but help had come too late: 'I did not answer.

[105] *LSB1*, 324. [106] *LSB1*, 311.
[107] Marc Slonim, *Le Bolchévisme vu par un Russe* (Paris: Brossard, 1921), 79.
[108] 'Lecture on André Gide', *IT*, 6 November 1936, 8; 'André Gide', *IT*, 16 January 1937, 4; Elizabeth Cullingford, *Yeats, Ireland and Fascism* (London: Macmillan, 1981), 236.
[109] André Gide, *Retour de l'URSS* (Paris: Gallimard, 1936), 67. In 1932, Beckett planned to write an essay on Gide for Chatto and Windus and, later, for the *New Statesman*.
[110] Herbert Read, *Poetry and Anarchism* [1938] (London: Freedom Press, 1941), 22–3.

Moscow is another journey'.[111] Some weeks later, in Dresden, old memories resurfaced: finding himself in the close company of exiled white Russians posing as aristocrats, he feels 'positively communist'.[112] It is somewhat bewildering that Beckett could consider, with the same ease, dedicating a year to political filmmaking in Moscow and spending six months wandering around German cities and museums bound by Nazi decrees. Peculiar forms of displacement and substitution are at work in his change of heart, and his capacity to make new plans so quickly poses important questions about his political coordinates during this period. The German Diaries confirm that his perspective had shifted – that he perceived Goebbels, notably, as the 'pupil' of Soviet techniques.[113] He embarked on his journey eager to learn about thorny subjects: a notebook he kept prior to his departure maps out the circumstances germane to war, featuring vocabulary lists that record the different roles of the Wehrmacht, the SS and the SA, and anticipate discussions of rearmament, the contested Alsace-Lorraine region and German colonial ambitions.[114] Clearly, fluency in Nazi political rhetoric was for Beckett essential, and, while in Germany, he dedicated much energy to apprehending the workings of Nazism as a political system. He watched propaganda films, initiated numerous conversations about German and European politics, and spent hours listening to speeches by Hitler, Goering and other Nazi dignitaries on economic planning, infrastructure and foreign policy broadcast on the wireless.[115] Long after his return, he remained persuaded that war was an inevitable prospect; in September 1938, from his new Parisian home on Rue des Favorites, he listened with dread to yet another speech by 'Adolf the Peacemaker',[116] who was by then preparing the ground for the invasion of the Sudetenland while presenting himself as the great negotiator for peace in Europe.

Nazism, as Victor Klemperer has powerfully demonstrated, had the singular power to turn the darkest political aspirations into the most innocuous words and phrases, and the German Diaries offer an encyclopaedic

[111] *LSB1*, 423.

[112] Mark Nixon, 'Solitude(s) and Creative Fidgets: Beckett Reading Rainer Maria Rilke', *Litteraria Pragensia* 17, no. 33 (2007): 6.

[113] Cited in James McNaughton, 'Beckett's "Brilliant Obscurantics": *Watt* and the Problem of Propaganda', in *Samuel Beckett: History, Memory, Archive*, ed. Seán Kennedy and Katherine Weiss (New York: Palgrave Macmillan, 2010), 55.

[114] See 'German Vocabulary Book', Beckett International Foundation, University of Reading, UoR MS 5006, f. 1, 3, 17, 27.

[115] Mark Nixon, 'Between Gospel and Prohibition: Beckett in Nazi Germany 1936–1937', *Samuel Beckett: History, Memory, Archive*, 34.

[116] *LSB1*, 642.

account of the all-too-mundane language of Nazism.[117] In his notebooks, Beckett copied statements by Goebbels and Rudolf Hess affirming the greatness of the German *Volk* and unconditional loyalty to the Führer. He reported on an exhibition of 'decadent' modern art in Halle, a precursor to the infamous Entartete Kunst exhibition.[118] As the months went by, he became intimately familiar with commonplace denunciations of international Jewish and Communist conspiracies, and watched the consolidation of a regime concerned with economic autarchy – as well as, ominously, colonial expansion. Many of his factual reports are studded with penetrating insights and powerful puns, and, as Nixon and McNaughton have shown, they are the work of someone acutely aware of the forces of censorship and propaganda. To readers anticipating indignation and revolt, it may come as a surprise that so many of Beckett's observations should be couched in seemingly disengaged shorthand, as though he was writing to evade the eye of a potential censor.[119] It is in the same spirit that he ended some letters to Reavey with variations around the Nazi salute, 'Heil, Sieg und fette Beute'.[120] This kind of greeting would have identified his missives as unworthy of scrutiny and, more mischievously, would have made his literary agent fear the prospect of seeing an obedient Nazi return. More broadly, Beckett's diary-keeping practice refracts the culture of indirect commentary prevalent in the fictional literature produced in Germany under Nazi censorship, which finds some of its most fascinating illustrations in Keun's early novels and their occasional humour about Hitlerism. Modernist writers such as Djuna Barnes, Christopher Isherwood and Virginia Woolf appropriated this mode of oblique subversion, reflecting on the mechanics of the Nazi regime with a limited awareness of the realities experienced by Jews, Communists and anti-Nazi dissenters.[121]

Like the vast majority, Beckett seems to have been numbed, rather than shocked, by sustained exposure to the Nazi mind. Nevertheless, the ironies of history startled him, and he retained an acute sense of imminent peril. While in Berlin, walking down the Judenstraβe, he notices that this is 'where Horst Wessel spent his youth!', and copies the text from the plaque

[117] For a recent reappraisal, see Thomas Pegelow Kaplan, *The Language of Nazi Genocide: Linguistic Violence and the Struggle of Germans of Jewish Ancestry* (Cambridge: Cambridge University Press, 2009).

[118] Nixon, *German Diaries*, 136–7.

[119] Nixon, 'Between Gospel and Prohibition', 34–6; James McNaughton, 'Beckett, German Fascism, and History: The Futility of Protest', *SBTA* 15 (2005): 101–16.

[120] *LSB1*, 400, 441.

[121] See Mia Spiro, *Anti-Nazi Modernism: The Challenges of Resistance in 1930s Fiction* (Evanston, IL: Northwestern University Press, 2013).

affixed to the house, celebrating the martyr who died for the Nazi cause.[122] Elsewhere, Nazism is persistently equated with an extreme verbosity of the worst kind; just as Goering can deliver an '[i]nterminable harangue' on the wireless, many of Beckett's new acquaintances surprise him with seemingly endless rants in response to his questions.[123] One figure proves particularly willing to educate him in German political history: his landlord from Berlin's Budapesterstraβe, Willy Kempt – a latecomer to the NSDAP, formerly prevented from joining, he explained, by his membership in the Stahlhelm. Kempt, Beckett remarks, is a remarkably gifted storyteller, and his diary records the extraordinarily detailed account of the failed coups against Hitler and the merciless rivalries between the SA and the SS that his inebriated landlord had delivered the previous night, in response to his prompt about Kurt von Schleicher's assassination.[124] Kempt's belief that Germany and Europe's finest hour has come does not hold water for Beckett, who is more sympathetic with the version of events offered by bookseller Axel Kaun, who perceives Hitler and Goering as the populist tub-thumpers serving Goebbels's Machiavellian vision.[125]

Behind all the bluster, there was an all-too-real political abyss, which Beckett discerned in the recesses of museums and when speaking to Jewish scholars fearing for their future, as Nixon has shown. His tastes – including his work on Proust, a 'non-Aryan', as he notes – marked him out as someone capable of political subversion and sedition, as did his manner: in Munich, at a charity event for the Hitler-Franco alliance featuring an SS brass band, he performed the Hitlerian salute with the wrong arm during the singing of Horst Wessel's Nazi anthem.[126] In Hannover, he was fined for wandering in a 'dangerous fashion'.[127]

The poignancy of his accounts lies precisely in the incommensurability between what he recorded and the reality that lay beyond what tourists could see. His entry for 20 December 1936, for example, records time spent in the claustrophobic company of two Nazi sympathisers in Berlin, and hearing about the buildings and cellars used for torture across the city.[128] On other days, his curiosity took him to places that would soon become laden with a sombre baggage: to the town of Lüneburg, for example, a

[122] Erika Tophoven, *Becketts Berlin* (Berlin: Nicolaische Verlagsbuchhandlung, 2005), 31–2.
[123] Nixon, *German Diaries*, 85.
[124] SB, German Diaries, Notebook 4, 19 January 1937, Beckett International Foundation, University of Reading, f. 17.
[125] Ibid. [126] *LSB1*, 389; Nixon, *German Diaries*, 86. [127] *LSB1*, 395.
[128] SB, German Diaries, Notebook 3, 20 December 1936, f. 7; Mark Nixon, 'Chronology of Beckett's Journey to Germany 1936–1937 (Based on the German Diaries)', *Journal of Beckett Studies* 19, no. 2 (2010): 257. Thanks to Mark Nixon for confirming the original entry.

privileged witness to Nazi military defeat in 1945, and the later site of the Bergen-Belsen trial. In the early days of 1937, he spent time wandering around Tempelhof airport, hankering for the enthralling sight of planes landing and taking off (he had, not long before, expressed a new wish: to become a pilot).[129] The same area had housed one of the first large Hitlerian camps: KZ Columbia-Haus, evacuated the previous year to make way for the expansion of the airport but not yet dismantled. The existence of a concentration camp by Tempelhof airport had come into focus abroad with the English publication of *All Quiet in Germany*, a testimony by a Communist Jew, Karl Billinger, which attracted widespread attention: it described flogging with horsewhips and lethal tortures perpetrated in cellars.[130]

Beckett seems to have expected a creative metamorphosis from his trip, a breakthrough towards another kind of writing. He encouraged himself to 'invent without scruple' for his 'Journal of a Melancholic', and to be less circumstantial in his writing.[131] His mother was unusually keen to see him publish: she encouraged him to pen an account of his travels for the newspapers, on the grounds that he could write 'at least as well as the Irishman Diarist' in the *Irish Times*.[132] Ultimately, the diaries were not put to any direct use, and the 'Journal of a Melancholic' remained unwritten. Nixon has traced the history of this prospective work, relaying Beckett's frustrated aspirations to find a form that would enable an 'absence of comment' and '[n]o social or political criticism whatever, apart from what the fact as stated implies'.[133] There was no model for the narrative perspective that Beckett wished to adopt as an external observer with an over-abundance of evidence at his command. That said, his aspirations resonate with the portrayals of Germany presented in anti-Nazi exile literature after 1933, which were realist for the most part, and often featured autobiographical elements and factual information extracted from the German press (nevertheless, many of these accounts, as Jean-Michel Palmier observes, were 'pure products of the imagination, even if the barbarism and terror were described and analysed with considerable verisimilitude').[134] The over-accumulation of first-hand evidence – that troublesome 'material of experience' – was not something to which Beckett responded well as a writer, and the subsequent Johnson project, which also began in a frenzy of evidence-driven note-taking, was discarded too. It is unsurprising that he should have renounced on all these fronts: at this juncture, he was not someone who retained an innate belief in the legitimacy of his political voice; he had had little success with

[129] Tophoven, *Becketts Berlin*, 34–5. [130] See 'In a Nazi Prison', *IT*, 20 July 1935, 7.
[131] Nixon, 'Solitude(s) and Creative Fidgets', 17; *Chronology*, 64. [132] *LSB1*, 423.
[133] Nixon, *German Diaries*, 122. [134] Palmier, *Weimar in Exile*, 393–409.

polemical writing, and no formal connections to the circles in which testimonies by anti-Nazi émigrés were published in Paris and London. Paris, in particular, was home to a growing body of anti-Nazi literature written by exiles, who had publishers and a press dedicated to their cause (when circumstances required discretion, texts were camouflaged in travel guides and cookbooks, and sometimes distributed in packets of tea).[135] In pre-war Paris, Beckett became acquainted with Otto Freundlich and Wolfgang Paalen, who had fled persecution in Nazi Germany and Austria, and he met other exiles who had previously lived in Germany – Jankel Adler and Wassily Kandinsky, for example. Any political discussion with them would have reinforced his sense that this was not a time for subtleties. As time went by and the prospect of war became a reality, transforming the raw material collected in his diaries must have seemed increasingly difficult.

A gulf separated Beckett's practice, and the relentless demands he made of himself, from the perspectives commonly nurtured by his contemporaries. The ideas that Stephen Spender articulated in 1935 in a letter to Isherwood are particularly telling: 'all a writer can do, the only completely revolutionary attitude for him today is to try and create standards which are really civilized'.[136] At the other end of the spectrum, however, Bertolt Brecht reappropriated the Nazi rhetoric crafted against the intellectual class; in his view, the essential problem was to understand how writers can 'become intellectual beasts, beasts in the sense that the fascists will fear for their domination'. 'How can we writers produce a writing that kills?' he asked.[137] Many visitors to Nazi Germany expected little of themselves on the terrain of testimony, even after decades had elapsed: in the briefest of terms, de Beauvoir – one of the many foreigners who had sleepwalked their way into the early days of Hitlerian rule – described a Berlin that, in February 1934, 'did not look as though it were crushed under a dictatorship'.[138] In 1960, she merely recalled pleasant strolls and somewhat conceited conversations with anti-fascist intellectuals for whom Nazism was a passing trend, soon to be defeated by the forces of reason. For Beckett, the months spent in Nazi Germany marked a peculiar creative hiatus, but also the start of a very different endeavour: shortly after his return, he began to dabble

135 Ibid., 203–5, 381–2; Egbert Krispyn, *Anti-Nazi Writers in Exile* (Athens: University of Georgia Press, 1978), 76.

136 Christopher Isherwood, *Christopher and His Kind, 1929–1939* (New York: Farrar, Straus & Giroux, 1976), 199.

137 Bertolt Brecht, 'Gefährlichkeit der Intelligenzbestien' [1937], in *Werke. Große kommentierte Berliner und Frankfurter Aufgabe*, vol. 22: 1 (Frankfurt am Main: Suhrkamp, 1993), 341.

138 Simone de Beauvoir, *The Prime of Life*, trans. Peter Green (London: André Deutsch and Weidenfeld and Nicolson, 1962), 145–6.

with writing poems in French and, still using his poetry as testing ground, took steps to make a name for himself in French literary circles. He had spent six assiduous months attempting to fathom totalitarianism at work, and the experience continued to resonate throughout the texts written in France during the occupation years and thereafter. Eventually, old memories resurfaced, in the novel trilogy, for example, in a context that raised even more troubling political questions.

'Red for a Change and Plenty of It': Beckett and Political Caricature

Since his first attempts at writing fiction, Beckett's sights had remained firmly set on a single political horizon: the Dublin he knew, torn by immense anxieties towards Soviet Russia and continental politics, and tangibly permeated by broader shifts to the right taking place across Europe. There is a strong continuity between his early work and the creative ambitions he nurtured while in Nazi Germany: indeed, his early texts pivot upon carefully crafted political symbols, proving remarkably alert to the ideological filters through which Nazism and Italian Fascism were received in the Irish Free State. In this regard, it is significant that political ideologies should converge so literally in Belacqua, the main character in *Dream of Fair to Middling Women* and *More Pricks than Kicks*. Belacqua is a member of the petty bourgeoisie, a class historically swayed by the messages of Fascism and Nazism; he is portrayed as a keen student of Italian, sporting a 'German shirt'.[139] His assiduous reading of the 'twilight Herald' or *Evening Herald*, however, aligns him with the Irish Catholic middle classes and the farming community, and with preoccupations far removed from continental politics.[140] For Belacqua, the *Herald* primarily appeals because he enjoys reading its 'Moscow notes' at the pub, and because the paper itself can be put to many domestic uses. He has little interest in political activity, however, and fears interruptions to his everyday routine from one 'brisk tattler' or other, 'bouncing in [. . .] with a big idea or a petition'.[141] The walk from College Street to Merrion Row is, for him, a 'perilous way, beset [. . .] with poets and peasants and politicians'.[142] Others are less averse to political enthusiasm. The Polar Bear, who is particularly susceptible to rapid mood shifts, perceives green and red as incompatible colours: '"Isn't there enough green in this merdific island? . . . If it's not the Stephen's Green

139 *MPTK*, 78.

140 *DFMW*, 201; *MPTK*, 54; John Horgan, *Irish Media: A Critical History since 1922* (London: Routledge, 2001), 6.

141 *MPTK*, 10. 142 *MPTK*, 54.

it's Green's bloody library. What we want" he screamed from the sidewalk "in this pestiferous country is red for a change and plenty of it"'. The outburst is greeted with silence, and the conclusion that '[o]nce again the Polar Bear had been let go unscathed'.[143] As the Polar Bear's invective suggests, the Dublin reimagined in Beckett's early fiction is not naturally inclined towards social revolution, but remains structured by secure landmarks of petty-bourgeois endeavour – the Bovril sign and the clocks of the Johnston, Mooney and O'Brien's bakery. Beneath the surface, however, change is underway: the city is bristling with concealed political activity, and is traversed by 'banned novelists', a 'communist painter and decorator fresh back from the Moscow reserves' and a 'phalanx of Grafton Street Stürmers' who, incidentally, melt into the landscape in *More Pricks than Kicks*, never to resurface.[144] The denomination evokes the *Sturm und Drang* movement as much as the Sturm-Abteilung, Hitler's Brown Shirts, and the readership of the anti-Semitic newspaper *Der Stürmer*.

There are occasional skirmishes: an episode in *Dream of Fair to Middling Women*, reproduced in 'A Wet Night', describes a dispute between the 'communist decorator' and a 'labour man', who administers a slap and calls him 'a bloody Bolshy'.[145] The decorator is recast as 'the glorious Komsomolet' in *More Pricks than Kicks*, in reference to the youth division of the Soviet Communist Party, and is granted a last appearance in 'Echo's Bones'.[146] However, if there is any lasting political turmoil around Belacqua, then its roots are to be found elsewhere – in the work of the 'eager young sociologists' who are assiduous readers of Célestin Bouglé, baptised as 'the Paris schoolman, the master and author of them that are anxious to have an opinion, the bearded bonhomme: *one commences to re-read Proudhon, or, perhaps better, one recommences to read Proudhon*'.[147] The statement – a citation from Bouglé's *La sociologie de Proudhon* – identifies the author, rather than Proudhon, as the corrupting influence.[148] As is the case with many facets of Beckett's novel, this narrative detail draws on personal knowledge: Bouglé, Durkheim's close collaborator, was Professor of the History of Social Economy at the Sorbonne and Deputy Director at the ENS; he had discouraged Beckett from applying for a doctorate on Proust and Joyce in 1929.

Political humour proliferates in Beckett's early work and is often disguised in non-sequiturs: in 'What a Misfortune', Hairy feels that exchanging conversational banalities leads to the 'wasting' of 'his own precarious

[143] *DFMW*, 157–8. [144] *MPTK*, 70–1. [145] *DFMW*, 220, 222. [146] *MPTK*, 73.
[147] *DFMW*, 160. [148] Célestin Bouglé, *La sociologie de Proudhon* (Paris: Armand Colin, 1911), v.

energies on a kind of rubber Stalin', while in 'Lightning Calculation', a short story eventually included in *Murphy*, the main character briefly associates his chest pains with a disease that killed his father and affected Stalin.[149] Incidentally, the figures known for ill-health and heart complaints in the British and Irish press of the 1920s and 1930s were Lenin and Trotsky, rather than Stalin.[150] 'Echo's Bones', situated in a spectral world between life and death, unfolds in a Stalinian hinterland inhabited by the figure of the 'machine-moujik' and a prostitute called Zaborovna, a name derived from the Russian for indecent or coarse, *zabornyj*.[151] The name has historical resonance: prostitution was banned as part of Stalin's first Five-Year Plan, and beggars and prostitutes were pushed out of cities and into 'special regime' camps.[152] What is significant is not so much the tokenistic aspect of these allusions in Beckett's text, but the fact that, in much the same way as his life, Belacqua's afterlife is punctured by shreds of political idiom, frequently misheard and misapprehended.

The political repertoire explored by Beckett in his early fiction has a specific context, and resonates with the tensions that escalated between 1931 and 1933 around Irish republicanism, the Irish labour movement and Irish communism. Prior to this point, the attempts of the Comintern to harness Irish communist sensibilities had been largely unsuccessful; internal memos sent to the Comintern's Executive Committee in 1929 deplored 'the derisory level of Marxist Leninist consciousness' in Ireland, describing an IRA 'terribly confused' about social questions and leftist organisations 'in the grip of the most paralyzing sectarianism'.[153] By the early 1930s, however, this was no longer the case, with political debate increasingly shaped by anxieties concerning the IRA's move towards the radical Left.[154] After October 1931, there were some violent confrontations, as the Catholic Church condemned Saor Éire for displaying communist leanings and subsequently encouraged attacks on suspected communist groups. March 1933 saw riots

149 *MPTK*, 144; J. M. B. Antoine-Dunne, 'Beckett and Eisenstein on Light and Contrapuntal Montage', *SBTA* 11 (2001): 319–20; Mark Nixon, 'Beckett and Romanticism in the 1930s', *SBTA* 18 (2007): 61–76.

150 For representative reports, see 'Lenin's Ill-Health', *IT*, 22 March 1922, 5; 'Leon Trotzky in France: Sick Man to Make His Home in Corsica', *IT*, 25 July 1933, 7.

151 SB, *Echo's Bones*, 5, 38, 59n.

152 See Dan Healey, 'Sexual and Gender Dissent: Homosexuality as Resistance in Stalin's Russia', in *Contending with Stalinism: Soviet Power and Popular Resistance in the 1930s*, ed. Lynne Viola (Ithaca: Cornell University Press, 2002), 152–3.

153 O'Connor, *Reds and the Green*, 149.

154 Enda Delaney, 'Anti-Communism in Mid-Twentieth-Century Ireland', *English Historical Review* 126, no. 521 (2011): 884; O'Connor, *Reds and the Green*, 3; English, *Radicals and the Republic*, 138–46, 155.

and severe disturbances on the streets of Dublin, including attacks against the Workers' College and Connolly House, which housed the Revolutionary Workers' Group.[155] Charlie Gilmore was among those who defended Connolly House (he was arrested, tried and acquitted).[156] The Bishop of Kilkenny called for the formation of anti-Bolshevik 'vigilance committees' in every parish.[157] Further clashes, attacks and parades were coordinated by members of the Catholic Young Men's Society and St Patrick's Anti-Communism League.[158] Anti-communist feeling also dominated the 1932 electoral campaign, bolstered by the perception that Fianna Fáil was as hostile to religion as communism itself. In February 1932, in a series of boisterous meetings, members of Cumann na nGaedheal sought to stir anti-communist feeling and presented Fianna Fáil as a threat, asking the Dublin public questions such as 'are you prepared to have the red flag flying?' and 'are you prepared to accept a foreigner as your leader?'[159] Pre-election posters and placards were inflected with the same rhetoric: a Cumann na nGaedheal poster bearing an Irish tricolour and a red flag was headed 'Keep your Red Rag off our Flag'.[160] Michael Tierney, campaigning for Cumann na nGaedheal, explained that 'the danger of communism [...] did not come from the working classes, but from the respectable young men and women who did not know what to do with their fathers' money'.[161]

The satires featuring in *Dream of Fair to Middling Women* and the concerns of Beckett's idle hero are given a new political immediacy by these dynamics. Beckett started work on the novel in May 1931 and submitted the whole text to Charles Prentice in June 1932, following a particularly intensive episode of writing in Paris in February 1932, the month of the Irish General Election that saw de Valera's accession to power.[162] His letters reveal that he was aware of sharpening divisions in the wake of the election: responding to MacGreevy, who had presumably remarked upon the enduring impact of the red scare on Irish political culture, he writes from London, in August 1932, of his surprise upon hearing of 'an undercurrent of communism' in Ireland.[163] His awareness of political nuance, at this point, was likely to have been limited, although his translation work for *Negro* provided new insights into political history and the work of Communist organisations. His notebooks suggest that he preferred to

[155] English, *Radicals and the Republic*, 177–8; Douglas, *Architects of the Resurrection*, 22–5.
[156] Michael Farrell, 'Anti-Communist Frenzy', *IT*, 29 March 1983, 10.
[157] Douglas, *Architects of the Resurrection*, 25. [158] O'Connor, *Reds and the Green*, 185–6.
[159] 'Noisy Dublin Meeting', *IT*, 11 February 1932, 8.
[160] 'Literature of the Elections', *IT*, 13 February 1932, 10.
[161] 'Dublin Meetings: Women Removed by Police', *IT*, 10 February 1932, 7.
[162] *Chronology*, 31, 35. [163] *LSB1*, 117.

read philosophical and literary surveys in which political history occupies a marginal position, and in which the subjects of socialism and communism are eschewed for other, less concrete, considerations. Yet much suggests that he was well-versed in the rhetoric of anti-communism: in early 1933, for example, he was absorbed in René Fülöp-Miller's *The Mind and Face of Bolshevism: An Examination of Cultural Life in Soviet Russia*. The lukewarm verdict he issued to MacGreevy conveys his sensitivity to the contradictions in Fülöp-Miller's account.[164] Resolutely hostile to its subject matter, the book draws attention to the endurance of a quintessential Russian soul, describes Bolshevism as a 'nameless beast', denounces the Komsomol as a depraved organisation, and designates revolutionary poetry and literature as attempts to 'mechanize' and 'de-soul' art.[165] This may have been Beckett's first encounter with the clowns Bim and Bom, figures who were to become dear to him: Fülöp-Miller comments on the tensions between their repertory, their role in the regime and their support of Stalin. In later years, Beckett continued to read about the history of the Soviet Union: during a holiday in Morocco in 1972, in letters to Bray, he recounts his immersion in Edmund Wilson's *To the Finland Station: A Study in the Writing and Acting of History* (1940), a comprehensive history of Marxist thought, revolutionary movements, socialism and communism. He begins by noting, 'Reading To the Finland Station with as much interest as I can muster for such vital matters'.[166] Three days later, he is coming to the conclusion of his reading, and is clearly intrigued and affected by the book: 'hate myself now even more while less Marxist-Leninist than ever'.[167] A few days later, he finds himself returning to and reflecting upon choice passages from Wilson's text.[168]

During the 1930s, Soviet Russia was clearly among Beckett's subjects of predilection. The relish with which he integrated affected and provocative allusions to Soviet Communism in many letters and critical essays is evident. For example, 'Les deux besoins', a discarded essay from 1938, alludes to the analogies between fascism and communism that became common among conservative critics of the Soviet regime in the 1930s, but does so tangentially by evoking the lynching of Hippasos, Pythagoras's disciple – a historical aberration, since Hippasos was 'neither fascist nor communist'.[169] His review of Devlin's *Intercessions*, published that year in *transition*, calls

[164] SB to MacGreevy, 27 January 1933, TCD MS 10402/45.
[165] René Fülöp-Miller, *The Mind and Face of Bolshevism: An Examination of Cultural Life in Soviet Russia*, trans. F. S. Flint and D. F. Tait (London: Chiswick Press, 1927), 1, 83, 152.
[166] *LSB4*, 282. [167] *LSB4*, lxxxi. [168] SB to Bray, 11 February 1972, TCD MS 10948/1/508.
[169] *D*, 56.

for a new art of 'need', proceeding from an artistic compulsion that is independent from public expectations and political diktats. The doctrines of socialist realism are invoked as an example of what the artist should strive *not* to emulate: 'Art has always been this – pure interrogation, rhetorical question less the rhetoric – whatever else it may have been obliged by the "social reality" to appear, but never more freely so than now, when social reality (*pace* ex-comrade Radek) has severed the connexion'.[170] The allusion to Karl Radek is of some significance: Radek, a leader of the Comintern, was tasked with promoting socialist realism; in a speech at the first Soviet Writers' Congress in 1934, he attacked *Ulysses* for lacking a social conscience due to its adherence to a realist cinematic aesthetic. The Stalinist purges were lethal to Radek: he was imprisoned and tried for high treason and terrorist conspiracy in 1936, and sentenced to ten years in a labour camp following the 1937 show trials, extensively discussed in a sympathetic Irish press.[171] Hence, Beckett's appraisal of Devlin's poetry is framed not simply by controversies around socialist realism, but by his keenness to situate Irish modernist poetry in a broader political context that, for many around him, should have no bearing upon Irish writing in the first place. The review ends with a parallel dismissal of Irish political pieties, and with the suggestion that '[t]he time is perhaps not altogether too green for the vile suggestion that art has nothing to do with clarity, does not dabble in the clear and does not make clear'.[172]

Political Symbols and the Brief Life of 'Trueborn Jackeen'

The peculiar circumstances through which Beckett honed his skill at political satire shed some light on the difficulties posed by 'Trueborn Jackeen', a mysterious project that absorbed his energies from the late autumn of 1933 until at least May 1934.[173] 'Jackeen' has a range of pejorative meanings denoting worthlessness; T. P. Dolan defines jackeen as 'a self-assertive Dubliner with pro-British leanings' and traces the etymology of the term back to the early eighteenth century, when Jack served as a familiar name for John Bull.[174] It was once thought that these notes were taken for

170 *D*, 91.

171 'Bolshevist Split', *IT*, 8 October 1936, 7; 'Thirteen Death Sentences', *IT*, 30 January 1937, 9; Quidnunc, 'Irishman's Diary', *IT*, 25 January 1937, 4; 'The Incredible Trial', *IT*, 26 April 1937, 5.

172 *D*, 94.

173 See John Pilling, 'A Critique of Aesthetic Judgment: Beckett's "Dissonance of Ends and Means"', in *A Companion to Samuel Beckett*, ed. S. E. Gontarski (Oxford: Blackwell, 2010), 64–5.

174 Terence Patrick Dolan, *A Dictionary of Hiberno-English: The Irish Use of English*, revised ed. (Dublin: Gill and Macmillan, 2006), 129.

Joyce, but Beckett's correspondence points elsewhere. To Nuala Costello, he described 'Trueborn Jackeen' as a satire in the fashion of Daniel Defoe's *The True-born Englishman*, 'though of course infinitely more amusing and competent'.[175] Two months later, he reported to Leventhal that the endeavour was too ambitious and had merely generated a few unsatisfactory fragments thus far. The coordinates he used to convey the impending abandonment of the piece borrow from a playful array of political and intellectual references, from Dostoievsky to the Russian pogroms.[176]

Of Beckett's efforts, all that remains are manuscript notes entitled 'Trueborn Jackeen' and a typescript entitled 'Cow'.[177] 'Trueborn Jackeen' consists of fragmentary notes on Irish history taken from the 1929 edition of the *Encyclopædia Britannica*, and 'Cow' consists of a list of jokes, puns, citations about the cattle trade and cattle rearing, and jottings about Irish medieval legends including the *Táin Bó Cúailnge*. The sources that Beckett used to compile the entries in 'Cow' include the *Saorstát Eireann Official Handbook* (1932), sponsored by W. T. Cosgrave's Ministry for Industry and Commerce,[178] and William Francis Collier's *History of Ireland for Schools* (1884), a school book favoured by Joyce, distinctive for its fanciful mixture of myth and matter-of-fact detail.[179] George Sandeman's *The Harmsworth Encyclopaedia: Everybody's Book of Reference* appears to be the source for Beckett's descriptions of cattle breeds and ailments.

As with other notebooks, the 'Trueborn Jackeen' notes acted as an imaginative repository to which Beckett returned when writing other texts, such as the short story 'Echo's Bones'.[180] The cultural currency of cattle seems to have obsessed Beckett: his *Dream* Notebook, compiled in 1931, frequently alludes to cattle, heifers, bullocks and milking, and many of these references entail comparing women to cattle, in a manner anticipating the novel's striking displays of misogyny.[181] A playful letter from 1936 adopts the cow as a powerful economic and political symbol, and mentions meeting 'a hard

[175] *LSB1*, 188. [176] SB to Leventhal, 7 May 1934, A. J. Leventhal Collection, HRHRC.

[177] TCD MS 10971/2, Trinity College Dublin; 'TCD MS 10971/2: Irish History', *Notes Diverse Holo*, 125–8.

[178] The *Handbook* was funded by Dublin businesses; funders and advertisers included Harris & Sinclair (the Nassau Street antiques business owned by the Sinclairs), James Beckett, Ltd. Builders and Contractors in Ringsend (founded by Beckett's great-uncle), and the Yeatses' Cuala Industries. See Bulmer Hobson, 'Introduction', in *Saorstát Eireann Official Handbook* (Dublin: Talbot Press, 1932), 15.

[179] William Francis Collier, *History of Ireland for Schools* (London: Marcus Ward, 1884). On Joyce, see Maria Tymoczko, *The Irish Ulysses* (Berkeley: University of California Press, 1994), 27, 119, 224, 300–1.

[180] See Mark Nixon, 'Belacqua Revividus: Beckett's Short Story "Echo's Bones"', *Limit(e) Beckett* 1 (2010); SB, *Echo's Bones*, 10, 65n.

[181] Pilling, *Beckett's Dream Notebook*, 11, 31, 32, 35.

hit publican in Bray [who] quoted Daniel O'Connell to prove there was no hope remaining for this country. A cow, a cow, my Free State for a cow'.[182] It seems that Beckett saw shades of Eisenstein in unlikely places: a letter to Arland Ussher from 1936 compares the poems of Cecil Salkeld to an allegorical scene featuring cattle in Eisenstein's *The General Line*, a film about the collectivisation of agriculture.[183] The beginning of the film relates the birth of a dairy cooperative and correlates the amount of food available to the population with the health of cattle. Incidentally, the film in general and this scene in particular are described in Rudolf Arnheim's *Film*, a book that Beckett read in early 1936, which features shot-by-shot analyses of recent films by Pabst, Eisenstein, Pudovkin and others.[184]

The satire that Beckett was attempting with 'Trueborn Jackeen' certainly bears the mark of his fascination for Jonathan Swift, and borrowed from other forms of literary polysemy: Anna McMullan has suggested a debt not simply to Defoe but to Charles Macklin's play *The True-born Irishman* (1762), which pits different social classes and political ambitions against one another.[185] The mention of the *Book of the Dun Cow* in Beckett's notes also reveals his interest in the most ancient text in the Irish language, *Lebor na hUidre*, which had been published in full in an accessible edition a few years previously.[186] The *Book of the Dun Cow* deals with warfare, conquest and settlement: it includes an early version of the *Táin Bó Cúailnge* as well as a number of other important manuscripts, translations and accounts of cattle raids.

Much in Beckett's notes from the *Encyclopædia Britannica* conveys his interest in crafting a historical epic. His manuscript replicates the encyclopaedia's account of prehistoric Ireland as an isolated territory, whose flaura and fauna were affected by insularity, and reproduces its anthropometric characterisation of Ireland's first inhabitants. Elsewhere, Irish history is presented as a long series of interrelated settlements, treatises, conversions, power struggles and legal wranglings around the Brehon Laws, the English Code and the Statutes of Kilkenny, which attempted to curb the influence of the Irish upon English settlers. Throughout, Beckett's notes pay particular attention to dominant patterns in racialist thinking, defining Irish history as driven by social and ethnic mixing in ways that echo Defoe's own denunciation of discourses on English racial purity. Among the many passages that attracted Beckett's eye, the *Encyclopædia Britannica* dedicates

182 *LSB1*, 299. 183 Ibid., 328.

184 Rudolf Arnheim, *Film*, trans. L. M. Sieveking and Ian F. D. Morrow (London: Faber, 1933).

185 'TCD MS 10971/2: Irish History', *Notes Diverse Holo*, 126.

186 R. I. Best and Osborn Bergin, eds., *Lebor na hUidre* (Dublin: Royal Irish Academy, 1929).

a paragraph to the period 1333–1399 and the restauration of English lordship, explaining that '[t]he capacity of this "middle nation", "Irish to the English and English to the Irish", to turn into temporary rebels was often to puzzle England'.[187] As McMullan notes, Beckett recorded this statement as a verdict about the present, in a manner that evinces his awareness of the political baggage inherited by his own social class.[188]

The typescript entitled 'Cow' develops a distinctive historical shorthand. It offers a list of facts about cattle breeding that closely parallels sections on Irish agriculture, cattle trade figures and cattle breeds in the *Saorstát Eireann Official Handbook*, echoing its anglicised spellings and discussions of the Cattle Spoil of Cooley, the Ogham inscriptions, the Ox Mountains and the *Book of the Dun Cow*. Other references to early Celtic history and heroic myths are laid out in exactly the same anglicised spellings as those offered in Collier's *History of Ireland for Schools*. The manner in which Beckett's two sets of notes separate myth from historical fact holds significance in light of wider methodological and ideological tensions permeating accounts of Irish history in the late nineteenth century and thereafter.[189] Collier's account is firmly at odds with that offered by T. W. Rolleston, for example, who sought to proceed from an anthropological basis, and treated Celticist accounts of history as mythical literature. If Collier discusses Tara as the central seat of power (his sources are Petrie, O'Curry and Leland), Rolleston describes Tara as 'the traditional seat of that central authority which was always a dream of the Irish mind, but never a reality of Irish history'.[190] Likewise, Collier's account of Cairbry the Cathead (which Beckett had clearly consulted) speaks of a legendary hero endowed with special powers, who 'wore a golden collar, which was believed to grow tight on his own neck, if he pronounced an unjust sentence'.[191] Rolleston concludes his evocations of Cairbry's life and the Battle of Gowra with a major caveat: 'All this sounds very matter-of-fact and probable, but how much real history there may be in it is very hard to say'.[192] Although 'Trueborn Jackeen' was soon abandoned, Beckett's readings informed some of his later texts. Celticism and Celtology fare equally badly in his writings, as suggested by the fanciful episodes in *Watt* surrounding Ernest Louit's fraudulous

[187] 'Ireland', in *Encyclopædia Britannica*, vol. 12, 14th ed., ed. J. L. Garvin et al. (London: Encyclopædia Britannica Company, 1929), 604.

[188] Anna McMullan, 'Irish/Postcolonial Beckett', in *Palgrave Advances in Samuel Beckett Studies*, ed. Lois Oppenheim (Basingstoke: Palgrave Macmillan, 2004), 93.

[189] See Sinéad Garrigan Mattar, *Primitivism, Science and the Irish Revival* (Oxford: Oxford University Press, 2004), 1–40.

[190] T. W. Rolleston, *Celtic Myths and Legends* [1911] (New York: Dover, 1990), 148.

[191] Collier, *History of Ireland for Schools*, 15.

[192] Rolleston, *Myths*, 305.

dissertation on *The Mathematical Intuitions of the Visicelts* and the mocking reference to Dr Killiecrankie's interest in Ossian in the French *Murphy*, which associates folklore-collecting with a lack of intellectual integrity and rigour.[193]

What Beckett aspired to produce with 'Trueborn Jackeen' can only be imagined. Nevertheless, these fragments reveal an attempt to work with precise political coordinates, and resonate with determining debates about Irish agriculture and the economy that, in the early 1930s, were enmeshed with the Anglo-Irish Tariff War, the rise and fall of the Blueshirts, and the transformation of Cumann na nGaedheal into Fine Gael. Cattle became a particularly weighted symbol as the campaign against the land annuities gained ground and discussions of agricultural policy became sharply polarised.[194] The problems posed by the land annuities had shaped political dynamics since the 1927 General Election, and galvanised support from republicans and socialists, with O'Donnell working hard to advance the debate.[195] The 1932 General Election campaign took a new turn when Fianna Fáil cast itself as the party of the small farmer, ultimately winning the vote with an economic programme opposed to the free trade doctrines of W. T. Cosgrave and Cumann na nGaedheal. De Valera promised that the annuities to be paid to the British government would be reduced by half, and dedicated the first years of his mandate to dismantling the economic provisions imposed by the Anglo-Irish Treaty.[196] Two weeks after his election, measures were introduced to withhold land annuities payments, and new tariff walls were imposed on British imports in order to support the cultivation of new Irish industries. The ensuing conflict had an immediate impact on the Irish cattle industry, which was directly dependent upon exportation to Britain. In retaliation, the British government introduced severe tariffs on Irish cattle and agricultural produce in 1932 and imposed a strict quota on Irish cattle in 1934, reducing imports drastically. Throughout 1933 and 1934, the Irish press surveyed cattle prices with anxiety, while political leaders – Cosgrave in particular – remained keen to be perceived as knowledgeable about milch cows and egg prices.[197]

[193] For a different reading, see Patrick Bixby, *Samuel Beckett and the Postcolonial Novel* (Cambridge: Cambridge University Press, 2009), 135–45.

[194] Alvin Jackson, *Ireland 1798–1998: War, Peace and Beyond*, 2nd ed. (Malden, MA: Blackwell, 2010), 289–90; *Speeches and Statements by Eamon de Valera, 1917–73*, ed. Maurice Moynihan (Dublin: Gill and Macmillan, 1980), 215.

[195] Ó Drisceoil, *Peadar O'Donnell*, 76, 47–8; English, *Radicals and the Republic*, 86–95; J. J. Lee, *Ireland 1912–1985: Politics and Society* (Cambridge: Cambridge University Press, 1989), 178.

[196] *Speeches and Statements by Eamon de Valera*, 196–202; F. S. L. Lyons, *Ireland since the Famine*, 2nd ed. (London: Fontana, 1973), 511–16, 611–12; Terence Brown, *Ireland: A Social and Cultural History, 1922–2002* [1981] (London: HarperCollins, 2004), 131–2.

[197] 'Free State Trade Declining', *IT*, 8 July 1933, 18; 'Mr. Cosgrave's Indictment', *IT*, 16 June 1933, 6.

These political developments, and the Economic War more generally, form the backdrop to Beckett's interest in historical narratives of national cohesion. Clearly, as far as the book trade was concerned, he was on the side of free trade, and 'Censorship in the Saorstat' presents all forms of Irish economic isolationism, past and present, as the same manifestation of blind ignorance, deploring national newspapers merely concerned about the 'latest snuffles from the infant industries'.[198] His later correspondence mentions 'Dev' at various points – sometimes, it seems, with affection – but his earlier comments about Fianna Fáil are mixed. A letter to MacGreevy from July 1932, written from London, reports on the breadth of responses to the recent election: for the Italian barber he has met at the Turkish baths, de Valera is a national hero; for the hotel porter from Dublin he has met elsewhere, his election spells catastrophe.[199] The 1933 General Election, which saw de Valera's sweeping victory and bolstered parliamentary support to Fianna Fáil, also leaves traces in Beckett's letters to MacGreevy. These are significant: state politics was a subject of discussion that they favoured less than others, and their political disputes mostly took place in another realm, around the idea of the national artist and MacGreevy's perception of Jack Yeats. In letters from January 1933, Beckett describes a family home deeply enamoured with Cosgrave.[200] He also relates his reading of Fülöp-Miller's history of Bolshevism, comments on the completion of his translations for Cunard's *Negro*, for which he received 'a few quid', and refers to the General Election that took place a few days previously, lamenting, 'And I sold my vote for a quid also'.[201]

This trade has interesting symbolic dimensions: it is indexed to Beckett's attempts to read widely about political history, and to the translations of anti-colonialist texts submitted to Cunard, which he presents as a corrective to his own political disaffection. There are different interpretations of Beckett's stance: for Anthony Cronin, Beckett supported de Valera; for Gerry Dukes, Beckett may have sold his vote to his father for a pound and hence voted for Cosgrave, perceived as the politician most able to defend the position of the Unionist upper-middle class; for McNaughton, who offers a more plausible verdict, the letter points to Beckett's unenthusiastic vote for de Valera and disinterest in Cosgrave.[202] It is certain that well-off Irish Protestants such as Beckett belonged to a difficult category for de Valera: their support would only be sought if it came with the relinquishing

[198] *D*, 86, 87. [199] See my *Samuel Beckett and the Problem of Irishness*, 12.

[200] See SB to MacGreevy, 19 January 1933, TCD MS 10402/44.

[201] McNaughton, 'The Politics of Aftermath', *Beckett and Ireland*, 61.

[202] *LM*, 188; Gerry Dukes, *Samuel Beckett* (Woodstock, NY: Overlook Press, 2002), 55–8; McNaughton, 'The Politics of Aftermath', 61.

of Protestant identitarian claims. This matter was made clear in February 1932, when de Valera addressed a rally at the gates of Trinity College Dublin and clarified his party's policy towards young Protestants. Recalling that the great political leaders of the past belonged to the Anglo-Irish ascendency, he urged all citizens, including young Protestants, to join forces with Fianna Fáil, and to bear in mind that 'the principles to be applied by a Fianna Fáil Government – being the principles of the majority – should be principles consistent with Catholicity'.[203] The connections between 'Trueborn Jackeen' and these political developments suggest that Beckett's efforts may have been spurred by a desire to satirise the mechanics of populism; presumably, as political tensions escalated, the scale of the task became so great as to necessitate abandonment.

Greens, Reds and the Rise of the Blueshirts

The period during which Beckett worked on 'Trueborn Jackeen' was also marked by the rise of Eoin O'Duffy's Blueshirts, who attempted to counter de Valera's economic policy with proposals for a corporative state following the model of Mussolini's Fascist Italy. The movement gained support and exposure throughout 1933; by the end of the year, blue shirt-wearing became increasingly common, and some Fine Gael members were seen wearing blue shirts in the Dáil and the Seanad.[204] In February 1934, as Fine Gael's newly elected leader, O'Duffy delivered a speech summarising the Blueshirts' economic strategy and proposing a new agricultural policy aimed at restoring trade with Britain until Irish agriculture became able to fund the national economy. More generally, O'Duffy aspired to create a corporative state in which a federation of vocational and professional unions would replace political parties and Parliament would have no other function than to pass legislation; the result of his 'Christian social' programme, as he termed it, would be an Ireland free of class tensions and Communist influence.[205] In February 1934, the rise of the Far Right also became visible in France: marches organised by far-right leagues in response to a wave of political scandals led to the dissolution of Daladier's government, and to a call for a general strike issued by many across the Left

[203] 'Mr. de Valera and Young Protestants', *Weekly IT*, 20 February 1932, 11.

[204] Mike Cronin, 'The Blueshirts in the Irish Free State, 1932–1935: The Nature of Socialist Republican and Governmental Opposition', in *Opposing Fascism: Community, Authority and Resistance in Europe*, ed. Tom Kirk and Anthony McElligott (Cambridge: Cambridge University Press, 1999), 84–5.

[205] Mike Cronin, '"Putting New Wine into Old Bottles": The Irish Right and the Embrace of European Social Thinking in the Early 1930s', *European History Quarterly* 27 (1997): 98–9, 100.

including the Surrealists, in response to the formation of a new repressive government led by the Right.[206] The Irish situation was somewhat different, and the relation between the Blueshirts and Italian Fascism is often perceived as deeply ambivalent. Some historical accounts dissociate the Blueshirts from continental fascism in strong terms, presenting them as poorly equipped rivals to Fianna Fáil, unable to match the skill and fascistic rhetoric of Fianna Fáil's own spokesmen.[207] Others, more persuasively, point to the Blueshirts' incapacity to rally a petty-bourgeois support already enlisted to republicanism, and discuss how the Blueshirts institutionalised their anti-Semitic position.[208] For Mike Cronin, the Blueshirts filled a gap that the Irish Left, divided, lacking a coherent discourse, and 'preach[ing] a message as alien to the Irish people as that of fascism', had failed to fill.[209] On the international stage, the political positioning of the Blueshirts came across as unambiguous in the early 1930s: from the perspective of Italian Fascist journals and their contributors, there was no doubt that the Blueshirts were true members of the Fascist International, and O'Duffy's contributions to pan-European Fascist leagues and societies were highly esteemed by their ultra-reactionary elements.[210]

May 1934 – the month Beckett abandoned 'Trueborn Jackeen', working instead on satire in another mode in 'Recent Irish Poetry' – was a good month for the Blueshirts: the movement reached its peak of 48,000 members.[211] Weekly marches, rallies and mass meetings were organised in every town and village where the Blueshirts had a branch.[212] No one reading the press could be oblivious to their prominence on Irish streets, the violence of their conflict with the IRA and Communist militants, or the strength of anti-communist feeling in Dublin. There are occasional allusions to these developments in Beckett's writings and correspondence, although nothing suggests that he witnessed the political rallies organised by the Blueshirts or their opponents first-hand (several anti-fascist demonstrations were organised in 1934 and 1935 at College Green). In early September 1933, after de Valera made various attempts to curb the

206 *Tracts surréalistes et déclarations collectives*, vol. 1, ed. José Pierre (Paris: Le Terrain Vague, 1980), 262–5.

207 See Lee, *Ireland*, 181–2.

208 Mike Milotte, *Communism in Modern Ireland: The Pursuit of the Workers' Republic since 1916* (Dublin: Gill and Macmillan, 1984), 139; Bryan Fanning, *Racism and Social Change in the Republic of Ireland* (Manchester: Manchester University Press, 2002), 68–9.

209 Cronin, 'The Blueshirts in the Irish Free State', 88.

210 Ledeen, *Universal Fascism*, 100, 122–4, 128.

211 Cronin, 'The Blueshirts in the Irish Free State', 88; Cronin, 'The Irish Right', 93.

212 Mike Cronin, 'The Blueshirt Movement, 1932–5: Ireland's Fascists?', *Journal of Contemporary History*, 30, no. 2 (1995): 316.

Blueshirts' progress and ban their marches, Beckett sent a brief appraisal of Irish and European politics to McGreevy, comparing the Irish Free State to a political backwater, the land of 'cockatoo Cosgrave arrayed as a Fascist',[213] and obliquely arguing that, at this precise moment, Spain would be a more promising prospect than Austria.[214] It is difficult to imagine what may have been said about Spain, where the Right was gaining ground, and about Austria, given that MacGreevy's letters have not survived. What is significant is Beckett's capacity to succinctly articulate the underlying malaise around the Blueshirts: Cosgrave recoiled from associations between Fine Gael and fascism,[215] and Beckett's comment is interesting for that very reason. Nonetheless, 'cockatoo Cosgrave' may not be Beckett's phrase: it chimes with the description of Cosgrave's 'cockatoo's crest' offered by H. V. Morton in *In Search of Ireland*, a travelogue presenting Cosgrave as an unlikely political leader.[216]

'What a Misfortune', written in July 1933, hints at the thrills offered by the Far Right, but describes marching for the Far Right as a French and hence alien occupation: an unnamed 'Deputy of the extreme Right' is quoted as saying, 'Il faut marcher avec son temps', among other non-sequiturs.[217] The Dublin of *More Pricks than Kicks*, organised according to trade and activity, seems naturally sympathetic with corporative aspirations. It features a petty bourgeoisie with a strong sense of its identity and interests: the grocer, for example, is defined as 'a small tradesman [. . .] with a small tradesman's sense of personal dignity and what was what'.[218] The professions that, in a recent past, were engaged in ruthless struggles for workers' rights and trade union activism have been pushed to the fringes of political activity: Belacqua's favourite pub is frequented by 'rough but kindly habitués', 'recruited for the most part from among dockers, railwaymen and vague joxers on the dole'.[219]

Beckett knew personally several of the figures who inspired the anti-democratic vision of the Blueshirts: W. B. Yeats, Starkie, Francis Stuart as well as Joseph Hone, who first sparked Yeats's interest in the state model offered by Italian Fascism.[220] Critical essays penned in 1934 allude to the rise of an Irish configuration of fascism in the literary arena. 'Recent Irish

[213] McNaughton, 'The Politics of Aftermath', *Beckett and Ireland*, 61.

[214] SB to MacGreevy, 7 September 1933, TCD MS 10402/54. [215] Cronin, 'Ireland's Fascists', 329.

[216] H. V. Morton, *In Search of Ireland* [1930] (London: Methuen, 1931), 14.

[217] *MPTK*, 155. This means 'one must keep up with the times', rather than 'one must march with the times' as Beckett's pun suggests.

[218] *MPTK*, 15. [219] *MPTK*, 44.

[220] Cronin, 'The Irish Right', 93–125; Cronin, 'Ireland's Fascists', 318; Joseph Hone, *W. B. Yeats, 1865–1939* (London: Macmillan, 1965), 467.

Poetry', for example, written between May and June 1934, while Beckett was in London, cites Yeats's *The Winding Stair and Other Poems*, portraying the poet as a 'born singer' and a 'fanatic heart' in perpetual search for a song.[221] These lines evoke Yeats's 'Three Songs to the Same Tune', originally written for O'Duffy's Blueshirts, and published in *The Spectator* in February 1934 with a short preface recalling Irish republican traditions.[222] It is likely that Beckett kept an eye on *The Spectator*: his reviews 'Schwabenstreich' and 'Proust in Pieces' were published in the magazine in May and June that year. In February 1934 also, Yeats was awarded the Goethe Plakette by the mayor of Frankfurt, a prize also attributed to NSDAP members Ernst Krieck and Hermann Stehr, and granted, as the *Irish Times* explained, 'in exceptional cases to persons distinguished in cultural life'.[223] The troubling questions raised by Yeats's politics have attracted extensive commentary; it is not my purpose here to rehearse these debates, but simply to point to ways in which Beckett's piece also stands as a critique of Yeats's political associations in early 1934.[224]

'Recent Irish Poetry', published under a pseudonym, appeared elsewhere – in *The Bookman*, Yeats's early critical turf. It had a noticeable impact upon publication: in an issue of *Poetry* from March 1935, Hone discussed in detail the mysterious article that had 'set everyone by the ears'.[225] Hone's article mostly consists of speculations about the author, Andrew Belis, identified as an 'extreme partisa[n] of the modernistic school and the anti-celticists', on the basis of his critique of Yeats's Irish Academy of Letters. As Hone points out, the review makes no reference to Beckett, author of the recently banned *More Pricks than Kicks*, but Hone concludes that Padraic Fallon, 'unaccountably absent' from Belis's account, 'has claims [. . .] to be regarded as the most promising of our younger men', and hence could be the author of the piece. Hone, who had been working closely with Yeats for some time, may have seen 'Recent Irish Poetry' as a precious opportunity to drive forward some ideas that he could not advance himself; his review gives a real consistency to Beckett's argument and

221 *D*, 71.

222 On Yeats's poems, see Edward O'Shea, '"An Old Bullet Imbedded in the Flesh": The Migration of Yeats's "Three Songs to the Same Tune"', *Yeats: An Annual of Critical and Textual Studies* 4 (1986): 121–42; Peter van de Kamp and Peter Liebregts, eds., 'Introduction', in *Tumult of Images: Essays on W. B. Yeats and Politics* (Amsterdam: Rodopi, 1995), 1–26; Foster, *W. B. Yeats: A Life*, vol. 2, 466–95.

223 'German Distinction for Dr. W. B. Yeats', *IT*, 16 February 1934, 7.

224 See, notably, Conor Cruise O'Brien, 'Passion and Cunning: An Essay on the Politics of W. B. Yeats', in *In Excited Reverie*, ed. A. Norman Jeffares and K. G. W. Cross (London: Macmillan, 1965), 207–78; Cullingford, *Yeats, Ireland and Fascism*, 144–64, 197–214; W. J. McCormack, *Blood Kindred: The Politics of W. B. Yeats and His Death* (London: Pimlico, 2005).

225 Joseph Hone, 'Letter from Ireland', *Poetry* 45 (1935): 331–5.

condemnation of the 'search for an external validation' that 'has been the bane of Irish poetry since Yeats'.

This was an improbable alliance, for Hone had frequently written in praise of Italian Fascism and French monarchism in *The Dublin Magazine.* Between 1923 and 1933, he published regular articles on Mussolini, Papini, Croce, D'Annunzio, Gentile and the Blackshirts.[226] Like many in Ireland and elsewhere, his interest in Mussolini endured beyond the war; he is known to have kept a signed copy of Mussolini's autobiography.[227] Hone's articles are unambiguous: in 1923, he depicts Charles Maurras as a 'man of genius' and 'the most talented and ingenious philosopher' of the anti-democratic 'counter-revolution'.[228] A sequel evokes 'the Jewish problem' in Europe and describes Zionism as a 'fiasco'.[229] Another piece presents Croce and Gentile as Italian counterparts to Yeats and George Russell, and stresses the resemblance between texts penned by Æ and by Gentile.[230] On occasion, Mario Rossi, Hone's close collaborator, also wrote for *The Dublin Magazine* and participated in Hone's efforts to disseminate information about the Fascist corporative state; his contributions include, in 1935, a piece dated from year XII, according to the Fascist calendar.[231] Rossi was not a member of the Fascist Party, but was a renowned advocate of fascism close to Gentile (the latter had enforced the Fascist cultural programme as Minister for Public Instruction).[232]

'Dull' and 'boring': this is how Beckett frequently described those who displayed fascist leanings during these years, in the wake of encounters with Stuart, Rossi or Pelorson. Rossi ranked particularly low in his esteem, but his appreciation for Hone grew over time.[233] There is evidence of an enduring dialogue on literary and philosophical questions: it is Hone who encouraged Beckett to read Berkeley in 1933; three years later, reciprocating the favour, Beckett encouraged him, tongue firmly in cheek, to consider translating André Breton's *Nadja* 'in the long winter evenings'.[234] Mussolini's Italy was a subject of interest for Beckett's closer friends too; in 1935, Devlin sent a letter to MacGreevy emphasising his 'pro-Italian' stance and lamenting that his diplomatic post in Geneva required him to work against

[226] W. J. McCormack, *'We Irish' in Europe: Yeats, Berkeley, and Joseph Hone* (Dublin: UCD Press, 2010), 185–9.
[227] Ibid., 75. [228] J. M. Hone, 'Charles Maurras', *Dublin Magazine* 1 (1923): 414–17.
[229] H., 'Foreign Correspondence', *Dublin Magazine* 2, no. 4 (1924): 223–6.
[230] J. M. H., 'Foreign Correspondence', *Dublin Magazine* 2, no. 6 (1925): 369.
[231] Mario Rossi, 'Foreign Correspondence', *Dublin Magazine* 10, no. 3 (1935): 70.
[232] McCormack, *Yeats, Berkeley, and Hone*, 15, 66–9, 72–5.
[233] *LSB1*, 149–50, 154; *Chronology*, 41; Bruce Arnold, *Jack Yeats* (New Haven: Yale University Press, 1998), 269.
[234] *LSB1*, 367.

Italian concerns.[235] For Alex Davis, this is not indicative of a sympathy for Italian Fascism, but is a corollary of Devlin's perspective on the invasion of Ethiopia and casual displays of racism elsewhere. Others have issued similar warnings: Ray Douglas, for example, has demonstrated how frequently Italian Fascism was commended for its political achievements in the Irish Free State, where Mussolini was widely admired.[236] Ultimately, the enthusiasm and political ignorance displayed by Yeats, Hone and so many others found little by way of a challenge. The coded and covert critiques issued by Beckett – who had spent time in Fascist Italy and would have been aware of the prestige that Mussolini enjoyed in the eyes of the Irish public – are part of the same problem, and reveal the difficulty of speaking against a political consensus mostly articulated as a matter of common sense and bolstered by powerful and established voices.

Situated in this context, Beckett's notes towards *Human Wishes*, compiled in the wake of his German trip, take on added significance. In a roundabout way, his detailed miscellany of Johnsonian anecdote also responds to the rise of an interest in the nationalist Far Right witnessed among his Irish contemporaries. I have written on this question in depth elsewhere,[237] and will merely stress that what may seem an idiosyncratic pursuit on Beckett's part was, in fact, a response attuned to wider attempts to reshape the Irish political landscape through successive reimaginings of eighteenth-century Anglo-Ireland. Throughout the 1930s, a steady stream of publications sought to reassess the origins of Berkeley, Swift, Goldsmith and Burke, in an attempt to outline the contours of an intellectual tradition founded by and for Irish Protestants and curb the erosion of their political authority. A. A. Luce, Beckett's former tutor at Trinity, published a study of Berkeley and Malebranche; Hone and Rossi completed biographies of Berkeley and Swift; Oliver St John Gogarty and James Starkey (Seumas O'Sullivan, editor of *The Dublin Magazine*) collaborated on a biography of Oliver Goldsmith; Stuart researched and wrote a novel set in late eighteenth-century Ireland; and Yeats celebrated the eighteenth-century Ascendancy in *The Winding Stair and Other Poems* and *The Words upon the Window-pane*. Beckett's letters reveal that he was aware of much of this work, and the *Human Wishes* notebooks suggest that he attempted to respond to it. Like the notes towards 'Trueborn Jackeen' and his critical essays, his planned 'Johnson blasphemy' says much about the political context of its genesis in the late 1930s.[238] The *Human Wishes* notebooks focus

[235] Davis, *A Broken Line*, 116. [236] Douglas, *Architects of the Resurrection*, 24–5, 33, 62–3.

[237] See my 'Beckett, Samuel Johnson and the "Vacuity of Life"', *Sofia Philosophical Review* 5, no. 1 (2011): 228–50.

[238] *LSB1*, 569.

on the same period of English literary history, but celebrate values normally considered incompatible with political thought and action: unreason, vacuity and melancholy. Reimagined by Beckett, Samuel Johnson is no beacon of English imperialism: he emerges as an advocate for the Irish cause, living among Irish exiles such as Arthur Murphy and Hugh Kelly; as an inadequate proponent of standardised English, who speaks with a strong Staffordshire accent and displays his affection for a former prostitute and a freed slave.

Censorship and Political Shadows in the Irish Free State

Overall, Beckett had little success with the pieces addressed to an immediate present. He had no luck at all with 'Censorship in the Saorstat', in which the author is recast as political commentator. The essay remained unpublished until its inclusion in *Disjecta* in 1983. It was originally written in August 1934 at the request of the *Bookman*, months before the ban on *More Pricks than Kicks*, and was revised in September 1935, at which point Beckett added a conclusion drawing attention to his assigned number in the Irish Register of Prohibited Publications. He then sent the piece to *transition* in May 1936, without success.[239] The text is a detailed commentary on censorship legislation in the Irish Free State, and it consists of an inventive montage of paraphrases and quotations from published parliamentary debates in the Dáil and the Seanad that arose at different moments in the successive mandates of Cumann na nGaedheal and Fianna Fáil. On the surface, Beckett's article merely transforms parliamentary discussions of the 1929 Censorship Act into a Swiftian postface, mocking the ambitions of 'the cephalopods of state' to purify the nation and sanctify 'the pure Gael'.[240] Behind this parody, however, lies an attack on the infiltration of racialist discourses and authoritarian politics: the two main targets of Beckett's ire – James Fitzgerald-Kenney (Minister for Justice until 1932) and Michael Tierney – were both staunch Blueshirt supporters. Fitzgerald-Kenney was, in 1934, leader of the Blueshirts' Youth Section, while Tierney, known as the Blueshirts' academic and political brain, was no longer a parliamentary representative by 1934, but remained active as a member of the Blueshirts, whom he was among the first to join.[241] In the early 1930s, Tierney reflected intensely on models of state organisation, publishing in 1934 a short pamphlet entitled

[239] *Chronology*, 49, 54, 57. [240] *D*, 87.
[241] Cronin, 'The Irish Right', 88, 93–125; Cronin, 'Ireland's Fascists', 318.

Some Aspects of the Social Structure of a Corporative State through Fine Gael.[242]

Beckett does not name Fitzgerald-Kenney but misquotes him as the Minister for Justice, and presents him as responsible for the specific configuration of censorship that he decries. 'Censorship in the Saorstat' begins with a citation from a Dáil committee debate of February 1929 that was largely driven by Fitzgerald-Kenney's observations about the degree of 'calculation' that might be involved in a text that 'suggest[s] or incite[s] to sexual immorality'.[243] Fitzgerald-Kenney contended that 'the expressed purpose' of the author and 'the effect [of] his thought' mattered, not 'what the author really meant'. Elsewhere in Beckett's article, 'Deputy Professor Tierney' emerges as the man who pulls the strings, particularly when it comes to sanctioning the make-up of powerful committees. Tierney is depicted as someone who 'could not bear the thought of any committee with only half a Jew upon it'.[244] At this point Beckett ventriloquises some significant moments in parliamentary debates from 1928 and 1929, including the Report of the Committee on Evil Literature, which had recommended that 'a permanent committee should be established of nine to twelve persons representative of the religious, educational and literary or artistic opinion of the Irish public'.[245] Both the number of committee members and the representative principle fostered heated debate in the Dáil.[246] Tierney attacked the measure, and described the Jewish community as less deserving of, and germane to, civic representation.[247] Tierney was not, sadly, the most vocal opponent to this measure, but Beckett's article transforms him into the leader of a submerged campaign against proportional representation, portraying Tierney's anti-Semitic stance in ways that are aligned with the political creeds that he popularised as supporter of the Blueshirts. Beckett's pointed gesture to an anti-Semitic stronghold in the Irish Free State finds correlation in the historical record: Bryan Fanning has drawn attention to the ways in which the Blueshirts discriminated against Jews and

[242] Michael Tierney, *Some Aspects of the Social Structure of a Corporative State*, Fine Gael Policy Series, Pamphlet No. 3 (Dublin: Fine Gael, 1934).

[243] 'Committee on Finance. Financial Resolutions. Censorship of Publications Bill, 1928 – Committee', 20 February 1929, *Dáil Éireann Debates*, vol. 28, no. 1, http://debates.oireachtas.ie/. All subsequent references to Dáil and Seanad Éireann debates are from this online archive.

[244] *D*, 84–5.

[245] 'Estimates for Public Services. Censorship of Publications Bill, 1928. Committee (Resumed)', *Dáil Éireann Debates*, vol. 28, no. 4, 27 February 1929. On SB's 'Che Sciagura' and the Committee on Evil Literature, see Bixby, *Samuel Beckett and the Postcolonial Novel*, 10–11.

[246] 'Censorship of Publications Bill, 1928. Second Stage', *Dáil Éireann Debates*, vol. 26, no. 6, 18 October 1928.

[247] 'Committee on Finance. Financial Resolutions. Censorship of Publications Bill, 1928', *Dáil Éireann Debates*, vol. 28, no. 1, 20 February 1929.

borrowed from the xenophobic rhetoric of continental fascist movements, notably by associating Judaism with Communism and foreign interference in national affairs.[248] The terms that Beckett employed in his letter to Leventhal admitting defeat with 'Trueborn Jackeen' suggest that these events preyed on his mind, somewhat confusedly.

'Censorship in the Saorstat' recasts Tierney's and Fitzgerald-Kenney's interventions in a different context, however, and does so rather creatively: the article merges parliamentary discussions on the censorship of publications advocating birth control that took place prior to the passing of the Censorship Act in July 1929 with later debates about birth control and the Criminal Law Amendment Bill, whose individual items were discussed in 1934.[249] Section 17 of the latter, which banned the sale and importation of contraceptives, was widely debated in the Irish press in June and July 1934, as the Bill was making its way through parliamentary chambers and was greeted by stern letters to the *Irish Times*.[250] Without differentiation, Beckett's satire associates these two different moments in Cosgrave's and de Valera's mandates, deploring an inability on the part of the Free State administration to offer an ideologically progressive and non-censorious political vision. 'Censorship in the Saorstat' presents the censorship board as an amateurish legislative body obsessed by its perceived moral authority, treating contraceptives and books as equivalents, and classifying advocates of birth control such as Margaret Sanger and Marie Stopes in the same category as a wide range of classical and contemporary writers. Some criticisms are specifically directed at Fianna Fáil: citing the party's adopted motto, 'government of the people, by the people, for the people', Beckett deplores that there are more urgent tasks at hand than regulating reading practices, wondering '[w]hether a government of the people by the people can afford these free shows'.[251]

The manner in which 'Censorship in the Saorstat' and 'Recent Irish Poetry' deal with the growing acceptance of Irish and continental fascism through layered allusions to political culture owes much to Beckett's own familiarity with the rhetoric of racial intolerance and prejudice. He saw Nazi anti-Semitism at work on many levels during his travels through Germany, and knew the kinds of persecutions German Jews faced through

[248] Fanning, *Racism and Social Change in the Republic of Ireland*, 68–9.

[249] See, notably, 'Local Elections (Dublin) Bill, 1929. Censorship of Publications Bill, 1928: Committee Stage (Resumed)', *Dáil Éireann Debates*, vol. 28, no. 5, 28 February 1929; 'Criminal Law Amendment Bill, 1934: Second Stage', *Seanad Éireann Debates*, vol. 19, no. 8, 12 December 1934.

[250] 'Letters to the Editor', *IT*, 9 July 1934, 4; 18 July 1934, 4.

[251] *D*, 87; see *Speeches and Statements by Eamon de Valera*, 92.

his Jewish uncle William 'Boss' Sinclair and his family, who were forced to leave Kassel in the summer of 1933, at a time marked by boycotts of Jewish shops and spectacular book burnings. Beckett's account of their return was dispassionate: in the letter commenting on Cosgrave's politics, he notes that Boss Sinclair and his family left Germany 'with not much more than pyjamas & toothbrushes' when the country became 'too hot'.[252] The reality was, of course, much more serious: Beckett's cousin Deirdre Sinclair had traumatic memories of witnessing an attack against a rabbi, being under surveillance from a group in SA uniform, and seeing anti-Semitic inscriptions on her father's shop.[253] Kassel, as later events confirmed, was a city where the SA were particularly brutal towards those whom they could identify as Jewish.[254]

The Dublin to which the Sinclairs returned came with few direct threats, but was nevertheless the site of a shrill and enshrined anti-Semitism, expressed particularly forcefully at the time of the Gogarty-Sinclair trial in November 1937.[255] Ultimately, the limericks that Gogarty had penned in his memoir against Harry and William Sinclair and their grandfather, Morris Harris, were recognised as libellous, and Gogarty was condemned to paying damages and legal expenses. The trial came in the wake of Gogarty's long parliamentary career in the Irish Seanad, where he had stirred anti-Semitic feeling particularly vehemently.[256] This moment is widely perceived as an important turn in Beckett's life and the origin of his decision to settle for good in France. Several accounts of the trial have been offered,[257] and all of them fail to convey the degree to which Judeophobic discourse remained ubiquitous, accepted and unchallenged. The innuendos and rumours relayed in Gogarty's memoir and at the trial were far more pernicious and serious than they have been made out to be: Gogarty's associations of Harris and the Sinclair brothers with usury, money-lending, adultery, pedophilia, money squandering and improvidence, and his derogatory references to Harris's physique, had an immediate origin in trials that took place in the year of Beckett's birth, when Gogarty also became known for his rabid anti-Semitism in Arthur Griffith's newspaper *Sinn Féin*. The same allegations about the Harris-Sinclair family were first

[252] Nixon, 'Between Gospel and Prohibition', 32–3.
[253] Jackie Blackman, 'Beckett Judaizing Beckett: A "Jew from Greenland" in Paris', *SBTA* 18 (2007): 328.
[254] Pegelow Kaplan, *The Language of Nazi Genocide*, 102–3.
[255] See also Douglas, *Architects of the Resurrection*, 38–41.
[256] Ibid., 36.
[257] Ulick O'Connor, *Oliver St John Gogarty: A Poet and his Times* (Dublin: O'Brien Press, 1999), 276–9; *SB*, 258–9; *LM*, 258–60; *DF*, 275–80.

relayed in late 1906 and thereafter by the press, in response to the divorce case that opposed Morris Harris to his wife Kathleen Hynes Harris. All allegations were proved untrue and were dismissed. As his letters reveal, Beckett was aware of this painful history ('All kinds of dirt will be raked up') and thought that taking action was necessary ('there are limits to scurrility, & to cynical laissez-faire').[258]

In 1906, Hynes filed a petition for divorce, proffering a series of spectacular allegations: she accused Harris of cruelty and violence, insults to her Catholic faith, blasphemy and indecency; she stated that her husband had sustained a long-term affair with his recently deceased sister-in-law and enticed young girls into his shop; she reported beatings, stealing, blasphemy and assault involving William and Harry Sinclair, whom Harris had brought up in the Jewish faith.[259] Only the *Irish Times* gave a full account of the questions asked of Hynes and the testimonies defending Harris. The *Freeman's Journal* and the *Irish Independent* presented the case as a failed inter-faith marriage that should not be emulated, and the *Sunday Independent* published a court drawing striking in its anti-Semitism. Much was made of their difference in age and religious faith. He was a former vice-president of Dublin's Jewish congregation; she had converted to Judaism, and her relation to Catholicism and Judaism was central to the hearings.[260] As part of the process of cross-questioning, some chilling facts emerged: that Hynes had been previously arrested for assault against Harris, that she threatened him constantly, that his family feared for his life, and that she had made violent threats against the Sinclair brothers.[261] The jury dismissed the charges of misconduct levied against Harris and cleared him of charges of adultery and child molestation, but withheld the charge of cruelty, and the divorce was pronounced.[262] Shortly after, Hynes opened a second case on the matter of alimony, alleging that Harris owned a considerable wealth that was not registered in his account books.[263] Again her accusations were found to be untrue.[264] Subsequently, she sought to

[258] *LSB1*, 495.

[259] 'Harris Divorce Case', *Freeman's Journal*, 9 November 1906, 3; 'Harris Matrimonial Suit', *IT*, 6 November 1906, 10; 'Humanity: Jew and Christian', *Sunday Independent*, 4 November 1906, 7.

[260] Dermot Keogh, *Jews in Twentieth-Century Ireland: Refugees, Anti-Semitism and the Holocaust* (Cork: Cork University Press, 1998), 7; 'Her Life a Hell', *Irish Independent*, 3 November 1906, 5.

[261] 'Harris Divorce Suit', *IT*, 7 November 1906, 9; 'Harris Matrimonial Suit', *IT*, 8 November 1906, 10.

[262] 'Dublin Divorce Suit', *Weekly IT*, 10 November 1906, 18; 'Harris Matrimonial Suit', *Weekly IT*, 17 November 1906, 20.

[263] 'The Law Courts', *IT* 27 November 1906, 3.

[264] 'Harris Divorce Case', *IT*, 4 December 1906, 7.

impeach his will, making further allegations of assault against Harris and the Sinclairs that were also disallowed.[265]

The offensive lines published by Gogarty in *As I Was Going down Sackville Street* were not simply generic slurs, but malicious attempts to ventriloquise the divorce trial and later proceedings. Displays of anti-Semitism were no less prominent at the 1937 trial that saw Beckett speak against the former senator. When hearings began, the press reports from 1906 occupied centre stage.[266] Thereafter, Gogarty's lawyer, J. M. Fitzgerald, returned repeatedly to the question of religion, stressing that there were differences between Jewish and non-Jewish names, describing the former as 'strange' and 'unpronounceable', and asking Beckett whether he was a Christian, a Jew or an atheist ('None of the three', he replied). Harry Sinclair's lawyer called for a fair trial, denouncing an evident prejudice. Beckett's interest in Proust was emphasised in the court and in the press; his essay on Proust, depicted by Fitzgerald as 'a man who indulged in the psychology of sex', bolstered claims that Beckett was a 'bawd', a 'blasphemer' and an unreliable witness.[267]

These attacks relayed other stereotypes: in November 1936, Ernest Dimnet – a French priest whose praise of Hitler, Mussolini and Franco was favoured by the *Irish Times* – gave a lecture to the Royal Dublin Society celebrating the insights of Maurice Barrès and making derogatory references to Proust's and Zola's Jewish origins.[268] Harry Sinclair, who had attended the lecture, wrote on two occasions to the *Irish Times* to denounce Dimnet's anti-Semitic slander.[269] These forms of prejudice and intolerance were familiar to Leventhal also: in an essay published in June 1945, at a time when negationism had begun to rear its head in Eire and the Dublin Jewish community was subject to further intimidation and threat, Leventhal evoked the forms of anti-Semitism to which he had been routinely exposed during his youth, detailing the common beliefs feeding stereotype ('That you are either a Rothschild or a Karl Marx; an international financier or a denationalising communist. [. . .] That you are a parasite but may not be your own host in the land of your fathers or anywhere else. That you are accused of being different and ostracised if you

265 'Harris Family Litigation', *IT*, 26 January 1907, 9; 'Will of the Late Mr. Harris', *IT*, 7 December 1909, 1; 'Dublin Will Case', *IT*, 5 February 1910, 5; 'Remarkable Probate Suit', *IT*, 8 Febrary 1910, 3; 'Harris Will Suit', *IT*, 28 June 1910, 7.

266 'Dr. Gogarty Sued for Libel', *IT*, 23 November 1937, 5.

267 '£900 Damages Awarded in Libel Action', *IT*, 24 November 1937, 5.

268 'Machiavelli of Statesmen', *IT*, 13 November 1936, 4; 'From a Paris Balcony', *IT*, 14 November 1936, 10.

269 'Letters to the Editor', *IT*, 17 November 1936, 9; 1 December 1936, 5.

assimilate').[270] Beckett witnessed prejudice at work in other settings: a letter to Arland Ussher from May 1938, for example, relates a series of unpleasant encounters in London, including a discussion with Edward Morrison, a Trinity alumni and physician known for his anti-Semitic position.[271]

There is another, more problematic connection between Beckett's polemical essays and the Gogarty trial that is important in understanding the context of Beckett's exile to France and the pressures he sought to escape. Yeats, as many in Dublin knew, was infuriated by 'Recent Irish Poetry', and a letter to Dorothy Wellesley from May 1937 suggests that his anger had little abated three years later. This derogatory letter, which evokes the Sinclairs and the Gogarty trial, was excised from the published volume of Yeats's correspondence with Wellesley, a copy of which Beckett owned.[272] Relaying the libellous rumours disseminated in 1906 and reignited by Gogarty, Yeats presents himself as a witness of sorts: he describes Harry Sinclair as 'the chicken butcher', clarifying that the denomination applies to someone who 'makes love to the immature'.[273] For his part, Beckett is designated as 'the informant' upon whom Gogarty's fate depends, and as a '"racketeer" of a Dublin poet or imatative [*sic*] poet of the new school', which leads Yeats to explain that 'He [Beckett] and the chicken butcher are Jews'. This comment invites associations with other problematic facets of Yeats's politics, and with other allegations of 'half-Jewishness' commonly levied in the political arena in order to marginalise opponents: in particular, the idea that de Valera was of Jewish parentage was frequently brandished after 1932.[274] Yeats's letter also echoes other perceptions of Beckett as 'half-Jewish': that which Lucia Joyce offered in another context, in an account of her life, for example.[275] The same letter refers to a lost review by Beckett of Yeats's 1936 *Oxford Book of Modern Verse*, of which this is the sole record, and suggests that Yeats's ire had other origins in a perceived personal slight: 'He [Beckett] hates us all – his review of the Anthology was so violent the *Irish Times* refused to publish it'. Clearly, something happened around Yeats's anthology, and there are a few hints of what it might have entailed. Decades later, Beckett responded to John

270 A. J. Leventhal, 'What It Means to be a Jew', *The Bell* 10, no. 3 (1945): 207–16. See also Douglas, *Architects of the Resurrection*, 220–4.

271 *LSB1*, 621–2, 623 n4.

272 Atik, *How It Was*, 69.

273 Yeats to Wellesley, 19 May 1937, *The Collected Letters of W. B. Yeats. Electronic Edition, vol. 4: Unpublished Letters (1905–1939)*, ed. John Kelly, Eric Domville, Warwick Gould, Ronald Schuchard, Deirdre Toomey et al. (Charlottesville, VA: InteLex, 2002).

274 McCormack, *Blood Kindred*, 108; Douglas, *Architects of the Resurrection*, 36–8.

275 Cited in David Hayman, 'The Papers of Lucia Joyce', in *James Joyce: The Centennial Symposium*, ed. Morris Beja, Phillip F. Herring, Maurice Harmon and David Norris (Urbana: University of Illinois Press, 1986), 202.

Fletcher's questions about a mysterious document he had described as a review of a 'late work by W. B. Yeats' by saying that he couldn't recall the details.[276] Around this time too, Beckett's relations with the *Irish Times* soured: this became manifest when R. M. Smyllie covertly turned down a tribute Beckett had written for his uncle William, who had passed away in May 1937, shortly after his return from Germany.[277] A few months previously, a resounding silence greeted the publication of Yeats's poetry anthology in the *Irish Times*, which gives credence to Yeats's complaint about a hostile review by Beckett that might have been pulled out unexpectedly. Yeats's anthology certainly invited criticism: it dismisses the poetry of the First World War on the grounds that 'passive suffering is not a theme for poetry', and suggests forgetting about suffering altogether, 'as we do the discomfort of fever, remembering our comfort at midnight when our temperature fell, or as we forget the worst moments of more painful disease'.[278] Instead of a review of Yeats's anthology, the *Irish Times* published a defensive and densely allusive article by F. R. Higgins that decried the 'newer thing' and the 'Dublin imitators' influenced by the Bloomsbury group, T. S. Eliot and French Surrealism. The piece obliquely appropriates the rhetoric of conspiracy and anti-cosmopolitanism prevalent in anti-Semitic discourse, while offering racialised metaphors that seem calculated to counter Beckett's comparison between Yeats and the 'mesozoic pelican' in 'Recent Irish Poetry'. The 'Dublin *dilettanti*' portrayed by Higgins belong to an undefined and threateningly international group: 'these are our literary birds of passage – the cosmopolitans – of no racial abode, of no background. Their insecure slickness, so negative and, [*sic*] unmanly, is promoted by those cultural racketeers who have recently terrorised even the journalistic high priests into submission'.[279]

These troubling anecdotes reveal the degree to which Beckett was labouring under the weight of many creative and political impossibilities. By the mid-1930s, he had increasingly little support in Dublin and seems to have violated some powerful political codes, knowingly and unknowingly. Much evidence points to his very real isolation; in October 1935, for example, Devlin wrote to Reavey reporting his efforts to attract attention to Beckett's work through new channels such as a subscription list and publicity posted to acquaintances; he admitted that, beyond his close circle of

[276] Raymond Federman and John Fletcher, *Samuel Beckett: His Works and his Critics* (Berkeley: University of California Press, 1970), 105.

[277] *LSB1*, 495.

[278] W. B. Yeats, ed., 'Introduction', in *The Oxford Book of Modern Verse, 1892–1935* (Oxford: Clarendon Press, 1936), xxxiv–xxxv.

[279] F. R. Higgins, 'The Poet and Modern Life', *IT*, 30 November 1936, 4; *D*, 72.

friends, 'Beckett is not popular here on account of the pundits (Higgins, F. O'Connor, O' Faolain etc, + the Professor people)'.[280] For his part, Beckett became increasingly concerned about his ability to speak in a critical capacity and take professional risks. He feared, for example, that accepting to review Devlin's poetry in *transition* might 'damage' the latter's reputation in Ireland.[281] When he was invited to translate and write a preface for Sade's *Les 120 journées de Sodome*, a book banned in France, he wondered about 'the practical effect on [his] own future freedom of literary action in England & USA'.[282] These anxieties were certainly founded, and should be considered in relation to the many tensions that shaped his education and political affirmations in British and Irish spheres. There is something poignant, if not tragic, about Beckett's inconclusive attempts to write about political history during the 1930s. Yet the discarded texts and fragments in which he sought to examine the 'material of experience' across a broader historical trajectory pose important questions about the legibility of political events during the interwar period, and about the artistic uncertainties that surround political articulacy, for Beckett as for other writers.[283] Ultimately, his move to France was not simply an escape from cultural dynamics that he found intolerable, but a tentative step towards another political identity. The France where he settled in late 1937 was rocked by economic instability and strikes, but nonetheless offered the promise of a different social model to many, including artists, who had seen their working rights and levels of unionisation strengthened under the Popular Front. This was the old France that Beckett remembered wistfully a decade later – an ideal that 'one clung to, that I still cling to'.[284] In this new climate, however, the possibility of political affirmation came with different obstacles and exigencies, and it would be some time before Beckett was able to speak, in his own name and with the same freedom and ease, about the political manoeuvres that he opposed.

[280] Devlin to Reavey, 22 October 1935, George Reavey Collection, HRHRC. It is unclear who the 'Professor people' are.

[281] *LSB1*, 562. [282] *LSB1*, 607–8.

[283] See Benjamin Kohlmann, *Modernism, Politics, and Left-Wing Literature in the 1930s* (Oxford: Oxford University Press, 2014).

[284] *LSB2*, 72.

CHAPTER 2

Another War Entirely

Internationalist Politics and the Labour of Translation

It is difficult to think of Beckett's long writing career without considering his continued involvement with translation, and yet many of his activities on this front remain obscure. Charting his parallel career translating work by other writers has proved an arduous task: many of his translations were published anonymously – when he reworked translations for post-war issues of *Transition*, for example, or acted as ghost writer or ghost translator for UNESCO.[1] He frequently dismissed such work, particularly that undertaken for the UNESCO-commissioned *Anthology of Mexican Poetry*. Just how little he remembered is clear from his declarations: in 1961, he confessed to having made 'quantities of anonymous translations, in Paris, to earn a living'; three years later, when presented with a list of texts that he may have translated or revised during the lean years of 'literary drudgery', he recognised only one, stressing that he had '[n]o recollection' of others.[2] Yet his correspondence suggests a different level of investment: in a letter from 1948 inviting Georges Duthuit to send him more to translate for *Transition*, Beckett portrays translation as a war that requires some conviction, describing himself as an unconvinced conscript trapped in the trenches of a new world war: a 'poilu peu poilu' who has no talent for fighting and remains tragically 'indifferent to causes, caught up since the beginning in another war, without hope of leave or armistice'.[3]

This is one of several letters in which Beckett, speaking of himself as an artist, correlates his disaffection from narratives of accomplishment with a wider historical chaos. The association between translation and militancy by proxy has other resonances: as translator, Beckett became enrolled in distinctive political struggles, including when translation was also a means of

[1] John Pilling and Seán Lawlor, 'Beckett in *Transition*', in *Publishing Samuel Beckett*, ed. Mark Nixon (London: British Library, 2011), 83–96; *LSB3*, 639 n11.

[2] D'Aubarède, 'En Attendant . . . Beckett', 7; *LSB2*, 666; *LSB3*, 637.

[3] *LSB2*, 90–1, 92. The term 'les poilus' (the hairy ones) designates the French soldiers who fought in the trenches during the First World War. George Craig translates Beckett's phrase as 'rankest of rankers'.

building a reputation or earning a living. The two voluminous anthologies to which he made vital contributions – Nancy Cunard's *Negro* and Octavio Paz's *Anthology of Mexican Poetry* – were not simply ambitious enterprises of translation, but important responses to larger debates about peace, justice and the capacity of literary writing to shed light on political history. It is through translation that Beckett became truly acquainted with the political idioms of the international Left: his translations for *Negro* include polemical manifestos and essays that are aligned with the international work of prominent anti-colonial organisations and the political campaigns articulated in confidential Surrealist reviews such as *Le Surréalisme au service de la révolution*. His translations for *Negro* and the *Anthology of Mexican Poetry* are important pieces of work that illuminate his political thinking, and convey the depth of his reflection on the long history of colonialism and imperialism as well as the political remit of translation itself.

Beckett's Parallel Career

When working on the anthologies edited by Cunard and Paz, Beckett took great liberties: his translations often rely on transposition and substitution, articulating views or critiques that were present only in residual form in the original. This approach was not uncommon: indeed, in his capacity as commissioned translator, he often subjected texts to drastic rewriting, particularly when the original discussed a political problem or situation that sparked his interest. The distinctive terminology that he employed bears the marks of an imaginative and interventionist approach: in the early days, he aspired to 'transpose' Surrealist poetry, while the last translation exercise that bears his name – the variations around Chamfort's *Maximes* published in the mid-1970s – was generated by a process of 'doggereliz[ing]' that led to new Beckettian aphorisms.[4] The practice of translation was, for Beckett, an ongoing subject of reflection, and discussions about the minutiae of translation are frequent in his correspondence. He worked closely with Elmar Tophoven and other translators, while Bray – a professional translator whose prolific career included translating French fiction and non-fiction authors, from Duras to Le Roy Ladurie – soon became his favoured interlocutor on matters of translation and composition.

The contexts in which Beckett acted as translator were immensely diverse, and he was remarkably versatile in the role: he most commonly

[4] *LSB1*, 146 n6; Seán Lawlor and John Pilling, eds., *The Collected Poems of Samuel Beckett* (London: Faber, 2012), 438. See also Pascale Sardin and Karine Germoni, '"Scarcely Disfigured": Beckett's Surrealist Translations', *Modernism/modernity* 18, no. 4 (2011): 739–54.

worked from French to English, but also translated Italian and Spanish texts into English. His career began with a protracted and, it seems, deeply ungratifying experience – the version of Joyce's 'Anna Livia Plurabelle' translated with Péron in 1929.[5] Nevertheless, this early collaboration marked the beginning of a long series of signed and unsigned translations, including many related to Dada and Surrealist endeavours. These translations were formative in other ways: their publication enabled Beckett to secure work and precious contacts in literary cultures where his own work in French had yet to be recognised and accepted.

Translation constituted but one in a series of sidelines, half-pursued endeavours and aborted possibilities: he sometimes nurtured other aspirations, which ranged from a pondered career as an air pilot to plans to move to Moscow, and from letting his friends believe that he was 'trying journalism in Paris' in the early 1930s to reflecting on the usefulness of working as editor for the review of the Irish Retail Grocery, Dairy and Allied Trades' Association immediately after the war.[6] He was well aware that working in the Irish civil service was not a possibility due to his ignorance of Irish Gaelic, and other options – such as working as 'agent to an estate (Lord Rathdowne's?) near Carlow' – were unappealing.[7] It seems that he resolved to turn to writing when other options failed to materialise: he told Rosette Lamont, for example, that he began writing in French 'in [his] mother's room' in Dublin in 1938 because '[t]here was nothing left to do but be a writer'.[8] Prior to that, his ambitions had remained shaped by family expectations and the common view of the 'Trinity man' as ready to 'go anywhere, do anything'.[9] In practice, for those of his social class, the realm of possibilities frequently coincided with the lineaments of the British Empire: Trinity had a long-established Indian and Home Civil Service School, and sent graduates to India until the end of British rule.[10] Some of Beckett's friends pursued successful careers in the colonial administration, while his brother Frank spent time in India before becoming a quantity surveyor at Beckett and Medcalf and acquiring, much to Beckett's dismay, 'a car and a bowler-hat'.[11] Beckett later recalled that his brother had

[5] Megan M. Quigley, 'Justice for the "Illstarred Punster": Samuel Beckett's and Alfred Péron's Revisions of "Anna Lyvia Pluratself"', *James Joyce Quarterly* 41, no. 3 (2004): 469–87.

[6] Sheehy Skeffington, *Skeff*, 63; *LSB2*, 29. [7] *LSB1*, 508; *SB*, 251.

[8] Cited in Rosette Lamont, 'Samuel Beckett's Wandering Jew', in *Reflections of the Holocaust in Literature*, ed. Randolph L. Braham (Boulder, CO: Social Science Monographs, 1990), 43.

[9] McDowell, *Trinity College Dublin, 1592–1952*, 451.

[10] The class lists in the *Dublin University Calendar* do not indicate that Frank Beckett undertook special training for the Indian Civil Service at Trinity, but the programme was running when he obtained a BA in Engineering in 1924.

[11] *LSB1*, 338, 112.

worked on 'some railway in India', while Belmont, drawing on faint memories, reported that Frank Beckett had been stationed in a Gurkha garrison guarding a high mountain pass of strategic importance to the British Raj, evoking the Khyber Pass as a possibility.[12] For Beckett, finding work after his resignation from his lecturing post at Trinity in January 1932 was an arduous task; thankfully the colonial world was, seemingly, his for the taking. He considered applying for a 'job as teacher of French in Technical School in Bulawayo, S. Rhodesia', and pondered a lectureship in Italian at the University of Cape Town, while voicing qualms at the prospect of living in a country that practised segregation.[13] The British Empire had brought fortune to some in his family: his uncle Edward Roe, who had sent his daughters to live in Cooldrinagh, was a plantation owner in Nyasaland. A letter of 1936 announcing his arrival predicts conversations about 'big game, angling[,] Wimbledon, arthritis, tobacco plantations, Mombassa and no money', concluding, 'until that is over I can't get away, even if I had the money'.[14] Translation provided an escape from these frustrations; yet it is certainly intriguing to imagine Beckett at work on the anti-imperialist and anti-capitalist texts selected by Cunard in a family home decorated with colonial memorabilia, leopard skins and kudu horns.[15]

Cunard's *Negro* was Beckett's first substantial experience of translation, and it bore a lasting influence on his approach to political history. He mined the anthology for creative resources, particularly in his later work, just as he continuously put to use other historical sources with which he was familiar. There is a peculiar irony in his reappropriations of Cunard's materials, not least because the scattered and residual allusions to the global history of colonisation and slavery that occasionally surface around his destitute European characters are articulated in ways that challenge the possibility of a legitimate connection. Lucky's plight in *Waiting for Godot*, for example, evokes the flogging and forced labour depicted in essays by Léon Pierre-Quint and Benjamin Péret, while the Unnamable's characterisation of himself as 'a kind of tenth-rate Toussaint l'Ouverture' owes much to the anthology's section on Haiti: notably, to the brief history by Jenner Bastien translated by Beckett, featuring a portrait of Toussaint l'Ouverture celebrated as 'the Black Napoleon'.[16]

Beckett's contribution to Cunard's anti-racist and anti-segregationist enterprise also paved the ground for later political engagements, particularly in the wake of the Algerian war. In 1963, he joined the first supporters

[12] *BR/RB*, 15; Belmont, *Souvenirs*, 164. [13] *LSB1*, 138–9.
[14] *LSB1*, 351–2, 354 n13. [15] See *DF*, 4, 14.
[16] *Trilogy*, 352; Jenner Bastien, 'Summary of the History of Hayti', trans. Samuel Beckett, in *Negro: Anthology Made by Nancy Cunard, 1931–1933* (London: Nancy Cunard at Wishart & Co.), 460–4.

of the Anti-Apartheid Movement chaired by the British Labour MP Barbara Castle, and endorsed an early call for a cultural boycott instructing literary agents 'to insert a clause in all future contracts automatically refusing performing rights in any theatre where discrimination is made among audiences on grounds of colour'.[17] The declaration was initially signed by fifty-four playwrights including John Arden, Shelagh Delaney, Daphne du Maurier, Spike Milligan, Iris Murdoch, John Osborne, Harold Pinter, Muriel Spark and Arnold Wesker. All signatories were British, except Beckett and Arthur Adamov. Genet, Sartre, O'Casey and Arthur Miller subsequently joined (ironically, Miller was identified as the sole non-British signatory in the British press). Castle had pledged to attract a hundred signatures; however, half of those she initially contacted refused to endorse the declaration.[18] The following year, as part of a group of twenty-eight Irish playwrights including O'Casey, Hugh Leonard and John B. Keane, Beckett joined Irish Playwrights Against Apartheid, which arose from the Irish Anti-Apartheid Movement and the efforts of Conor Cruise O'Brien and others. Over the years, he continued to adhere to the pledge, taking steps to ensure that his work would not be performed to segregated audiences.[19] In the late 1980s, he agreed 'instantly' to the reprinting of 'Murderous Humanitarianism', the Surrealist manifesto he had translated for *Negro*, in a tribute to Nelson Mandela supported by the Irish Anti-Apartheid Movement, and he contributed a poem entitled 'Brief Dream' to another volume celebrating Mandela's political message – *For Nelson Mandela*, the English version of Jacques Derrida and Mustapha Tlili's tribute, published by Richard Seaver.[20]

For Beckett, South Africa and apartheid were not distant realities: during the 1930s, his cousin Morris Sinclair worked as a private tutor in the Eastern Cape; during the 1950s, he translated *Molloy* with Patrick Bowles, who had emigrated from South Africa to Europe on political grounds, and he tried to assist Aidan Higgins, who was living in Johannesburg. Some snippets in his correspondence convey his admiration for Lionel Rogosin's *Come Back, Africa* (1960), a political documentary exposing the workings of segregation in South Africa, the apartheid system of migrant labour and black life in the townships.[21]

[17] '48 Playwrights in Apartheid Protest', *Times*, 26 June 1963, 12.

[18] 'Playwright Strike at Segregation', *Washington Post*, 27 June 1963, E9; Dorothy Connell Carroll, 'Cultural Boycott: Yes or No?', *Index on Censorship* 4, no. 1 (1975): 3444.

[19] *LSB4*, 287–8, 398.

[20] Chris Agee and Bill McCormack, 'In the Prison of His Days', *Linen Hall Review* 5, no. 3 (1988): 11; W. J. McCormack, ed., *In the Prison of His Days: For Nelson Mandela* (Dublin: Lilliput, 1988); Jaques Derrida and Mustapha Tlili, eds., *For Nelson Mandela* (New York: Seaver Books, 1987).

[21] *LSB3*, 297.

Other letters evidence a continued interest in American race politics, pointing to Beckett's interest in the American civil rights movement and the theatre of the Black Arts Movement. In 1964, during his stay in New York, he witnessed a performance of *The Dutchman* by LeRoi Jones (Amiri Baraka) – a notable event, since Beckett never frequented theatres assiduously.[22] Shortly after its publication, he read Adrienne Kennedy's *Funnyhouse of a Negro*, describing the play as a 'wild affair' that was, while 'beyond' him, an interesting performance counterpart to *Play*.[23] His interventions in this political arena could be concrete and direct: in 1978, he made a donation to a French committee headed by Maria Jolas and set up to assist George Brown, Jean and Melvin McNair, and Joyce Tillerson – four members of the Black Panther Party who had hijacked a plane to travel to the Black Panther base in Algiers and were detained in France.[24] The subsequent appeal protesting their extradition to the United States was signed by figures long involved with anti-imperialist movements, such as Claude Bourdet, de Beauvoir and Schwartz. In Beckett's eyes, his Irish nationality did not enable him to sign a document that took an explicit position on French law, yet making a financial contribution was a different question.[25] This and other moments at which Beckett supported similar forms of political militancy take on a new significance when considered alongside his involvement in Cunard's political enterprise. Many haunting political revelations separate the elderly writer, militant and compassionate, from the complacent youth who thought appropriate to start his first published essay, 'Dante . . . Bruno. Vico . . Joyce', by comparing philosophy and philology to 'a pair of nigger minstrels'.[26] Without doubt, Cunard's *Negro* led Beckett to recognise the prejudiced and racist mindset common to his affluent, secluded familial upbringing, and enabled him to learn how to think differently.

Beckett, Nancy Cunard and the Internationalist Left

Negro was a major political and creative undertaking that demanded an unusual level of commitment from its translators: indeed, preserving the historical, political and rhetorical qualities of the selected texts required

[22] *LSB3*, 588. [23] *LSB3*, 571; *NABS*, 140.

[24] Maria Jolas, 'Lettre de Fleury-Mérogis', *Esprit* 1 (1978): 104–9.

[25] 'Correspondence 1978–1979', Fonds Beckett, Institut Mémoires de l'Edition Contemporaine (hereafter IMEC).

[26] *D*, 19.

great care and critical acumen. The volume includes more than 220 contributions, most of which were originally written in English, by some 150 authors, and features essays on historical and political topics, poems, songs, letters, bibliographies, maps, musical scores, press articles, photographs, photostats of manuscripts and proverbs. Beckett was one of the main contributors, alongside Raymond Michelet and Cunard herself.[27] He translated most of the French-language originals – nineteen texts including contributions by René Crevel, Georges Sadoul, Benjamin Péret and many others, published in sections dealing with imperialism and racial politics entitled 'Negro Stars', 'Music', 'West Indies and South America', 'Europe', 'Africa' and 'Negro Sculpture and Ethnology'. The published volume was dedicated to the black jazz pianist Henry Crowder – Cunard's former companion and collaborator, who had opened her eyes to the realities of segregation in the United States.

The vagaries of history have added weight to Beckett's translations, since several texts have not survived in any other form. Despite the efforts of Cunard's loyal neighbours, who saved some of her archive at great personal risk, most of the originals were destroyed during the Second World War, when Cunard's Normandy house was ransacked with the blessing of the local mayor, who encouraged German officers to destroy her belongings.[28] She featured on a Gestapo black list of British intellectuals earmarked for arrest, and the German military commandant who supervised the looting of her house saw it as Hitler's personal order that she be hung, should she be found.[29] As early as March 1940, during the 'phoney war', the French police had visited her house in La Chapelle-Réanville, searched for books and papers, and confiscated some of her publications.[30]

Within Beckett studies, *Negro* has mostly been perceived as an idiosyncratic episode, and the translations have attracted little attention in spite of Alan Warren Friedman's pioneering work. In other fields, however, Cunard's volume has been celebrated as a landmark in anti-colonial and anti-racist movements. Its historical reach is vast: *Negro* offers a response

[27] McCormack, 'Samuel Beckett and the *Negro Anthology*', 73–92; Friedman, 'Introduction', *Beckett in Black and Red*, xi.

[28] John Banting, 'Nancy Cunard', in *Nancy Cunard: Brave Poet, Indomitable Rebel, 1896–1965*, ed. Hugh Ford (Philadelphia: Chilton Book Company, 1968), 181; Nancy Cunard, *These Were the Hours: Memories of My Hours Press, Réanville and Paris, 1928–1931*, ed. Hugh Ford (Carbondale: Southern Illinois University Press, 1969), 199–205.

[29] 'If Britain Had Been Conquered: 2300 Names on Nazi Black List', *Dundee Evening Telegraph and Post*, 14 September 1945, 8; Lois Gordon, *Nancy Cunard: Heiress, Muse, Political Idealist* (New York: Columbia University Press, 2007), 303.

[30] Ibid., 199–200.

to Alain Locke's 1925 anthology *The New Negro*, but also stands as a political landmark situating the work of different communist and anti-colonial groups in the same political sphere, and as a forerunner to later studies of slavery and capitalism.[31] Jane Marcus, Renata Morresi, Carole Sweeney and Laura Winkiel have documented Cunard's work in defence of civil rights, while tracing the tensions between her political commitments and a personal life marked by an antagonistic relation to the Cunard family, who entertained privileged relations with the upper classes and aristocrats of Europe.

The original title – *Negro: Anthology Made by Nancy Cunard, 1931–1933* – reflects the labour involved in the making of the work. Cunard began collecting appropriate documents in April 1931, by means of an open-ended circular that evoked the conception of a 'new book on COLOR' to be published 'as soon as enough material has been collected'.[32] Beckett was enrolled as translator in October 1931, and his involvement continued until early 1933. The book was published by Cunard in February 1934, in association with Wishart & Co., the radical London publisher linked to the British Communist Party. Its publication chimed with profound evolutions in political thinking about colonialism, the emergence of the Négritude movement in Paris and related developments around the Harlem Renaissance.[33] The anthology also arose from circumstances specific to Cunard's political work with the League Against Imperialism and Colonial Oppression in London, the Negro Workers' Association and the International Labor Defense.[34] She was particularly dedicated to the work undertaken by the ILD, the legal wing of the American Communist Party that supported the Scottsboro Boys – the nine teenage black boys accused of rape of two white women in Alabama – through the infamous series of trials that began in 1931.

In 1931, in anticipation of new developments in the Scottsboro affair, Cunard issued an appeal to garner support and funds in copies of her pamphlet *Black Man and White Ladyship*. The appeal was initially circulated to friends with the first edition of the pamphlet, printed privately in 1931, and it was reproduced in the edition published later that year by

31 See, for instance, Eric Williams, *Capitalism and Slavery* (Chapel Hill: University of North Carolina Press, 1944).

32 Quoted in Chisholm, *Nancy Cunard*, 191.

33 Carole Sweeney, *From Fetish to Subject: Race, Modernism, and Primitivism, 1919–1935* (Westport, CT: Praeger, 2004), 71–94.

34 Susan D. Pennybacker, *From Scottsboro to Munich: Race and Political Culture in 1930s Britain* (Princeton: Princeton University Press, 2009), 6, 67; Maroula Joannou, 'Nancy Cunard's English Journey', *Feminist Review* 78 (2004): 141–63.

the Utopia Press, a London press affiliated with the British Communist Party that printed the *Daily Worker* and other Communist publications.[35] This is the first political appeal that Beckett endorsed, and Cunard's personal list, which identifies signatories by profession, categorises him as a writer.[36]

Cunard's appeal offered a brief account of the Scottsboro case, stressed that the appeal to the Alabama Supreme Court for a second trial had been won, and argued for the 'imperative urgency and necessity to free the 9 innocent working class victims of American race hatred'.[37] The text concluded with the following plea: 'If you are against the lynching and terrorisation of the most oppressed race in the world, if you have any innate sense of justice,/sign this protest/and contribute towards the defense funds'. Morresi has shown that the appeal was supported by a large group of artists, academics and journalists, with some also sending messages of support. The signatories from a list dated 1933 include, among others, Gide, H.D., George Antheil, Salvador Dalí, Paul Eluard, Alberto Giacometti, Robert Graves, Walter Lowenfels, Len Lye, Dorothy and Ezra Pound, Arthur Symons, Yves Tanguy and Rebecca West. Beckett signed the appeal alongside Michelet, René Crevel, Henri Lavachery, Benjamin Péret and Georges Sadoul – other contributors to *Negro*, whose texts he translated.

Negro afforded Cunard the possibility of broadening her vision of political writing as well as her work in support of the Scottsboro Boys. The foreword she wrote in 1933 positions the anthology as a response to the Scottsboro affair, characterising the latter as one instalment in a long series of lynchings, murders and persecutions, and a turning point in a long fight for social justice. Every facet of the anthology was shaped by Cunard's political activities: the cost of producing the volume, for example, was covered by damages that the English press had been forced to pay in compensation for republishing racial slurs previously disseminated in the American press about her 1932 research trip to Harlem with Crowder.[38] By the time work

[35] Renata Morresi, *Nancy Cunard: America, modernismo, negritudine* (Urbino: QuattroVenti, 2007), 78–84; Morresi, 'Black Man and White Ladyship (1931): A Manifesto', in *Recharting the Black Atlantic: Modern Cultures, Local Communities, Global Connections*, ed. Annalisa Oboe and Anna Scacchi (New York: Routledge, 2008), 98–100. Earlier studies date the appeal to 1933 without going into specifics.

[36] Cunard, *Hours Press*, 128–9; Morresi, 'Black Man', 100; Morresi, *Nancy Cunard*, 802, 167 n77. Beckett did not send an additional statement when he signed the appeal. Warm thanks to Renata Morresi for sharing this information and for directing me to Beckett's 'From the Only Poet to a Shining Whore'.

[37] Morresi, *Nancy Cunard*, 79–80.

[38] Jane Marcus, *Hearts of Darkness: White Women Write Race* (Brunswick, NJ: Rutgers University Press, 2004), 128, 139.

on *Negro* had commenced, Cunard had come to be perceived as a political activist worthy of being placed under FBI watch. Internal US State Department reports from 1933 describe her as a determined and 'ultra-leftminded' activist, who seems 'capable of sharing her last £10 with any organisation connected with the I.L.D.' and continues 'improvident and impenitent' to work on an anthology that is thought to be 'pretty well the last shot in her financial locker'.[39] In London, Cunard, like many other politicised intellectuals, fell under the surveillance of MI5 and Special Branch agents, and there is evidence of intercepted correspondence and tailing by detectives.[40] Nor did her activities go unnoticed in France, where a satirical newspaper reporting on the anthology went so far as to suggest that she might one day be marched out of the country.[41]

After *Negro*, Cunard turned her eyes towards other political horizons. She spent a month in Moscow before returning to France, where she remained until 1940, becoming a journalist affiliated with the Associated Negro Press.[42] She also wrote articles for the *Manchester Guardian* on the plight of Spanish republican refugees in French internment camps, the advances of Nazism in Africa, the involvement of African troops in the war and Pan-Africanism. Her work remained part of global debates about decolonisation long after *Negro*: Michelet's 'African Empires and Civilisation' was republished in 1945 in a pamphlet series edited by George Padmore, for which T. R. Makonnen, Jomo Kenyatta, Wallace Johnson, C. L. R. James and Peter Abrahams acted as advisory editors.[43] During the 1930s, however, Cunard and her contributors encountered some difficulty in reaching their readership: *Negro* was banned for seditiousness in Trinidad and Tobago, and for communist subversion elsewhere in the West Indies, while in Kenya and other British colonies and protectorates it was subject to anti-sedition ordinances.[44] The ban was denounced in the British House of Commons in July 1936, in a debate acknowledging the anthology as a masterpiece.[45]

39 Ibid., 140.

40 James Smith, *British Writers and MI5 Surveillance, 1930–1960* (Cambridge: Cambridge University Press, 2012), xi, 161 n17; 163 n19, 155.

41 'La France d'outre-mer: Miss Nancy Cunard', *Bec et ongles*, 14 May 1932, 11.

42 Maureen Moynagh, ed., 'Introduction', in *Essays on Race and Empire*, by Nancy Cunard (Peterborough, Ontario: Broadview, 2002), 9–63.

43 Raymond Michelet, *African Empires and Civilisation, International African Service Bureau No. 4*, trans. Edward Cunard, foreword by Nancy Cunard (London: Panaf, 1945).

44 'Negro Anthology Banned by Trinidad as Seditious', *NYT*, 13 April 1934, 21; Chisholm, *Nancy Cunard*, 222.

45 Colonial Office, *House of Commons Debates* 314, 9 July 1936, 1495–7, Hansard Online, http://hansard.parliament.uk/.

Long before work on the anthology began, Cunard became persuaded that her commitment to publishing would involve taking great personal risks: even in the late 1920s, at the time of her relationship with Louis Aragon, she speculated that her printing press might be used for underground anti-fascist publications one day, should a fascist *coup d'état* take place in France.[46] Unlike many of her acquaintances, she was not a card-carrying Communist, but was nevertheless identified as such in US State Department files by virtue of her alliances with figures such as Padmore.[47] Her political convictions were mixed, as some of her friends noted after her death. Charles Duff described her as a conservative thinker who had little understanding of communism, yet presented herself as communist when her own humanitarian principles benefited from it.[48] For Charles Burkhart, she was simply an anarchist, animated by a strong anti-authoritarian impulse.[49]

Cunard's lack of political orthodoxy makes her an easy target for mockery in Beckett's correspondence with MacGreevy. Letters from the early 1930s deride her work in Harlem and in Jamaica with the Marcus Garvey Association.[50] Yet by January 1938, writing from a hospital bed in Paris, Beckett alludes more warmly to her work in support of Spanish refugees and anti-fascist groups ('Nancy Cunard bounced in the other evening from Spain. I was very glad to see her').[51] Subsequently, the pair met regularly, but Beckett often reverted to his former tone, complaining that she had 'submerged [him] in left wing literature', and that he had 'never seen so many bad poems' as in the short poetry collections about the Spanish Civil War that Cunard printed in 1937.[52] Yet, he conceded, the poems by Lorca and Alberti had merits.[53] Later correspondence expresses his continued solidarity with Cunard's endeavours and his fond memories of *Negro*, of which he owned a copy.[54] The friendship remained immensely important to Cunard as well, to the extent that Beckett, along with Sadoul and Aragon, were said to be the only friends whom she longed to see on her deathbed.[55]

The success of Cunard's literary and political ventures relied heavily upon her friendships, and *Negro* was no exception. Michelet was her companion, while Sadoul had been her faithful assistant at the Hours Press.[56]

[46] Georges Sadoul, 'The Fighting Lady', *Cunard: Brave Poet*, 146.
[47] Marcus, *Hearts of Darkness*, 140.
[48] Charles Duff, 'Nancy Cunard: The Enigma of a Personality', *Cunard: Brave Poet*, 188.
[49] Charles Burkhart, 'Letters from Nancy', ibid., 329. [50] *LSB1*, 112. [51] *LSB1*, 584.
[52] Chisholm, *Nancy Cunard*, 145. [53] SB to MacGreevy, 11 February 1938, TCD MS 10402/156.
[54] *LSB2*, 611. [55] Raymond Michelet, 'Nancy Cunard', *Cunard: Brave Poet*, 132.
[56] Gordon, *Nancy Cunard*, 161; Cunard, *Hours Press*, 75.

Members of the Surrealist group such as Crevel were old friends and contributed on this basis. Some were enrolled through friends' recommendations: Jean-Joseph Rabearivelo, for example, recalled that he was invited to contribute at the suggestion of Claude McKay and Henri Barbusse.[57] Others were members of organisations supported by Cunard: Francis Jourdain, one of the many authors translated by Beckett, was a member of the French branch of the League Against Imperialism and is introduced as such in the anthology. That this link is clearly stated is not insignificant: the league, founded in Brussels in 1927 as the Ligue contre l'Impérialisme et l'Oppression Coloniale, was one of the first organisations to emerge from the anti-colonial work of the Communist International.[58] The main objectives of the league, split into national branches working under the command of the Comintern, were to campaign for the civic and national liberties of oppressed peoples and to cultivate communist and socialist alliances. Its leaders and members were originally dispersed across a broad political spectrum, and included Jawaharlal Nehru, Messali Hadj, Willi Münzenberg, Jim Larkin and Ernst Toller. Its first Congress, opened by Barbusse (at the time, one of the organisation's honorary presidents along with Albert Einstein), focused on three main issues: struggles for emancipation in China, American imperialism in Latin America, and the black liberation struggles in South Africa, the Caribbean, African colonies and North America. Subsequent gatherings focused on the nature and mode of operation of the league's anti-imperialist struggle. This broad church of political interests offers a compelling corrective to the accepted notion that *Negro* was conceived to raise funds for the French Communist Party.[59] This seems unlikely: the Surrealists' relations with the French Communist Party were strained, and relations between Cunard and the British Communist Party equally so, not least because the party had a habit of laying claim to the funds that she had raised for the International Labor Defense.[60]

Many facets of *Negro* accord with the concerns of the League Against Imperialism: Cunard's foreword, for example, declares her ambition to bring together the energies of communism and anti-imperialist thought to curb the hold of racialist ideologies in the United States and elsewhere.

[57] J. J. Rabearivelo, 'Notre grande consultation sur les aspirations indigènes vues par les Malgaches', *Le Madécasse*, 7 October 1936, 1.

[58] Michel Dreyfus, 'La Ligue contre l'Impérialisme et l'Oppression coloniale', *Communisme: Revue d'études pluridisciplinaires* 2 (1982): 49–71.

[59] W. J. McCormack, *From Burke to Beckett: Ascendency, Tradition and Betrayal in Literary History* (Cork: Cork University Press, 1994), 386.

[60] Chisholm, *Nancy Cunard*, 209.

Most of the essays, however, do not make a case for the emancipatory role of communism but describe the realities of slavery, colonial exploitation and racism, while accounts of segregation and struggles for civil rights remain primarily focused on the United States, allowing only marginal representation to the colonial histories of North Africa and South America. A short section is dedicated to South Africa, offering brief information about the pass laws and the exploitation of black labour. As Tory Young notes, the anthology is not an encyclopaedia, but a 'call to arms', and should be read as such.[61]

The idiosyncratic nature of Cunard's call to arms is evidenced in the prominent position given to Crevel, Jourdain, Péret and Sadoul, whose ties to the Surrealist circle and the French Communist Party were shifting. Their contributions to *Negro* were all translated by Beckett. Cunard's decision to grant such political significance to their work has a distinctive context, and intersects with the action taken by different branches of the League Against Imperialism against the 1931 International Colonial Exhibition, held from May to November in Paris.[62] In March 1931, the German Liga gegen Imperialismus und für Nationale Unabhängigkeit began to plan a counter-exhibition in Berlin; in May, a Paris counterpart organised by the Ligue Contre l'Impérialisme et l'Oppression Coloniale was announced.[63] This counter-exhibition – in which Cunard played an unacknowledged role – was put together by the Surrealists, led by Aragon, Sadoul and Thirion, and ran between September 1931 and February 1932, coinciding with one of Beckett's numerous stays in Paris.[64] Its title, 'La vérité sur les colonies' (The Truth about the Colonies), conveys its focus on the politics of forced labour, poverty, armed repression and colonial subjugation.[65] Some parts of the exhibition celebrated the Soviet regime; others dealt with the atrocities of the tsarist system and with global patterns of colonial conquest. The event had little to do with the 1936 London exhibition with which Beckett's translations of Eluard became directly associated. The latter event featured colonial exhibits selected solely on aesthetic

[61] Tory Young, 'The Reception of Nancy Cunard's *Negro Anthology*', in *Women Writers of the 1930s: Gender, Politics and History*, ed. Mary Joannou (Edinburgh: Edinburgh University Press, 1999), 115.

[62] See Morresi, *Nancy Cunard*, 87–93.

[63] Catherine Hodeir and Michel Pierre, *L'Exposition coloniale de 1931*, revised ed. (Brussels: André Versailles, 2011), 161.

[64] On Cunard's contribution, see Morresi, 'Black Man', 93–4.

[65] Amanda Stansell, 'Surrealist Racial Politics at the Borders of "Reason": Whiteness, Primitivism and Négritude', in *Surrealism, Politics and Culture*, ed. Raymond Spiteri and Donald LaCoss (Aldershot: Ashgate, 2003), 116–19; Morresi, *Nancy Cunard*, 90; Hodeir and Pierre, *L'Exposition coloniale de 1931*, 157–69.

grounds and was emphatically *not* designed as an exhibition exposing the workings of imperialism.[66]

The inclusion in *Negro* of 'Murderous Humanitarianism', a manifesto written in May or June 1932,[67] carries particular significance, since the statement (signed by Breton, Crevel, Eluard, Péret, Tanguy, Roger Caillois, René Char, Jules Monnerot, André Thirion, Pierre Unik and Pierre Yoyotte) contributes to a series of polemical responses to the 1931 Colonial Exhibition. These included an article by Blin (then associated with Surrealist circles) that was discussed in the French National Assembly[68] as well as articles and photographs in *Le Surréalisme au service de la révolution*. The Surrealists issued two collective manifestos: the first, from May 1931, expressly asked French audiences not to visit the Colonial Exhibition, attacked the myths and hypocrisy that bolstered the empire, and encouraged the public to demand the immediate withdrawal from the colonies; the second, from July 1931, denounced the cultural politics of the exhibition and reported on its many human and organisational fiascos.[69]

'Murderous Humanitarianism', presented in Beckett's translation as the work of 'the Surrealist group in Paris', is directly aligned with the preoccupations voiced in these manifestos and *Le Surréalisme au service de la révolution*. The original French text has not survived; it does not seem to have been written expressly for *Negro*, and it seems more likely that it was conceived for the ephemeral journal of the Ligue Contre l'Impérialisme et l'Oppression Coloniale. This journal, *Contre l'impérialisme*, produced only one special issue in May 1932, which was dedicated to the threat of a second world war and included articles by Jourdain on French presence in Indochina and a call by Aragon to campaign against French imperialism.[70] The year 1932 witnessed numerous ideological disagreements within the Surrealist group as their affiliations with the Communist Party came under considerable strain: in January, notably, the Surrealists discovered that only card-carrying party members (Alexandre, Aragon, Sadoul and Unik) would

[66] *Surrealism: Catalogue, The International Surrealist Exhibition, Thursday, June 11th to Saturday, July 4th 1936* (London: New Burlington Galleries, 1936).

[67] Gérard Durozoi, *History of the Surrealist Movement*, trans. Alison Anderson (Chicago: University of Chicago Press, 2002), 305.

[68] Odile Aslan, *Roger Blin and Twentieth-Century Playwrights* (Cambridge: Cambridge University Press, 1988), 11–22, 58; Roger Blin, 'Le scandale du village canaque', *La dépêche africaine* 38, 1 July 1931.

[69] *Tracts surréalistes*, vol. 1, 194–5, 198–200; Hans T. Siepe, '"Ne visitez pas l'exposition coloniale': Quelques points de repère pour aborder l'anticolonialisme des Surréalistes', in *Surréalisme et politique – Politique du Surréalisme*, ed. Wolfgang Asholt and Hans T. Siepe (Amsterdam: Rodopi, 2007), 169–80.

[70] Dreyfus, 'Ligue', 69 n20.

be accepted into the Association des Ecrivains et Artistes Révolutionnaires, an organisation sponsored by the Communist Party that they supported but that did not support them.[71] Their relation with this new organisation was tainted by hierarchical tensions and a wave of exclusions from the Communist Party and the Association itself. Aragon, Sadoul and Unik, for whom Communism had replaced Surrealism as the chosen cause, left the Surrealist group in March, in the wake of the 'Aragon affair' that had also erupted in January. In many ways, the idea that the French colonial enterprise was a political disaster was one of few issues around which the Surrealists could still rally in 1932, without any disagreement or tension. As such, 'Murderous Humanitarianism', like many collective statements issued by the Surrealists, symbolised a fleeting political alliance created largely for the purposes of the appeal itself: the text binds to the core Surrealist group the Martiniquan writers Yoyotte and Monnerot, who were not considered members of the Paris elect, and were involved in *Légitime Défense*, a short-lived Surrealist review tied to the Négritude movement and dedicated to Caribbean writing.[72] These allegiances, tensions and ruptures give a different dimension to the work of translation that Beckett conducted in the shadows.

The *Negro* Anthology in the Making

Beckett's voice remained concealed in the 1934 edition of *Negro*: his name appears in neither table of contents nor acknowledgements, and only in the body of the texts for which he is credited as translator.[73] His contribution did not expose him; Cunard, however, received a substantial amount of hate mail during the making of the anthology and following reports of her relationship with Crowder in the American press.[74] Where Beckett stood in relation to the controversies sparked by Cunard's work is not always clear, and he seems to have been alternately aware of and oblivious to the obstacles that Cunard and Crowder encountered as a couple. He sometimes referred to their partnership in ways that recall the racism that they faced from other close friends: he wrote, for example, about their 'comparing colours'.[75] His letters to MacGreevy give little sense of Crowder's talent

[71] Carole Reynaud Paligot, *Parcours politique des Surréalistes* (Paris: CNRS, 2010), 118; Durozoi, *History of the Surrealist Movement*, 233–5.

[72] *Tracts surréalistes*, vol. 1, 235–7.

[73] However, in Hugh Ford's abridged edition from 1970, Beckett's name features more prominently.

[74] Chisholm, *Nancy Cunard*, 197–8. The hate mail is part of the HRHRC's Nancy Cunard collection.

[75] Robert L. Allen, 'Epilogue', in *As Wonderful as All That?*, by Henry Crowder and Hugo Speck (Navarro, CA: Wild Trees Press, 1987), 195, 189–201; *DF*, 133.

and stature as a jazz musician; they caricature Crowder's Southern drawl and mock his perceived lack of erudition.[76] Yet some of Beckett's poems from that period enter in dialogue with the political work of Cunard and the artistic work of Crowder in a different way. The only poem by Beckett to feature an in-text dedication is a tribute to Crowder the musician: 'From the Only Poet to a Shining Whore. For Henry Crowder to Sing'. The dedication also marks the continuation of a dialogue between Beckett and Crowder begun with *Whoroscope*, which had been printed by Crowder and typesetter Maurice Rigaud at the Hours Press.[77] 'From the Only Poet' was written to be set to music by Crowder; it appeared in *Henry-Music* (1930), a collection also published by the Hours Press featuring striking cover designs by Man Ray and other poems by Richard Aldington, Harold Acton, Walter Lowenfels and Cunard, as well as Crowder's scores for their texts. Beckett's poem is a peculiar combination of ventriloquised references to Dante; it revolves around Dante's representation of Rahab in *Paradiso*, and her capacity to abide by her principles, alone and in all circumstances, even when doing so leads to the destruction of her world, the city of Jericho. While maintaining an insistent focus on shades of whiteness and brightness, the poem also introduces a meditation on domination and marginalisation – issues of pressing importance to Crowder and Cunard, who had taken high personal risks to pursue their political and artistic ideals. It seems that both of them recognised Beckett's poem as an expression of friendship and solidarity: in her memoir, Cunard described Beckett as the friend who appreciated Crowder's charm and musical talent the most, presenting his poem as an illustration of their friendship; her words become particularly meaningful in light of her own dedication of *Negro* to 'Henry Crowder/my first Negro friend'.[78] Crowder's memoir concurs: he was clearly fond of Beckett and retained warm memories of him.[79]

It is likely that, by the time he started work on the anthology, Beckett had come to understand something of the workings of racism, and of the difficulties encountered by Crowder in particular in the United States and in Europe. In the years that followed, Beckett had further occasions to become acquainted with prejudice; he always retained bitter memories of the anti-Irish racism he encountered in London in particular.[80] Calder recalls meeting a very annoyed Beckett at Heathrow airport in later years,

[76] *LSB1*, 25, 43.

[77] On *Whoroscope*, see Anthony Barnett, *Listening for Henry Crowder: A Monograph on His Almost Lost Music with the Poems and Music of Henry-Music* (Lewes, Sussex: Allardyce Books, 2007), 94, 24.

[78] Cunard, *Hours Press*, 155.

[79] Crowder, *As Wonderful*, 76.

[80] McMillan and Fehsenfeld, *Beckett in the Theatre*, 183.

after an immigration officer had asked him, 'How long are you staying Paddy?'[81] In France, Beckett also encountered manifestations of intolerance, in a somewhat different register; in 1962, for example, the academician Marcel Achard described Beckett's work as worthless and void, emphasising that it was inappropriate to mix apples and oranges – or, here, his own theatre and the 'new theatre'. His conclusion was without appeal: 'besides', Beckett is 'not French'.[82]

When Cunard invited Beckett to translate texts for *Negro*, Beckett had no experience of translation beyond his aborted Joycean exercise with Péron and versions of short Italian texts by Eugenio Montale, Raffaelo Franchi and Giovanni Comisso, which involved much radical rewriting, yet little translation, and were published as a 'miniature anthology' in *This Quarter*. Interestingly, Beckett was entrusted with several of the more difficult and controversial texts to appear in *Negro*. Beckett, Cunard and her cousin Edward translated Michelet's essays, whose assessment of the workings of colonialism emerges as the most virulent and lucid in the collection, and Beckett was also tasked with an essay by Léon-Pierre Quint, biographer of Proust and Gide, which examined the conditions according to which an international, anti-colonial and interracial movement might emerge. Beckett's first contribution was a translation of another polemical text, Crevel's 'The Negress in the Brothel', a vitriolic portrayal of racism and colonial subjugation.[83] Crevel wrote the text specifically for *Negro* in August 1931 during a holiday at Dalí's home in Port-Lligat and at the same time as an essay entitled 'Le patriotisme de l'inconscient', which appeared in *Le Surréalisme au service de la révolution*.[84] Cunard knew that Crevel's text would constitute a delicate addition, and the essay does not feature in the table of contents to the 1934 edition. Weary of surveillance and potential interference, she arranged for the setting and printing of the English text to be done separately by the Utopia Press in London, and inserted Beckett's translation into copies of the anthology herself when the volumes were bound.[85]

Cunard seems to have treated Beckett – who, if his letters from that period are to be trusted, could be immensely unpleasant, petulant and

[81] Calder, *Pursuit*, 327.

[82] Cited in Claude Sarraute, 'Rien n'est plus beau que le métier de faire rire les gens', *Le Monde*, 14 September 1962, 15.

[83] *LSB1*, 60.

[84] Jean-Michel Devésa, 'René Crevel et le monde anglo-saxon', *Mélusine: Cahiers du Centre de Recherche sur le Surréalisme* 22 (2002): 236; Crevel, *Correspondance de René Crevel à Gertrude Stein*, ed. Jean-Michel Devésa (Paris: L'Harmattan, 2000), 242; Crevel, 'Le patriotisme de l'inconscient', *Le Surréalisme au service de la révolution* 4 (1931): 3–6.

[85] Marcus, *Hearts of Darkness*, 139; Laura Winkiel, *Modernism, Race and Manifestos* (Cambridge: Cambridge University Press, 2008), 186.

immature – with great indulgence and generosity. This treatment extends to the anthology: Beckett's correspondence indicates that he asked for money early on and received payment for some translations on at least one occasion; his plaintive tone suggests that he was indeed expecting some remuneration. Yet the anthology was reliant on good will rather than payment, and this led to incidents with some contributors: Claude McKay broke contact when he discovered that no fee was forthcoming, and the poet Sterling Brown, who protested that he could not write for nothing, was eventually paid.[86] Beckett, for his part, appears to have previously benefited from Cunard's generosity, but without particular reason: Crowder recalls in his memoir that, shortly after he first made Beckett's acquaintance, Cunard gave Beckett 'quite a large sum of money', 'because he seemed to be in need' and 'she felt like doing it'.[87]

It may well be that Cunard was so supportive and trusting because she perceived special affinities with Beckett (she was very proud of her own Irish ancestry) and sympathised with his feelings of estrangement towards his maternal family. The history of the Roe family, whose fortune was built through connections with the rest of the British Empire, makes Beckett's relation to the anti-imperialist remit of *Negro* at least as complicated as Cunard's. Beckett was intimately familiar with the colonial and racist rhetoric exposed in Cunard's anthology; his boyhood readings included the children's magazine *Union Jack*, which published stories of adventure, travel and conquest around the British Empire and at the American Frontier – precisely the kind of publication that capitalised on the enshrined assumptions and racial stereotypes denounced in the essay by Sadoul that he translated for *Negro*.

The letters to MacGreevy in which Beckett comments on the anthology offer some uncomfortable and contradictory insights. In October 1931, he reports that he has been translating 'surréalistes inédits for Nancy's nigger book'; he describes Crevel's text as 'Miserable rubbish' and complains: 'I'll have about 11 more to do. About 8 pages each. I asked her £25 for the whole job. Is that too much? Tzara next'.[88] The same letter features an unkind pun on Crevel's poor health, spelling his name as 'Creve(l)' or *crevé* (Crevel suffered from chronic ill-health and exhaustion, and a diagnosis of tuberculosis culminated in his suicide a few years later).[89] Twelve months later, his tone has changed, and he suggests that further translations for *Negro* would be a welcome prospect.[90] In early January 1933, he writes that he

[86] Chisholm, *Nancy Cunard*, 205–6; Morresi, 'Black Man', 97.
[87] The sum was a hundred pounds. Crowder, *Wonderful*, 76; Chisholm, *Nancy Cunard*, 152.
[88] Friedman, 'Introduction', *Beckett in Black and Red*, xxxiv n41. [89] Ibid.
[90] *LSB1*, 128.

is 'doing stuff for Nancy at present – some interesting (Congo Sculpture) some balls (Madagascar). There's one there waiting ['Murderous Humanitarianism'] about the usual assassin signed by the whole surrealiste guild. And a long one by Péret'.[91] A few weeks later, he reports: 'I have finished all translations for N.C., poem & prose – Thank God. Such fizzle she sent a few quid anyhow'.[92]

At this point in his career, Beckett remained reliant upon a system of patronage comparable to that which might be imposed by a literary 'guild'. While his letter suggests that he viewed the Surrealist group as a small literary monopoly whose actions were not in keeping with their collectivist ideals, he nonetheless remained keen to present himself to MacGreevy as an insider acquainted with their political work. Whenever his letters to MacGreevy touch upon the political realm, his comments are inconclusive and troubling, bearing testament to a distinctive capacity to anticipate the reactions of his correspondent and adjust his tone accordingly. Most significantly, none of Beckett's reflections on Cunard and the anthology conveys the care, attention and thought that he put into translating, and sometimes rewriting, the texts assigned to him.

The *Negro* Anthology Translations

There are many indications that Beckett did not remain indifferent to the factual and political content of *Negro*, even in the early days. There are, for example, troubling coincidences between the anthology's subject matter and Beckett's rendering of Arthur Rimbaud's 'The Drunken Boat', written in the early months of 1932 with a view to publication in *This Quarter*. Beyond its visionary reveries, Rimbaud's poem also deals with the materiality of colonial trading, and Beckett's translation brings to the fore the poem's vision of colonialism as a spent force. His translation voices a stronger and clearer indictment of colonial rule than in the original; its opening stanzas carry a more ominous tone, assimilating colonial trade to a physical strain or burden that will eventually be removed.[93]

His translations for Cunard's anthology betray a similar sensitivity to historical and political nuance. These are not transparent, non-committal renderings of the original texts, but partisan interventions that approach the question of historical reporting with seriousness and gravity. Clearly, he took a keen interest in polemical essays and densely researched historical surveys, but had less sympathy for superficial readings such as the potted

91 *LSB1*, 149. 92 McNaughton, 'The Politics of Aftermath', *Beckett and Ireland*, 61.

93 See, notably, the first six lines in SB, *Collected Poems*, 64.

history of Madagascar offered by Rabearivelo. His translations often accentuate the tone of the original texts, particularly when dealing with suffering, poverty, distress and the work of colonial administrations; at other points, Beckett tempered obscenity and sexual allusion, elided references to Judaism suggesting prejudice and transformed singular examples of violence and oppression into key features of a wider economic system. Some translations are fanciful: Louis Armstrong, reimagined by Beckett, speaks Irish English, a slippage that introduces into the anthology some challenging resonances between the growing American civil rights movement, Irish political nationalism and the Irish diaspora.

Beckett's rendering of Crevel's bellicose essay 'La Négresse des Bordels' offers rather striking illustrations of his method of transposition and rewriting. The translation minimises sexual innuendo, accentuating instead other passages addressing the systemic ills of imperialism. Notably, Beckett italicises a statement associating class stratification with the effects of colonisation and, in doing so, offers a politically charged account of colonisation as a phenomenon 'suffered': 'But since such an attitude is impracticable in capitalistic societies stinking of class consciousness (*coloured men and women being assimilated to the proletariat because they happen to have suffered colonisation*), it becomes necessary to annihilate the imbecile ideology that is precisely the cause and the sanction of that social degradation'.[94] Crevel's conclusion also undergoes a radical transformation. The original text presents rape and sexual exploitation as the staples of colonial subjugation: 'Vraiment ce serait à vous ôter l'envie d'aller porter sa goutte militaire, sa goutte religieuse aux sauvages' (176). Here Crevel plays upon the multiple and colloquial connotations of *goutte*, associating the enterprise of colonisation with the transmission of gonorrhoea and forcible conversion to Catholicism. Beckett substitutes this sentence with another of his own invention, which introduces a parody of middle-class liberal sentiment and strengthens Crevel's acerbic parody of social relations: 'After that I propose to withdraw my subscription from the Society for the Diffusion of the White Man's Moral and Physical Complaints among Savage Peoples' (72–3). These additions and modifications gain added significance in light of Crevel's international work: Crevel was among the first in French Surrealist circles to enter into contact with British and American writers, who either ignored his political views or perceived them as incomprehensible.[95]

[94] *Beckett in Black and Red*, 72 (hereafter cited parenthetically).
[95] See Devésa, 'René Crevel et le monde anglo-saxon'.

'Black and White in Brazil', Beckett's translation of an essay by Péret, is exempt from such playfulness. The original text is imbued by other political concerns, arising from Péret's work with the Brazilian Communist League, a Trotskyist group that he founded in early 1931, and his parallel efforts to document the history of slavery in Brazil. Péret was, at the time, engaged in an archival study of the 1910 Revolt of the Lash, an endeavour that led to his incarceration and expulsion from Brazil, and his return to Paris at the end of 1931.[96] In his translation, Beckett grants added significance to Péret's depiction of colonial trade, and alters the text slightly to draw attention to the strategic use of starvation and forced labour. The systemic aspects of the slave trade between the African coast and Bahia are not expressly stated in the original, but Beckett's translation is unambiguous: it renders the journey of the slaves as a trial yielding 'few survivors', in which thirst and starvation are 'calculated' to keep people at the threshold of life (41). The translation also introduces an element of moral judgement: emphasising the relentless imprisonment of the slaves, held in chains even in slumber, Beckett's text renders forced labour as a factory routine in which even flogging methods display a 'frenzy of industry' (41). Péret evokes an empire of slavery reliant on slave owners in Brazil ('s'appuyait sur les propriétaires esclavagistes'), while the empire described by Beckett is clearly corrupt, 'in the pocket of the slave proprietors' (190, 44). Beckett's version also augments the effect and scope of the abolitionist movement: Péret's text speaks of an empire 'pressé' or pressured by the anti-slavery movement, while Beckett evokes an empire 'harassed by' – and hence unable to resist – 'the anti-slavery campaign' (190, 45). The translation also brings to the fore a reflection on economics confined to the margins of the original. Péret, when describing the abolition of slavery in Brazil, evokes the 'frightful misery' ('misère effroyable') of the freed slave, forced out of the towns and back to the plantations after 1889 (190). Beckett speaks of different conditions: of a people thrown into a 'distress [. . .] so appalling that they were soon obliged to return to the plantations which they had just left' (45). This nuanced tweak is significant, because it involves the transformation of an economic problem – a state of frightful misery – into the logical outcome of an immoral system of exploitation. Elsewhere, when turning to modern history and the future of Brazil, Beckett's translation expands on the radical register utilised by Péret; 'le combat' (the struggle) is rendered as 'the revolutionary element', and the phrase 'solidaires contre l'ennemi commun'

[96] Daïnis Karepovs, 'Benjamin Péret et la Ligue Communiste du Brésil', *Cahiers Léon Trotsky* 47 (1992): 11–18; Fulvio Abramo and Daïnis Karepovs, 'Benjamin Péret, poète révolutionnaire au Brésil', *Cahiers Léon Trotsky* 25 (1986): 75–6.

(in solidarity against the common enemy) is translated as 'united in opposing the common enemy' (192, 48). Describing the general strikes that raged in the 1910s, Péret states that the government capitulated, lacking the means to resist the united workers' movement ('Le gouvernement capitula, faute de moyens de leur résister') (192). The state is even less immune to protest in Beckett's translation: 'The government had no choice but to capitulate' (47). Furthermore, where Péret evokes farmers presently submitted to a regime that often recalls slavery ('soumis à un régime qui rappelle souvent l'esclavage'), Beckett speaks of 'agricultural workers' who work 'as often as not under conditions that do not greatly differ from those of slavery' (191, 46). Ultimately, through such emendations and additions, the political history recounted by Péret becomes more momentous and sharply delineated in the translation.

Beckett's other translations place greater emphasis on the nature of colonial authority and its lack of political legitimacy. These questions bear particularly strongly upon the translation of Pierre-Quint's 'Races et Nations', which draws upon Gide's *Voyage au Congo: Carnets de route* (1927). Gide's widely read diary of a journey to the Congo offered such revealing accounts of the system of 'porterage' or forced labour, the regime of concessions and the conditions in which the railways were built that the book was debated at the French National Assembly upon publication.[97] Yet it remains difficult to read Gide as an advocate of racial equality along the lines suggested by Pierre-Quint: Gide denounces some economic realities, but as part of a straightforward humanist critique of the horrors of which humankind is capable. Pierre-Quint's essay transforms Gide into a vociferous anti-colonial thinker, and presents observations confined to footnotes and addenda in Gide's journal as a historical thesis on colonial trade and exploitation. Beckett's translation, meanwhile, features minor factual additions that strengthen Pierre-Quint's transformation of Gide's account. For example, where Pierre-Quint's text emphasises the explosive nature of the situation described by Gide upon his arrival in Libreville, Beckett's translation adds new details that both corroborate Gide's original text and confer greater emphasis and precision on Pierre-Quint's statements.[98] Commenting upon the delivery of spoilt goods, Pierre-Quint's text remains imprecise and does not indicate the quantity and mode of transport ('Bordeaux a expédié des conserves, mais elles sont avariées') (193). Beckett's translation,

[97] *JORF*, 95, 24 November 1927, 3178–9; *JORF*, 54, 15 June 1929, 2059–60.

[98] André Gide, *Voyage au Congo: Carnets de Route* (Paris: Gallimard, 1927), 16.

however, evokes a 'cargo of tinned food sent from Bordeaux' that 'arrives unfit for use', following the details provided in Gide's diary (60).

At other points, historical facts are given added significance: Beckett transforms a sentence evoking the public 'emotion' that greeted the discovery in the 1820s of the shackles, chains and whips utilised by the slave traders into an invocation of a French public 'stirred to a great movement of sympathy' upon its discovery of 'the slave-trader's stock-in-trade' (194, 62). Where Pierre-Quint speaks of Europeans schoolboys being educated to believe that they should go to the colonies to deliver the benefits of civilisation ('pour y apporter les bienfaits de la civilisation'), Beckett evokes a whole culture driven by the belief that 'the European in the colonies is actuated exclusively by the desire to propagate the bounties of civilization' (194, 62). Pierre-Quint's nondescript evocation of Congolese regions is transformed into a political topography; a vast stretch of land consisting of regions that are 'quite independent' (and keen to remain so). Elsewhere, Beckett renders as an unwarranted aggression the power relationship that Pierre-Quint traces in the European fascination with African arts; the translation turns a simple statement about conquest ('cette influence du vaincu sur le vainqueur n'a jamais empêché ce dernier d'exercer jusqu'au bout son pouvoir de domination, d'absorption ou de mort') into a commentary on violence and aggression: 'the aggressor can submit to the influence of his victim without ceasing to exercise his prerogative of domination, absorption and death' (197, 66). Even mistranslations serve a rhetorical purpose: the words *exaction* and *exactions*, designating abuse, violence or severe brutality in French, are rendered according to their literal English meaning – as extortions, and hence a feature of an economic system that dispossesses and oppresses. For example, Pierre-Quint's description of a general 'régime de force et d'exaction' in colonial Africa is rendered as 'a regime of coercions and exactions' (196, 65).

Beckett's translation recasts Pierre-Quint as a more articulate and credible campaigner against racial discrimination on several levels. The original text features arguments about Judaism and racial pride that Beckett partially transforms and omits,[99] and his translation adds rhetorical and factual depth to Pierre-Quint's commentary on race as a socially determined concept. Pierre-Quint's discussion of Enlightenment legacies stresses a concept of race which 'n'a plus rien d'absolu. Il ne sépare pas plus les hommes que ne les séparent, au sein d'une même famille, leur taille, la couleur de leurs yeux

[99] This argument is woven through the essay, and Beckett omits its most direct articulations (notably, the following sentence: 'Cependant, ironie du destin, ils [in the original, the Hebrews] sont devenus les hommes les plus vilipendés du monde' (195–6)).

ou de leurs cheveux' (195). Beckett adds considerable rhetorical flourish and emphasis: 'From this point of view the historical concept of race loses its importance. It has no longer any absolute value. It can no more separate man from his neighbour than accidents of physique, variously coloured eyes and hair, can separate members of the same family' (64). For Pierre-Quint, the French Revolution marked a turning point, as a moment at which 'les hommes osent manifester cette pensée, à savoir que les injustices ne sont pas une nécessité ici-bas et que la fonction sociale ou la couleur de la peau ne crée pas nécessairement des privilèges' (196). In Beckett's hand, this sentence becomes: 'It was not until '89 that men dared formulate the idea that human injustice is not a necessity and that privileges are not automatically conferred by accidents of social status and cuticular pigmentation' (65). There are fewer ambiguities about future political horizons in Beckett's text. Where Pierre-Quint evokes the Hindus and the people of Indochina rejecting the invader ('rejetteront l'envahisseur'), Beckett speaks of two peoples who 'will cast off the yoke' (196, 65). Questions of collective responsibility are foregrounded in Beckett's conclusion: where Pierre-Quint portrays resistance against racial prejudice as a specific duty for the intellectual, Beckett imagines a generic 'opponent of racial prejudice' (198, 66); where Pierre-Quint evokes the continuation of specific anti-colonial struggles in the present, Beckett's text speaks of an 'effort towards emancipation' and a generic 'oppressed race [. . .] capable of opposing and vanquishing the invader' (67). And if the original concludes with a non-specific vision of social equality ('C'est, au contraire, de l'atténuation des frontières raciales, (de même que des frontières internationales) que peut sortir un monde social nouveau'), the translation bequeaths a greater specificity and some visionary Swedenborgian undertones to Pierre-Quint's internationalism: 'Racial and international frontiers must be abolished before the new social Jerusalem can arise' (198, 67).

Similar techniques are deployed in Beckett's translation of Sadoul's 'Le Nègre à l'usage des enfants', an essay that exposes French hypocrisy and denounces the racism prevalent at every level of the economy, from popular children's magazines to the factory. For Sadoul, '[l]a bourgeoisie Américaine et la bourgeoisie Française agissent de même avec la basse main d'œuvre, que ce soit la langue ou la couleur qui les distingue. Elle se sert de ces différences ethniques pour diviser le prolétariat' (202). In Beckett's translation, the argument resonates with renewed force: 'Sweated labour, whether denoted by language or colour, meets with the same treatment at the hands of both the French and the American industrial systems: racial peculiarities exploited to disunite the proletariat' (53). The translation, retitled 'Sambo Without Tears', adds variation to Sadoul's historical register: Beckett's text alternately borrows from an English colonial idiom, presumably to reinforce Sadoul's attacks against systemic racism ('enfants du Congo' becomes 'Congo piccaninnies' (199, 49)), and renders literally the French context of the original ('boche', the French wartime pejorative for the Germans, becomes 'Boches' (200, 51)). Sadoul denounces the hypocrisy of the French middle classes, who are themselves eager to denounce the racial segregation practised in the United States, but clearly despise the colonial labour they need to man both army and factories. Sadoul refers to the writer Maurice Martin du Gard, who, in the name of French settlers in the colonies, had requested the segregation of black troops in metropolitan France as well as new forms of 'sexual segregation'; to this Beckett adds inverted commas and a smattering of contempt, describing Martin du Gard as 'distinguished' and 'talented' (201, 52). Sadoul's depiction of the French industrial economy undergoes similar transformations in Beckett's hand; the 'basse main d'œuvre industrielle' lured from Italy, Poland and the North African colonies becomes a workforce 'employed at starvation wages' in the factories (201, 53). The essay appears to have been drafted in Moscow, after Sadoul attended the Conference of Revolutionary Writers in Kharkov with Aragon in late 1930, the circumstances of which enabled him to flee from a prison sentence sanctioning a slanderous article discrediting the military academy Saint-Cyr.[100] Sadoul makes clear that his observations about children's education in the Soviet Union are based on first-hand evidence and concludes that the children's magazines he discovers in Moscow do not disseminate the racialist ideology ubiquitous in the readings of the French bourgeoisie. Beckett's translation suggests that educational ills can be addressed, and it speaks of a publishing culture without any intermediary agent, 'imposed upon the children of the French bourgeoisie' (54). Ultimately, 'Sambo Without Tears', as it appears in *Negro*, transforms Sadoul's evocation of a shared struggle 'contre le capitalisme de toutes couleurs' (of all colours) into a fight 'against capitalism of whatever colour' (202, 54). By 1934, these observations garnered greater imperative: Sadoul was then editor of a children's magazine financed by the French Communist Party and crafted to have a broad appeal.[101]

Beckett's letters to MacGreevy suggest that, among the translations with which he was entrusted, he was most interested in the essays about sculpture – precisely the contributions that fail to interrogate racial politics

[100] See Mark Polizzotti, *Revolution of the Mind: The Life of André Breton* (London: Bloomsbury, 1995), 356.

[101] See Valérie Vignaux, 'Georges Sadoul rédacteur en chef de *Mon Camarade* (1933–1939). Un magazine illustré pour une culture de jeunesse communiste?', *Strenæ* 10 (2016), http://strenae.revues.org/.

altogether. Yet it is in these essays that Beckett tries most consistently to improve on the style of the originals and to politicise their terminologies. Henri Lavachery's essay on statuary in the Congo clearly benefits from Beckett's stylistic efforts: for example, the phrase 'les oeuvres d'art les plus parfaites qu'ait produit le Congo belge' (literally, the most perfect artworks that the Belgian Congo has produced) is rendered as 'the indisputable masterpieces of Belgian Congo' (183, 94). Lavachery does not speak of white profit and exploitation, yet Beckett renders Lavachery's denunciation of the neglect that threatens to annihilate the arts in Africa as a strictly political matter, translating 'les blancs' (the whites) as 'the white man' and 'those intruders' (186, 98). Beckett also gives to Lavachery's generic associations between western civilisation and progress a new anti-colonial flavour. Lavachery suggests that, 'Si l'on veut réellement que les Noirs d'Afrique accèdent à ce stade de civilisation où celle-ci n'est ni un jouet dans ses produits, ni un esclavage dans son travail, il faut que l'on facilite et entretiennent [*sic*] la renaissance de leurs arts' (186) (literally: if one really wants the Black peoples of Africa to access the stage of civilisation at which the work of civilisation is neither a mere toy in the process of production nor slavery, one must facilitate and nurture the revival of their arts). To this Beckett adds further allusions to forced labour and the time-honoured trade of trinkets against valuable colonial goods, redistributing Lavachery's terms into a clear economic equation: 'If it be desirable honestly for the black peoples of Africa to attain that degree of civilization where civilization will not signify only a supply of useless trifles and labour spell slavery, the revival of their arts must be encouraged and maintained' (98). B. P. Feuilloley's essay on 'Magic and Initiation among the Peoples of Ubanghi-Shari' is subject to similar treatment; in Beckett's hand, it becomes an account of ethnography as a practice of colonisation, which puts in its service all the people and goods it encounters. Such additions and emendations were crucial to the kind of political intervention that Cunard wished to make. She must have been pleasantly surprised: in Beckett's hands, the exuberant and provocative lyricism deployed in many of these difficult texts was given new rigour, and a precision appropriate to the demands of her anthology.

Taking Sides: The Spanish Civil War and the New Idioms of Republicanism

The dialogue between Beckett and Cunard on political history continued beyond *Negro* to *Authors Take Sides on the Spanish War*, a pamphlet published in 1937 by the *Left Review*. Although presented as a group enterprise, the pamphlet was primarily Cunard's work, and marked the continuation of another project: the same year, her printing press served the very anti-fascist activities she had once hoped for,and was used for a series of six *plaquettes* of poetry entitled *Les poètes du monde défendent le peuple espagnol*, conceived with the help of Pablo Neruda, which were sold to raise funds for Spanish Republican Relief in Paris.[102] The poets featured included Neruda, as well as Rafael Alberti, Vicente Aleixandre, W. H. Auden, Nicolás Guillén, Brian Howard, Langston Hughes, Federico García Lorca, Tristan Tzara and Randall Swingler – the eminent poet of the British Communist Party and editor of the *Left Review*. For *Authors Take Sides on the Spanish War*, Cunard collected 173 statements and published 148 of them.[103] The contributors responded to a call specifically addressed to 'the Writers and Poets of England, Scotland, Ireland and Wales' that aspired to '[reflect] faithfully the frame of mind of British authors to-day'. Writers were asked two questions: 'Are you for, or against, the legal Government and the People of Republican Spain?' and 'Are you for, or against, Franco and Fascism?'[104] This model had precedents; in 1925, Barbusse, Aragon and the Paris Surrealist group had published an appeal condemning the Moroccan Rif War, asking 'intellectual workers' to answer with 'yes' or 'no'.[105]

The canvassing technique that Cunard employed was strikingly effective and has left a trace in the history of contestation: thirty years later, a pamphlet entitled *Authors Take Sides on Vietnam* was conceived according to the same model, and was signed by many of the writers who had featured in the *Left Review* in 1937.[106] Beckett's name does not feature in this sequel, but there are other connections between his work and the protests taking place against the Vietnam War that reflects the distinctive ways in which his work has often been mobilised in support of pacifist campaigns and movements: in 1970, sixteen signed volumes of original editions of Beckett's texts were donated to a large New York auction organised by the American group Publishers for Peace; this was held at the Gotham Book Mart, with which Beckett had associations. The proceeds were intended to support the election to Congress of candidates opposed to the continuation of the Vietnam War.[107]

[102] Nancy Cunard, 'Spain', *Cunard: Brave Poet*, 164–70; Cunard, *Hours Press*, 196.

[103] Andy Croft, *Comrade Heart: A Life of Randall Swingler* (Manchester: Manchester University Press, 2002), 68.

[104] *Authors Take Sides on the Spanish War* (London: Left Review, 1937), n.pag.

[105] *Tracts surréalistes*, vol. 1, 51–3.

[106] Cecil Woolf and John Bagguley, Introduction, *Authors Take Sides on Vietnam: Two Questions on the War in Vietnam Answered by the Authors of Several Nations* (London: Peter Owen, 1967).

[107] Other auctioned items were works and manuscripts by Marianne Moore, Lawrence Ferlinghetti, Nelson Algren, Norman Mailer, Bertrand Russell, Allen Ginsberg, W. S. Merwin, John Steinbeck

Cunard was immensely proud of *Authors Take Sides on the Spanish War*, and later recalled that the 3,000 copies 'sold out immediately'.[108] The pamphlet opens with a preface entitled 'The Question', signed by Aragon, Auden, Cunard, Neruda, Spender, Tzara and others, and dated Paris, June 1937. In this commentary, the contributors emphasised the necessity to 'take sides', reminding readers that '[t]he equivocal attitude, the Ivory Tower, the paradoxical, the ironic detachment, will no longer do'. The pamphlet made a dedicated effort to situate the Spanish Civil War in a wider context marked by 'murder and destruction by Fascism' in Italy and Germany (the land 'of social injustice and cultural death'), the Italo-Abyssinian War and the continuation of colonial exploitation. The preface also emphasised that 'To-day, the struggle is in Spain. To-morrow it may be in other countries – our own'. The choice of contributors coincided with the contours of a colonial empire either vanished or under threat; some of the authors polled were from the Irish Free State and Northern Ireland, Jamaica and India, and the contributors included Mulk Raj Anand, Boyle, O'Flaherty, O'Casey, Sean O'Faolain and Louis MacNeice. T. S. Eliot and Pound both issued statements classified as 'neutral?', while the majority of the contributors stated their opposition to Franco, with many reflecting on the war's historical significance. Marcus Garvey, who had met Cunard in Jamaica during the preparation of *Negro*, described fascism as 'the cult of organised murder, invented by the arch-enemies of society', which 'tends to destroy civilisation and revert man to his most barbarous state', concluding: 'Mussolini and Hitler might well be called the devils of an age, for they are playing hell with civilisation'.

Beckett – who had only a modest record as a writer at that point – contributed a one-word statement that mirrored the anti-fascist slogan '¡No pasarán!': '¡UPTHEREPUBLIC!' The pamphlet certainly accommodated this format and features other comparably brief statements, for example, Rose Macauley's 'AGAINST FRANCO'. The war's historical coordinates were familiar to Beckett, through his Irish and French acquaintances and as a consequence of his personal interests. He had briefly considered a trip to Spain in 1935,[109] a year before the outbreak of hostilities, when visiting Spain had little to do with taking up arms. There are scattered traces of his interest beyond the letters: for example, the list of censored books and authors that he draws up in 'Censorship in the Saorstat' includes Barbusse

and William Styron. Henry Raymont, 'War Foes to Sell Two Russell Essays', *NYT*, 23 August 1970, 2; 'Anti-War Auction to Assist Candidates Put Off to Oct. 8', *NYT*, 12 September 1970, 25; 'Peace Group Gains $9,000 at Auction', *NYT*, 10 October 1970, 1.

[108] Cunard, 'Spain', *Cunard: Brave Poet*, 165. [109] *Chronology*, 54.

and the contributors to *The Spanish Omnibus*, an anthology published in 1932 and edited by Julián Gómez García or Julián Gorkin, the later leader of the Workers' Party of Marxist Unification (POUM). Barbusse's introduction to the anthology charts developments in Spanish-language literatures since the late nineteenth century against the backdrop of recent political history and concludes that the primary duty of the writer is to safeguard the legacy of the April revolution.[110]

'¡UPTHEREPUBLIC!' and its obscure referentiality have received much attention, and have even earned Beckett a place in the recorded history of the Spanish Civil War.[111] James McNaughton has pointed to the political polysemy of Beckett's statement, noting that the slogan 'Up the republic' was associated with IRA action during the Irish Civil War and with the pro–de Valera side in the 1932 General Election.[112] Beckett's statement, through its telegrammatic form, also connects to a longer and more hazardous history of revolutionary action. The same form was used by the Surrealist group to convey political urgency in the first issue of *Le Surréalisme au service de la révolution* in July 1930, which opened with a question and answer defining the nature of the revolution Surrealism intended to serve. The reproduced exchange consisted of a telegram from Moscow asking what the Surrealist position would be if world war were to be declared against the Soviet Union, and a reply from Breton and Aragon asserting that the Surrealists fully supported the French Communist Party and stood ready to offer all the support that intellectuals could provide.[113] In the context of Cunard's pamphlet, however, Beckett's statement also intersects with the history of republicanism in a specific Irish sense. One of the first objectives of the 1916 Easter Rising was to gain control over communications, particularly over the Irish School of Wireless Telegraphy on O'Connell Street, and it is from there, using a ship's transmitter and Morse code, that a text written by James Connolly announcing the proclamation of the Irish Republic was broadcast to the world.[114] The telegrammatic form of Beckett's statement and its attempt to mimic the workings of the Spanish language have a wider significance in the context of the pamphlet: his contribution brings

[110] Henri Barbusse, 'Introduction', in *The Spanish Omnibus: Being a Collection of Stories Representing the Work of the Leading Spanish Writers of To-Day*, trans. Warre B. Wells, ed. J. G. Gorkin (London: Eyre and Spottiswoode, 1932), vii–xxvi.

[111] Hugh Thomas, *The Spanish Civil War*, 3rd ed. (London: Penguin, 1986), 347 n3.

[112] McNaughton, 'The Politics of Aftermath', *Beckett and Ireland*, 57.

[113] 'Télégramme envoyé à Moscou', *Le Surréalisme au service de la révolution* 1 (1930): 1.

[114] See Maurice Gorham, *Forty Years of Irish Broadcasting* (Dublin: Talbot Press, 1967), 2–3; Christopher Morash, *A History of the Media in Ireland* (Cambridge: Cambridge University Press, 2009), 125–30.

the work of the Spanish republican front in line with these precedents and creates a correlation with the overthrow of British colonial rule in Ireland, suggesting that the overthrow of fascism is a task for all republics. This sentiment resonates with Liam O'Flaherty's own contribution, which emphasises that Spanish republicanism is a struggle, like its Irish precedent, 'against landlordism and foreign Imperialism'.

Only if the doctrine of non-intervention had not prevailed in Europe at this point would '¡UPTHEREPUBLIC!' read as a mocking declaration of international solidarity. In some ways, the dominant idea that one could take side recast the Spanish Civil War as a conflict around communism, which served Franco well. The stakes were terrifyingly high: this was, as Hugh Thomas emphasises, a 'world war in miniature', which Hitler seized as a strategic opportunity to re-arm Germany and bolster the political strength of his regime across Europe.[115] In France, the Left saw Spain at war, in the words of André Chamson, as the 'symbol of liberty in peril' and the 'prefiguration of our own future'.[116] Much confusion raged in Britain, where responses to the war became more indicative of the state of British political culture.[117] For Thomas, the war gave British intellectuals 'a sense of freedom, the thought of rubbing shoulders with the dispossessed in a half-developed country, above all the illusion that their "action" could be effective'.[118] The coordinates of the debate in the Irish Free State were different: Spanish republicanism became associated with Irish socialist republicanism, and Franco with the defence of Catholicism against communism. Donal Ó Drisceoil identifies the outbreak of the war as the point at which old ideological and cultural battles resurfaced.[119] The *Irish Independent*, the Catholic Church and Fine Gael joined forces to support Franco – a manoeuvre denounced in November 1936 at a meeting led by George Gilmore, Owen Sheehy Skeffington, Ernie O'Malley and Peadar O'Donnell.[120] Some former Blueshirts, following O'Duffy's lead, formed an Irish Brigade and joined Franco's army, while Frank Ryan and his volunteers joined the Spanish republican forces. Tensions rose in the Dáil. In November 1936 also, Cosgrave asked the Dáil to take steps to recognise Franco's government, on the basis that the war raging in Spain was 'for the victory or defeat of communism and all it stands for, with its denial of Christian principles, individual liberty and democracy'.[121] De Valera

[115] Thomas, *The Spanish Civil War*, 356. [116] Ibid., 348.

[117] Tom Buchanan, *The Impact of the Spanish Civil War on Britain: War, Loss and Memory* (Brighton: Sussex Academic Press, 2007).

[118] Thomas, *The Spanish Civil War*, 347. [119] Ó Drisceoil, *Peadar O'Donnell*, 95.

[120] English, *Radicals and the Republic*, 246–7.

[121] *Speeches and Statements by Eamon de Valera*, 285.

delivered a meandering response advocating caution and non-intervention, in keeping with the pact signed by France and Britain. He emphasised that communism in Ireland had virtually vanished, and related the debate around the Spanish war to the red scares that had surrounded Fianna Fáil's election.[122]

In light of these debates, Beckett's contribution to *Authors Take Sides on the Spanish War* takes on a new dimension, as a reminder of the history of Irish republicanism and a response to Irish perceptions of the Spanish Civil War. Whether his response also reflects a resentment at being categorised as British by virtue of being Irish, as intimated in the call to writers that initiated the pamphlet, is a matter open to speculation. As usual, his correspondence suggests that no serious thinking took place: a letter to Hone mentions the 'Spanish business' and relates that Cunard 'wrote again, to demand amplifications'.[123] For Cunard, Beckett's cryptic statement acquired new meanings in retrospect: her memoir recalls this moment by association, emphasising that Beckett 'took side with some purpose' during the war, and that his Resistance activities 'counted effectively in the Allied effort'.[124] It is certain that Beckett remained committed to the idea of opposing Franco, whom he perceived, like many French intellectuals of his generation, as a symbol of brutal repression. Various anecdotes testify to his continued concern about levels of censorship in Spain. In 1963, he sent 'a wire of sympathy' (somewhat reluctantly, it seems) in response to an appeal from his Italian publisher, Giulio Einaudi, the son of a former Italian president, who was canvassing for support when his anthology of anti-Franco songs contributed to a lasting diplomatic crisis between the Italian and Spanish governments.[125] Sanctions included being forbidden from entering Spanish territory, and in Italy Einaudi was sued for blasphemy and obscenity and for offending a Head of State.[126] In 1966, Beckett donated a manuscript of 'Enough' – certainly an interesting choice – to a Paris auction organised at the Palais Galliera, to contribute to the payment of fines levied by the Spanish government against a group of Spanish professors, novelists, poets, painters and architects from Barcelona, and against another group of intellectuals and artists from Madrid. All were fined for attending meetings pressing for students' unions free from official control, and for protesting against the violent repression of a demonstration in Barcelona, during which Catholic priests who had questioned the mistreatment of an imprisoned student leader were subject to police

[122] Ibid., 287. [123] *LSB1*, 508. [124] Cunard, *Hours Press*, 118.
[125] *LSB3*, 525, 526 n2; 'Spain-Italy Relations Growing Icy', *Washington Post*, 24 January 1963, 21.
[126] 'Synopsis', *Guardian*, 22 February 1963, 9.

beatings. The auction was organised by a committee presided by the art historian Jean Cassou, and Sartre, de Beauvoir, Picasso, Alexander Calder, Max Ernst and Joan Miró donated artworks and manuscripts.[127] The following year, Beckett sent a plea for Arrabal to a Madrid tribunal, as part of a series of statements issued by other writers and artists including Ionesco, Achard, François Mauriac, Jean Anouilh and Jean-Louis Barrault. The context of Beckett's decision to intercede in Arrabal's favour is well known: Arrabal, then a French resident, was arrested during a trip to Spain and convicted of treason and blasphemy for writing in one of his books a dedication deemed unpatriotic and obscene ('Me cago en Dios, en la patria y en todos lo demás' [I shit on God, my country and everything else]).[128] The letter that Beckett wrote to the Spanish tribunal deploys a rhetoric conceived to impress: he evokes Arrabal's youth, describes him as mentally and physically fragile, and praises Arrabal as 'a profoundly Spanish talent' who has integrated a quintessential national quality into his work. The letter concludes that the court should '[l]et Fernando Arrabal return to his own sentence', on the grounds that he 'will have to suffer considerably to give us what he still has to give'.[129] This gesture and many of Beckett's public statements are inscribed in a long reflection on justice and freedom which began with *Negro* and owes much to Cunard's belief in Beckett's political voice.

Beckett, Surrealist Circles and Cultures of Translation

Cunard's anthology furthered Beckett's career in other ways: it marked his proximity to Surrealist political activities and affirmed his reputation as translator of Surrealist texts. Alongside and beyond his work for *Negro*, Beckett translated a substantial number of other prose texts and poems by Breton, Soupault, Eluard and Crevel. It is likely that he translated more Surrealist texts, which were published unsigned. His translations were pioneering: in the early 1930s, the French Surrealists rarely published outside of their own reviews, and the channels through which Surrealist work was disseminated abroad were few. Jolas's *transition* was the first magazine to introduce Surrealism to an Anglo-American readership.[130] In 1932, the Surrealist

[127] 'MSS Sold to Aid Spanish Artists', *IT* 27 June 1966, 5; Tad Szulc, 'Art Auction Aids Fined Spaniards', *NYT*, 27 June 1966, 13.

[128] Peter L. Podol, *Fernando Arrabal* (Boston: Twayne Publishers, 1978) 20; 'Autograph Leads to Arrest', *Chicago Tribune*, 25 July 1967, 4; 'Spanish Playwright Held on "Blasphemy" Charges', *NYT*, 25 July 1967, 28.

[129] 'La situation en Espagne', *Le Monde*, 28 September 1967, 5.

[130] Paul C. Ray, *The Surrealist Movement in England* (Ithaca: Cornell University Press, 1971), 79.

issue of Edward Titus's *This Quarter*, featuring many texts translated by Beckett, followed in its footsteps in bringing Surrealism to the attention of a wider public. Surrealist work was also disseminated via *New Verse* and the Europa Press directed by Reavey, who was close to the British Surrealists.[131] Other than Beckett, Devlin and Coffey, early translators of French Surrealist texts into English included Man Ray, e.e. cummings, Eugene Jolas, Kay Boyle, David Gascoyne and Humphrey Jennings.

Among the artists associated with British Surrealism, Beckett befriended the painter John Banting, whom he had met through Cunard.[132] Banting, a militant communist and anti-fascist, was one of Cunard's close allies: he designed banners for demonstrations in support of the Scottsboro Boys, helped her collect materials for *Negro* – to which he also contributed – in New York, and later joined her on a trip to besieged republican territories in Spain.[133] Beyond Banting, however, British Surrealism remained a world largely unknown to Beckett: he met Gascoyne much later, in the early 1950s, through Duthuit.[134] His letters convey his lack of sympathy for the variety of Surrealism manufactured by Herbert Read; fortunately for Beckett, the influential Read thought more highly of his work. Read's Surrealism was firmly aligned with English writing traditions, and with an aesthetic that obscured social and political dimensions.[135] His parallel attempts to theorise of the role of the artist often led him to blur the distinctions between political creeds, and to present the poet as 'the agent of destruction in society', who 'must oppose all organized conceptions of the State, not only those which we inherit from the past, but equally those which are imposed on people in the name of the future'.[136]

Information about Beckett's contacts with the Paris Surrealist group is largely anecdotal, but even in the early days, he remained a step ahead of MacGreevy, Devlin and Coffey; a letter from Devlin to MacGreevy from September 1933 states that Beckett has met both Breton and Eluard, and relays Beckett's observations: 'Breton impressed him and Eluard inspires

[131] *New Verse* 5 (1933); Dougald MacMillan, *transition 1927–38: The History of a Literary Era* (London: Calder and Boyars, 1975), 79–89; Céline Mansanti, 'Between Modernisms: *transition* (1927–38)', in *The Oxford Critical and Cultural History of Modernist Magazines*, vol. 2, ed. Peter Brooker and Andrew Thacker (Oxford: Oxford University Press, 2012), 729–36; Mark Nixon, 'George Reavey: Beckett's First Literary Agent', *Publishing Samuel Beckett*, 45; Kohlmann, *Modernism, Politics, and Left-Wing Literature in the 1930s*, 41–50.

[132] Michel Remy, *Surrealism in Britain* (Aldershot: Ashgate, 1999), 66.

[133] John Banting, 'Nancy Cunard', *Cunard: Brave Poet*, 182–4.

[134] Robert Fraser, *Night Thoughts: The Surreal Life of the Poet David Gascoyne* (Oxford: Oxford University Press, 2012), 266.

[135] Ray, *The Surrealist Movement in England*, 149, 108–33.

[136] Read, *Poetry and Anarchism*, 15.

affection; which is proper'.[137] Beckett's correspondence indicates that he perceived Eluard's poetry as an important precedent and continued to work in imaginative proximity to Eluard. In 1938, he toyed with the idea of giving to Eluard a recently assembled corpus of poems in French and, possibly, of asking Marcel Duchamp to act as intermediary.[138] Many of his friends and collaborators shared such informal ties to the Surrealist circle: the world of Peggy Guggenheim, for example, revolved around Breton, Eluard, Duchamp, Calder, Mesens and Tanguy at the time of her tumultuous affair with Beckett.[139] From the late 1920s through to the 1950s, Beckett frequented Surrealist disciples and associates of every imaginable stripe, from Philippe Soupault – who wrote the first exploration of automatic writing with Breton, *Les champs magnétiques* – to Duchamp, Giacometti, Paz and Patrick Waldberg. The literary circles in which Beckett worked regularly intersected with Surrealist cultures of protest: Cunard, Duthuit, Jean Lurçat, Giacometti, Ernst, Paz and Soupault, for example, endorsed some of the many manifestos, protests and appeals issued by the Surrealists over time. Many of those who were sympathetic to Surrealism entertained an ambivalent relation to the core Paris group, whose internal dynamics were deeply fractious and involved numerous attempted slights, perceived betrayals, withdrawals and verdicts of exclusion. Some of Beckett's close friends were involved with the radical Surrealist fringe: Blin joined several Surrealist offshoots during the 1930s, including the revolutionary group Contre-Attaque, and endorsed a number of Surrealist manifestos between 1934 and 1939.[140] Prior to meeting Beckett, the Montreal-born painter Jean-Paul Riopelle signed several Surrealist tracts and appeals; he exhibited paintings at the 1947 Surrealist exhibition in Paris, and joined the pro-Breton group that dissociated itself from the French Communist Party that year.[141] Many of Beckett's letters and essays demonstrate his continued interest in Surrealism and its legacies, and attest to his careful scrutiny of texts and paintings by André Masson, Ernst, Paalen and Freundlich throughout the 1930s and after 1945.

There are other connections between Beckett's own writing and Surrealist political cultures. Péron's translation of 'Alba', for example, appeared in the last issue of an anti-fascist review tied to Surrealism and entitled *Soutes:*

[137] *LSB1*, 169 n4. [138] *LSB1*, 630, 645.

[139] Peggy Guggenheim, *Out of this Century: Confessions of an Art Addict* (London: André Deutsch, 1980), 162–96.

[140] Aslan, *Roger Blin and Twentieth-Century Playwrights*, 11–22, 58.

[141] *Tracts surréalistes et déclarations collectives*, vol. 2, ed. José Pierre (Paris: Terrain Vague, 1982), 30–6.

Revue de culture révolutionnaire internationale.[142] This was the first of Beckett's poems to appear in a French publication, and the choice of *Soutes* is significant: the review, which was conceived and delivered at the same time as the French Popular Front, was characterised by its political militancy and internationalist ambitions. Prior to 1938, *Soutes* published volumes of antimilitarist poetry, Spanish republican poetry and a long poem about the Spanish Civil War by Jacques Prévert denouncing the collusion between Franco and the Catholic Church; these books were sold at popular gatherings, at political meetings and on picket lines.[143] The review's founder and main editor, Luc Decaunes, was Eluard's son-in-law, and the editorial board included Péron, Decaunes and Jean Marcenac – who, like Decaunes, was a member of the French Communist Party. In 1938, *Soutes* was infused with melancholic evocations of the heady summer of 1936 and the Popular Front spirit; the Spring issue featuring 'Alba' included texts by Decaunes, Péron, Tzara, Marcenac and others who had ties to Communism and Trotskyism, and later rallied the anti-Nazi Resistance.

These affiliations were to prove crucial for Beckett's career in the war's immediate aftermath, when Eluard and Aragon enjoyed immense influence as the poets of the liberation, and when those who still believed in Surrealism rallied around Breton and Péret to redefine the political remit of artistic endeavour and create a new literary scene. Fortunately for Beckett, his pre-war translations had made a lasting impression: Blin, for example, recalls that Beckett was more widely recognised in Parisian circles as translator of Surrealism than as poet or novelist.[144] Tzara, widely known for his support to Stalinism and long-standing associations with different strands of the French Left, was rumoured to be acting as Beckett's literary 'advisor' at that point, and Maurice Nadeau later recalled that Tzara worked hard to attract attention to Beckett.[145] As for Blin, he stated that he knew of Beckett's work long before their first encounter, through Tzara, who had spoken to him about *En attendant Godot.*[146] There are indications that, for long-standing Surrealist renegades also, Beckett could offer a model of literary activity: in 1969, the year the Surrealist group eventually disbanded,

[142] SB, 'Alba (traduit de l'anglais par A.R. Peron)', *Soutes: Revue de culture révolutionnaire internationale* 9 (1938): 41.

[143] Jacques Prévert, *La crosse en l'air. Feuilleton* (Paris: Soutes, 1936); J.-E. Béry, Luc Decaunes, Louis Guillaume, Jacques Prévert and Michel Rochvarger, *Cinq poèmes contre la guerre* (Paris: Soutes, 1937); Arturo Serrano Plaja, Rafaël Alberti, Pascual Pla y Beltrán and José-Luis de Gallega, *No pasarán!!! 5 Poèmes espagnols*, trans. Luc Decaunes (Paris: Soutes, 1937); Pascal Ory, *La belle illusion: Culture et politique sous le signe du Front Populaire*, revised ed. (Paris: CNRS, 2016), 216–19.

[144] Blin, *Souvenirs*, 80.

[145] Maurice Nadeau, *Grâces leur soient rendues* (Paris: Albin Michel, 1990), 364.

[146] Blin, *Souvenirs*, 80.

Aragon published a long article entitled 'I had voted for Samuel Beckett' that contrasts sharply with the flow of press commentaries on Beckett's Nobel Prize emphasising or deploring the complexity of Beckett's national attachments. Aragon stated his admiration for Beckett's writing, presented himself as an assiduous reader of his work, and explained that Beckett had been on his mind constantly during the composition of his most recent essay, *Je n'ai jamais appris à écrire ou Les Incipit* (1969). His tribute is certainly moving. 'Go on? I will only have known my beginning. I have never learnt how to write'.[147]

Translating Surrealism

The translations that Beckett contributed to *Negro* hold particular significance in the political history of Surrealism. By positioning Surrealist texts alongside studies of the Harlem Renaissance and documents related to the work of the League Against Imperialism, Cunard's anthology inscribed Surrealist political affirmations in a longer series of historical struggles against racial and social injustice. Yet the literary reviews that commissioned and published Beckett's translations during the 1930s could not be further removed from such model: Jolas's *transition*, Reavey's Europa Press and Titus's *This Quarter* manufactured a nihilistic and depoliticised version of Surrealism that had little to do with the activities of the movement. Their versions of Surrealism were entirely dissociated from the polemical work published in reviews such as *Le Surréalisme au service de la révolution* – which made a concerted attempt to document the history of colonial oppression over the course of its short life between July 1930 and May 1933 – and contrast sharply with the account of Surrealist political aspirations offered by Gascoyne a few years later.[148]

transition, in particular, published manifestos that echoed the mystical aspirations of Surrealism but did not emulate their political focus and anticolonial persuasion. When Jolas and writers from the *transition* circle proclaimed the 'revolution of the word' in 1929, they also called for a revolution divorced from politics and from 'sociological ideas'.[149] In a later attempt to elaborate on the concept, Jolas explained that the revolution of language would operate in the realm of metaphysics, according to a kind of

[147] Louis Aragon, 'J'avais voté Samuel Beckett', *Les Lettres françaises*, 29 October 1969, 4.
[148] David Gascoyne, *A Short Survey of Surrealism* (London: Routledge, 1935).
[149] Eugene Jolas, Kay Boyle, Stuart Gilbert and others, 'Proclamation', *transition: An International Quarterly for Creative Experiment* 16–17 (1929): 13.

mysticism that 'owe[d] nothing to Surrealism'.[150] Similarly, 'Poetry is Vertical' – published in March 1932 and bearing Beckett's signature – borrowed from a revolutionary register to call for a non-political revolution occurring through word, syntax and the invention of new hermetic languages. The text proclaimed 'the autonomy of the poetic vision', 'the hegemony of the inner life' and the necessity to safeguard 'orphic forces [. . .] from deterioration, no matter what social system ultimately is triumphant'.[151] The manifesto was aligned with Jolas's Vertigralist philosophy, which encompassed strictly linguistic and psychic phenomena, and upheld a mysticism recalling the 1924 Surrealist Manifesto, but deprived of political implications. The signatories of 'Poetry is Vertical' also included MacGreevy and Hans Arp, who had just broken away from Surrealist circles. Beckett later denied involvement in the composition of Jolas's manifesto, and his own perspective on it remains unclear.[152] It seems likely that he agreed to see his signature added to it because the same issue of *transition* featured another text by him, 'Sedendo et Quiescendo', an excerpt from *Dream of Fair to Middling Women* categorised by Jolas as an example of 'anamyth' or 'psychograph'.[153] The June 1936 issue of *transition* featuring Beckett's 'Malacoda', 'Enueg II' and 'Dortmunder' confirms this alignment and presents Beckett as a disciple of Jolas's Vertigralism. The issue, published shortly before the 1936 Surrealist exhibition, ends with a manifesto explaining that *transition* will bring about a 'metaphysical revolution' capable of overturning the 'world-crisis and its resultant suicidal nihilism', concluding with the call, 'DREAMERS OF THE WORLD UNITE!'[154]

The Surrealist issue of *This Quarter*, published in September 1932 and featuring translations by Beckett, was enmeshed in similar uncertainties concerning the ways in which Surrealist political activity might be represented to an English-speaking readership. Its editor, Edward Titus, was hostile to Surrealist revolutionary aspirations, and, under his editorship, *This Quarter* became in many ways a vanity project, financed by his wife Helena

[150] Eugene Jolas, 'What Is the Revolution of Language?', *transition: An International Workshop for Orphic Creation* 22 (1933): 125. Beckett may have had this moment in mind when he later wrote about an article by Jolas that was more revolutionary than usual, or 'plus révolutionnaire que nature' (*LSB2*, 264).

[151] Hans Arp, Samuel Beckett, Carl Einstein, Eugene Jolas, Thomas MacGreevy, Georges Pelorson, Theo Rutra [Eugene Jolas], James J. Sweeney and Ronald Symond, 'Poetry is Vertical', *transition: An International Workshop for Orphic Creation* 21 (1932): 148–9.

[152] Ruby Cohn, *A Beckett Canon* (Ann Harbor: University of Michigan Press, 2001), 34; Thomas Hunkeler, 'La poésie est-elle verticale? Remarques à propos d'une signature', *SBTA* 11 (2001): 416–24.

[153] *transition* 21 (1932): 4.

[154] Eugene Jolas, 'Vertigral Workshop', *transition: A Quarterly Review* 24 (1936): 109, 112, 113.

Rubinstein and her cosmetics company.[155] In his foreword, Titus explained that his aim was to disseminate unfamiliar Surrealist texts and that Breton, his guest editor, had been expressly asked to '[eschew] politics and such other topics as might not be in honeyed accord with Anglo-American censorship usages, although entirely permissible in France'.[156] In his own introductory essay tracing the history of Surrealism, Breton graciously noted that Titus had provided a precious opportunity to present Surrealist work to British and American readers 'at more effectual length than has been possible hitherto', explaining that 'the more or less rigorous controls to which publications in English are subjected in English-speaking countries obliges us to pass over in silence whatever in [Surrealist] activity bears on social conflicts and morals'.[157] Yet, by 1932, the association between the French Surrealist group and the French Communist Party was old news. Breton, Aragon, Eluard and Péret had stated their adherence to Marxism and joined the French Communist Party in early 1927, and their intricate trajectories around the French Communist Party and the Comintern during the 1930s and beyond are well known. Their political concerns inflected their poetry: even Eluard, then the least demonstrative in the political arena, published in 1931 in *Le Surréalisme au service de la révolution* a poem that proclaimed his hatred of the ruling bourgeoisie, police and Church.[158]

The selection of texts in *This Quarter* alludes to the controversies ignited by the Surrealists at several points, but these allusions are so scattered and muted that their political dimension comes across as unconvincing and somewhat delusional. An example is the unsigned translation of Crevel's 'The Period of Sleeping-Fits', which claims that '[t]o draw frontiers between the different psychic states is no more justifiable than to draw them between geographical states. It is for surrealism to attack both, to condemn every kind of patriotism, even the patriotism of the unconscious'.[159] This call to redefine the relation between the imagined and the real is echoed elsewhere, for example, in his essay against patriotism in *Le Surréalisme au service de la révolution* from the same period, but it loses its political resonance in the context of *This Quarter*. Elsewhere, in his potted history of Surrealism, Breton mentions briefly the polemic generated by

[155] See Gregory Baptista, 'Between Worlds: *Gargoyle* (1921–2); *This Quarter* (1925–32); and *Tambour* (1929–30)', *The Oxford Critical and Cultural History of Modernist Magazines*, vol. 2, 690–1.

[156] Edward W. Titus, 'Editorially: By Way of Introducing This Surrealist Number', *This Quarter* 5, no. 1 (1932): 6.

[157] André Breton, 'Surrealism: Yesterday, To-Day and To-Morrow', trans. E. W. Titus, *This Quarter*, 7–8.

[158] Paul Eluard, 'Critique de la poésie', *Le Surréalisme au service de la révolution* 4 (1931): 14.

[159] René Crevel, 'The Period of Sleeping-Fits', *This Quarter*, 188.

Aragon's 'Le Front Rouge' (1930), a poem calling for violent revolutionary action against institutional socialism, designating Léon Blum and partisans of social democracy as targets.[160] Aragon was prosecuted for 'incitation to military insubordination and provocation to murder', a charge questioned by hundreds of writers and intellectuals who expressed their support for him.[161] The signatories of the Surrealist tract issued in Aragon's defence included Cunard and some of Beckett's later friends (Duthuit, Lurçat, Giacometti), but none of his Dublin and London acquaintances. In the wake of the controversy, Aragon, Unik and Sadoul left the group to seek new political outlets. Throughout 1932, the Surrealists were ensnared in this controversy and continued to issue pamphlets and statements. The portrait of Surrealism offered in *This Quarter* could not have been further removed from their activities and concerns at that point.

The contribution that Beckett made to Titus and Breton's Surrealist issue was substantial and includes signed translations of poems by Breton and Eluard, prose texts from *Les champs magnétiques* by Breton and Soupault, and other prose excerpts by Crevel, Breton and Eluard. The overall selection is distinctive and presents the Surrealists as hedonistic anarcho-libertarians, trapped in hermetic disagreement with the figureheads of French psychiatry in the wake of their controversial experiments with automatic writing – in other words, an inoffensive aesthetic movement, unlikely to imagine alternative forms of social and political organisation, or to influence the course of international events. Such version of Surrealism was reinstated with the publication of *Thorns of Thunder*, a collection edited by Reavey featuring Beckett's translations of Eluard's poems. The volume was published to coincide with the 1936 International Surrealist Exhibition in London – an event widely publicised in the British press that, for Roland Penrose, marked the genuine beginnings of Surrealism in Britain.[162] Reavey was keen to involve his team of translators and made plans for a public reading by Eluard, with readings of translations by other contributors including Beckett. Beckett declined the invitation, and his correspondence suggests that he protested against Reavey's original plan because he had not been consulted.[163] In the end, the event took another shape: Eluard read excerpts from his own poetry as well as poems by Lautréamont, Baudelaire,

[160] Aragon, 'The Red Front', trans. e.e. cummings, *Literature of the World Revolution* 3 (1931): 35–7.

[161] *Tracts surréalistes*, vol. 1, 204–5, 208–22; Durozoi, *History of the Surrealist Movement*, 231–2, 725 n51; Maurice Nadeau, *The History of Surrealism*, trans. Richard Howard (New York: Collier Books, 1967), 175–82.

[162] Roland Penrose, *Quatre-vingt ans de surréalisme* (Paris: Cercle d'Art, 1981), 60–2.

[163] *LSB1*, 340, 342 n5.

Rimbaud, Cros, Jarry, Breton, Mesens, Péret and Picasso, while Gascoyne, Jennings and Reavey read translations of Eluard's poems and English Surrealist verse.[164] Arguably, Beckett's response was also an attempt to dissociate himself from an emerging strand of British Surrealism that he found confused and opportunistic. The London exhibition attracted other expressions of dissent, notably from three Birmingham artists who pointed out that the criteria determining the choice of exhibits were too loose and broad to be designated as Surrealist.[165]

Thorns of Thunder resonates with the domesticated version of Surrealism presented at the 1936 exhibition: it portrays Eluard's poetry as solely driven by mysticism, ekphrasis and classical traditions of love poetry.[166] Reviewing the volume in *The Dublin Magazine*, Leventhal presented Beckett as uniquely able to 'catch' Eluard's 'elusiveness' and seized the opportunity to explicate Surrealist political sentiment: his article points to the tensions between the Surrealists and the Communist Party, arguing that it is necessary 'for the man in the literary tavern' to know how 'to discuss surrealism, albeit superficially', and to learn to 'distinguish between Leninism and Marxism' more generally.[167] Leventhal's praise of Beckett's skill also foregrounded other coded literary insights: Beckett's 'Cascando', a poem featuring a muted allusion to the Irish laws on abortion and contraception, appeared next to poems by Ernie O'Malley in the same issue.

Cunard's *Negro* anthology was, then, the first English-language publication to give substance to the idea of a Surrealist political front, tied to major internationalist movements for equality and social justice. Situated in this context, Paz's *Anthology of Mexican Poetry*, a large-scale translation project commissioned by UNESCO, also becomes far more than the product of a simple accident of fate, as Beckett liked to portray it. Like *Negro*, Paz's anthology required considerable investment, and yet is rarely evoked in studies tracing Beckett's career, so much so that the 1985 Grove Press reedition was opportunistically presented as a lost Beckett text, its dust-jacket gloss claiming the work as a collaboration that the young Beckett, fresh out of Trinity College Dublin, had once undertaken with Paz.[168] The task of producing the anthology was monumental: the published edition

164 Michel Remy, 'Londres 1936, l'année de tous les dangers', *Mélusine* 8 (1986): 128.

165 Ibid., 129–30.

166 Paul Eluard, *Thorns of Thunder: Selected Poems, with a Drawing by Pablo Picasso*, ed. George Reavey, trans. Samuel Beckett, Denis Devlin, David Gascoyne, Eugene Jolas, Man Ray, George Reavey and Ruthven Todd (London: Europa Press and Stanley Nott, 1936).

167 A. J. Leventhal, 'Surrealism or Literary Psycho-Therapy', *Dublin Magazine* 11, no. 4 (1936): 72, 66.

168 Octavio Paz, ed., *Mexican Poetry: An Anthology*, trans. Samuel Beckett (New York: Grove, 1985).

features 103 poems, but Beckett initially translated many more. The minutiae of translation absorbed much of his time between January and April 1950, and may have required further spurts of work thereafter: a letter to MacGreevy from September 1952 complains that too much time has been taken up with yet another UNESCO task.[169] The volume saw light after considerable delays, a decade after Beckett first applied to UNESCO for translatorial work. It was published by Indiana University Press in December 1958 – six years after the French version.

UNESCO and the Cultural Politics of Translation

The *Anthology of Mexican Poetry* had diplomatic, rather than literary origins: it arose from a special agreement with the Mexican government in the wake of the 1948 UNESCO conference in Mexico City, and it was commissioned for UNESCO's Collection of Representative Works, which aspired to make masterpieces of world literature available predominantly in French and English.[170] This large and ambitious translation project, initiated in 1948, was then in its infancy, and Paz's anthology was the second instalment in a subseries dedicated to Latin America. Both French and English editions present the anthology and, more broadly, the Collection of Representative Works as contributions to a wider endeavour to promote reconciliation between nations liberated from totalitarianism: the anthology is earmarked as an attempt to 'emphasize the essential solidarity of creative artists in different nations, languages, centuries, and latitudes'.[171] These aspirations were aligned with UNESCO's foundational remit and its constitutional aim to contribute to peace and security by promoting the principles of the United Nations Charter. Naturally, aspirations to peace, security and collaboration also made for fraught political negotiations: as Gail Archibald has shown, UNESCO was the political medium through which the American government sought to implement its own moral and economic models in the wake of a war it had reluctantly joined.[172]

If the *Anthology of Mexican Poetry* was a long time in the making, this was due to circumstances shaped by UNESCO's internal politics and the shifting position that Mexico occupied in a larger game of political chess

[169] SB to MacGreevy, 19 September 1952, TCD MS 10402/183.
[170] See Edouard J. Maunick, *The UNESCO Courier* 39, January 1986, 5–8.
[171] UNESCO statement, in *Anthology of Mexican Poetry*, ed. Octavio Paz, trans. Samuel Beckett (Bloomington: Indiana University Press, 1958), 4. See also *Anthologie de la poésie mexicaine*, ed. Octavio Paz, trans. Guy Lévis Mano (Paris: Nagel, 1952), 8. Both are hereafter cited parenthetically.
[172] Gail Archibald, *Les Etats-Unis et l'UNESCO, 1944–1963* (Paris: Publications de la Sorbonne, 1993).

played out beyond UNESCO. The volume also owed much to networks established around Spanish republicanism that would have been familiar to Paz since the days of the Spanish Civil War – Paz had travelled to Spain in 1937 to attend the Second International Congress of Antifascist Writers and later attempted to join the republican army.[173] The idea of publishing an anthology of Mexican poetry was initiated by the critic and translator Ricardo Baeza, a Spanish republican in exile who worked for UNESCO and provided Paz with a link to the institution.[174] Gerald Brenan was later enrolled to proof Beckett's translations prior to publication; he had authored a landmark study of Spanish political history, *The Spanish Labyrinth*, and had also been associated with republican circles. Guy Lévis Mano, who translated the French version, entitled *Anthologie de la poésie mexicaine*, had published Surrealist poems expressing opposition to Franco at the time of the Spanish Civil War. It is certainly intriguing that, in this context, Beckett should be positioned as a counterpart to Lévis Mano, an artisan with a unique portfolio of work as typographer, printer and editor, a prominent figure in the Parisian world of Surrealist poetry and political writing – and the person to whom Cunard, incidentally, had sold one of her printing presses after *Negro*, for his Editions GLM.[175]

For Beckett, the *Anthology of Mexican Poetry* would remain a sorry episode and an unwelcome reminder of lean times. Reviews were mostly lukewarm and seemed only to confirm the sentiment: one reviewer thought that the originals were 'superbly' rendered, observing that the whole volume was, nevertheless, 'very far removed from the grisly slob-lands of the Beckett country', while others described 'uninspired' translations that occasionally succeeded in rendering the feel of the originals.[176] Beckett's letters to Mary Hutchinson and Kay Boyle issue damning verdicts on the volume, lamenting the inclusion of poor poems and his uneven grasp of Spanish.[177] As was the case with Cunard's *Negro*, Beckett's affirmations about the

[173] Nick Caistor, *Octavio Paz* (London: Reaktion, 2007), 35–43.

[174] Octavio Paz and Eliot Weinberger, 13 July 1994, 'Afterword: A Conversation with Octavio Paz', in *The Bread of Days: Eleven Mexican Poets; El pan de los dias: Once poetas mexicanos* (Covelo, CA: Yolla Bolly Press, 1994), 121–2; Froylán Enciso, *Andar fronteras: El servicio diplomático de Octavio Paz en Francia (1946–1951)* (Mexico: Siglo XXI Editores, 2008), 127.

[175] On Lévis Mano, see Edwy Plenel, 'La fidélité Maspero', in *François Maspero et les paysages humains*, ed. Bruno Guichard, Julien Hage and Alain Léger (Lyon: Fosse aux Ours, 2009), 13; Cunard, *Hours Press*, 196.

[176] Thomas Hogan, 'Books', *Manchester Guardian*, 13 February 1959, 6; George G. Wing, 'Review of *An Anthology of Mexican Poetry*', *Books Abroad*, 33, no. 4 (1959): 465; David Paul, 'Colonial Muse', *Observer*, 8 February 1959, 20.

[177] See SB to Boyle, 20 November 1960, Beckett Collection, HRHRC; SB to Hutchinson, 6 February 1959, Mary Hutchinson Collection, HRHRC.

Anthology of Mexican Poetry do not convey the intensity of attention and insight that he dedicated to the task. The selected poems were immensely challenging and the work involved far more than simple translation, for the anthology was also a political enterprise that came with its own tensions, disputes and solidarities.

There was much rewriting and discontent behind the scenes, not least because Paz, as his foreword reveals, felt uneasy about both the Spanish-language remit of the anthology and its exclusion of pre-conquest and contemporary poetry. Before the French volume was completed, he related his dissatisfaction to Reyes, complaining that the intense process of revising had not succeeded in improving Lévis Mano's 'unfaithful' translations; furthermore, the selection was fundamentally unsatisfactory, and the confused introduction by the 'sectarian' Paul Claudel, previously known for his pro-Franco stance, was, he felt, inappropriate to a discussion of Mexican poetry, due to Claudel's theological and Eurocentric fixations.[178] No such problems arose in response to Beckett's translations, and it seems that Paz wished to see them appear as written. However, when plans to publish the English anthology resurfaced some years later, Indiana University Press wrote to Beckett, informing him of the necessity to correct his sometimes 'awkward', 'infelicitous' or 'florid' translations.[179] It seems that, initially, either Brenan or Indiana University Press wanted to include the line 'revised by Mr Gerald Brenan' on the book cover, although there were no clear reasons for this: thirty years later, Brenan asserted that he and his wife had found only one minor error in Beckett's manuscript.[180]

Paz's recollections of the anthology were as ambivalent as Beckett's. He remained for a long time unwilling to discuss this episode, and sent an irate response to Deirdre Bair when she contacted him in 1974 about the anthology.[181] In the 1990s, however, he gave a fuller account to Eliot Weinberger, explaining that he had taken over the enterprise because he was, at the time, employed by the Mexican embassy in Paris and was in need of money. Much of the content had been imposed, but he was at least given the freedom to choose his translators. He would have preferred to edit an anthology of Latin American poetry more closely aligned with his internationalist beliefs, he claimed, and resented the conditions imposed by the Mexican poet Jaime Torres Bodet, UNESCO's Director-General, who directed the publications list.[182] To Paz's dismay, Torres Bodet

[178] Enciso, *Andar fronteras*, 127–8. [179] *LSB2*, 511 n2.
[180] *LSB2*, 666; *SB*, 410. Beckett thanked Brenan for his assistance in a translator's note.
[181] *SB*, 695 n49.
[182] Paz and Weinberger, 'Afterword', 122; Weinberger, 'Introduction', *The Bread of Days*, x.

commissioned introductions by Claudel for the French edition and by the Oxford scholar C. M. Bowra for its English counterpart; he also decided that the anthology would conclude with the work of Alfonso Reyes, thus excluding the contemporary Mexican poets admired by Paz. Ultimately, the only living poets included in the anthology were two former diplomats: Reyes and Enrique González Martínez. The anthology's fate remained tied to Torres Bodet's career; he resigned from his UNESCO post in 1952 over a budget controversy shaped by Cold War dynamics and tensions with American representatives over the cultural role of UNESCO.[183] It is likely that the 1952 publication of the French volume, in an extended edition that reproduced the original Spanish poems, and the long-delayed publication of its English version owed much to tensions over the institution's grants and future.

As translator, Beckett was not at all at home with UNESCO. The liberal humanism sponsored by the organisation and its internal politics were deeply alien to him, and he had nothing positive to say about its internationalist ambitions. His letters deplore 'an atmosphere of futility & incredulity' and conclude that UNESCO may not last, or perhaps only 'in a very modified form'.[184] Fortunately for his term as translator, this was not the case, and UNESCO supplied him with a steady trickle of commissions. He worked on a tribute volume to Goethe published in 1949 in Zurich, revising some English translations including 'Message from Earth', a translation of 'Recado Terrestre' by the Chilean poet Gabriela Mistral.[185] This poem reads as a homage to Goethe's wisdom; it is also phrased as a mock-prayer for a new state of grace, on behalf of a warring world in agony. Such translation tasks required a deft hand: Goethe's work had been mined by the Nazis to bolster their nationalist iconography, and the post-war reinterpretation of his work was a large-scale endeavour fraught with many cultural and scholarly anxieties.[186] UNESCO's reappraisal anticipated the growth of a new consensus around Goethe and returned to Nietzsche's view of Goethe as a 'good European' who resisted the pressures of nationalist sentiment.[187] The volume implemented a reconciliation of another order, bringing very different political trajectories together. The

[183] Vincenzo Pavone, *From the Labyrinth of the World to the Paradise of the Heart: Science and Humanism in UNESCO's Approach to Globalization* (Plymouth: Lexington Books, 2008), 78.

[184] *LSB2*, 75.

[185] *Chronology*, 106; Federman and Fletcher, *Samuel Beckett: His Works and His Critics*, 98.

[186] See Gerhart Hoffmeister, 'Reception in Germany and Abroad', in *The Cambridge Companion to Goethe*, ed. Lesley Sharpe (Cambridge: Cambridge University Press, 2002), 248–53.

[187] See William H. F. Altman, *Friedrich Wilhelm Nietzsche: The Philosopher of the Second Reich* (Lanham, MD: Lexington, 2013), 18.

contributors included writers with staunch political ambitions and politicians and diplomats harbouring literary ambitions – Senghor, Spender and Reyes, as well as Benedetto Croce; Thomas Mann; Carl J. Burckhardt, Swiss ambassador to France and director of the International Committee of the Red Cross between 1945 and 1948; Sarvepalli Radhakrishnan, later vice-president and president of India; the Egyptian writer, academic and politician Taha Hussein Bey; and Jules Romains, newly appointed to the French Academy to replace Abel Bonnard. The preface to the volume, meanwhile, reproduces a statement by Torres Bodet asserting UNESCO's ambition to overcome enshrined political tensions through the medium of culture. Paraphrasing Nietzsche's verdict, Torres Bodet presents Goethe as 'a great European' and 'a great universalist', and asserts that UNESCO, in keeping with its aims of 'harmonizing and reconciling', is 'proud to salute Goethe's memory and to recognize in it an imperishable testimony to what the human mind can accomplish when its desire for knowledge, that is for analysis and awareness, is combined with the power of understanding'.[188]

Later in 1949, Jean-Jacques Mayoux and Emile Delavenay, who worked for UNESCO alongside other *normaliens*, again invited Beckett to act as ghost writer, for a collection entitled *Interrelations of Cultures: Their Contribution to International Understanding*, which grew out of an international UNESCO colloquium promoting cultural diversity, cooperation and a reflection on 'the present stage of the indigenous cultures of the various peoples of the world'.[189] The topic was also a response to global anxieties regarding the possibility of a new world war, and the volume emphasised UNESCO's commitment to human rights and progressive economic ideals. The conference proceedings gathered academic essays on a range of questions pertaining to philosophy, anthropology, sociology, musicology, economics, archaeology, history of art and literature. At the request of Mayoux and Delavenay, Beckett revised an essay by Shih-Hsiang Chen entitled 'The Cultural Essence of Chinese Literature'; more precisely, he retranslated into English the extant French translation of the essay by Louis Cazamian, for the sum of $200 – a significant fee at a time of successive currency devaluations in France.[190]

[188] Preface, *Goethe: UNESCO's Homage on the Occasion of the Two Hundredth Anniversary of His Birth* (Paris: UNESCO, 1949), ix–xi.

[189] Introduction, *Interrelations of Cultures: Their Contribution to International Understanding* (Paris: UNESCO, 1953), 7.

[190] Emile Delavenay, 'Beckett, dernier recours', in *L'UNESCO racontée par ses anciens* (Paris: Organisation des Nations Unies, 2006), 171–2; *Chronology*, 108.

Clearly, old networks of contacts played a role in Beckett's appointment as translator for the *Anthology of Mexican Poetry*. ENS alumni occupied prominent posts at UNESCO, as they did in many other spheres of state administration and government in France: René Maheu, for example, became Torres Bodet's Director of Cabinet in 1948, Deputy Director General in 1954 and eventually Director General. Delavenay, who had been Beckett's student at the ENS, later explained that it was Mayoux who had initially recommended Beckett to Paz.[191] For his part, Paz mentioned his interest in Beckett's French-language fiction as the trigger for his appointment: he had read 'L'Expulsé' in *Fontaine*, which also published his own poetry, and admired Beckett's novella.[192] Ironically, this is one of the texts in which Beckett deploys most successfully and strikingly a whole array of translation effects outside of the process of translation.[193] It seems more likely that Paz chose Beckett on the basis of his translations for *Negro* and *This Quarter*: the Surrealists – Péret and Breton above all – maintained a long-standing fascination with Mexico, and Paz, a well-connected poet in both Mexico and Paris, was close to Breton and knew Péret well.[194] Perhaps Breton refreshed Paz's memories: Breton and Beckett met in April 1948,[195] a few months after Péret's return from seven years in Mexico, just as Breton and Péret were seeking to rekindle old partnerships and rebuild the Surrealist group.

Translating the *Anthology of Mexican Poetry*

There is little documentation of the translation process as such, but ample evidence of the difficulties that Beckett encountered, and the pains he took to render the specificities of flora and fauna while respecting prosody.[196] His grasp of Spanish – a language he attempted to learn in 1933 and thereafter, but never mastered – was poor, and the poems featured many challenging Mexicanisms. Having found that he had unwittingly omitted some lines, stanzas and even whole poems, he had to revise all his translations at the end of the process. To Paz, Beckett made clear that he didn't speak Spanish and said that he would rely on his Latin and the assistance of a friend, likely the unknown helper dismissed in correspondence as an arrogant 'petit normalien' (Beckett had other Hispanist friends – Coffey,

[191] *LSB2*, 184 n5. [192] Paz and Weinberger, 'Afterword', *Bread of Days*, 121.
[193] See my *Samuel Beckett and the Problem of Irishness*, 58. [194] Caistor, *Octavio Paz*, 63–4.
[195] *Chronology*, 103.
[196] María José Carrera, '"And Then the Mexicans": Beckett's Notes toward *An Anthology of Mexican Poetry*', *SBTA* 27 (2015): 159–70.

for example).[197] Interestingly, Paz was never daunted by Beckett's lack of fluency and retained a boundless faith in his capacities. In the 1990s, he explained that he and Beckett were on friendly terms and met occasionally to resolve translation problems; he also recalled that they shared a dislike of the Mexican Romantic poets, and an admiration for modern poets such as José Juan Tablada and Ramón López Velarde, as well as seventeenth-century poets such as Luis de Sandoval y Zapata and Sor Juana Inés de la Cruz (the latter, however, does not feature in the published volume). Beckett's correspondence conveys his enduring admiration for others, such as Miguel de Guevara and the only female poet he translated, Sor Juana de Asbaje.[198] Paz also emphasised Beckett's dedication to the task and the beauty of his translations. He had little sympathy for Beckett's personality, however, and stated that Beckett 'was not interested in anything exterior, only his own philosophical and existential problems', that '[h]e had no anthropological interest or curiosity'. 'He was a man of his time, a certain moment in Western civilization. He never showed any interest in the Americas or even in the United States, as Kafka did. He was too much a prisoner of himself, of his own obsessions. His country was his room'.

These declarations are important, not simply because they repeat common myths about Beckett prevalent since the 1950s. Beckett's contribution to the anthology contradicts this verdict, offering a subtle rewriting of the original poems into a broader history of imperialist conquest across the globe. His translations speak of a colonial violence inflicted and felt, charting a haunted territory animated by mysterious forces capable of taking over. These aspects of Beckett's translations are certainly at odds with other sections requested by UNESCO. Bowra's foreword and Paz's short history of Mexican poetry evade questions of conquest, ascendency and indigeneity; while Bowra barely mentions Mexico at all, Paz celebrates the exoticist baroque that brought Spanish and indigenous traditions together, describing the poetry of the colonial period as a derivative art without commenting on the cultural imaginary that such poets replicate but do not own. His treatment of the Mexican revolution is confined to the raising of minor points about the formal innovations of López Velarde, portrayed as the father of modern Mexican poetry. Overall, Paz's introduction offers abstract evaluations of poetic forms and posits a purely formal teleology between poetry from the early days of conquest and modernist poetry, concluding that 'the only true revolutionary poetry is apocalyptic poetry', but

[197] Paz and Weinberger, 'Afterword', 121–3; *LSB2*, 179.
[198] SB to Boyle, 20 November 1960, Beckett Collection, HRHRC.

without entering into specifics about how poetry 'transmutes' history (41). For Paz, poetry simply provides the ultimate refuge from 'the domination of history', which in his view has never been greater (44). Paz's notes to the poems, however, render the pressure of historical circumstance more clearly, discussing the poets' social origins and political relations between Spain and the colonies. These notes Beckett translated particularly faithfully.

At times, the divorce between poetry and history described by Paz reverberates in the selections chosen for inclusion. For example, the anthology features a fragment from Ignacio Rodríguez Galván's 'Profecia de Guatimoc', a poem that presents a speaker estranged from his beloved, friends and family, who engages in a dialogue with the spirit of Cuauhtemoc, the last Aztec emperor, imprisoned and tortured by Cortés. In the full-length poem, his dialogue with the ghost of the martyred emperor addresses the ways in which indigenous American peoples have lost their status, wealth and power, and yields political prophecies foretelling the downfall of a corrupt elite ruling Mexico and the collapse of Paris and London, ultimately expressing the hope that justice will be done and that the time of revenge will come for Mexico's indigenous peoples.[199] Paz's anthology transforms the poem into a declaration of existential anguish: the only sections included in the volume are those bracketing the dialogue between ghost and speaker, which focus exclusively on the isolated speaker's thoughts and visions of death and resuscitation.

There are many tensions between the framing of the anthology and Beckett's translation choices. These are perhaps most readily discernible in the opening poem by Francisco de Terrazas, which is permeated by spectral references to the Spanish conquest of Mexico that are largely introduced by the translation. The original text is a love poem, which relates the speaker's dream of being thrown off from a rock ('una peña') by the woman he loves. Beckett's translation, however, presents a poetic voice under the sway of something other than love: it offers an apocalyptic vision in which terror and powerlessness have overwhelmed the spectrum of possible feelings. Beckett's speaker dreams of being 'thrown from a crag/by one who held my will in servitude,/and all but fallen to the griping jaws/of a wild beast in wait for me below' (49). Other translations introduce new historical undertones and accentuate the political predicament that informs the originals. For example, Beckett's translation of Manuel José Othón's

[199] See Jorge Cañizares-Esguerra, *Nature, Empire, and Nation: Explorations of the History of Science in the Iberian World* (Stanford: Stanford University Press, 2006), 133; Benjamin Keen, *The Aztec Image in Western Thought* (New Brunswick, NJ: Rutgers University Press, 1971), 366.

'Idilio Salvaje' slightly alters the register of the original, where, in the midst of horrific visions of devastation, a 'wild' Indian woman appears to the speaker, who tries in vain not to forget. The lines 'Flota en todo el paisaje tal pavura/como si fuera un campo de matanza' (107) are rendered in a manner that introduces a proximity to ritual sacrifice, animal or human ('Such horror hovers over all the scene/as on a place steeped in the blood of slaughter') (132). The French translation opts for 'champ de meurtre', field of murder, the distinctive nineteenth-century French usage of which invokes the military battlefield (107).

Some of Beckett's most delicate translation choices strengthen a historical dimension that is only half-stated in the original poems, and bring together coded signifiers of colonial conquest and imperialist custom. The translation of Reyes's 'Yerbas del Tarahumara' introduces a reference to *cúscus*, the Spanish word for couscous, in a description of the Tarahumaras' pharmacopeia: Beckett renders the line 'yerbaniz, limoncillo, simonillo' (or mint marigold, lime, horseweed) as 'mint and cuscus and birthroot' (190).[200] The French translation by Lévis Mano, however, remains neutral, opting for 'menthe, piloselle, simonillo' (152). For Weinberger, this is one of several slippages resulting from Beckett's unfamiliarity with indigenous Mexican cultures, and it reflects Beckett's neglect for his sources more generally.[201] This seems doubtful: on the contrary, a close reading of Beckett's translations illuminates his experiment with historical logics. The medicinal practices of the Tarahumaras, and their use of peyote in particular, were far from obscure in the wake of Antonin Artaud's accounts of his travels to Mexico and to the land of the Tarahumaras, published in different forms from 1937 onwards.[202] Many details in Beckett's translation convey the care with which he rendered the complexities of the original poem, which stands as the most direct evocation of colonial plunder, exploitation and forcible conversion in the anthology. In Beckett's hands, Reyes's poem becomes a tribute to the nobility and philosophical insights of the Tarahumaras – issues that, in another context, had also preoccupied Artaud. To this effect, Beckett's translation introduces many antiquated terms, exotic references and baroque grammatical reversals, and is considerably more solemn than its French counterpart. Gradually, Beckett's speaker becomes alienated from the documented history invoked in the original: in a

[200] See also Alfonso Reyes, *Obras completas*, vol. 10 (Mexico City: Fondo de Cultura Económica, 1959), 122.

[201] Weinberger, 'Introduction', xi.

[202] See ***, 'D'un voyage au pays des Tarahumaras', *Nouvelle Revue Française* 287 (1937): 232–47; Antonin Artaud, *D'un voyage au pays des Tarahumaras* (Paris: Editions Fontaine, 1945).

subsequent stanza, Don Felipe Segundo is rendered as 'Don Philip the Second', a seemingly provincial ruler who shares little with Philip II and the golden age of the Spanish Empire. Beckett's stylised reworkings resonate with other reimaginings of Mexican geography: his rendering of the Aztec calendar stone as a 'stone of sun' (another demonstration of his ignorance, for Weinberger) anticipates the 'pierre de soleil' that Péret celebrated over a decade later in his translation of Paz's *Piedra de sol.* Such creative additions and subtle rewriting contrast with Lévis Mano's more literal approach. Paz, who believed in translation as a creative process, was unlikely to take issue with Beckett's choices.[203]

Throughout his translations, Beckett counters the anti-historical impulse that frames the collection, deploying various forms of historical remapping and shadowy references to Scotland, Ireland and North Africa. These minute shifts are significant: the Mexican poets included in the anthology are mostly of Spanish origin, and the original poems remain haunted by colonial history in ways that are largely coded or implicit. At times, Beckett's translations edge close to Irish and Scottish balladry; for example, the lines 'no queda ya ni un resto de verdura,/ni una brizna de hierba, ni un abrojo' from Manuel José Othón's 'Elegía' (101) become, 'there survives not a trace of verdure,/not a blade of grass, not a thistle' (128). 'Thistle' is not in itself an incorrect or improbable translation but certainly differs from the literal French, 'ronce' or bramble, and resonates with Beckett's persistent rendering of *peña* as 'crag'. Elsewhere, Beckett introduces a historical shading absent from the original; his translation of José Juan Tablada's 'El ídolo en el atrio' renders 'Y en pleno día las caudas de los quetzales/suben y giran como fuegos artificiales' (133) as 'And in broad day the quetzels' tails soar and whirl like Catherine wheels' (157), playing upon the dual meaning of the Catherine wheel, as both a type of fireworks and a torture instrument used to crush limbs in Roman times and during the Spanish Inquisition. Other translations acquire a Parisian flavour, evoking 'this grisaille that never is/lit up by any colour' (127), or a mock Sartrean flavour ('what a nausea of self-disgust!') (133).

Ultimately, Paz's anthology offers precious insights into the manner in which Beckett, in his humble capacity as translator, participated in a wider reflection on the formation of new international dialogues arising from a reshaped and frequently occluded imperial past. Beckett's own rendering of political history, here as in *Negro*, wrestles with unresolved questions often

[203] Octavio Paz, 'Literature and Literalness', in *Convergences: Essays on Art and Literature*, trans. Helen Lane (London: Bloomsbury, 1987), 196–200.

half-glimpsed in the recesses of the original texts. To wars long gone or raging far away he was never indifferent, and the vast body of translations that he crafted and honed reveals the attention and care with which he represented the political anxieties of others. As translator, he worked according to his own principles and aspirations, unburdened by inherited political affiliations, but armed with a body of historical knowledge acquired from decades of literary engagement. It is in these translations – precisely when he attempted to render histories and landscapes far removed from those he intimately knew – that his dedication to political thought appears in its bluntest and most unmediated form.

CHAPTER 3

Aftermaths
The 'Siege in the Room' and the Politics of Testimony

When Beckett was awarded the Nobel Prize in 1969, the Swedish Academy paid tribute to his historical insight and to the courage he had displayed in the French Resistance. His work, it said, was about 'what happened afterwards', about coming to terms with 'the lengths to which man can go in inhuman degradation'.[1] Clearly, in the eyes of the Nobel committee, Beckett's work shared the same literary and historical coordinates as war testimonies: a list of potential Nobel nominees drawn as early as 1963 featured Beckett alongside Nelly Sachs and Charles de Gaulle, who had just published the three volumes of his military memoirs.[2] The Nobel Academy's verdict followed a broader consensus: notably, in a televised debate from 1968, Fischer and Adorno concurred that Beckett's texts were written 'in the ashes of Auschwitz' – a view that Adorno had also developed in his own work, which draws attention to the capacity of Beckett's texts to represent the aftermath of the Holocaust through their very omission of clear historical landmarks.[3] These various appraisals have paved the ground for more recent readings by trauma theorists. Dominick LaCapra, for example, describes Beckett as belonging to a tradition of 'testimonial art' alongside Blanchot, Paul Celan and Franz Kafka, each having produced a 'writing of terrorized disempowerment as close as possible to the experience of traumatized victims without presuming to be identical to it'.[4]

The idea that Beckett's writing remains inextricably bound to the aftermath of the Second World War and its traumas may well be the only line of interpretation around which his critics have rallied unanimously. Indeed, the literature of the Holocaust is made up of a complex array of

[1] 1969 Nobel Award Ceremony Speech by Karl Ragnar Gierow of the Swedish Academy, www.nobelprize.org/nobel_prizes/literature/laureates/1969/press.html.

[2] 'Candidates for the 1963 Nobel Prize in Literature', 2 January 2014, www.nobelprize.org/nomination/literature/1963.html.

[3] Adorno, *Notes sur Beckett*, 152.

[4] Dominick LaCapra, *Writing History, Writing Trauma*, revised ed. (Baltimore: Johns Hopkins University Press, 2014), 105–6.

diasporic texts and translations in which the most challenging and mysterious aspects of Beckett's writing seem strangely at home.[5] But this consensus around Beckett's historicity has had some curious and lasting effects. It has obscured the difficult relation that the work maintains to historical testimony on the one hand, while, on the other, preventing a full recognition of the manner in which processes of referentiality and abstraction function around the summoning of historical events and political idioms, in a writing also marked by a peculiar and far less comfortable closeness to detective fiction, the misery memoir and the literary hoax. Distinctive political preoccupations shape these features of Beckett's writing: although their idiosyncratic and experimental forms may suggest otherwise, the texts that he wrote in French prior to *L'Innommable*, between 1946 and 1948 in particular, remain concerned with the war's political legacies, and ask pressing questions about the role of the state that are closely indexed to French experiences of internment and deportation, to the forms of anti-Semitism that grew under the Vichy regime, and to continuities and ruptures in French cultural politics. The motifs of war and displacement so prevalent in Beckett's work of that period also respond to the rise of a new testimonial literature focused on France under Nazi occupation, revolving around the realities of rationing, partition and resistance, and journeys from ignorance to knowledge.[6] With their characters frequently identified as lapsed authors, detectives or representatives of mysterious bodies in charge of inscrutable investigations, Beckett's texts reverse the premise of such a literature, rendering history as unintelligible, and the process of telling as burdened by too many demands to enable the articulation of testimony.

The 'Siege in the Room'

The war years, which were entirely dedicated to survival and resistance, were not germane to sustained writing and did not provide anything other than dangerous and precarious circumstances for creative thought. With the work that Beckett conducted for Gloria SMH – a Resistance cell under

[5] See Alan Rosen, ed., *Literature of the Holocaust* (Cambridge: Cambridge University Press, 2013).

[6] Margaret Atack, *Literature and the French Resistance: Cultural Politics and Narrative Forms, 1940–1950* (Manchester: Manchester University Press, 1989). Scholarship on Beckett and post-war French culture has recently taken a new historical turn; see, notably, Angela Moorjani, 'Beckett's *Molloy* in the French Context', *SBTA* 25 (2013): 93–108; Andrew Gibson, 'Beckett, de Gaulle and the Fourth Republic 1944–49: *L'Innommable* and *En attendant Godot*', *Limit(e) Beckett* 1 (2010), www.limitebeckett.paris-sorbonne.fr/; Gibson, 'French Beckett and French Literary Politics 1945–52', in *The Edinburgh Companion to Samuel Beckett and the Arts*, ed. S. E. Gontarski (Edinburgh: Edinburgh University Press, 2014), 103–16.

the command of the SOE, the British intelligence service – came a new proximity between writing, translation and coding: the military information that Beckett collated, translated and typed was reportedly concealed among his own papers, and the translation of *Murphy*, on which Péron and Beckett were collaborating, provided a ready alibi (the manuscript had already accompanied Beckett when he and Suzanne joined the mass exodus of June 1940 and fled Paris for Vichy). The *Watt* notebooks, which absorbed Beckett's attention throughout the war years, are laden with a wartime baggage that haunts their rich adornments, fragmentary messages, lists and calculations. Indeed, the proximity between these jottings and secret code once seemed so obvious that the London War Office withheld the notebooks to scrutinise them when Beckett returned to Dublin via London in April 1945.[7]

The period that followed, which Beckett memorably baptised as 'the siege in the room', was immensely prolific. The 'siege in the room' designates not simply a deep immersion in writing, but also the emergence of new political idioms and coordinates in Beckett's writerly imagination, at a time when he feared a new world war according to new parameters. The phrase itself deserves close scrutiny: 'siege' hints at a political regime enshrined in the French constitution – the *état de siège*, whose legal peculiarities have attracted the attention of Giorgio Agamben and others.[8] As Anne Simonin points out, the period between September 1939 and October 1945 unfolded as successive states of siege, encompassing the military defeat of 1940, Nazi occupation, the anti-collaborationist purges known as the Epuration and three different political regimes. All of these regimes were legally sanctioned by the same constitutional state of exception known as *état de siège*.[9] In 1945, the state of siege also provided the frame for the sanction of 'national indignity' levied against Vichy officials and collaborationists, and their trials for high treason, intelligence with the enemy and plotting against the State.[10] This legal context is particularly important for understanding Beckett's novel trilogy: its very terminology, as Andrew Gibson points out, has affinities with the discourse of the anti-collaborationist

7 See David Murphy, 'Paddy fait de la résistance. Les Irlandais dans la Résistance française et la section F du SOE, 1940–1945', *Revue historique des armées* 253 (2008), http://rha.revues.org/; Laura Salisbury, 'Gloria SMH and Beckett's Linguistic Encryptions', *The Edinburgh Companion to Samuel Beckett and the Arts*, 153–69.

8 Giorgio Agamben, *State of Exception*, trans. Kevin Attell (Chicago: University of Chicago Press, 2005), 4–5, 11–14.

9 Anne Simonin, *Le déshonneur dans la République: Une histoire de l'indignité, 1791–1958* (Paris: Grasset, 2008), 365, 366–90.

10 See Philippe Bourdrel, *L'Épuration sauvage* (Paris: Tempus, 2008); Joseph Kessel, *Jugements derniers*, ed. Francis Lacassin (Paris: Tallandier, 2007).

purges, which much resembled a civil war at their beginnings in 1944.[11] These legal and political tensions also informed the context in which Beckett's novels were first read: *Molloy* and *Malone meurt*, for example, appeared shortly before Jean Paulhan's *Lettre aux directeurs de la Résistance*, also published by the Editions de Minuit. Paulhan's controversial pamphlet questioned the political uses and abuses of the Epuration, reviving debates that had remained unresolved since the fall of the Vichy regime.[12]

Years later, Beckett vividly recalled the urgency and determination that animated this period. A nostalgic letter to Rosset deplores his growing entanglement 'in professionalism and self-exploitation', concluding: 'What I need is to get back into the state of mind of 1945 when it was write or perish. But I suppose no chance of that'.[13] There was, however, little time to write in 1945, and 1946 was equally, if not more, momentous. January 1946 began with Beckett's resignation from his post with the Irish Red Cross in Normandy. The texts he wrote thereafter include 'La Fin' (initially 'Suite et Fin'), *Mercier et Camier*, 'L'Expulsé', *Premier amour* (initially 'L'Amour') and 'Le Calmant'. *Eleutheria* followed at the start of 1947, then *Molloy*. In late 1947 Beckett started work on *Malone meurt*, then entitled 'L'Absent', in a manuscript sequel to the *Watt* notebooks, and, in 1948, he turned to *En attendant Godot*. The trajectories of these texts from manuscript to print were very different. 'Suite', for example, was conceived to be followed by a second instalment, 'Fin', but only the first half of the text appeared in 1946 in *Les Temps Modernes*, which led to Beckett's infamous dispute with de Beauvoir. *Mercier et Camier* and *Premier amour* were published after Beckett's Nobel Prize, *Eleutheria* was published posthumously, and other fragments and translations appeared in literary reviews such as Duthuit's *Transition* and *Les Temps Modernes* prior to full publication. For Beckett, the texts from *Watt* to *Malone meurt* belonged to the same series, and indeed there are many echoes between their portrayals of devastation, deprivation, warfare and return.[14] The recurrence of the same narrative concerns has been frequently noted: Alysia Garrison has commented on the possibility that Beckett – like many others who witnessed the aftermath of horrific events experienced indirectly – might have suffered from 'secondary traumatization', while Jackie Blackman, David Houston Jones and Daniel Katz have traced the many references to Judaism featuring in his texts, as well as connections to Holocaust testimonies and philosophical debates

[11] Gibson, *Samuel Beckett*, 97–127, 121–3.

[12] On Paulhan, see Simonin, *Les Editions de Minuit*, 404–15.

[13] *LSB3*, 177.

[14] *LSB2*, 80.

about the ethics of telling.[15] The manner in which Beckett harnessed his memories of the Resistance to write *En attendant Godot* has also attracted sustained attention.[16]

This aspect of the work's critical reception is torn between contrary impulses, however. In Beckett scholarship and in modernist studies alike, Beckett is celebrated for his wartime bravery, and his discretion concerning his war decorations (which was such that their number and designation have remained shrouded in mystery)[17] is perceived as an illustration of his integrity. Outside of these fields, however, Beckett does not enter the historical record. His name does not appear in the major histories of wartime and post-war France, in which a literary identity such as his – a foreign writer, citizen of a neutral country, dissociated from major political currents and yet ready to risk his life – does not fit neatly with established trajectories of collaboration and resistance. In parallel, much is known about the role played by Pelorson and other alumni of the Ecole Normale Supérieure who worked for the Vichy regime and disseminated pro-Nazi propaganda, and about members of the French Resistance including Péron, Beaufret and Lurçat, whom Beckett considered as friends.[18] This chapter seeks to craft a different narrative around Beckett's transformation from an obscure Irish francophone writer struggling to publish his work into a Nobel prizewinner able to offer unique insights into the catastrophe of recent history: it examines the tensions between the political concerns that permeate Beckett's writing and the literary cultures in which his French-language fiction was first published, and discusses the thwarted accounts that Beckett offered of Nazi occupation, tracing the internalisation of other difficult histories that he observed at some remove.

[15] Alysia E. Garrison, 'Faintly Struggling Things: Trauma, Testimony, and Inscrutable Life in Beckett's *The Unnamable*', *Samuel Beckett: History, Memory, Archive*, 100–1; Jackie Blackman, 'Beckett's Theatre "After Auschwitz"', ibid., 71–87; David Houston Jones, *Samuel Beckett and Testimony* (Basingstoke: Palgrave Macmillan, 2011); Daniel Katz, 'What Remains of Beckett: Evasion and History', in *Beckett and Phenomenology*, ed. Ulrika Maude and Matthew Feldman (London: Continuum, 2009), 144–57.

[16] See Marjorie Perloff, '"In Love with Hiding": Samuel Beckett's War', *The Iowa Review* 35, no. 1 (2005): 76–103; Paul Sheehan, 'Waiting for Nothing: Commitment, Resistance, and Godot's Underground Ancestry', in *In Dialogue with Godot: Waiting and Other Thoughts*, ed. Ranjan Ghosh (Lanham, MD: Lexington, 2013), 99–112.

[17] See Sarah Alyn Stacey, '*Patria non immemor*: Ireland and the Liberation of France', in *Southern Ireland and the Liberation of France: New Perspectives*, ed. Gerald Morgan and Gavin Hughes (Bern: Peter Lang, 2011), 10–12.

[18] Péron, for example, was awarded the Légion d'Honneur, Croix de Guerre, Médaille de la Résistance and Certificate of Service posthumously. Sirinelli, *Génération intellectuelle*, 587; Sirinelli, *Sartre et Aron*, 190, 190 n80.

States of Transition

Beckett's letters suggest that he looked upon French politics after 1944 with a mixture of amusement, fascination and irritation. He followed attentively the trials of the former heads of the Vichy government: his correspondence comments on Philippe Pétain's performance at his hearing in 1945 as 'the poor old misled man and hero of Verdun', refers to the attempted assassination of Pierre Laval, once the effective head of the Vichy government, prior to his trial and execution, and mentions the attempt of Marcel Déat, a former *normalien*, prominent collaborationist minister and representative of the Vichy militia, to flee the country.[19] An exchange with Arland Ussher suggests that Beckett perceived little difference between 1944 and 1946, and that the collaborationists and the military still served the same function. Ussher had sent him an essay that situated French collaborationism in a broader historical continuum reaching back to the eighteenth century and described the two world wars as the outcome of the nineteenth-century 'religion of nationalism'.[20] Beckett's account of the political situation in December 1946 is very clear: 'Flourishing, particularly the military representatives, they are happily engaged in reorganising the salvation of the country. They are prepared to forget and forgive – the so rude interruption'.[21]

Other letters commenting on French literary life are indignant: in August 1945, for example, Beckett notes that '[t]he same crowd, writing & painting, tops the bill that has topped it since the liberation'.[22] De Beauvoir's memoir features the negative image of Beckett's remark: 'The men now in power had been in the Resistance and, to a greater or lesser extent, we knew them all. [. . .] Politics had become a family matter, and we expected to have a hand in it'.[23] In his letters to Duthuit, Beckett greeted these developments with contempt. Their dialogue has an external referent: Duthuit's short-lived review, *Transition*, which published occasional commentaries in English on the post-war purges and more specific matters including Louis-Ferdinand Céline's situation.[24] In 1952, for example, Beckett comments upon an issue of *Combat* in which Breton evoked his certainty that the war would eventually end, even in the darkest

[19] *LSB2*, 19.

[20] Arland Ussher, 'The Meaning of Collaboration', *The Nineteenth Century: A Monthly Review* 140, no. 1333 (1946): 331.

[21] *LSB2*, 47. [22] *LSB2*, 19–20.

[23] Simone de Beauvoir, *Force of Circumstance*, trans. Richard Howard (London: André Deutsch, 1965), 4.

[24] 'The Case of Céline', *Transition Fifty*, no. 6 (1950): 132–4.

hours of Nazi occupation. Beckett's response, 'Veinard, va' (lucky devil), is clearly a jibe at Breton's decision to move across the Atlantic at that precise moment.[25] The same letter dismisses ungainly metaphors in an essay that nevertheless advances views similar to his own: Julien Gracq's 'La littérature à l'estomac', which portrays a 'republic of letters' in which the sharp political divergences of 1945 have not been mended and anti-intellectualism is on the rise.[26] A translation of the essay – one of many to which Beckett contributed – was published in *Transition*.[27] Beckett's diagnoses are certainly apt: Gisèle Sapiro has shown that the post-war purges did not foster radical transformations in Parisian literary production, but a generational passing of powers and the formation of literary alliances that merely exacerbated dynamics created long before the war, around nationalisation and the conquest of autonomy.[28] The war's aftermath was also the terrain of a 'counterpurge' that saw the arrests of former Resistance members for their activities in the anti-collaborationist purges, the formation of a committee requesting Pétain's liberation, and the publication of many books attempting to justify Vichy policies.

Some hints in Beckett's correspondence reveal a wartime experience shaped not simply by resistance action, but by continued friendship with writers who stood on the other side, such as Léon-Paul Fargue, who was associated with Drieu La Rochelle's *Nouvelle Revue Française* and other collaborationist publications during the war.[29] In later conversations, Beckett talked about collaborationism with some indulgence: he joked that he had never met Céline – who had been 'a bit foolish' during the war, he thought – because they were both on the run, he from 1942 and Céline from 1944, 'but in the other direction' (Céline recounted his time in Sigmaringen with the exiled Vichy government in novels that featured in Beckett's personal library).[30] He also associated his decision to join Gloria SMH with taking 'the Péron side', diametrically opposed to the choices made by Pelorson, who 'got into trouble in the war'.[31] These are a few of Beckett's euphemisms on the subject of the Vichy regime, a context that has attracted relatively little attention in Beckett scholarship. Beyond Beckett studies, however, much is known about Pelorson's political work, and he has been described as 'one of the more curious characters' spawned by the Vichy regime, and as

25 *LSB2*, 194. 26 Julien Gracq, *Préférences* (Paris: José Corti, 1961), 12–13.

27 Pilling and Lawlor, 'Beckett in *Transition*', 90; *LSB2*, 79 n1.

28 Gisèle Sapiro, *La guerre des écrivains, 1940–1953* (Paris: Fayard, 1999), 561–2, 636–45, 690.

29 *LSB4*, 618; Sapiro, *La guerre des écrivains*, 60, 419, 421.

30 *BR/RB*, 264–5; Van Hulle and Nixon, *Beckett's Library*, 266. 31 *BR/RB*, 41.

a 'disliked and mistrusted' figure, endowed with a personality fundamentally 'favourable to collaboration'.[32]

Pelorson's political career began after his return from a prisoner of war camp in Germany; he was appointed to governmental posts and became head of the Ministry of Youth's propaganda unit for the occupied zone in February 1941. After June 1942, as Deputy of Georges Lamirand, then National Secretary for Youth, Pelorson promoted Pétain's National Revolution in schools and universities, and reported on manifestations of dissent with noted zeal. His task, as he described it, entailed the 'civic and social education' of the French youth.[33] There are several accounts of his rapid ascent at the Ministry of Youth, where his ideological position accorded with the views of the new Minister of Education, Abel Bonnard, his superior, who supported him. Beyond his official duties as propagandist, Pelorson manoeuvered to ensure that officials who displayed pro-Gaullist opinions would be dismissed from their posts; he denounced the schools and educational institutions that breached the Vichy edicts, and he attempted to engineer the expulsion of Jews from a youth organisation over which he had some jurisdiction, the Auberges Françaises de la Jeunesse, in return for financial incentives.[34] His actions were aligned with the policies of the Ministry of Education and with a regime that relied upon corruption, conspiracy, trafficking and denunciations. Pelorson was dismissed when Lamirand was replaced in March 1943, and his deputy post remained vacant. By this point, officials at the Ministry of Youth and Pétain's entourage alike had become weary of his extremism.[35]

The anti-collaborationist purges, which sanctioned Nazi and fascist intellectuals as severely as Vichy administrators, but through different tribunals,[36] put Pelorson in a difficult position since his literary activities had continued throughout the war years alongside his political career. The blacklist of collaborationist writers published in the French press in September 1944 featured Pelorson alongside the most influential voices of the Vichy regime – Brasillach, Céline, Drieu La Rochelle, Charles Maurras

[32] W. D. Halls, *The Youth of Vichy France* (Oxford: Clarendon Press, 1981), 136; Daniel Lee, *Pétain's Jewish Children: French Jewish Youth and the Vichy Regime* (Oxford: Oxford University Press, 2014), 231.

[33] Mariane de Rochcau, 'M. Georges Pelorson, secrétaire général adjoint à la jeunesse, commente pour *Le Petit Parisien* le role des futures "équipes nationales de jeunes"', *Le Petit Parisien*, 24 July 1942, 1.

[34] Halls, *Vichy*, 137–8, 149; Lee, *Pétain's Jewish Children*, 109, 107.

[35] Giroud, 'Transition to Vichy', 237.

[36] Robert O. Paxton, *Vichy France: New Order, 1940–1944* (New York: Knopf, 1972), 333–4; Simonin, *Le déshonneur*, 361–584.

and Paul Morand.[37] In 1947, Pelorson was sentenced by the Court of Justice of the Seine to fifteen years of forced labour and to 'national degradation' – the loss of civic and professional rights incurred by those recognised guilty of 'national indignity'; this was presumably commuted to a lighter sentence, as was commonplace.[38] Under his new name, Georges Belmont, he led a prolific career as translator of English texts, starting with Evelyn Waugh and later extending to Gandhi and Nehru. In 1944, none of this seemed likely; like many of his friends, his future was hanging by a thread. In his memoir, Maurice Girodias relates that Pelorson was detained with Lucien Combelle in one of the prisons improvised by the FFI for collaborators, in this case a hotel in the Montparnasse area. At the last minute, Pelorson was freed by an unidentified man who – curiously – stated that he feared another miscarriage of justice, and recommended that he find a new name and leave Paris.[39] Combelle, who was formerly associated with *Volontés*, had no such luck and was condemned to a heavy sentence for his work as editor of the collaborationist weekly *Révolution nationale*: confiscation of property, national degradation and fifteen years of forced labour, eventually commuted to seven.[40] Severe sanctions were also levied against the collaborationist intellectuals who had previously been among the 1928 class whom Beckett had been appointed to teach at the ENS. Brasillach, editor of the collaborationist newspaper *Je suis partout*, was executed in 1945; Claude Jamet, from the same cohort, was sentenced to seven years of forced labour; Maurice Bardèche had various wranglings with the courts from 1944 onwards, and subsequently continued to play an important role in far-right movements.[41] Pelorson's superiors had very different fates. Lamirand was amnestied by virtue of the support he gave to the Resistance; Bonnard, lacking redeeming connections, was condemned to capital punishment *in absentia*, national degradation for life, confiscation of property and banishment from the national territory for ten years.[42]

[37] Sapiro, *La guerre des écrivains*, 458–9, 572–3.

[38] My thanks to Daniel Lee for elucidating this matter. Lee, *Pétain's Jewish Children*, 52 n30; Henry Rousso, 'L'Epuration en France: Une histoire inachevée', *Vingtième siècle, revue d'histoire* 33 (1992): 78–106; Simonin, *Le déshonneur*, 468–70.

[39] Maurice Girodias, *Une journée sur la terre, II: Les jardins d'Eros* (Paris: La Différence, 1990), 77–80.

[40] Giroud, 'Transition to Vichy', 229; Assouline, *Le fleuve Combelle*, 76, 98.

[41] De Montety, *Thierry Maulnier*, 241–60; Ghislaine Desbuissons, 'Maurice Bardèche, écrivain et théoricien fasciste?', *Revue d'histoire moderne et contemporaine* 37, no. 1 (1990): 148–159; Rubenstein, *What's Left*, 31, 137–63.

[42] Peter Novik, *L'Epuration française, 1944–1949* (Paris: Balland, 1985), 336, 338; Jean-Michel Barreau, 'Abel Bonnard, Ministre de l'Education Nationale sous Vichy, ou l'éducation impossible', *Revue d'histoire moderne et contemporaine* 43, no. 3 (1996): 466; Yves-Frédéric Jaffré, *Les tribunaux d'exception, 1940–1962* (Paris: Nouvelles Editions Latines, 1962), 344, 346.

Beckett only ever alluded to Pelorson's role in the Vichy administration in covert terms. His correspondence with Belmont evidences a warm friendship and is punctuated by attempts to assist him in getting his work published under his new identity. The earliest archived letters date from 1951, but they were clearly in contact prior to that point.[43] Beckett displayed the same magnanimity towards Francis Stuart, known to have worked for the Abwehr in Berlin during the war, who was aware of Beckett's Resistance decorations and was humbled by his response.[44] He treated Ezra Pound with the same clemency when the latter visited Paris in the 1960s and 1970s, and merely commented on how the aggressive temper that Pound had displayed in his youth, when he was a 'literary dictator', had subsided into silence.[45] Among common acquaintances, Beckett seems to have been the only one willing to engage with Pelorson-Belmont after the war; Raymond Queneau, asked to intercede in Pelorson's favour, refused to assist, on the grounds that the political choices made by his former friend could not be redeemed or forgotten.[46] Later, Maria Jolas spoke of Pelorson with great contempt after seeing footage of him calling a group of French boys to pay allegiance to Pétain's National Revolution in Marcel Ophüls's film *The Sorrow and the Pity*.[47]

Although Beckett's letters suggest scepticism towards self-righteous Resistance veterans, there are many signs that he perceived his own political identity through the lens of the French Resistance. The first text he wrote in French in 1945, an essay on Geer and Bram van Velde, was for *Cahiers d'Art* – a review that, throughout the war years, had remained one of the nevralgic centres of the Parisian intellectual resistance; its offices were turned into an underground publishing hideaway after its imposed closure by the Nazis.[48] It is also clear from the reviews to which Beckett submitted his novellas and poems, *Les Temps Modernes* and *Fontaine*, that he actively sought to align his French-language work with the newly established literature of the Resistance movement. *Les Temps Modernes*, which began to appear as a monthly in October 1945, under Sartre's directorship, brought together fiction, testimony, life writing and political essays; early issues were divided into sections entitled 'Vies' (Lives), 'Témoignages' (Testimonies), 'Exposés' (Reports) and 'Documents'. The issues published in 1945 and 1946 mostly focus on wartime losses, resistance and internment, and offer

[43] See Folder 17.15, Carlton Lake Collection of Samuel Beckett, HRHRC.
[44] *BR/RB*, 63. [45] Stern, *One Person*, 43. [46] Girodias, *Une journée*, 79.
[47] Giroud, 'Transition to Vichy', 223.
[48] Herbert R. Lottman, *The Left Bank: Writers, Artists, and Politics from the Popular Front to the Cold War* (Boston: Houghton Mifflin, 1982), 199.

contrasting accounts of Jewish and German lives and of the war damages caused by the Allied bombings in France and in Berlin, documenting the workings of the French militia, heroic evasions from the German prisoner of war camps and the process of selection in the Nazi camps, and addressing pressing political issues arising from the execution of Pierre Laval and currency devaluation. Some authors (particularly in the 'Lives' sections) remained anonymous, while others published their work under their initials. The texts marked as 'Lives' and 'Testimonies' were frequently published in instalments, with the final text simply labelled as 'Fin'. It is this specific taxonomy that Beckett emulated for his own 'Suite et Fin' when he submitted 'Suite' to *Les Temps Modernes* in June 1946. That same year, *Les Temps Modernes* became home to a self-styled literature of 'fragments' and published excerpts from David Rousset's *Les jours de notre mort* and poetry and essays by Jean Cayrol.[49] 'Suite' appeared alongside a report on the Nuremberg trials and an essay returning to a heated national debate: whether Marcel Petiot, the serial killer who had joined the Resistance and the FFI, should be considered a 'fake' Resistant or not. The November 1946 issue featuring Beckett's 'Poèmes 38–39' covered similar topics. This context informs Beckett's decision to address, in 'Suite', a subject that remained firmly in the margins of *Les Temps Modernes*: the unknown future that awaited survivors of deportation upon their return. To understand de Beauvoir's antagonism towards 'Suite' and her refusal to publish the second half of the text, one should look no further than its subject matter: the original text is shaped to respond to the canon of life-writing pioneered in *Les Temps Modernes*; it borrows many of its details from historical fact, but is clearly framed as an imagined historical testimony exposing the indifference of those unaffected by deportation.

Fontaine had a different political remit and had long been positioned at the literary vanguard of the Resistance. Its founding editor, Max-Pol Fouchet, was widely recognised for his wartime achievements: he was, for example, nominated as the representative of the anti-Nazi intellectual resistance in overseas French territories at the powerful Comité National des Ecrivains in November 1944.[50] *Fontaine* had, he asserted a few months later, acted as 'the review of refusal, in broad daylight', showing the way in the literary 'combat of cunning and intransigeance' belatedly joined by

[49] David Rousset, 'Les jours de notre mort (Premier fragment)', *Les Temps Modernes* 1, no. 6 (1946): 1015–44; 'Les jours de notre mort (Deuxième fragment)', *Les Temps Modernes* 1, no. 7 (1946): 1231–61; Jean Cayrol, 'Lectures', *Les Temps Modernes* 1, no. 9 (1946): 1604–12.

[50] 'Les lettres et les arts', *Ce soir*, 23 November 1944, 2.

others.[51] Throughout the war, the review – founded in 1939 in Algiers, the later capital of de Gaulle's Free French government – published important texts from occupied France alongside work by French writers in exile, using the Swiss post to transmit manuscripts. The rhetoric of universal resistance was invoked regularly: the issue published in the wake of de Gaulle's appeal to the Resistance in July 1940 claimed 'We are not vanquished', while issues published after the Allied landings in North Africa identified *Fontaine* as the review 'of the free world'.[52] In the eyes of the French shadow Ministry of Foreign Affairs, *Fontaine* became, in early 1942, the publication destined to represent no less than the virtues of the 'French spirit' to the world.[53] By that point, Fouchet's work extended to the airwaves: he presented regular broadcasts based on *Fontaine* publications on French radio and, occasionally, on the BBC. The review itself had a large international circulation and was allegedly disseminated on every continent; a clandestine digest was also printed in London on Bible paper, and was parachuted by the RAF into parts of the French *maquis*.[54]

From early on, *Fontaine* had a broader literary remit than other reviews and dedicated special issues to British and American literature in translation. Its international dimension became particularly pronounced in 1945, in issues featuring work by Eliot, Kafka, Lorca, Karl Jaspers, Elizabeth Bowen and William Faulkner. These factors may have influenced Beckett's decision, in late 1946, to submit 'L'Expulsé', his first sustained exploration of cultural and linguistic displacement, to *Fontaine*. Fouchet held Beckett in great esteem from this early point, and described him in 1949 as one of the greatest writers of his time.[55] These interlaced circumstances reveal how Beckett's French-language work became intuitively aligned with the profile of the Editions de Minuit long before the start of Lindon's editorship. By 1945, Beckett's future publisher also had a celebrated record among the publishers of anti-Nazi France; the editors Jean Bruller (known as Vercors) and Pierre de Lescure, keen to bolster their position, reasserted the ideals that had animated their underground wartime catalogue: to 'bear testimony to the world of the spiritual constancy of a France that has not resigned'.[56]

[51] Max-Pol Fouchet, 'Brève histoire de *Fontaine*', *Fontaine* 41 (1945): 170.
[52] Max-Pol Fouchet, 'Nous ne sommes pas vaincus', *Fontaine* 10 (1940): 49–51.
[53] M-P F, 'Le mouvement artistique et littéraire', *L'Echo d'Alger*, 18 February 1942, n.pag.
[54] Max-Pol Fouchet, *Un jour, je me souviens. Mémoire parlée* (Paris: Mercure de France, 1968), 130–1; Caroline Hoctan, *Panorama des revues à la Libération* (Paris: IMEC, 2006), 26.
[55] Simonin, *Les Editions de Minuit*, 292.
[56] Jacques Debû-Bridel, *Les Editions de Minuit: Historique et bibliographie* (Paris: Minuit, 1945), ii.

If Beckett felt that his work fitted with the editorial remit of *Fontaine* and *Les Temps Modernes*,[57] this is also because the texts he wrote in French in 1946 and 1947 engage, mostly in coded ways, with the vernacular and coordinates of the French Resistance. It is well known that the extreme conditions in the Nazi camps generated distinctive vocabularies, and a similar phenomenon was at play in Resistance movements, in a context in which secrecy, double meanings and coded allusion remained vital. Beckett was familiar with this vocabulary; a letter from 1957 to Boyle about *Waiting for Godot* alludes affectionately to a metaphysical 'Nono zone' – a translation of the Resistance slang for the *Zone Non-occupée* or 'free' zone controlled by the Vichy regime, known as 'la zone nono' (its inhabitants were sometimes designated as 'les Nonos').[58] As Serge Kastell has shown, the French and Belgian Resistance developed a remarkably varied, intelligent and humourous political idiom, predicated upon displacement, concealment and the hijacking of common cultural conventions.[59] 'To enter the fog' was to go underground; a 'coffin' designated a buried arms chest; 'up there' referred to Germany, notably as a place of deportation, or to the population living in the occupied zone. 'Hospital' and 'hotel' became synonymous with prison. 'National' meant 'of poor quality' and was associated with a wide range of ill-tasting substitutes for everyday foods and poor-quality shoes and garments provided by the system of rationing (coffee substitute became known, for example, as 'café national', 'jus national' or 'national'). To 'aryanise' Jewish children meant to secure false papers that ascertained their non-Jewish roots, in a mocking allusion to the procedures implemented by the Vichy regime, following the model of the Nuremberg laws. The 'promenade' could designate the daily promenades in prisons, but also summary execution. A 'valise' (suitcase) was a radio transmitter and receiver, and a 'valisard' (suitcase-carrier) someone involved in the black or grey market. An 'agent' referred to someone recruited, instructed, controlled and paid by an intelligence or security service to obtain information, or to a member of a Resistance network. An 'asile' or asylum designated the temporary accommodation or hiding places secured by Resistance cells, and 'auberge', or inn, the network who would provide shelter. 'Excursion' applied to armed action, and 'excursion touristique' (tourism excursion) qualified the industrial and railway sabotages executed by members of the SOE. The excursionist was, in this context, the person responsible for the sabotage. The connections between Beckett's French texts and this wartime

[57] *LSB3*, 636. [58] *LSB3*, 56.

[59] Serge Kastell, *Dictionnaire du français sous l'Occupation: Les mots de la Résistance, de la Collaboration et de la vie quotidienne, France-Belgique (1940–1945)* (Paris: Grancher, 2013).

idiom can be literal as well as symbolic, direct as well as indirect, and raise interesting questions about the ways in which the political unconscious of the work and the war's subterranean legacies can surface in the most banal terms and phrases. The lexicon of the Resistance, which became known through the abundant testimonial literature published after 1944, gives a very different dimension to the mundane details and props central to Beckett's post-war fiction and plays: to the characters' suitcases, promenades, excursions, inns and asylums, and to the obstacles put by mysterious 'agents' who commonly sport pseudo-military attire.

Beckett's manuscript drafts also relay other political idioms, and, in this regard, 'L'Absent' – the discarded title that features in the manuscript of *Malone meurt* dated November 1947–January 1948 – holds particular significance. Before 1944, 'les absents' designated, in the political rhetoric of Pétain and Vichy officials, the soldiers who had died in combat in 1939 and 1940 and the men requisitioned to work in Germany by the Service du Travail Obligatoire (STO). The political stakes were high: the figure of the prisoner of war fed a discourse of national redemption that rendered the loss of men to Germany as a preparatory stage for national rebirth, calling for a France purged from the weaknesses, temptations and perversion that had led to military defeat in 1940.[60] Various charitable societies, many of which had a military and fascistic bent, were created around prisoners of war and their families, and 8 October was named Day of the Absents across the occupied and free zones.

After the liberation of Paris, the meaning of the term shifted to qualify the unspeakable: the Minister for Prisoners, Deportees and Refugees, Henri Frenay, designated as 'absents' all of those who should have been on national territory, but were not.[61] A Week for the Absents was organised between 24 December 1944 and 1 January 1945 to commemorate the disappeared and those due to return. In parallel, concerted attempts were made to inform the public about the camps, particularly in Paris, where two large exhibitions were organised at the Grand Palais in quick succession. The first, entitled 'Le front des barbelés' (the barbed wire front) – which ran between December 1944 and February 1945, at a time when Beckett was living in Paris – was organised by Frenay's Ministry and inaugurated by de Gaulle, and dealt with the STO and life in the stalag. It was followed by a large-scale exhibition on German war crimes ('Crimes hitlériens'), which in the early days of planning had involved Edgar Morin, Marguerite

[60] Pieter Lagrou, *Mémoires patriotiques et occupation nazie. Résistants, requis et déportés en Europe occidentale, 1945–1965* (Paris: Complexe, 2003), 107–9.
[61] André Kaspi, *La libération de la France, juin 1944–janvier 1946* (Paris: Perrin, 1995), 263.

Duras and Dionys Mascolo, but in its final form eschewed many of the historical nuances that they had wanted to bring to it.[62] These exhibitions were also an attempt to respond to a prior event organised by the French Red Cross under Pétain's patronage, entitled 'L'âme des camps' (the soul of the camps), which dealt with the life of the French in German labour camps. In parallel, the Provisional Government headed by de Gaulle issued posters and guides to dispel myths about the camps disseminated in Nazi and Vichy propaganda. The evocative power of the word 'absent' made it an ideal literary referent, and the term was used twice as title for books published by the Editions de Minuit: in January 1948, for a collection of short stories by Robert Mathy (*Le Phénomène, suivi de Le Voyageur et l'Absent*), and in 1960, for a novel by Christian Nègre (*L'Absent*). References to departures under coercion and to the possibility of absents returning permeate many of Beckett's texts – including *Fragment de théâtre I* (or *Rough for Theatre I*), a play first written in French in 1956, riddled with allusions to military combat, rationing and the eventual return of those who might 'try and settle again', 'look for something they had left behind, or [. . .] someone they had left behind'.[63]

The texts by Beckett that allude most clearly to the murky period of political transition in France after 1944 are those that were most ruthlessly modified in translation. *Mercier et Camier*, in particular, was considerably abbreviated in the transfer from French to English. It seems that the 'French atmosphere' that Beckett aspired to retain when translating *En attendant Godot* originated in historical and political markers that, this time around, were politically too specific to enable translation.[64] The most marking feature of the French text is the sense that the characters have had dealings with the old and the new political regimes. In a passage later emended in the English text, Mercier and Camier come across a business-minded inn-keeper who speaks shreds of English and German in the same breath to attract them to his rooms, both 'cosy' and 'gemütlich'.[65] The German word is uttered in a lower tone of voice, out of precaution. Like many of the places along Mercier and Camier's journey, the inn has an uncertain status: the inn-keeper initially dismisses them, objecting that his property is known as 'la Maison Clappe et Fils', wholesale suppliers of fruit and vegetables; they respond by asking whether or not the building also serves as

[62] Laure Adler, *Marguerite Duras* (Paris: Gallimard, 1998), 236. [63] *CDW*, 229.

[64] Cited in Barney Rosset, 'Remembering Samuel Beckett', *Conjunctions* 53 (2009): 15. See also Andrew Gibson, 'Franco-Irish Beckett: *Mercier et Camier* in 1945–6', in *Samuel Beckett: Debts and Legacies*, ed. Peter Fifield and David Addyman (London: Bloomsbury, 2013), 19–38.

[65] SB, *Mercier et Camier* (Paris: Minuit, 1970), 66.

fish market, and are let in. These non-sequiturs find a new meaning in the light of the Resistance idiom that I have evoked. The inn-keeper, whom they call Monsieur Gall, is also designated as Monsieur Gast, the German word for visitor or guest. In the French text, he comes across as a skilled chameleon: his ominous interventions and comments recall, in equal measure, the culture of anti-Semitic denunciation that flourished under Nazi occupation, the culture of the pro-Nazi French militia and anti-Resistance surveillance, and the culture of denunciation that subsequently drove the anti-collaborationist purges. Likewise, *Eleutheria* presents a fawning bourgeois class who, sensing that the wind has turned, promptly changes allegiances or tries to conceal its political persuasions. Eventually, Dr Piouk comes to believe that he can work honourably for 'the commission', a term that brings to mind the Purges Commission or Commission d'Epuration that tried collaborators. This is wishful thinking: Piouk knows all too well the irredeemable differences between his generation ('Les vieux, les lâches, les salauds, les pourris, les foutus') and that of Victor ('les jeunes, les purs, les gars de l'avenir').[66] The latter category accords not simply with Gaullist sentiment, but with the lyrics of the pre-war socialist anthem 'La jeune garde'. The Glazier sings another hymn, 'La France est belle', a song used by Christian missionary organisations in French colonies in Africa. Its verses evoke the nation's immortality and the duty to take up arms in its defence.[67]

Every snippet of dialogue in *Eleutheria* is indexed to the three years of intense political turmoil that preceded the conception of the play. When asking Mrs Meck about her recently deceased husband, Mrs Piouk confuses 'le général' with 'le maréchal', the terms used to designate de Gaulle and Pétain in common parlance (34). Dr Piouk has similar difficulties when trying to forget the Third Republic, and he associates the defunct regime with the invocation of 'chancres' – a term commonly utilised by anti-Semitic organisations under the Vichy regime (112).[68] Other identities

[66] SB, *Eleutheria* (Paris: Minuit, 1995), 160. The English translation differentiates between '[o]ld people, cowards, bastards, the corrupt, the defeated' and 'the young, the pure, the young men of the future'. SB, *Eleutheria*, trans. Barbara Wright (London: Faber, 1996), 162.

[67] The song (by Jean-Jacques Porchat) features, for example, in *Chants de l'Alliance chrétienne universelle*, vol. 1 (Paris: Agence de l'Alliance Chrétienne Universelle, 1860), 52–3. The text was sometimes modified to advocate sacrifice to the French nation, notably in Cameroon; see Louis Ngongo, *Histoire des forces religieuses au Cameroun: De la Première Guerre Mondiale à l'Indépendance* (Paris: Karthala, 1982), 131.

[68] The Institut d'Etudes des Questions Juives published anti-Semitic pamphlets such as *Le chancre qui a rongé la France*, which presented 'national reconciliation' as depending on the 'definitive liquidation of Jewish questions'. *Le chancre qui a rongé la France* (Paris: Institut d'Etudes des Questions Juives, n.d.), n.pag.

are indexed to both old and new regimes: Joseph, who escorts Mrs Meck to Victor's room, works for a mysterious organisation that recalls the wartime French militia, and was formerly a wrestler employed by her deceased husband, a military hero who gave his last breath to the nation. The Glazier is, alternately, a political educator, a spy and an interrogator who is conversant with the workings of rogatory commissions and speaks in the service of 'le parti' (necessarily, in accordance with common usage, the French Communist Party). Like *Mercier et Camier*, *Eleutheria* flirts with the limits of social critique and exposes the workings of a double political economy, with its double standards and multiple compromises. Ironically, the figure who becomes the natural receptacle for what is left of the Vichy spirit is the Spectator. His anti-Semitism soon turns against the play's author, identified as 'Béquet' and as a 'a cross between a Jew from Greenland and a peasant from the Auvergne' ('juif groenlandais mâtiné d'Auvergnat'), blamed for delivering a nonsensical script (136).

Remembering the War

Aidan Higgins has described Beckett, in later years, as a man haunted by the events that had unfolded on his doorstep: 'Certain hidden factors of the Occupation festered in his mind, with the knowledge that an authentic torture chamber was operating in Paris at X. In those years he lived in the sixteenth *arrondissement* at Y, and would have passed it on his way to Z'.[69] The flow of news footage and press reports in late 1944 and 1945 articulated what many had known for years: for example, the existence of torture chambers in the Paris buildings that had housed the Gestapo and the Nazi administration. Mourning the deaths of Cavaillès, Péron, Robert Desnos and other friends, de Beauvoir later wrote of her 'shame at having survived' and her feeling of being 'thrust [. . .] back into horror' when reading the press reports on torture and mass graves.[70] It seems that Suzanne Déchevaux-Dumesnil experienced similar feelings; like Beckett, she had narrowly escaped torture and deportation, but unlike him, she was once interrogated by the Gestapo and saw danger looming very close indeed.[71] In 1948, to Duthuit, Beckett described Suzanne as 'inconsolable at living'.[72]

[69] Aidan Higgins, 'Introduction', in *Samuel Beckett: Photographs*, by John Minihan (London: Secker and Warburg, 1995), 16. Rue des Favorites is in the fifteenth *arrondissement*.

[70] De Beauvoir, *Force of Circumstance*, 32, 10. This section naming Péron and other friends was first published in *Les Temps Modernes* between April and June 1963. It attributes the historical responsibility for these deaths to Brasillach and other contributors to collaborationist newspapers.

[71] See SB's own account of this episode in Salisbury, 'Gloria SMH', 154.

[72] *LSB2*, 96, 98.

Duthuit probably confronted the same difficult mixture of relief and consternation: following a denunciation to the Gestapo, his wife Marguerite had been tortured and imprisoned, and had miraculously escaped deportation to Ravensbrück. In his letters, Beckett's own depictions of writing as an activity shift significantly. Notably, in 1949, he writes to Duthuit that he is 'no longer capable of writing *about*'.[73] His statement takes on a new historical weight when envisaged alongside Blanchot's parallel decision to withdraw the word 'récit' or story from his writings. 'Un récit? Non, pas de récit, plus jamais', is the memorable ending of *La folie du jour* (1947–1949).[74]

Beckett's period of activity in Gloria SMH, which he joined through Péron, lasted from 1 September 1941 until 16 August 1942, when the cell was denounced to the Gestapo. This is a familiar story, but it continues to yield new mysteries and insights.[75] Within the cell, '[e]verybody knew everybody', as Beckett later put it,[76] and the common precautions to conceal identities and preserve secret information were not taken in many circumstances. Denunciation was lethal. Twelve members of Gloria SMH were shot, and a further ninety were deported to Ravensbrück, Mauthausen and Buchenwald, after periods of incarceration in the Fresnes and Romainville prisons for many.[77] The sinister fate that would have awaited the Becketts, had they been caught, can be inferred from the memoirs of Anise Postel-Vinay (née Girard), whose role in Gloria SMH involved collecting first-hand information on German military troops, sky-borne infrastructure in and around Paris and, occasionally, the impact of the British bombings in Normandy.[78] Postel-Vinay would bring this information to Beckett's contact, Jimmy le Grec, for transmission to Beckett, whom Postel-Vinay remembers as the 'comrade' who worked in the shadows, admired for his command of translation. When Postel-Vinay was arrested on 15 August 1942, she was taken to the Paris headquarters of the Sipo-SD and interrogated; thereafter, she spent a year in solitary confinement, first at the Santé

[73] *LSB2*, 137, 141.

[74] 'A story? No. No stories, never again'. Maurice Blanchot, *La folie du jour* (Paris: Gallimard, 2002), 30. See Sarah Kofman, *Smothered Words*, trans. Madeleine Dobie (Evanston: Northwestern University Press, 1998), 14–15.

[75] Notably, Tillion's memoir identifies Gilbert T., Alesch's assistant, as the key denunciator and comments on Alesch's trial between 1945 and 1948. Germaine Tillion, *Fragments de vie*, ed. Tzvetan Todorov (Paris: Seuil, 2009), 168–73.

[76] Cited in *BR/RB*, 80.

[77] David Murphy, '"I Was Terribly Frightened at Times": Irish Men and Women in the French Resistance and F Section of SOE, 1940–5', in *Franco-Irish Military Connections, 1590–1945*, ed. Nathalie Genet-Rouffiac and David Murphy (Dublin: Four Courts, 2009), 273.

[78] Alain Navarro, *1945: Le retour des absents* (Paris: Stock, 2015), 120–4; Anise Postel-Vinay, with Laure Adler, *Vivre* (Paris: Grasset and Fasquelle, 2015), 19–47.

prison, where she was temporarily marked off for the firing squad, then at the Fresnes prison. Subsequently, she was sent to the Fort de Romainville, which served as a transit camp, then to a prison in Aix-la-Chapelle and eventually to Ravensbrück, where she was classified like Germaine Tillion and others as 'Nacht und Nebel', as a special political prisoner doomed to vanish without a trace. In Ravensbrück, Postel-Vinay befriended Tillion and Geneviève de Gaulle-Anthonioz, and she later contributed important documents to Tillion's studies of the Nazi camp system. She is the only surviving member of Gloria SMH to have published a testimony of imprisonment and deportation.

The years that Samuel and Suzanne Beckett spent 'on the run' and in hiding were never exempt from danger, and they continued to be at the mercy of denunciations. Literary activity was often synonymous with political activity, at least in the eyes of the Nazi and Vichy administrations, which looked upon literary work and artistic aspirations with utmost seriousness. If uncovered, Beckett's associations with Cunard and with Surrealism would have ignited suspicion, even in the context of a benign interrogation by the local police. The Surrealists were under watch, as Breton soon discovered, although in the eyes of Vichy inspectors he did not qualify as a Communist but was merely a 'parlor anarchist'.[79] Several friends from the Surrealist circle of the 1920s and 1930s – those of Jewish ancestry, those classified as 'enemy aliens' – were interned in French and Nazi camps. Others were deported for acts of resistance or were imprisoned for insubordination. Max Ernst and Hans Bellmer were interned in the Camp des Milles in the South of France; Desnos, deported for acts of resistance, died after his liberation from the Terezin concentration camp; Max Jacob died in Drancy, and Freundlich died in Majdanek. Their tragic fates shed light on the political trauma and loss experienced by those who survived the war unscathed. Beckett, with his characteristic indirection and elusiveness, was one of the many in mourning, and one of the many who perceived a continuity between their wartime responses to Nazi occupation and the principles they defended as artists.

The precariousness of Beckett's own position in occupied France should not be underestimated. On a prosaic level, 'Samuel' and 'Beckett' were dangerous names to bear at a time when overzealous Nazi sympathisers were at work at all levels of the police and administration, on the lookout for names indicating possible Jewishness and foreignness. In many circumstances, evidence that one's mother tongue was English would have been

[79] Polizzotti, *Revolution of the Mind*, 492–3.

inherently incriminating; few would have been aware of, or concerned about, the differences between British accents and Irish accents north and south of the border. Numerous British citizens were sent to internment camps in France, and round-ups against French Jews and foreigners were common (late August 1942 was a particularly dangerous time, marked by mass round-ups targeting foreign Jews in the Free Zone). Freedom and survival involved a great deal of luck and probably some minor miracles: Beckett was forgetful, gave his real name when doing so posed serious risks, grew a moustache that owed something to the style embraced by British military officers, and let himself be identified as a citizen of 'Dublin, England' in the Roussillon register of foreign residents.[80] Other anecdotes, however, suggest that he had faith in his own flair and capacity to identify potential denunciators; he is reported to have said, for example, 'There were always those whom no one took seriously, neither the *résistants* nor the Gestapo. Sartre seemed to many people to be among these'.[81]

In Beckett scholarship, Beckett's decision to join Gloria SMH is commonly perceived as his clearest, most powerful and enduring political act and, occasionally, as evidence of his alignment with the international Left.[82] These questions deserve to be examined closely: such critical consensus does not account for the political make-up of Resistance movements, which encompassed the whole spectrum of political allegiances from the Far Right to the Far Left, and reflected a wide range of positions on French national sovereignty, republicanism and German occupation. It is clear that Beckett himself was driven by an ideal of service to the military front: as early as April 1939, he affirmed that he would put himself 'at the disposition' of France, should a war break out, and he '[f]led back to France' from Greystones the day after the declaration of war.[83] During the 'phoney war', he remained keen to serve in the French army, first in an undefined capacity, then as ambulance driver,[84] and he later worked for the Irish Red Cross in Saint-Lô, in an area devastated by successive German and Allied bombings. Accordingly, his contributions to British military intelligence and the SOE are situated in the grey zone between patriotic and anti-fascist resistance. Much has been said, also, about the singularity of Beckett's experience as an Irish citizen fighting in a guerrilla war in which his native

[80] Lois Gordon, *The World of Samuel Beckett, 1906–1946* (New Haven: Yale University Press, 1996), 172; *DF*, 321, 317, 337.

[81] Cited in Deirdre Bair, *Simone de Beauvoir: A Biography* (London: Jonathan Cape, 1990), 254.

[82] Eagleton, 'Political Beckett?', 69.

[83] *LSB1*, 656; *LSB4*, 427.

[84] *LSB1*, 669–70, 679. Alfred Péron served in the British Field Ambulance in 1939.

country had no direct political stakes. Yet his situation was far from isolated: many foreign residents were involved in the French Resistance, and numerous other Irish citizens played an important role in intelligence gathering, evasion networks, the Free French forces and the SOE, as David Murphy has shown. The idea of a unified Resistance that provides an explicit or implicit background to many accounts of Beckett's decision to serve in Gloria SMH should be approached with caution, for it is one of many Gaullist myths forged in the context of emerging Cold War tensions, when de Gaulle became increasingly keen to counter the ideological advances of the French Communist Party.[85] During the war, only the Communist Resistance and the *maquis*, mostly aligned with the Left, had a clear ideological unity.[86] When Beckett joined Gloria SMH, the tensions between the different strands of the Resistance were particularly fierce, not least because the Communist Resistance aspired to create a 'government for national liberation', a plan that de Gaulle opposed.[87] Beyond the early Communist cells, which employed the same combat tactics, each group and, to some degree, each member was fighting a different war, for different political reasons. This was certainly true of the cells that had preceded Gloria SMH; for example, the Musée de L'Homme group, to which Tillion (a staunch Gaullist from the early days) belonged, and in which all political currents were represented except communism.[88] Everything suggests that Gloria SMH was configured in the same way.

In practice, many contributed to the work of different cells: Péron, for example, is said to have been affiliated with the Resistance groups of the Musée de l'Homme and Lycée Buffon, and with Etoile, the Combat network and Gloria SMH.[89] Like Beckett, he had no faith in Sartre as a potential resistant; nonetheless, he attended meetings of Socialisme et Liberté – Sartre's resistance group, formed primarily for *normaliens*, which by all accounts was deeply chaotic and ineffectual. At these meetings Péron made audacious proposals, formulating in 1941, for example, a plan to attack the Renault factories of Boulogne-Billancourt – the factories, which manufactured tanks for the Wehrmacht, were bombed by the RAF in March

[85] See Henry Rousso, *The Vichy Syndrome: History and Memory in France since 1944*, trans. Arthur Goldhammer (Cambridge, MA: Harvard University Press, 1991), 10–11, 15–20, 27–32.

[86] Henri Michel and Boris Mirkine-Guetzévitch, *Les idées politiques et sociales de la Résistance: Documents clandestins (1940–1944)* (Paris: PUF, 1954).

[87] Stéphane Courtois, *Le PCF dans la guerre: De Gaulle, la Résistance, Staline* . . . (Paris: Ramsay, 1980), 233–5. The Communist and non-Communist strands of the Resistance merged between November 1942 and February 1943.

[88] Taos Aït Si Slimane, interview of Germaine Tillion, www.fabriquedesens.net/A-voix-nue-avec-Germaine-Tillion.

[89] Gordon, *The World of Samuel Beckett*, 155; Bair, *Simone de Beauvoir*, 254; *Samuel Beckett: An Exhibition Held at Reading University Library*, ed. James Knowlson (London: Turret Books, 1971), 43.

1942, in a spectacular raid that Beckett watched from his flat.[90] Beckett himself owed much to the solidarities between resistance movements: he attributed his successful escape in 1942 to some of Suzanne's Communist friends, who hid them in Paris while they procured forged papers.[91] Their identity remains unknown, but it is likely that Suzanne had these privileged contacts with the Communist Resistance because she was born in Argenteuil, a working-class town outside Paris where the Communist Party had a very large following.

Through his own activities, Beckett abided by this general principle of solidarity and participated in different types of resistance action, sometimes informally. The editors of the *Letters*, for example, relate how he used his Irish passport to deliver documents and money on behalf of André Salzman, one of Suzanne's acquaintances, who secured funds for clandestine publications.[92] Elsewhere, rumours have circulated about his possible involvement in the Musée de L'Homme cell in late 1940 and the help he gave to Jewish friends, but these rumours cannot be corroborated.[93] Jean Rouaud also recounts an interesting anecdote relayed by Roger Louis, chief of the Resistance cell in Roussillon. The group, which met in the café that Beckett also frequented, noticed Beckett listening to their discussions, exactly as an informer would do, and pondered a radical response. One day, Beckett offered his services to Louis, explaining that, as an Irish citizen, he held privileges that enabled him to transmit messages. Louis, still persuaded that Beckett was dangerous, pretended not to understand, but from this point plans to eliminate Beckett were dropped.[94] The rest – Beckett helping the Roussillon *maquis*, joining the FFI in May 1944 and marching in the liberation parades – is part of a well-charted history, although biographical accounts tend to differ on the details. Joining the FFI was an important step, not least because it gave Beckett a different status. The FFI, created by de Gaulle in February 1944 to federate the armed wings of the Resistance, recruited extensively from the *maquis* but had a different remit and organisation.[95] At the start of June 1944, a few weeks after Beckett joined, the FFI were formally integrated into the French army and were subject to the same legal provisions and obligations.[96]

[90] Sirinelli, *Sartre et Aron*, 171; Huguette Bouchardeau, *Simone de Beauvoir* (Paris: Flammarion, 2007), 113; Cohen-Solal, *Sartre: A Life*, 167, 159–77; Patrick Bowles, 'How to Fail: Notes on Talks with Samuel Beckett', *PN Review* 20, no. 4 (1993): 27–8.

[91] *BR/RB*, 80. [92] *LSB2*, xvi.

[93] Assouline, 'Enquête sur un écrivain secret', 28; Curtis, 'Beckett Remembered', 25.

[94] Jean Rouaud, *Un peu la guerre* (Paris: Grasset, 2014), 200–4.

[95] Brian Crozier, *De Gaulle: The Warrior* (London: Eyre Methuen, 1973), 299–300.

[96] 'Ordonnance du 9 juin 1944 fixant le statut des Forces Françaises de l'Intérieur', in Charles de Gaulle, *Mémoires de guerre: L'unité, 1942–1944* (Paris: Plon, 1956), 694.

Beckett's statements about the war are striking, not for what they relate, but for the manner in which they eschew historical complications and separate the personal from the political. In 1977, he explained to Richard Stern that he had decided to join the Resistance '[w]hen the business with the Jews started in '41 or '42. The yellow star and everything. It wasn't politics. Just a human thing. I couldn't stay detached from that'.[97] To John Kobler, in 1964, he declared that he was 'so outraged by the Nazis, particularly by their treatment of the Jews, that [he] could not remain inactive'.[98] To Alan Simpson, Beckett portrayed his activities in the French Resistance as a 'fight [. . .] against the Germans, who were making life hell for my friends'.[99] To Alec Reid, a few years later, he suggested that anger spurred him to take action when seeing Jews obliged by the Nazis to wear the Star of David and witnessing the retaliatory execution of hostages.[100] In conversations with Mel Gussow during the 1980s, he recalled his 'fury at the treatment of Jews, who had to "crawl away", with stars of David affixed to their clothes'.[101] Echoing reports by Mira Avrech and Rosette Lamont, Richard Ellmann recalled Beckett 'mourn[ing] the killing of Jewish friends by the Nazis as if it had happened yesterday'.[102] His correspondence does not offer such insights and rarely evokes wartime events; 'hell' and 'hellish' appear to be the only words that Beckett was willing to commit to writing when thinking about the Drancy camp or the Warsaw ghetto.[103]

Yet the inventory of his library confirms that he continued to think about the war's legacies.[104] The books he owned include Charles Duff's *A New Handbook on Hanging*, a 1956 treatise against the British death penalty that also discusses the Nazi system of concentration and extermination camps, and François Maspero's fictionalised memoir *Le sourire du chat*, which describes resistance action, military struggle and the liberation of France. Further archive records show that, in September 1959, he purchased from the Editions de Minuit a copy of Wiesel's *La Nuit* (*Night*), a testimony whose initial Yiddish version had remained largely unnoticed, and which became internationally celebrated following its republication in abbreviated form by Lindon and its English translation.[105] There are many intersections between Beckett's writings and artistic reflections and the

97 Stern, *One Person and Another*, 43. 98 *SB*, 308.
99 Alan Simpson, *Beckett and Behan, and a Theatre in Dublin* (London: Routledge and Kegan Paul, 1962), 64–5.
100 Reid, *All I Can Manage*, 13–14. 101 Gussow, *Conversations*, 62.
102 Richard Ellmann, 'Samuel Beckett: Nayman of Noland', in *Four Dubliners: Wilde, Yeats, Joyce and Beckett* (London: Penguin and Sphere Books, 1988), 81–2.
103 *LSB4*, 639, 689. 104 See Van Hulle and Nixon, *Beckett's Library*, 268, 278.
105 'Correspondence 1958–1959, Droits étrangers', Fonds Beckett, IMEC.

memory of Nazi occupation, and some take peculiar forms – through Resnais, for example. Beckett admired his 1956 film *Nuit et brouillard* (*Night and Fog*),[106] the celebrated documentary scripted and narrated by Cayrol, which begins by pointing out that, at the end of every quiet country road and in the recesses of every landscape, there is a concentration camp. Resnais was approached in 1958 to undertake the film adaptation of *Tous ceux qui tombent* – one of many abandoned projects.[107] The film was eventually shot by Michel Mitrani in 1963 for the ORTF, the French television and broadcasting service; eleven years later, Mitrani made a film about Nazi occupation and the Vel d'Hiv round-up, *Les Guichets du Louvre* (*Black Thursday*).

It is likely that, for Beckett, personal memories took on added significance over time, as friends and acquaintances began to write about deportation, death and survival. In 1945, Leventhal published articles about anti-Semitism, negationism and the problems faced by homeless and stateless survivors of the Nazi camps.[108] The Beckett scholar Raymond Federman, whom Beckett befriended, had escaped the Vel d'Hiv round-up in 1942 and published a celebrated memoir in 1979.[109] Other close friends included the painter Avigdor Arikha, who spoke frequently about his time in the Jewish ghetto of Mogilev-Podolsk in Transnistria, which also functioned as a labour camp under German control, and about the long and lethal marches that he and his family were forced to join.[110] It was at the camp that he began to draw, and he drew beatings, corpses and gravediggers' tools. Beckett's later tribute to Arikha is attuned to these circumstances and reads as a celebration of the faculty of bearing testimony: this brief text from 1966 invokes the capacity of Arikha's paintings to show 'the marks of what it is to be and be in face of'.[111] Beckett also took a deep interest in Celan's poetry ('beyond him', he said), and wondered whether Celan would, in everyday life, manifest his sorrow.[112] Curiously, in the wake of a missed encounter that Adorno had sought to arrange in Paris, Celan described Beckett as 'probably the only man here [he] could have an understanding with'.[113]

[106] *LSB3*, 246. [107] *NABS*, 45.

[108] A. J. Leventhal, 'The Future of the Jews', *IT*, 8 September 1945, 2; 'What It Means to Be a Jew', 207–16.

[109] Raymond Federman, *The Voice in the Closet/La Voix dans le cabinet de débarras* (Madison, WI: Coda Press, 1979).

[110] Arikha, *Major/Minor*, 79–91, 97–100, 134–6, 143–5, 168–74. [111] *D*, 152.

[112] Bernold, *L'Amitié de Beckett*, 58 n15.

[113] Adorno, *Notes sur Beckett*, 152; John Felstiner, *Paul Celan: Poet, Survivor, Jew* (New Haven: Yale University Press, 1995), 282.

During the war, Beckett's everyday life routinely exposed him to the realities of collaboration. Yet his declarations are strangely removed from historical fact, and unaligned with other reported discussions revealing his excellent memory for the tiniest of details. His accounts of joining Gloria SMH, in particular, seem more closely indexed to the chronology of anti-Jewish persecution in Germany, where the yellow star was introduced in September 1941. In France, the yellow star was imposed in June 1942, shortly before Beckett's cell was dismantled. Similar slippages permeate his last conversations with Knowlson in 1989. When discussing his decision to join the Resistance, Beckett recalled the moment when an unspecified 'they' 'round[ed] up all the Jews, including all their children, gathering them in the Parc des Princes ready to send them off to extermination camps'.[114] This scene does not resemble the successive roundups of 1941, but relates more closely to the notorious round-up of July 1942 at the Vel d'Hiv stadium, which was orchestrated by the Paris police.

The many elisions in Beckett's statements about the war revolve around difficult historical questions, relating to the zeal with which the French administration implemented and sometimes anticipated the orders of the German occupation forces, organising mass round-ups of Jewish and Roma residents and orchestrating their detention in camps across the country. Michael Marrus and Robert Paxton have shown that the anti-Semitic Vichy laws, in October 1940 and thereafter, went further than German ordinances and prepared the ground for the rapidity and efficiency with which the French administration complied with Nazi demands and enforced the deportation of foreign Jews in 1941 and French Jews in 1942.[115] It may well be that Beckett was only too aware of these uncomfortable facts to point to them, and it is certain that many of his generation in France were also haunted by non-specific and distorted memories of the war. Of course, these questions would have been of minor interest to many of Beckett's interlocutors, who were probably more receptive to a simplified version of Hitlerism that eschewed the problem of collaboration. Most importantly, Beckett's retrospective declarations about his political motives respond to their immediate context and resonate with the immensely fraught debates about anti-Semitism, the Holocaust and the French Resistance that emerged in the 1960s, the decade during which his acquaintances and interviewers frequently asked him to talk about his war experiences.

[114] *BR/RB*, 79.

[115] See Michael R. Marrus and Robert O. Paxton, *Vichy France and the Jews* (New York: Basic Books, 1981), 5, 12–13, 224–8.

It is during the 1960s that the Jewish Holocaust began to be widely discussed and recognised, and that the Gaullist myth of a resistant France – which Beckett obviously resented – ceased to be consensual, due to the immense political pressures imposed upon this myth by the Algerian War of Independence.[116]

It is well known that compassionate references to the Holocaust surface frequently in Beckett's texts of the 1940s and 1950s, and I discuss some of these resonances and their political contexts in what follows. At this juncture, however, it is important to emphasise that this facet of Beckett's writing ran against the dominant tide in the war's aftermath: the relation between resistance action, anti-Semitic persecution and the legacy of the Vichy regime was then fraught with immense tension. With the liberation of France came a new body of legislation that annulled any precedent set by the Vichy regime and declared all its constitutional and legislative acts 'null and of null effect'.[117] Deportation and repatriation were inscribed into a new military history of resistance and victory: de Gaulle's Provisional Government presented deportation as the sole realm of a heroic Resistance, using a rhetoric that obscured the political, ethnic and religious dimensions of the Holocaust. Upon their return in 1945, the 'racial prisoners' or 'racial deportees' – the terms used to designate Jewish survivors of the Nazi camps – were met with far greater unease than the 'political prisoners' or 'political deportees', deported for acts of resistance. The men drafted in the German factories and labour camps by the compulsory STO – known as the 'work deportees' or the 'malgré-nous' (despite-ourselves) – also had an awkward status.[118] The voices that were heard were not theirs: the majority of testimonies about the Nazi camps published in France between 1945 and 1947 were by Resistance members deported for anti-Nazi activities, not by Jewish men and women.[119] Thereafter, public interest dwindled and the flow of information gradually ran dry.[120] The key documents and films from this period reflect this phenomenon of occultation; Resnais's *Nuit et brouillard*, for example, makes one marginal reference to the deportation of the Jews, and mentions neither genocide nor collaboration. The

[116] On these shifts, see Jean-Michel Chaumont, *La concurrence des victimes: Génocide, identité, reconnaissance*, revised ed. (Paris: La Découverte, 2010), 93–125.

[117] 'Ordonnance du 9 août 1944 relative au rétablissement de la légalité républicaine sur le territoire continental', *JORF*, 9 August 1944, 7.

[118] Navarro, *1945*, 18, 28.

[119] See Annette Wieviorka, 'Penser Auschwitz: Indicible ou Inaudible? La déportation: Premier récits (1944–1947)', *Pardès* 9–10 (1989): 23–59; Jean-Pierre Vittori and Irène Michine, eds., *Le grand livre des témoins* (Paris: L'Atelier and Editions Ouvrières, 2005), 349–50.

[120] Kaspi, *La libération*, 269–72.

catalogue of the Editions de Minuit after 1944 also reflects this consensus, and includes books examining the historical and legal circumstances that shaped the 1940 armistice, texts by the French Surrealists and writers banned by the Nazis – and, after 1945, Jean Moulin's journal *Premier combat*, publications by the Conseil National de la Résistance and re-editions of wartime writings by Vercors. Under Lindon's later editorship, the Editions de Minuit published documents related to the post-war purges, some of which were connected to the work of his father Raymond Lindon, a magistrate who played an important part in the trials of high-profile collaborationists and industry magnates.

For Jewish survivors of the Nazi camps, the return to France was shaped by silence, memories of 'contempt', 'permanent humiliation' and 'shame', to borrow from the words of Elie Wiesel and Simone Veil – not to mention the problem of spoliation.[121] Jewish survivors, as Wiesel and Veil later made clear, were considered as victims rather than heroes, and their voices were given minimal representation in a public space dominated by the 'political deportees' of the Resistance, portrayed in Gaullist rhetoric as saviours of the nation. Sartre briefly drew attention to this silence in *Réflexions sur la question juive* in 1954, but the occultation of Jewish victims otherwise ignited little protest at that point.[122] These tensions were manifested on many levels. The Fédération Nationale des Déportés et Internés de la Résistance, of Gaullist persuasion, prided itself in accepting only former Resistance members designated as 'political deportees'. The Fédération Nationale des Déportés et Internés Résistants et Patriotes, of Communist persuasion, accepted all former deportees but required 'racial deportees' to give proof of deportation.[123] There is no sign that Beckett joined any of the organisations gathering Resistance veterans, and it is certainly no coincidence that he should have so persistently dismissed his wartime activities as 'boy scout stuff' and as something that did not warrant particular pride. The comparison with the scouts is not without historical resonance: those who rallied the section of the Jewish *maquis* issued from the Jewish scouts – the strand of the *maquis* that Lindon had joined at the age of eighteen – made exactly the same comparison.[124] In any case, Beckett's reported declarations about the war rarely stretch beyond brief evocations of the Resistance, especially when he was invited to make broader comments. In response to a parallel drawn between *Waiting for Godot* and the Auschwitz

[121] Chaumont, *La concurrence*, 25–90.
[122] Jean-Paul Sartre, *Réflexions sur la question juive* [1954] (Paris: Gallimard, 2005), 77–8.
[123] Chaumont, *La concurrence*, 37–9.
[124] Lucien Lazare, interview with Julie Clarini, 'Résister toujours', *Le Monde*, 10 July 2015, 10.

memorial museum, for example, he evoked Péron's death after his release from an unspecified camp, without mentioning Mauthausen, and issued a verdict that evaded further discussion of their clandestine work: 'We were amateurs, and therefore naïve, vulnerable'.[125] This is one of many moments at which his conflicted recollections are clearly sutured to a French cultural memory marked by various forms of silence, corrosion, suspicion, imposture and fracture.[126]

There is no doubt that Beckett's activity in Gloria SMH is indexed to a clear political chronology and rooted in the summer of 1941, which marked the beginning of a dramatic period that aimed to crush the Communist Resistance and saw many retaliatory executions in response to a wave of sabotages and shootings of German soldiers by Communist cells in Paris. The moment at which Beckett joined Gloria SMH also coincides with the acceleration of round-ups within the occupied zone. These developments began in Paris in May 1941, when those identified as foreign and stateless Jews received letters summoning them to their local police stations and were taken by train to the camps of Pithiviers and Beaune-la-Rolande. Soon after came the mass internment of Polish and foreign Jews, and, in 1942, the mass round-ups and deportations, first from the occupied zone and then from the unoccupied zone, to Nazi camps in Germany and Poland. Some aspects of the operations were coordinated by the Gestapo and the SS; others were handled by the French police and *gendarmerie*. In August 1941, during a five-day Gestapo round-up in Paris, Parisian Jews between fourteen and seventy-two years old who featured in a 1940 census were sent to the Drancy camp.[127] The camp was, at the time, under the joint responsibility of the SS, the German military commandment for the occupied zone, the French *gendarmerie*, the Paris police headquarters and the *préfecture* for the Seine *département*. It remained under joint command until May 1943, when the SS took over the administration of the camp, retaining the services of the *gendarmerie*. Paul Léon, Joyce's Jewish collaborator, was arrested on the second day of the round-up, on 21 August 1941. Beckett met Léon on the street the previous day, when police blockades were erected in the 11th *arrondissement*, and urged him to leave Paris immediately (Léon explained that he was unable to do so: his son was taking the baccalaureate examination the following day). The Léons were old acquaintances from the

[125] Lamont, 'Samuel Beckett's Wandering Jew', 43, 37.

[126] See Pierre Laborie, *Le chagrin et le venin: La France sous l'Occupation, mémoire et idées reçues* (Paris: Bayard, 2011).

[127] Annette Wieviorka and Michel Laffitte, *A l'intérieur du camp de Drancy* (Paris: Perrin, 2012), 21–3, 27–32, 218–19.

Joyce circle, and Beckett had become closer to them in occupied Paris; the memoir that Lucie Léon published shortly after the war relates a friendship that revolved mostly around the sharing of food, of which there was certainly little.[128] For Knowlson, Léon's arrest was the turning point that spurred Beckett to join the Resistance.[129]

The situation was complicated. To begin with, Paul Léon's arrest was far from unexpected: this much is clear from Lucie Léon's later application for American citizenship, which gives an account that differs considerably from her exchange with Knowlson and from the memoir familiar to Joyce scholars. Furthermore, the statement she submitted to the American Congress indicates that she found herself in great danger after narrowly escaping arrest in mid-July 1941 (one of Paul Léon's former pupils, who was in the Resistance, had warned her that her name featured on a list of arrests and deportations); she had to leave the family home immediately and moved from one precarious address to another for eight months.[130] Prior to that, there had been innumerable home visits from the Gestapo and interrogations at the Gestapo headquarters, during which the couple were accused of being spies, and she was accused of 'hiding and aiding British paratroopers'. Long after Paul Léon's arrest, Gestapo officers returned to search their flat, looking for valuable first editions of Joyce's works.

As early as 1940, Paul Léon had anticipated the persecutions to come: to save their belongings, he handed ownership of their flat over to French friends.[131] From the overcrowded Drancy camp, beset by an acute penury of food and epidemics, he would transmit to his wife clandestine letters evoking Joyce, Beckett and his own work plans, and wishing that he could work on *Ulysses* with Beckett.[132] Beckett would add his bread and cigarette rations to the packages that Lucie Léon prepared for her husband.[133] To maintain contact, she joined the Service of Civil Internees of the Red Cross the day after his arrest and was affected to Drancy, where the sanitary situation was periodically under watch. In December, Léon and eight other prominent detainees were transferred from Drancy to the Royallieu camp in Compiègne; he was subsequently deported to Auschwitz, where he was

[128] Lucie Noel, *James Joyce and Paul L. Léon: The Story of a Friendship* (New York: Gotham Book Mart, 1950), 31.

[129] *DF*, 304.

[130] 'Relief of Elizabeth Lucie Léon (also known as Lucie Noel). March 4, 1959. Committed to the Committee of the Whole House and Ordered to be Printed', *US Congressional Series Set*, 86th Cong., 1st sess., vol. 8, No. 12165, H. Rpt. 175, 6–7. Available evidence suggests that Lucie Léon was of Russian Orthodox faith.

[131] Ibid., 7. [132] Noel, *James Joyce and Paul L. Léon*, 48–9. [133] *DF*, 304.

shot.[134] Lucie followed him to the Royallieu camp with other relief staff: riding on the Red Cross truck 'almost daily', she would distribute food packages to men 'dying of starvation, cold and malnutrition', soon smuggling letters, money and more food.[135] She and her son were allowed to say goodbye: they witnessed Paul Léon's deportation to Silesia – 'a death march with all typical trimmings', as she later described it.[136] As a 'stateless' Russian-born widow, with a brother in the Resistance who was hunted by the Gestapo, Lucie Léon was immensely vulnerable; she subsequently found refuge in Monaco, where she lived in hiding until the American landings. Thereafter, she served as interpreter for the American army in various locations across liberated France. In May 1945, she returned to her flat in Paris, and worked under oath for the War Crimes Commission formed by the Allied governments, 'allotting numbers to the criminals all day long' in the Central Registry of War Criminals and Security Suspects.[137] Beckett, who never divulged personal information about friends and acquaintances, only alluded to Paul Léon's life as a Jew in occupied Paris in the vaguest terms. In later conversations, he mentioned only that Léon had 'died in transit. In that place on the edge of Paris, where his wife visited him. No, it was en route to Auschwitz or one of those places'.[138]

This run of events raises the question of what Beckett knew of the French and Nazi camps. Gloria SMH was set up to deal with naval and maritime intelligence and, occasionally, military evasions, and had no direct involvement with other Resistance groups working to hide and help Jewish men, women and children. When discussing Beckett's historical awareness, scholars have stressed his probable familiarity with Georges Loustanau-Lacau's two war memoirs, which describe the two years he spent in Mauthausen, the efforts that he and others deployed to protect Péron from tasks that could have proved lethal, and Péron's death from starvation and exhaustion after his release from Mauthausen. Loustanau-Lacau's testimonies, however, make for an awkward read and rank among the most troubling and controversial documents of the period: he had been a soldier, an aide of Pétain, and was associated with the Cagoule, a far-right armed group. His second autobiography relates that he had been involved in political plots at such a high level in the Vichy administration that he was taken to Vienna's main prison to be interrogated during his internment in Mauthausen.[139] Everything separated Loustanau-Lacau from Péron, and it

[134] Wieviorka and Laffitte, *Drancy*, 88; Noel, *James Joyce and Paul L. Léon*, 41, 60–1.
[135] 'Relief of Elizabeth Lucie Léon', 6. [136] Ibid. [137] Ibid., 7.
[138] Stern, *One Person*, 46–7.
[139] Georges Loustanau-Lacau, *Mémoires d'un Français rebelle* (Paris: Robert Laffont, 1948), 323–5.

seems that the two men only knew each other by virtue of the ways in which nationality often shaped solidarity in the Nazi camps.[140]

Other testimonies give a better sense of what was common knowledge among members of the Resistance who had a profile similar to Beckett's. In her first testimony about Ravensbrück, published in December 1946, Tillion gave a detailed account of what she knew – and, in her view, anyone with an interest in politics would have known – about Nazi practices in 1942. Tillion, a former member of the pioneering Musée de l'Homme cell, had continued her resistance activities and was arrested after the denunciations that dismantled Gloria SMH. In 1942, she knew that, in Germany, 'those who were mad, those whom they call the mentally retarded, the elderly who are supposed to be incurable, and the elderly in need' were killed by gas or injection. She also knew, 'in a vague and very uncertain way', that 'entire trains of Jews' had been gassed in Germany (but she 'ignored in what exact conditions and to what ends'). She had long known that 'the concentration camps existed', and had read a first-hand testimony about the Hitlerian labour camps in the years before the war.[141] She also explained that, '[a]bout the executions in France, the tortures committed by the Gestapo, the treatment of prisoners in German prisons, I was informed with great exactitude and precision, particularly from the Spring of 1941, when the first arrests in my Resistance cell took place'.[142] It is unlikely that Beckett was informed with the same precision in 1941 and 1942 – although he probably knew much about the camps in Drancy and Compiègne through Lucie Léon – but he would have had a clearer sense of the mechanics of anti-Semitic persecution and the deployment of the Nazi camp system than many of his contemporaries. Information about the Hitlerian labour camps was widely available long before his trip to Germany: the *Irish Times*, for example, began to publish articles on Dachau and Sachsenhausen in 1933 and discussed the common use of political executions and penal facilities at other points during the 1930s.

It is certain that, in the war's immediate aftermath, Beckett's daily existence held many reminders that life could have taken a different turn. His residence in wartime Paris, Rue des Favorites, was close to the Cherche-Midi prison on Boulevard Raspail, which functioned as a German

[140] See Germaine Tillion, *Ravensbrück, Les Cahiers du Rhône* 65 (Neuchâtel: Cahiers du Rhône, 1946), 42; *Ravensbrück* (Paris: Seuil, 1988), 195–208, 211–12. On international solidarities and political beliefs, see Michel Pollak, *L'Expérience concentrationnaire: Essai sur le maintien de l'identité sociale* (Paris: Métailié, 1990).

[141] This was Wolfgang Langhoff's *Les soldats du Marais sous la schlague des nazis* (Paris: Plon, 1935).

[142] Tillion, *Ravensbrück* [1946], 65, 11–12.

military prison for those accused of anti-German activities, and to the former headquarters of the Ministry of Air, requisitioned by the Truppenunterkunft, whose basement was used for summary executions of Resistance members.[143] On the immediate outskirts of Paris were the Fort de Romainville and the Fresnes prison, where many political prisoners were detained and executed, and the Drancy camp, from which trains departed to other French camps and Nazi camps in Germany and Poland. The Drancy camp had acted as a site of detention since 1939 (the first detainees were Communists) and was used thereafter as a repository of hostages to be traded and for retaliatory executions. Further north were the Aincourt transit camp and the Royallieu camp, designated as 'the camp of slow death' by Jewish survivors.[144] To the south of Paris were the camp of Linas-Montlhéry, set up as a camp for 'nomads', as the Roma were designated; the camp of Jargeau, which was put to different uses over the course of the war; and the camps of Pithiviers and Beaune-la-Rolande, which functioned mostly as transit camps and sent large numbers to Auschwitz. There were many other camps throughout Vichy France, and they were supplemented by other structures including 'regroupment centres' for foreigners, or 'Centres de rassemblement des étrangers'. Roussillon, where Beckett spent the rest of the war after his escape from Paris, was close to camps in Arles, Aspres-sur-Bûech and Reillanne, and the Camp des Milles near Aix-en-Provence, which closed in 1943 and was used for detention and deportation.[145] It is important to note that the history of the French camp system stretches further and begins in February 1939, when camps were set up for Spanish republican refugees in the south of France, imposing living conditions that many found alarming – including Cunard, who was then reporting on the side-effects of the Spanish Civil War for the *Manchester Guardian*.[146] Denis Peschanski has scrutinised the transformations of the French camp system, showing how the camps developed from temporary structures for Spanish refugees into internment camps under the Vichy regime, with some eventually serving as concentration camps for German

[143] Cécile Desprairies, *Ville lumière, années noires: Les lieux du Paris de la Collaboration* (Paris: Denoël, 2008), 100–1, 262–3.

[144] Jean-Jacques Bernard, *Le camp de la mort lente: Compiègne 1941–42* (Paris: Albin Michel, 1944).

[145] Anne Grynberg, 'Les camps du sud de la France: De l'internement à la déportation', *Annales. Economies, Sociétés, Civilisations* 48, no. 3 (1993): 557–66; Irène Herrmann and Daniel Palmieri, 'Le Comité international de la Croix-Rouge (CICR) et les camps de concentration nazis, 1933–1939', *Matériaux pour l'histoire de notre temps* 95, no. 3 (2009): 65–74; Denis Peschanski, *La France des camps: L'internement, 1938–1946* (Paris: Gallimard, 2002), 167, 320.

[146] Nancy Cunard, 'The Camp at Argelès', *Manchester Guardian*, 14 February 1939, 6; 'Misery in the French Refugee Camps', 17 February 1939, 15; 'The Spanish Refugees in France', 23 August 1939, 5; 'Tour of the Refugee Camps in France', 31 July 1939, 5.

and French political prisoners placed under Allied watch in 1944. A few sites – for example, the camp of Gurs, where Hannah Arendt was interned – continued to be utilised in all circumstances.

Beckett's writings allude to this topography of confinement at various points. *Watt* relates a sudden encounter with a garden 'surrounded by a high barbed wire fence', whose purpose is to dissuade, to 'impal[e]', to trap those who lack the wherewithal to turn back, in the hope that they will 'bleed to death, or be eaten alive by the rats, or perish from exposure, long before their cries were heard'.[147] The makeshift nature of this garden works by analogy and recalls the intermediary transit and detention camps close to Paris, mostly run by the local police and *gendarmes*, which (like the camp of Pithiviers) were set up within towns and near train lines, and consisted of wood barracks and barbed wire fences. As is the case elsewhere in Beckett's texts when the subject of deportation is invoked, the questions that are raised pertain not simply to Nazi ideology but to the manner in which totalitarian regimes are nurtured by passivity, wilful blindness and ignorance. Likewise, in *Eleutheria*, all discussions about Victor, absent from the family home, are indexed to a landscape that persistently recalls occupation, internment and deportation. Mrs Krap has taken to safeguarding the memory of her son by marking off his places of predilection with barbed wire, and Mrs Piouk recalls seeing Victor's fiancée in Evian – a place commonly used as a point of entry into Switzerland by those seeking to escape anti-Semitic persecutions – at a moment that coincides with Victor's own disappearance two years previously. What happened to Victor remains a mystery; he is haunted by visions of death, fire and destruction, and remains driven by a desire to shoulder the weight carried by other victims. His speeches read as requisitories against those who 'come across an infinite number of mysteries every day', and yet 'pass by on the other side': 'Saints, madmen, martyrs, victims of torture – they don't bother you in the least, they are in the natural order of things. [. . .] You turn away from them. [. . .] It's not worth worrying about. Nothing to do with you' (144–5). Memories of unspeakable distress, horror and destruction also recur in Beckett's fiction. His narrators inexplicably recall things German at inopportune moments: Moran cites Goethe in the original German to invoke self-sacrifice as a life principle, and the narrators of the post-war novellas nurture ambivalent and blurred memories of the religious architecture of Saxony; the grave of Carl Hagenbeck, trader in wild animals and people;

[147] SB, *Watt* [1953] (London: Calder, 1976), 155. For a different reading, see McNaughton, 'Beckett's "Brilliant Obscurantics"', 53–5.

and Lüneburg Heath, the large stretch of land where the Bergen-Belsen camp was erected and the German army surrendered to the Allied forces in 1945.

Aftermaths and Returns: Paris, Dublin, Saint-Lô

When Beckett attempted to bear testimony, he did so to an Irish public, about the military facets of the war, and by evoking his experience in Saint-Lô in liberated France. Saint-Lô – renamed by American troops and French newspapers 'the capital of the ruins' – was widely represented as a martyred town, since the scale of destruction exceeded the damage suffered elsewhere in Normandy. The short poem 'Saint-Lô', published in the *Irish Times* in June 1946 as 'SAINT-LO 1945', vindicated Beckett's proximity to a material devastation that few could imagine, although its contents – like its predecessor, 'DIEPPE 193?', published a year previously – eluded direct historical association. In contrast, 'The Capital of the Ruins', a mysterious text dated June 1946 and intended for broadcast on Radio Éireann, offers a detailed account of the slow reconstruction of Saint-Lô by German prisoners of war and casual labourers, while discussing the role fulfilled by the new Irish Red Cross hospital and its staff. The text seeks to elicit feelings of horror and empathy by describing what surely must have been the worst nightmare of its imagined audience: a rural town 'bombed out of existence in one night'.[148] To Beckett's imagined listeners this unspecified circumstance would have evoked the German bombings experienced in Great Britain, Northern Ireland and, temporarily, in Eire. Saint-Lô was not rased to the ground by German bombings, but by an American air raid in June 1944, which pushed the inhabitants into a tragic repetition of the exodus of 1940; the ensuing battle to establish control over German-occupied territory destroyed most of what remained. The Radio Éireann audience for whom Beckett wrote this text was unlikely to know the precise situation of the population, since coverage of the Allied landings in the Irish press had focused exclusively on the movements of Allied troops, not on the means taken to secure victory. There are other shadowy zones in Beckett's text. If the new Red Cross huts were locally called 'the Irish hospital', as Beckett emphasises, this was also because they replaced the municipal public hospital, destroyed in the American raid, and because the German occupation forces, not long before, had built an underground hospital under the town

[148] SB, *The Complete Short Prose, 1929–1989*, ed. S. E. Gontarski (New York: Grove, 1995), 277.

walls,[149] which had never run as the German hospital or another kind of hospital, but had been utilised as a shelter during the Allied bombings by the local population.

In summoning these historical spectres, Beckett's piece also offers an indirect response to the ideological war fought in 1945 between de Valera and Churchill on the airwaves. In a radio broadcast from May 1945 responding to Churchill's attacks against Irish neutrality, de Valera did not call for solidarity, but for an inward look, a self-reliant economy and reduced importations. He concluded by promising a small contribution to support the reconstruction of Europe, commensurate with the size of the country and with Christian obligations.[150] The Irish Red Cross provided some solutions: de Valera assigned to it the tasks of bringing relief to Europe and coordinating all donations from Irish individuals and businesses.[151] Neutrality was a subject that seemed to spur Beckett's indignation when he reached Dublin in early April 1945, as suggested by his oft-cited declaration that 'Ireland gorges while my friends eat sawdust', and by a letter describing a city 'lousy with guzzling tourists'.[152] He was certainly marked by the years of rationing, and his friends were shocked to see how thin he had become.[153] 'The Capital of the Ruins' draws attention to neutrality as a historical privilege, and it is on those terms that it responds to de Valera's post-war speeches on the unavoidable necessity of neutrality. Beckett's account is permeated by one assumption: that the country wants to hear that it got its money's worth. He concludes, 'in the hope that it will give general satisfaction', that the Irish Red Cross staff 'got at least as good as they gave' (278). Elsewhere, he describes 'the Irish bringing gifts' (276) – a rebuke to Irish press headlines, which frequently associated the Irish Red Cross with gifts bestowed to the warring continent. Beckett's text also points to the derisory level of relief that an improvised hospital might bring to a territory reduced to rubble, evoking the vital need for imported Irish penicillin, the incomplete process of demining and children playing with detonators. 'The Capital of the Ruins' had the same uncertain fate as the majority of Beckett's polemical texts, and it seems unlikely that it was ever broadcast as intended, although the circumstances are sufficiently blurred to warrant speculation.[154] In any case, Beckett's account could not be

[149] 'A la découverte du souterrain de Saint-Lô', *Ouest France*, 7 August 2013, www.ouest-france.fr/la-decouverte-du-souterrain-de-saint-lo-703483.

[150] *Speeches and Statements by Eamon de Valera*, 473. On Irish domestic policy, see Wills, *That Neutral Island*, 344–426.

[151] 'Ireland's Relief for Starving Europe', *IT*, 19 May 1945, 1.

[152] *SB*, 339; *LSB2*, 29.

[153] Brian Coffey, 'Memory's Murphy Maker', *Threshold* 17 (1962): 35.

[154] Phyllis Gaffney, 'Dante, Manzoni, De Valera, Beckett . . . ? Circumlocutions of a Storekeeper: Beckett and Saint-Lô', *Irish University Review* 29, no. 2 (1999): 260–3.

further removed from that of the *Irish Times* Paris correspondent, who in August 1946 described the Saint-Lô hospital as a remarkably 'happy' place where visitors were 'pleasantly entertained', in the midst of a region that still had much to offer to the sightseer.[155]

Ultimately, despite its epidemics, penuries and material dangers, Saint-Lô was a safer and less controversial place to be than many others: from 1944 onwards, numerous Red Cross missions were conducted at huge risk, particularly on German roads, where the advances of the Red Army ushered the lethal evacuations of the Nazi camps and the death marches.[156] It is important to note that the actions of the International Committee of the Red Cross were never perceived as politically neutral: its responses to the Nazi camps and strategy of providing selective humanitarian aid without intervention were questioned by many.[157] In France specifically, and without doubt in Saint-Lô, there was also much debate about the Allied bombings, due to the fact that they transformed strategic coastal and border areas into ruins soon to be placed under Allied military control, resented as another form of occupation.[158]

The few letters that Beckett sent to MacGreevy offer an interesting picture, pointing to 'all kinds of obscure tensions between the local people, the medical crowd and the Red X in Paris'.[159] He misdates the American raid, mentioning 'the night of 5th to 6th June', the date of the Allied landings in Normandy, instead of 6–7 June 1944. He also relates his 'impression that the locals would like the stuff, but don't want us (very reasonable attitude) and that the French Red X., for reasons unclear, insist on an Irish staff'. The latter issue had much to do with the fact that Irish staff, coming from a neutral and mostly Catholic country, were likely to be more widely accepted, as indeed they were. Beckett left in January 1946; in August, tensions escalated between the local doctors, the Irish hospital staff, the Saint-Lô council and the Red Cross headquarters in Paris and Dublin, in the wake of a resolution voted by the regional doctors' union, which demanded the withdrawal of the Red Cross, on the grounds that France had regained its sovereignty.[160] Relations were mended thereafter, and, in April 1948, Irish Red Cross workers were decorated by the French State in a Dublin ceremony, during which

[155] 'The Irish Red Cross Hospital at St. Lô', *IT*, 21 August 1946, 4.
[156] Henri Frenay, *La nuit finira, vol. 2: Mémoires de Résistance 1943–1945* (Paris: Robert Laffont, 1973), 265–6.
[157] Jean-Claude Favez, *The Red Cross and the Holocaust* (Cambridge: Cambridge University Press, 1999).
[158] Richard Overy, *The Bombing War: Europe 1939–1945* (London: Allen Lane, 2013), 556–82.
[159] *LSB2*, 18.
[160] Phyllis Gaffney, 'A Hospital for the Ruins: The Irish Hospital at Saint-Lô', *Southern Ireland and the Liberation of France*, 114–7.

Beckett was awarded (*in absentia*) the Médaille de Bronze de la Reconnaissance Française for his work as 'storekeeper-interpreter' in Saint-Lô.[161]

There are many obscure zones in this period of Beckett's life, and the citation for his Croix de Guerre, awarded in March 1945, conveys some confusion around his wartime activities. It rewarded Resistance work conducted across the course of two whole years, which exceeds the period during which Beckett served as 'sergeant-chef' and 'sous-lieutenant' in Gloria SMH.[162] This and some other elements raise important questions about the events of October 1944. He and Suzanne were so impoverished that they had to borrow money from their Roussillon neighbours to pay the train fare to Paris.[163] They found their flat nearly intact, but several sources indicate that Beckett stayed at the Lutetia hotel for some of that month, using 'poste restante' for correspondence sent to Rue des Favorites.[164] He seems to have had an emotional attachment to the Lutetia – a luxury hotel much loved by Joyce, Reavey, Adorno and many others – since he continued to hold meetings there in later years. It is unclear how long Beckett spent at the Lutetia; what is certain is that, by that point, the hotel had long ceased to be a place of leisurely residence. It was, like other major hotels, a site of strategic importance.

From 1940 onwards, the Lutetia housed the French headquarters of the Abwehr, the Wehrmarcht's counter-espionage and intelligence service in charge of tracking down members of the Resistance, as well as some Gestapo services. After the liberation of Paris, at the end of August 1944, the Lutetia was assigned to the French Ministry of War and was put to military use until its next transformation in April 1945.[165] Some records indicate that the hotel was requisitioned for the staff of General Noiret, previously chief of the Free French forces in Britain, who was in charge of putting appropriate infrastructure in place for French army staff and the new government in Paris.[166] Many other buildings were rapidly reallocated: the building of the Commissariat Général aux Questions Juives, the executive arm of Vichy's anti-Semitic legislation, became the Personnel Department of the Ministry of Culture (it previously belonged to the Louis-Dreyfus Bank). Number 11, rue des Saussaies, which had housed the Sipo-SD, was transferred to the

[161] 'French Awards for Irish Red Cross Workers', *IT*, 12 April 1948, 3.

[162] On Beckett's grades, see Murphy, 'Paddy fait de la résistance'; Murphy, 'Irish Men and Women', 272.

[163] *Chronology*, 93.

[164] Ibid.; *LSB2*, 6.

[165] *JORF: Débats de l'Assemblée consultative provisoire*, vol. 2, 6 February–31 March 1945, 157.

[166] See Pierre Assouline's archival research in his *Lutétia* (Paris: Gallimard, 2005), 325; Kaspi, *La libération*, 285; Desprairies, *Ville lumière, années noires*, 103; Roger Noiret's French National Assembly biography, www.assemblee-nationale.fr/sycomore/.

French Ministry of the Interior, which had owned the building until 1940. The headquarters of the French Communist Party, once the headquarters of the French militia for the Northern zone, were returned to their former function in 1946.[167] These were extreme circumstances, and to stay at the Lutetia in October 1944, at a time when France and Europe were in the throes of armed combat, was necessarily to be involved in the work conducted by the Allied forces and the infant French administration. As the experience of Lucie Léon shows, competent translators were highly sought after during that crucial period; as for Beckett, the activities he undertook are among the many secrets he took to his grave.

Beckett left Paris for London on 8 April, before making his way to Dublin. A week later, the Lutetia underwent a radical transformation: it became 'centre Lutetia', the heart of a gigantic operation of repatriation led by Henri Frenay and what he called his 'Ministry of Suffering', the Ministry for Prisoners, Deportees and Refugees, created in response to the moving frontlines in Germany, where prisoners of war and concentration camp detainees were forced onto the roads after the summer of 1944. The evacuations continued throughout 1945 on a larger scale. Repatriation was a large-scale task fraught with immense uncertainty, since the number of displaced and interned people was unknown, and ultimately proved far superior to the most daring estimates. For this reason, some historians have argued that repatriation ultimately posed greater challenges to political leaders and administrations across Europe than the material destructions caused by bombings and moving frontlines.[168]

In mid-April 1945, the Lutetia and its 343 rooms were requisitioned, and the hotel played a vital role until August as a place of rest and recovery, a centre for medical examinations and interviews, and a meeting place publishing lists of Nazi camp survivors. To secure sufficient facilities, Frenay requisitioned everything that could be put to use in Paris: train stations, swimming pools, some military barracks formerly used by the French militia, the Vel d'Hiv, all large Paris cinemas including their staff and entertainers, and even the major Parisian Pinder circus, complete with cages and loudspeakers.[169] The procedures for deportees and most prisoners of war were the same: disinfection with DDT powder, medical examination and interrogation. Deportees were given papers ascertaining their identity, some clothing and a small sum of money. Many testimonies recall the hall

[167] Desprairies, *Ville lumière, années noires*, 66–7, 172–3, 208–9.

[168] Lagrou, *Mémoires patriotiques*, 85; Christophe Lewin, *Le retour des prisonniers de guerre français: Naissance et développement de la FNPG, 1944–1952* (Paris: La Sorbonne, 1986), 64–70.

[169] Frenay, *La nuit finira*, 283–4; Navarro, *1945*, 40; Kaspi, *La libération*, 285–7.

of the hotel covered in notices, photographs and messages from families hoping to see their loved ones again.[170] In *La Douleur* (1985), one of the many books translated by Bray, Duras described the work of documentation that she conducted at the Lutetia while waiting for Robert Antelme's return from Dachau in April 1945.[171] Maspero's *Le sourire du chat* relates the trips of the child narrator to the Lutetia in search of news and dedicates several chapters to his wait for his parents' return from Ravensbrück and Buchenwald.[172] Charlotte Delbo's testimony also described the disorientation and dismay of survivors at the hotel and the peculiar manifestations of solidarity, curiosity and indifference that they witnessed there.[173] A recent book by Pierre Assouline, based on the hotel's archives and military documents, recreates everyday life at the Lutetia, relating the interviews conducted to unmask the kapos and the SS masquerading as survivors, and detailing the stratagems that the hotel staff conceived to feed survivors by requisitioning the proceeds of black market seizures left over from the occupation years.

The mass repatriations continued from mid-April to August 1945; Beckett spent these months in Dublin and made his way to Saint-Lô, via London and Paris, in early August. The press reports and images documenting the liberation of the camps were, for the most part, disseminated while he was in Dublin. In a later conversation with Knowlson, he briefly evoked the horrific moment when '[t]he forces just opened up the extermination camps as they came through'.[174] His letters relate the non-return of Desnos and Léon, and announce Péron's death 'in Switzerland, on his way home May 1st 1945'.[175] The wording conveys his immense sorrow upon hearing of Péron's death on Labour Day, after years in a camp renowned for taking forced labour to horrific heights. Two decades later, in the same economical terms, he alluded to 'the "tourmente"' that had swallowed Freundlich's life.[176]

These concerns bear heavily upon the narrative of return developed in 'Suite', published in *Les Temps Modernes* in July 1946. The subject matter of this abbreviated text differs considerably from the version of 'La Fin' published in *Nouvelles et textes pour rien* and from the two versions of 'The End' translated with Richard Seaver for *Merlin* and the *Evergreen*

[170] See, for instance, Olga Wormser-Migot, *Quand les Alliés ouvrirent les portes: Le dernier acte de la tragédie de la déportation* (Paris: Robert Laffont, 1965), 195, 212, 219.

[171] Marguerite Duras, *La Douleur*, trans. Barbara Bray (London: Collins, 1986), 5, 15, 36.

[172] François Maspero, *Le sourire du chat* (Paris: Seuil, 1984), 277–8, 281–2.

[173] Charlotte Delbo, *Auschwitz et après III: Mesure de nos jours* (Paris: Minuit, 1971), 21–39.

[174] *BR/RB*, 86. [175] *LSB2*, 16, 19. [176] Storm or turmoil. *LSB1*, 646 n7.

Review (likewise, the version of 'L'Expulsé' that appeared in *Fontaine* subsequently underwent extensive rewriting). Beckett's narrator has freshly returned from a long period of absence, marked by starvation, exhaustion and extreme deprivation. Everything from his former life is long gone and long lost, and streets and buildings once familiar are no longer recognisable. Many narrative details resemble the procedures implemented at the Lutetia in 1945, and these are precisely the facets of the text that were edited out and rewritten in later versions. The narrator of 'Suite', for example, recalls a recent stay in a hotel – emphatically not situated in London – where he was unable to rest: 'Que de fois j'avais essayé de me reposer a l'hôtel, sans succès. Si j'avais été à Londres, ou dans ses environs, j'aurais cherché quelque chose dans le quartier Euston-King's Cross-Islington' (literally: I had tried so many times to rest at the hotel, without success. If I had been in London, or in its surroundings, I would have looked for something in the Euston-King's Cross-Islington neighbourhood).[177] Other passages cut from subsequent versions describe in detail his bare skull and his infected wounds, which recall the symptoms of malnutrition visible on the bodies of many concentration camp survivors. His extreme physical weakness is emphasised by means of small touches: he is, for example, fed fish by someone he knew from a prior time in life, while later versions present him as capable of feeding himself alone; fish is simply given to him. In later versions, he complains that he is not feeling well, but in 'Suite' he states that he is not feeling sufficiently strong, and he is made aware that his weakness will last. The charitable institution that temporarily looks after him has considerable resources at its disposal: the narrator offers to help in the garden and in the kitchen, and ponders asking for a whole loaf of bread, 'de la sorte qu'on appelle couronne' (110). In subsequent versions, however, he merely hopes for a small chunk of bread and for the possibility of making himself useful in an undefined capacity.

The opening, which describes the clothes donated to the narrator, underwent similar shifts. In later versions, these clothes have been recuperated from a deceased man. In 'Suite', the clothes have been freshly fumigated, and their previous owner is not identified as dead but fell victim to a mysterious medical appointment, in circumstances that recall the arrangements made by the French police to stamp the identity papers of Jewish men and women, and the appointment letters issued prior to the mass round-ups of 1941 and 1942. 'Il avait dû s'endimancher pour aller à la consultation. C'était probablement la première fois. Toute sa vie il l'avait renvoyé au

[177] SB, 'Suite', *Les Temps Modernes* 10 (1946): 111.

lendemain' (107) (literally: He had probably put on his Sunday best to go to the consultation. It was probably the first time. All his life he had postponed it to the next day). The narrator is also given a small allowance to cover his 'frais de route' – the term historically used to designate the retribution of the expenses incurred by soldiers, released prisoners or penal convicts; later versions state that this money was to get him started ('me faire démarrer'). Beyond these divergences, the different versions concur on one front: this is a world in which nothing is as it seems, and every object and every place carry conflicting memories.[178]

Mercier et Camier summons the spectres of deportation and return less directly, through a secondary character called Monsieur Conaire, who has returned by foot 'from the very core of the metropolitan gas-chamber', and believes that his experiences have left such heavy marks upon his body that no one can possibly guess his real age.[179] The English text is less weighted, but in the French text there are few ambiguities about his journey: he recalls that those who got off trains in Frankfurt would see the word 'HIER' (here in German, yesterday in French) in giant letters of fire, and he is haunted by memories of being brutally catapulted from a time of plenty to a time of starvation – from a past in which cakes were ubiquitous to a future that can only bring dry bread and stones (79, 102). Post-war testimonies of deportation also loom heavily over the procedures detailed in *Malone meurt* and *Malone Dies*. At the House of Saint John of God, where Macmann lives as 'number one hundred and sixty-six', the 'prisoners' wear a 'striped cloak', and remain thankful for being subject to 'a minimum of persecution and corporal punishment'.[180] Their 'keepers', with 'white clothes, armed with sticks and lanterns', commonly issue threats of 'the direst reprisals' (276). Everyday life is submitted to strategic forms of classification: the kitchen, for example, differentiates between the 'excursion soup' and the 'common or house soup': the latter is 'uniformally liquid', while the former, delivered upon 'written order', features 'a piece of fat bacon intended to keep up the strength of the excursionist until his return' (283). The soup classification recalls the distributions routines used in the Nazi camps, not least because it benefits only the strong and powerful – in this instance, Lemuel, who steals a bucket of excursion soup, eats the bacon and throws the remains back in the soup. No one can ascertain the precise status of the House of Saint

178 For a reading of the later version, 'La Fin', through Arendt and the plight of the stateless, see Lyndsey Stonebridge, *Placeless People: Rights, Writing and Refugees* (Oxford: Oxford University Press, in press).

179 SB, *Mercier and Camier* [1974] (London: Calder, 1999), 51.

180 *Trilogy*, 279 (hereafter cited parenthetically).

John of God – not even Lemuel, who remains 'plunged in thought' when asked whether this is 'a private institution or run by the State, a hospice of the aged and infirm or a madhouse' (267–8). His response is in keeping with the logic proper to the institution and its consecrated assaults on all certainties: this, after all, is a place where 'no questions were ever asked', but 'stern measures were simply taken, or not taken, according to the dictates of a peculiar logic' (277).

Inquests and Investigations: Beckett and the Aftermaths of the Vichy Regime

The first-person narratives born out of the 'siege in the room' have many affinities of subject matter. They tell not only of internment but of forced displacement and dangerous journeys undertaken through a ruined landscape; blackouts, rationing and penury; encounters with police officers, war veterans and members of mysterious militias; dealings in shifting currencies; people of different nationalities and social classes looking for shelter, living under threat and involved in trafficking, spying and denunciations. This is a writing that interrogates the remit of historical testimony in a very distinctive way, through an appropriation of the rhetoric of detective fiction, and, by the same token, raises troubling questions about the workings of political coercion and social consent. In this regard, Beckett's provocative approach to political history is aligned with the remit of the Editions de Minuit during the 1950s, and with its move towards more controversial accounts of Nazi occupation and resistance: examples include *Le coup d'état* (1950), a novel by David Scheinert that focused on the problem of collaborators reinventing themselves as members of the Resistance to escape prosecution, or Léon Weinigel's *Malgré nous* (1955), which dealt with Alsacian men who had joined the Wehrmacht under coercion.

Beckett was always a keen reader of detective fiction, especially during the early 1950s, when he was frequently immersed in Agatha Christie whodunnits in both English and French.[181] His interest in thrillers, crime and mystery novels by Christie, Edgar Wallace, Erle Stanley Gardner, Len Deighton and Rex Stout, however, continued long after this point. It seems that he mostly read British and American crime fiction, and that he had less interest in French crime authors writing under Americanised pseudonyms, as was then commonplace, although he kept abreast of the adventurous

[181] See *DF*, 390, 553, 562; Gussow, *Conversations*, 126; Mira Avrech, 'A Friend Recalls Affectionately a Shy Nobel Prize Playwright Named Samuel Beckett', *People* 15, 13 April 1981, 79.

explorations of the genre published by Robbe-Grillet and Robert Pinget at the Editions de Minuit. His own dialogue with detective fiction takes on many forms after *Watt*, which Frederik Smith reads as an anti-detective novel subverting the syllogistic thinking developed in Conan Doyle's Sherlock Holmes novels, familiar to Beckett since childhood.[182] The premises of detective fiction also fuel the cultural and political imaginary of his post-war fiction, from the quest of the private investigator Camier across a war-torn landscape to Moran's search for Molloy, through to the humble investigations underlying Malone's stories. These novels, however, offer an uneasy juxtaposition of historical frames (some characters are enthralled by the ideals of Vichy's National Revolution; others are dimly aware of the realities of persecution and deportation) and an uneasy fusion of genres (they toy with the conventions of detective fiction as well as autobiography, travel narrative and testimony). Connections to the recording of historical experience are sometimes expressed literally: Malone asserts his appreciation for the small piece of pencil at his disposal, while *Mercier et Camier* alludes to the ubiquitous last tenth of pencil, from which many testimonies of imprisonment and torture have historically been born. In a passage elided from the English text, Camier – whose business card emphasises his talent for discretion and tailing – reads from his notebook and describes cases and disappearances that recall the round-ups of the Vichy era. His notebook features reports seemingly copied from newspaper advertisements and seemingly issued by despairing relatives, evoking a fourteen-year-old girl called Lise Joly, who disappeared on her way to school ('Pas vue en classe'), and a sixty-eight-year-old lady called Gertrude Hamilton, wearing a veil, a black dress and a Russian fur hat; in this case the report concludes, 'Peut rentrer crise finie' (Can come home crisis over) (88).

Molloy is also haunted by the ghosts of persecution, denunciation and underground action, and the French text is considerably more ominous than its English counterpart, not least because Moran has received the order to 'take care of' Molloy ('s'occuper') – a task that the English text renders as less threatening (he is simply asked to 'see about Molloy').[183] The terms according to which he imagines Molloy are racialised and invoke the prejudices disseminated under the Vichy regime against those designated as 'Israelites': 'difforme', 'sans être noir, de couleur sombre', 'hirsute' and 'grimacier' – crooked, of a dark skin colour but without being black, wild-haired and prone to grimacing (154–5). If an execution is to take place, then

[182] Frederik N. Smith, 'Watt, Watson, and Sherlock Holmes: *Watt* as Detective Fiction', *SBTA* 16 (2006): 299–318.

[183] SB, *Molloy* (Paris: Minuit, 1982), 125; *Trilogy*, 92.

it will be one of many killings: Moran defines himself as a simple 'agent' in an immense network composed of other agents and messengers, who, like Gaber, have honed forms of coding that are so sophisticated that they are allowed to carry a notebook. Moran, for his part, is merely entrusted with 'missions' and 'interventions' (186–7). He answers to a 'patron' whose sinister name, Youdi – a term of abuse designating a Jew in colloquial French, used in the late nineteenth century and revived under the Vichy regime – further invokes the shadow of wartime persecutions. Molloy proves an elusive target, for he knows how to travel unseen: when walking at night he oscillates like a stealth bomber, 'en rase-mottes, dans l'obscurité, par les petits chemins déserts de la campagne' (89). 'En rase-mottes', hedgehopping, is specifically connected to aviation; in contrast, the English version renders this passage as 'swinging low in the dark over the earth, along the little empty country roads' (66). Being 'inquiété' – being caught, persecuted, arrested or attacked – is a permanent concern (89). The English text evades these connotations and uses the term 'molested' (66). In the French text, Molloy has legitimate reasons for operating in this way: the morning hours are the scene of an 'épuration' conducted by 'techniciens', a time of constant exposure to lynching (90). He emphasises the primordial necessity of hiding in the morning, in order to escape denunciation by those who yearn for order and justice ('They wake up, hale and hearty, their tongues hanging out for order, beauty and justice, baying for their due' (66–7)). For his part, he would prefer slavery over 'mise à mort' (91) or 'being put to death' (68). These threats are at work on a larger scale too: Molloy recalls a swamp between his hometown and the sea, where an incalculable number of human lives were swallowed ('où s'engouffrait chaque année un nombre incalculable de vies humaines' (102)). Public works, it is suggested, have been undertaken but may have seen more of the same 'lente extermination' (slow extermination). The word 'extermination' disappears from the English text, which merely refers to 'adversity, setbacks, epidemics' and condemns 'the apathy of the Public Works Department' (76).

There are fewer differences between *Malone meurt* and *Malone Dies*: both texts are littered with allusions to disappearances and conspiracies masterminded by unnamed powers and institutions, which, in turn, frame the attempts of Malone and his creatures to find, identify and connect material traces, sequences of events and explainable causes. The narrative is punctured by visions of mass graves and a 'tangle of grey bodies', 'perhaps clinging to one another', 'together in a heap, in the night' (289). This is a deeply precarious context for deductive thinking, and Malone tries to preclude linguistic imprecisions such as those that might emerge from inappropriate reasoning methods, concluding that he 'ha[s] no proof' of what little he is able to guess (219). The narration is not focused on reaping insights into a clearly defined social reality, but on honing mechanics of deduction that remain valid across the lower middle-class world of the Saposcats and the rural world of the Lamberts, and encompass the semi-secretive bodies of cleaners, guardians, nurses and doctors that dominate the institutions to which Malone and his creatures are confined. What binds these different social bodies is a shared celebration of work, family and fatherland, and obedience to the immemorial France of the Vichy regime. The daily life of the Saposcats, for example, is ruled by many 'axioms', 'of which one at least established the criminal absurdity of a garden without roses and with its paths and lawns uncared for' (187–8). The line separating personal thought from state politics is here very thin, if not inexistent, recalling the definition that Claude Lefort has offered of totalitarianism as a political order in which politics is integral to all domains of social life and intimate thought, and forbids their separation.[184]

The novel's lengthy descriptions of agrarian life have a distinctive political dimension as open satires of Pétain's vision for the French nation. In speeches celebrating the law of the soil and a land that 'does not lie', Pétain called for a National Revolution around a strong state that would function as the antithesis of the Popular Front, and in which the right of the family would be 'anterior and superior' to the rights of the individual.[185] This new state, inspired from military models, would be led by an elite and function without political parties, through an organisation of war veterans mediating between the government and the public.[186] Pétain's attempt to emulate Mussolini's and Hitler's governments was explicit: his appeal to the nation in September 1940 called for the formation of a corporatist state, organised around individual professions and their interests, and emphasised that the French spirit was naturally aligned with national socialist models of work and social organisation, in harmony with the German spirit.[187] The National Revolution had cultural ambitions too: the Vichy regime worked hard to buttress regionalist literatures, creating a museum of popular arts and traditions, regional commissions charged to invigorate and disseminate

[184] Claude Lefort, *The Political Forms of Modern Society: Bureaucracy, Democracy, Totalitarianism*, ed. John B. Thompson (Cambridge: Polity, 1986), 79.

[185] Jean Thouvenin, *La France nouvelle II: D'ordre du maréchal Pétain* (Paris: Sequana, 1941), 89–90.

[186] Philippe Burin, 'Vichy', in *Lieux de mémoire: Les France*, vol. 3, ed. Pierre Nora (Paris: Gallimard, 1982), 333.

[187] Thouvenin, *La France nouvelle*, 94.

local folklore, and a new literary prize in July 1942 destined to 'encourage, support and reward literature dedicated to peasant life', over which the Ministry of Agriculture and Supply had oversight.[188] Beckett's satires of country life and of the war veteran in *Mercier et Camier* and elsewhere owe much to the rhetoric of the National Revolution. The purposeless wanderings of Molloy and Moran also harbour a parodic dimension, not simply of the pastoral ideal that Beckett had encountered in the Irish state imagined by de Valera, but of a political reality that he saw at work, with far more sinister consequences, in wartime France.

In *Malone Dies*, the causes of death and disappearance remain hermetic, but it is clear that mass murder and imprisonment derive from the implacable logic of state institutions at liberty to administer a slow death to some and a quick death to others. Malone, beyond his prime, not fully sane and unable to work, belongs to a social category whom the Vichy regime subjected to slow starvation in psychiatric hospitals, hospices and internment camps.[189] His only source of counsel is Jackson, an 'Israelite' long since vanished; he emphasises that no assistance could be obtained elsewhere, especially not from Watson ('Johnson, Wilson, Nicholson, and Watson, all whoresons' (218)). The body social is defined by means of exclusion; possible classifications as understood by Malone include the 'abnormal', 'the inferior races, red, yellow, chocolate, and so on', 'the plague-stricken' and 'the insane', among whom he has, thus far, failed to find another 'kindred spirit' (218–19). Malone's creations have fully assimilated the requirements of racialist legislation and Aryan certificates: Lemuel is particularly keen to discount the Hebrew origins of his name, and emphasises without being prompted that '[his] parents were probably Aryan' (267). In *Molloy*, seemingly benign details are also framed by anti-Jewish decrees: the idea of owning a bicycle (a forbidden commodity for Jews according to Nazi and Vichy edicts) is unimaginable for Moran's son, although the trade of second-hand bicycles is thriving, even in the most remote villages. Invoking Goering – 'Who is this bicycle for, I said, Goering?' – becomes, for Moran, the only way to convey to his son that the bicycle he has been asked to buy is for him (143). The line belongs to the realm of the blackest humour: in the wake of the 1936 Four-Year Plan, Goering became the 'iron man' in

[188] Christian Faure, *Le projet culturel de Vichy. Folklore et révolution nationale (1940–1944)* (Paris: CNRS and Presses Universitaires de Lyon, 1989); Anne-Marie Thiesse, *Ecrire la France: Le mouvement littéraire régionaliste de langue française entre la Belle Epoque et la Libération* (Paris: PUF, 1991), 261–89.

[189] Isabelle von Bueltzingsloewen, *'Morts d'inanition': Famine et exclusions en France sous l'Occupation* (Rennes: Presses Universitaires de Rennes, 2005).

charge of boosting and coordinating steel production.[190] Moran's joke also resonates in sinister ways with Goering's role in setting up concentration camps from which Nazi leaders extracted an enormous fortune.

It is through such narrative details that Beckett's novels reimagine the anti-Semitic laws that provided the keystone of the Vichy regime and collaboration. Michael Marrus and Robert Paxton have shown that the growth of this new racialist State, which began during the summer of 1940, with the repeal of an executive order that had outlawed expressions of racial hatred in the press, was bolstered by the 'Loi portant au status des juifs', which introduced the notion of 'Jewish race' into French constitutional legislation in October 1940.[191] The insults, hesitations, omissions and silences in the stories of Moran and Malone develop around a shadowy referent – the anti-Semitic and racialist State, enforcing particular forms of internalisation and social organisation to further its ideological ends. As they attend to these historical shadows, Beckett's texts also ask powerful questions about the historical ability of totalitarianism to generate mass readiness to collaborate, and about its reliance on terms, phrases and forms of reasoning that impose restrictions upon critical thought. These are questions that attracted much international attention in the war's immediate aftermath, and found particularly powerful and influential answers in the thought of Hannah Arendt and the reflections of Victor Klemperer on the functioning of Nazism as a political ideology.[192] In *Malone Dies*, the work of coercion performed by the State penetrates all levels of existence; this is a State that incarcerates and criminalises those who are deemed socially marginal, isolates the working class, divides urban and rural economies, differentiates between the 'Aryan' and the 'Israelite', and keenly aspires to present itself as being at peace, rather than at war. Yet the shadow of war looms close: the sky is lined with airplanes moving noisily at fast speed, and London, in the English and French texts, remains an important landmark and the place where ambitions are fulfilled. At the House of Saint John of God, the Bank of England stands as a reliable frame of comparison for detainees who are unwilling to give away their possessions to the institution.

Historical landmarks tend towards overdetermination, further revealing the political and legal apparatus that feeds Beckett's imaginary. Within

190 Karl A. Schleunes, *The Twisted Road to Auschwitz: Nazi Policy toward German Jews, 1933–1939*, 2nd ed. (Urbana: University of Illinois Press, 1990), 164–5.

191 Marrus and Paxton, *Vichy France and the Jews*, 3–4.

192 Hannah Arendt, *The Origins of Totalitarianism* [1951], revised ed. (New York: Schocken, 2004), 507–92; Victor Klemperer, *The Language of the Third Reich: LTI-Lingua Tertii Imperii: A Philologist's Notebook*, trans. Martin Brady [1947] (London: Athlone Press, 2000).

Malone's evocation of 'the match king, Schneider, Schroeder, I forget' (275), for example, different allusions are juxtaposed: to the interwar financial scandal around the misdemeanours of Ivar Kreuger, the Swedish 'match king' and main creditor of a bankrupt Europe, also invoked in *More Pricks than Kicks*; to the industry magnate Kurt von Schroeder, whose long-standing support to Hitler attracted intense scrutiny after the Second World War; and to the Schneider-Creusot company, a French steel company that was involved in murky financial dealings with the German pre-war National Socialist government, and subsequently manufactured armaments for the German army. The integration of these clues into the narrative posits cryptic connections between a totalitarian state, industrial capital and structures of confinement and persecution. In less speculative forms, these connections are central to historical testimonies such as Rousset's *L'Univers concentrationnaire* (1945–1946) and Tillion's 1946 study of Ravensbrück, which described the proximity between the Nazi labour and concentration camps and the German industry, to which the camps provided an infinitely exploitable and profitable workforce. Tillion, who had trained as a sociologist in Algeria, gathered evidence of the profit that Ravensbrück generated for Himmler, its owner and main shareholder, and for the German companies (Siemens, textile companies and quarries) that relied upon the detainees' labour.[193] Both testimonies were driven by the strong beliefs of their authors in the power of evidence-gathering and deduction, and by their awareness of just how fragile and fraught the process of conducting sociological and historical enquiries truly was in the war's immediate aftermath. Their work extended to the legal sphere: Tillion, for example, represented the Association des Déportées et Internées de la Résistance at the trial of Ravensbrück camp officials in Hamburg, and later served in the commission formed by Rousset to investigate concentration camp systems in the Soviet Union and beyond.

Malone's modest investigations, of course, stand as little other than feeble fictional counterparts to historical testimonies. But these echoes offer precious insights into the ways in which Beckett uses the detective enquiry to point to the inadequacy of narrative forms in coming to terms with the rationalisation of persecution and genocide. Detective fiction is a social and political genre, and many have explored its political logic: Siegfried Kracauer, Ernst Bloch, Bertolt Brecht, Walter Benjamin and, most recently, Luc Boltanski. Boltanski argues that the detective novel – through the deployment, staging and resolution of an enigma – has a unique ability to

[193] Tillion, *Ravensbrück* [1946], 46, 50; Tillion, *Ravensbrück* [1988], 214–38.

interrogate the ways in which the social world takes as its premise the lineaments of a reality that has been stabilised to give rise to foreseeable anticipations of, and solutions to, social anomalies such as those arising through crime.[194] For Boltanski, the conspiracies and inquests at the heart of detective novels problematise, through their very form, their own relation to an evolving historical reality, posing important questions about the status of the institutions that regulate the social order and relate social events to identifiable causal sequences. The causality explored in the detective novel is, in his view, indicative of a deeper political turmoil indexed to its relation to the Nation-State – a State that pretends to know, control and arrange the reality experienced by those living under its authority. Boltanski's study accounts, on the one hand, for the influence that research on psychological ailments such as paranoia retained upon early detective novels, and, on the other, for the development of later detective novels that portray the State as the corrupt source of social crime.

Boltanski's analysis provides a useful background for Beckett's idiosyncratic flirtations with the genre in *Mercier et Camier* and *Molloy*, and makes it possible to apprehend *Malone Dies* and its French counterpart as texts that speak to the interstices between opposing representations of the State; the novel relates, albeit cryptically, a series of crimes that cannot be identified, let alone elucidated, because they are performed, staged and sanctioned by powers affiliated to the State. It presents but does not resolve this enigma: the entity that gives Malone shelter and food eludes enquiry, yet Malone knows that his survival depends upon the decisions of an all-knowing body able to administer life or death. 'They' take on different forms, from 'the agents of a consortium' to 'the powers that be' to the mysterious figures conducting 'visits' (254, 183, 269). Periodically, a deathly silence descends: the 'noises [...], cries, steps, doors, murmurs' sometimes cease 'for whole days' (222). The house 'across the way' also harbours 'queer things' (184). Malone's apprehension of the building shifts: he may be 'on the mezzanine', 'a kind of vault' or 'a wide trench or ditch with other vaults opening upon it' (219). Gradually, the 'plain ordinary house' becomes an immeasurable series of floors inhabited by 'people coming and going' and 'multitudes of fine babies', 'which the parents keep moving about from one place to another, [...] in anticipation of the day when they will have to move about unaided' (219). With its modern lines, carefully designed architecture and imprisoned children, the building that

194 Luc Boltanski, *Mysteries and Conspiracies: Detective Stories, Spy Novels, and the Making of Modern Societies*, trans. Catherine Porter (Cambridge: Polity, 2014), 5–9, 11–13, 15–17, 170–223.

emerges from Malone's descriptions bears an affinity to the Drancy camp, a modernist social housing project built before the war, called the Cité de la Muette. Partly unfinished by the time of its transformation into a camp, it featured medium-rise buildings towering over a central yard; its distinctive architecture and many modifications were widely remembered.[195] The peculiar architecture of confinement delineated in Beckett's novel, with its prisons within prisons, finds other counterparts in testimonies of deportation. Members of French Resistance networks were often detained in state prisons before their transfer to a camp, and many testimonies draw attention to the existence of 'Bunkers' or solitary confinement units within concentration camps: the Bunker played an important part in the functioning of Ravensbrück, Dachau and Neuengamme, where it served to incarcerate prisoners thought to pose an immediate political threat.[196] Even the Drancy camp had a prison, known by the common colloquial term as 'le gnouf'.[197]

French Cultural Politics and the Idea of Testimony

In 1947 already, long before the publication of many of his texts, the peculiar fusion of testimony and detective fiction offered by Beckett caused some unease. This is evident from the reports issued by the publishing house Le Seuil rejecting the novellas and *Molloy*. Hervé Serry has offered a detailed account of this episode, pointing out that Beckett's novellas were submitted shortly before the highly anticipated publication of Jean Cayrol's fictionalised account of deportation, *Je vivrai l'amour des autres*, co-published in December 1947 by Le Seuil and the Cahiers du Rhône, the press that also published Tillion's testimony in 1946. Le Seuil turned Beckett's novellas down because some of them were already published, and because Beckett's use of a narrative aesthetic emulating literal translation was seen as an opportunistic attempt to emulate Boris Vian's detective pastiche *J'irai cracher sur vos tombes*, published the previous year under the pseudonym Vernon Sullivan. The novel, presented as a translation of an American roman noir, caused great controversy: it was seen as an apology for an American genre glorifying a type of violence and immorality

[195] See, for instance, Georges Wellers, *De Drancy à Auschwitz* (Paris: Centre, 1946), 114.

[196] Simone Saint-Clair, *Ravensbrück, l'enfer des femmes* (Montreal: Variétés, 1945), 167; Office of United States Chief of Counsel for Prosecution of Axis Criminality, *Nazi Conspiracy and Aggression*, vol. 4 (Washington, DC: US Government Printing Office, 1946), 1043; Olga Wormser-Migot and Henri Michel, *Tragédie de la déportation, 1940–1945: Témoignages de survivants des camps de concentration allemands* (Paris: Hachette, 1954), 375–6.

[197] Wieviorka and Laffitte, *Drancy*, 66–8.

unwelcome in France, and led Vian and his editor into long-lasting legal difficulties.[198] This precedent, from the perspective of the readers appointed by Le Seuil, posed a serious problem. The readers' reports also perceived Beckett's text as a hoax – as an example of a 'fabricated, re-written, calculated writing' that parodied Kafka, but with the 'heaviness and childishness of an American'.[199] These are politically weighted criticisms, not least because, at that particular point, many in France believed that the principal design of the American government was world domination. A poll published in *Les Temps Modernes* in June 1946 revealed the divergences between French and European perceptions on this score.[200] Earlier in 1947, the American government had begun to fund mainstream publications on culture and current affairs as part of a large-scale diplomatic enterprise to influence French perspectives favourably, and funding later extended to a handful of private magazines and publications in the context of the Marshall plan.[201]

Molloy invited other reservations, by virtue of its awkward historical dimension and obvious framing as false testimony. In his report, Louis Pauwels objected: 'One feels that Beckett has touched the depths of the reality of being without faith. [. . .] But one cannot get rid of the feeling that, if he really had touched the depths, he would not dare to use his experience like that'.[202] There are indications that the novel was perceived as dangerously provocative long after this; the Strasbourg printer who worked for the Editions de Minuit, Müh-Le Roux, who normally printed texts on ancient art, refused to put his name to the first print-run of *Molloy* in March 1951. The first edition was presented as the work of the 'Imprimerie spéciale des Editions de Minuit', the stock phrase alluding to the publisher's illustrious record in the Resistance, utilised when a book seemed likely to be censored.[203]

The troubling freedom with which Beckett experiments with the limits of testimony has a distinctive literary context, and chimes with broader debates in France in the late 1940s and early 1950s. Rousset and Cayrol, notably, attempted to redefine the parameters of testimony in texts that merged their own experiences of the Nazi camps with memories of other

198 Martine Poulain, 'La censure', *L'édition française depuis 1945*, 561–4.

199 Hervé Serry, 'A Publishing Decision under Constraint: Samuel Beckett and Le Seuil Publishers in 1947', trans. Helena Scott, *JoBS* 21, no. 1 (2012): 71.

200 'Opinions', *Les Temps Modernes* 9 (1946): 1722.

201 Brian Angus McKenzie, *Remaking France: Americanization, Public Diplomacy, and the Marshall Plan* (New York: Berghahn, 2005), 193–229.

202 Serry, 'A Publishing Decision', 78.

203 Henri Vignes, *Bibliographie des Editions de Minuit: Du Silence de la mer à L'Anti-Oedipe* (Paris: Librairie Henri Vignes, 2010), 119, 371.

'political deportees'.[204] Their reflections on the historical status of fiction accord on several levels, although they had no political affinities (Rousset, a former Trotskyite, was a long-standing militant of the internationalist Left, and Cayrol, a Catholic humanist, was involved with the nationalist and right-leaning strands of the Resistance during the war, and with Catholic left-leaning publications after the war). In a foreword to *Les jours de notre mort*, a novel based on his own experience and other testimonies, Rousset emphasised that, although his book relates authentic facts and events, he chose to utilise the techniques of the novel due to 'a mistrust of words', to portray a universe that is 'singularly out of proportion with the everyday reactions of ordinary men, and yet close and intimate'. It would have been 'puerile to invent', he concluded, 'since reality far exceeded the imaginary'.[205] Cayrol, in contrast, sought to interrogate the category of the imaginary in its own right. An essay published in *Les Temps Modernes* in 1948 explored shared patterns in the dreams of concentration camp detainees and their capacity to provide hope: Cayrol writes about the significance of dreams of salvation and return, and about the nightmares experienced by survivors who have returned to a world unwilling to acknowledge what they have confronted.[206] For Cayrol, the dreams of dismemberment, slow death and torture that haunt survivors also reveal the abyss separating those who have lived through the horror of the camps from those who have not.

Cayrol, like Péron, had been sent to the Fresnes prison and to Mauthausen following his arrest. By the early 1950s, he had grown increasingly weary of fictionalised accounts of the Nazi camps; in an essay published in *Esprit* in 1953, he questioned the ethics of novels by Robert Merle and Erich Maria Remarque, denouncing their transformation of a historical problem into 'an image, a fiction, a fable'.[207] These were Merle's *Death Is My Trade* (*La mort est mon métier*, 1952), a fictional autobiography based on the testimonies of Rudolf Höss, commandant of Auschwitz, at the Nuremberg trials, and Remarque's *Spark of Life* (*Der Funke Leben*, 1952), a controversial fiction about daily life in a German concentration camp informed by testimonies collected by the author.[208] For Cayrol, these novels merely represented the rise of a new kind of opportunism, and he deplored that

[204] On the Holocaust as a 'radical historical *crisis of witnessing*', see Shoshana Felman and Dori Laub, *Testimony: Crises of Witnessing in Literature, Psychoanalysis and History* (New York: Routledge, 1992), xvii.

[205] David Rousset, *Les jours de notre mort: Roman* (Paris: Pavois, 1947), 11.

[206] Jean Cayrol, 'Les rêves concentrationnaires', *Les Temps Modernes* 36 (1948): 520–35.

[207] Jean Cayrol, 'Journal à plusieurs voix: Témoignage et littérature', *Esprit* 21 (1953): 575.

[208] On fictionalised testimonies, see Sue Vice, *Textual Deceptions: False Memoirs and Literary Hoaxes in the Contemporary Era* (Edinburgh: Edinburgh University Press, 2014), 142–202.

the concentration camp, whose existence had been met with shock, surprise and suspicion in public debate in 1945, should have so quickly and problematically become the source of 'nice, quaint historical subjects'; all that is required for literary success, he noted, is a 'good concentration camp intrigue', a 'home-based executioner', 'a few skeletons' and 'a wisp of crematorium smoke'. Between 1948 and 1950, in his essays and in a related book entitled *Lazare parmi nous* (1950), Cayrol conceptualised a different kind of literature – a 'littérature concentrationnaire', a literature of the concentration camps, driven by a concern for the expressive challenges that arise when survivors of deportation attempt to remember their experiences, and when writers attempt to represent historical atrocities. In interrelated reflections on a 'romanesque concentrationnaire' (concentration camp romance) and 'art lazaréen' (Lazarean art), Cayrol defined a new type of narrative, appropriate for victims who have nothing left to express, operating in a mode which renders even the most familiar events as incomprehensible, reprehensible, irritating and unrevealing.[209] This Lazarean model invited reflections on authorship and literary representation from Blanchot and François Mauriac, and echoed with Charles Vildrac's *Lazare*.[210] Underlying Cayrol's reflection is a 'littérature d'empêchement' that does not seek to explicate the Nazi camps but conveys the enigmatic nature of a world that no longer tolerates metaphysical questions. Cayrol's term, defined in *Esprit* in September 1949, qualifies a literature that arrests its characters into non-communication and non-development, like Lazarus before his resurrection; in his view, such a literature is uniquely able to represent the intense solitude experienced at the threshold of death, through a focus on human beings unable to enter into a defined history and a defined story.[211] These ideas coincide with Beckett's own call for an art of *empêchement*, impediment or hindrance, in 'Peintres de l'empêchement', an essay written in March 1947 and published in 1948.[212]

As utilised by Beckett, *empêchement* applies to a modern painting of acceptance, which takes as its premise a state of deprivation that is material and ontological in equal measure. For Beckett, the 'motif peinture empêchement' was an important, albeit unwitting critical insight on

[209] Jean Cayrol, 'D'un romanesque concentrationnaire', *Esprit* 17 (1949): 340–3.

[210] Maurice Blanchot, *La condition critique: Articles 1945–1998*, ed. Christophe Bident (Paris: Gallimard, 2010), 178–81; François Mauriac, 'Avant-propos', in *La Nuit*, by Elie Wiesel [1958] (Paris: Minuit, 2007), 28; Charles Vildrac, *Lazare* (Paris: Minuit, 1946).

[211] Cayrol, 'D'un romanesque concentrationnaire', 346.

[212] Gary D. Mole also points to this coincidence in *Beyond the Limit-Experience: French Poetry of the Deportation, 1940–1945* (New York: Peter Lang, 2002), 1.

modern painting that he continued to defend.[213] His work speaks in powerful ways to Cayrol's argument for a historical literature of atrocity in which surprise or revolt no longer exist. *Malone Dies* begins as a Lazarean narrative in reverse, haunted by a suffering and death that have already happened and recurred: 'I have only to open my eyes to have them begin again, the sky and smoke of mankind. [. . .] Dark and silent and stale, I am no prey for them. I am far from the sounds of blood and breath, immured. I shall not speak of my sufferings' (186). Likewise, 'The Calmative' begins with a narrator confessing his inability to remember the moment of his death, and expressing relief that he is 'no longer with these assassins, in this bed of terror'.[214] Of course, like those writers criticised by Cayrol, Beckett writes of a history of horror witnessed at a remove, but without ever attempting to reclaim it as his own. A world separates the highly controversial tradition of false and embellished testimony that emerged in the 1950s from Beckett's fragmentary narratives, in which the process of telling is subject to an evident and relentless assault: his is a literature retracing the boundaries and recesses of the political imaginary, through literary forms commonly indifferent, if not averse, to the extremes of historical experience. The territory charted by Beckett reimagines those very elements – cowardice, passivity, stupidity and social hatred – that realist historical fiction seldom attempts to render. His turn away from the 'material of experience' and towards the 'material of expression' in the war's aftermath was not merely an aesthetic break, but the continuation of his investigation into political memory.

[213] *LSB2*, 152. [214] SB, 'The Calmative', in *Three Novellas* (London: Calder, 1999), 24.

CHAPTER 4

Turning Points

Torture, Dissent and the Algerian War of Independence

'All that is left is the desert. And even then, it is a desert without issue, a desert without desertion'.[1] It is in this manner that the theatre programme for *Acte sans paroles I*, performed with *Fin de partie* at the Paris Studio des Champs Elysées in 1957, speculated on the predicament of Beckett's silent protagonist and its resemblance to the situation of a French deserter in Algeria. This interpretation of Beckett's mime probably seemed fanciful and certainly fell on deaf ears: indeed, to most of Beckett's contemporaries, there was no clear relation between his plays and the immediate present. A few years thereafter, the British playwright John Arden denounced Beckett's failure to write plays 'about Algeria' publicly; speaking up in Beckett's defence, Alan Schneider replied that his plays were all – metaphorically – about Algeria.[2] Schneider was right to a degree: the Algerian war marked a crucial moment for Beckett as a writer, and altered the remit of political writing more generally. Yet, overall, it has proved tempting to discount Beckett's proximity to the Algerian war,[3] and the conflict has remained a timid, if not an absent temporal landmark in a vast body of criticism that describes Beckett as lacking interest in political debate and political action. His biographers have not been particularly loquacious on the subject of the Algerian war, preferring to focus on Beckett's actions in the French Resistance when describing the kind of political turmoil to which his work responds. The ground is, nevertheless, beginning to shift: the

[1] Maurice Jacquemont, 'Acte sans paroles', theatre programme, *Studio des Champs Elysées, Saison 1956–1957*, n.pag.

[2] Mel Gussow, 'Beckett Distils His Vision', *NYT*, 31 July 1983, 3. No date is given, but other evidence points to a drama conference organised by John Calder and Kenneth Tynan in Edinburgh in August-September 1963. See Calder, *Pursuit*, 245, 250.

[3] For counter-readings, see Anthony Uhlmann, *Beckett and Poststructuralism* (Cambridge: Cambridge University Press, 1999), 99–103; David Lloyd, *Irish Culture and Colonial Modernity 1800–2000: The Transformation of Oral Space* (Cambridge: Cambridge University Press, 2011), 198–220; Adam Piette, 'Torture, Text, Human Rights: Beckett's *Comment c'est/How It Is* and the Algerian War', in *Around 1945: Literature, Citizenship, Rights*, ed. Allan Hepburn (Montreal: McGill-Queen's University Press, 2016), 151–74.

introduction to the third volume of Beckett's *Letters*, published in 2015, points to the Algerian war as one of the broader contexts shaping *How It Is*.[4] The war was far more than a backdrop to Beckett's middle career, however: it was a pressing political reality to which he responded by recourse to different artistic and material means. His experience certainly differentiates him from the vast majority of his contemporaries, who mostly thought of the Algerian war as a distant abstraction and perceived protest as the preserve of politically marginal circles and individuals.[5]

The Algerian war was a particularly murderous, unpredictable and damaging war, which differed vastly from colonial conflicts and uprisings in Indochina, Morocco and Tunisia. In France, the Algerian war was met by a mixture of unease, fear and indifference from the vast majority, but nonetheless mobilised the energies of small politicised groups, in Paris in particular, who advanced the Algerian cause in publications, talks, demonstrations and anti-war committees.[6] Ultimately, however, the international diplomatic campaign led by the Algerian National Liberation Front (FLN) would come to have a more profound influence on the course of events than military operations, particularly as Cold War tensions escalated and successive French governments were confronted by international crises of great magnitude over the issue of torture.[7] This was a time during which writing and dissent, publishing and protest became inextricably and durably enmeshed for many of Beckett's closest collaborators, and Lindon in particular. There are many traces of Beckett's attempts to record the political idioms that crystallised around the repression of a conflict that few were willing or able to acknowledge publicly as a war: references to guerrilla war, desertion, torture and interrogation proliferate in texts from this period, particularly *Pochade radiophonique* or *Rough for Radio II*, *Fragment de théâtre II* or *Rough for Theatre II*, and *Comment c'est* or *How It Is*. This facet of the work, in turn, is intimately tied to the debates about legality and sovereignty that marked the Algerian war and coloured much of the catalogue of the Editions de Minuit.

[4] *LSB3*, xiv–xvii.

[5] See Jean-Pierre Rioux, ed., *La Guerre d'Algérie et les Français* (Paris: Fayard, 1990); Raphaëlle Branche and Sylvie Thénault, eds., *La France en guerre 1954–1962: Expériences métropolitaines de la guerre d'Algérie* (Paris: Autrement, 2008).

[6] Sirinelli, *Intellectuels et passions françaises*, 194–224; Schalk, *War and the Ivory Tower*, 61–111; James D. Le Sueur, *Uncivil War*, 2nd ed. (Lincoln: University of Nebraska Press, 2005).

[7] See Matthew Connelly, *A Diplomatic Revolution: Algeria's Fight for Independence and the Origins of the Post-Cold War Era* (Oxford: Oxford University Press, 2002), 132; Paul Clay Sorum, *Intellectuals and Decolonization in France* (Chapel Hill: University of North Carolina Press, 1977), xi–xii, 29, 34, 174–5, 177; Todd Shepard, *The Invention of Decolonization: The Algerian War and the Remaking of France* (Ithaca: Cornell University Press, 2006), 63–73.

Beckett, the Algerian War and Political Writing

Beckett's notebooks of the 1930s offer ample evidence of an interest in the long history of colonial politics: the 'Trueborn Jackeen' notes locate the Plantation of Ulster, the Williamite Penal Acts and the Great Famine within a broader continuum of mass killings, conquests and civil wars, and present an account of the Elizabethan Reformation and the Desmond Wars that registers the vital role played by political euphemisms such as 'pacification' in the chain of massacres and confiscations leading to colonial subjugation.[8] In another register, the notes for *Human Wishes* relay Samuel Johnson's attack against the 'barbarous debilitating policy' of the Hanoverians in Ireland – an 'unrelenting persecution' that ignored the rule of law and led to impoverishment and starvation.[9] Beckett was also familiar with the doctrine of pacification implemented by successive French governments: his 'Murderous Humanitarianism' translation relays with considerable verve the Surrealist belief that 'pacification' is nothing but a 'fresh impulse' to 'war, that reliable colonial endemic'.[10] For Breton and his cosignatories, this 'godsent euphemism' provided a French government 'in throes of pacifism' with fresh motives to launch the Moroccan Rif War and send 'tried and trusty thugs' to 'plunder' the colonies, after that hiatus of 'the intercapitalistic butchery', the First World War. This and the other critiques of the French 'civilising mission' in the Caribbean and Madagascar that Beckett translated for *Negro* find pointed resonances in the debates about the Algerian war and pacification that marked the 1950s.

Pacification, the keystone of French colonial policy in Algeria after 1956, encompassed the repression of guerrilla war in the countryside and the mountains, the implantation of military forces to quell uprisings, the burning of rebellious villages and the forced removal of rural populations. Many other euphemisms developed around torture and internment, reflecting not simply an attempt to nurture a national consensus around the necessity of pacification, but also the emergence of a new political discourse indexed to emergency and censorship legislation. In April 1955, the government declared a state of emergency in Algeria and passed a law giving public authorities in Algeria, France and overseas territories the power to 'take all measures necessary to keep control over the press and all publications, no matter their nature, and over radiophonic broadcasts, cinematic

[8] The inverted commas feature in Beckett's source; see *Encyclopædia Britannica*, vol. 12, 606–7.
[9] See my 'Beckett, Samuel Johnson and the "Vacuity of Life"', 242.
[10] *Beckett in Black and Red*, 56.

projections and dramatic performances'.[11] In March 1956, powers of censorship were strengthened and extended to 'all means of expression' including telecommunications, in a body of legislation giving 'special powers' to the government and the army in order to maintain public order and 'safeguard' the national territory in Algeria.[12] The French press remained subject to frequent censorship, although the military state of emergency was implemented on metropolitan territory only in times of acute political crisis, in May and June 1958, and from April 1961 to May 1963. Numerous publications were censored; nevertheless, a considerable number of polemical testimonies, reports and essays continued to circulate, first on torture, between 1957 and 1959, and then, between 1960 and 1962, on insubordination and desertion, the emergence of the Third World, and the resurgence of far-right nationalism.[13] In the wake of the Battle of Algiers, the publishing strategies of Lindon, Pierre Jean Oswald, Nils Andersson and François Maspero proved critical, and focused public debate on the illegality of torture and its incompatibility with French republican ideals and post-war human rights legislation.

Contrary to other colonies and protectorates, Algeria was categorised as an ensemble of French departments and provinces, and its political, territorial and symbolic status embedded the conflict into many layers of unspeakability. There are clear correlations between the elision of the war, the devising of an illusory peace and enshrined beliefs in France's 'civilising mission' and 'modernising mission'.[14] The word 'war' was largely banished from public discourse, to avoid giving credence to the idea that a civil war was tearing the nation apart, and was commonly replaced by euphemisms such as the 'Algerian problem', 'counter-insurgency operations', a 'law-and-order problem' and 'pacification'.[15] Famously, in 1960, the word 'war' could not be uttered during the trial of the *porteurs de valise* or 'suitcase carriers' led by Francis Jeanson, who provided material and financial support to the FLN; witnesses were asked to refer to 'police operations'.[16] The war was

[11] 'Loi no. 55–385 du 3 avril 1955 instituant un état d'urgence et en déclarant l'application en Algérie', *JORF*, 7 April 1955, 3480.

[12] 'Décret no. 56–274 du 17 mars 1956 relatif aux mesures exceptionnelles tendant au rétablissement de l'ordre, à la protection des personnes et des biens et à la sauvegarde du territoire de l'Algérie', *JORF*, 19 March 1956, 2665.

[13] Benjamin Stora, *Le dictionnaire des livres de la guerre d'Algérie* (Paris: L'Harmattan, 1996).

[14] Benjamin Stora, *La gangrène et l'oubli* (Paris: La Découverte, 1998), 38; Connelly, *A Diplomatic Revolution*, 27–8; Shepard, *The Invention of Decolonization*, 6, 186–90.

[15] Martin S. Alexander, Martin Evans and J. F. V. Keiger, eds., 'The "War without a Name", the French Army and the Algerians: Recovering Experiences, Images and Testimonies', in *The Algerian War and the French Army, 1954–62* (Basingstoke: Palgrave Macmillan, 2002), 3, 12.

[16] Marcel Péju, *Le procès du réseau Jeanson* (Paris: Maspero, 1961), 102.

rendered unspeakable by other colonial realities, shaped by French assimilationist aspirations, the unconditional support of a large community of French settlers or *pied-noirs* to a French Algeria, and the tiered system of civic and voting rights that had categorised the majority of Algerians as French subjects, but not French citizens. The Evian Accords ending the war in 1962 did not address its obscured status but declared a moratorium on the prosecution of all acts of violence committed during the 'events' and on opinions voiced about the 'events' before the 1961 referendum on Algerian self-determination.[17] Further amnesties for the police and the army were declared in 1966 and 1968. It is only in 1999 that the conflict became officially recognised as a war, and this transformation was the subject of a law in its own right.[18]

The troubled political memory of the Algerian war has posed many challenges, not least to historians, who have frequently turned to Freudian notions of screen memory, repression and neurosis to elucidate its workings. Henry Rousso, for example, has borrowed his political metaphors from Freudian models, tracing the symptoms and resurgences of the 'Vichy syndrome' in debates about republicanism during the Algerian war.[19] Michael Rothberg has coined the term 'multi-directional memory' to describe the relation between the narrativisation of the Holocaust and the submerged articulations of colonial memory that emerged later in Algeria and France.[20] More recently, drawing on Freud's work on screen memory, Max Silverman has traced the relation between the 'palimpsestic memory' of the Algerian war in France and repressed memories of collaboration with Nazism.[21] In the political history of Algeria, the relation between the War of Independence and the Second World War remains deeply fraught: for many, the conflict found its political impulse on 8 May 1945, the day marked by V-Day celebrations across the world, when marches organised in Sétif and Guelma by Algerian nationalist militants gave rise to their massacre by French forces, marking the continuation of a century of violent repression.

Throughout this period, Beckett worked in artistic and intellectual quarters dominated by opposition to the war. Lindon became an important representative of the movement of dissent, particularly in the courts, where he

[17] 'Accords d'Evian', *JORF*, 20 March 1962, 3020.

[18] 'Loi no. 99–882 du 18 octobre 1999 relative à la substitution, à l'expression "aux opérations effectuées en Afrique du Nord", de l'expression "à la guerre d'Algérie ou aux combats en Tunisie et au Maroc"', *JORF*, 20 October 1999, 15647.

[19] Rousso, *The Vichy Syndrome*, 10–11, 15.

[20] Rothberg, *Multidirectional Memory*, 14–16, 267–308.

[21] Max Silverman, *Palimpsestic Memory: The Holocaust and Colonialism in French and Francophone Fiction and Film* (New York: Berghahn, 2013), 15–17.

was frequently called to testify and defend the Editions de Minuit. His pool of authors included Jacques Vergès, the FLN's unofficial lawyer, Jeanson and former soldiers who had deserted the French army. There is no doubt that Beckett and Lindon were exceptionally close; Lindon acted as Beckett's representative on many fronts, dealing with a wide range of administrative, legal and financial tasks. Beckett manifested solidarity with Lindon's political activities publicly and privately on numerous occasions, and their professional relationship brought him in proximity to important controversies about the practices of the French army and intelligence services. Taking sides, in this context, did not necessarily involve embracing a particular political current: the campaign against torture championed by the Editions de Minuit and in other channels federated political dissent across left and right, just as the later bombing campaign led by the far-right Organisation de l'Armée Secrète (OAS) rallied opposition from across the political spectrum. Nevertheless, in the context of the Algerian war, the Editions de Minuit remained broadly affiliated with the Left; this general political orientation had been established since the late 1940s, when Lindon took over as editor and occasionally supported causes defended by the French Communist Party.[22] Lindon's personal commitments were firmly with the socialist Left. After serving in the *maquis*, he adhered to the Rassemblement Démocratique Révolutionnaire, a short-lived party founded in 1948 by Sartre, Rousset and other intellectuals from the non-communist Left as a third way between the French Communist Party, of Stalinist obedience, and the SFIO. In April 1960, Lindon joined the Parti Socialiste Unifié (PSU), a new political party gathering dissident Communists and small parties of the secular and Catholic Left, which was founded to pursue new political alternatives and respond to de Gaulle's return to power. His allegiances shifted after the Algerian war; in the mid-1960s, he supported de Gaulle publicly, even if his editorial position a few years previously had led him to speak against the policies implemented by de Gaulle and his predecessors in the army and justice systems.[23]

During the Algerian war, Lindon's personal frame of reference remained Nazi occupation and the French Resistance; he later explained that the risks inherent in publishing testimonies of desertion and torture involved, at worst, book seizures or bankruptcy, never deportation nor death.[24] He

[22] Simonin, *Les Editions de Minuit*, 268.

[23] Ibid., 266, 504; Pascal Fouché, 'Le militant', *Livres Hebdo* 422, 20 April 2001, 7; Anne Simonin, *Le droit de désobéissance: Les Editions de Minuit en guerre d'Algérie* (Paris: Minuit, 2012), 41; Pierre Vidal-Naquet, 'Une fidélité têtue: La résistance française à la guerre d'Algérie', *Vingtième siècle, revue d'histoire* 10 (1986): 6–7.

[24] Simonin, *Le droit*, 38.

presented his role in the anti-war campaign as a commitment to French republican values, in the service of social emancipation, civic rights and human rights.[25] He frequently stressed that his position was that of a French citizen; when he was tried for publishing an account of desertion, Maurienne's *Le Déserteur*, he pointed out: 'I am not Algerian, and the cause of the FLN is not my cause'.[26] Many years later, he was asked why he had decided to document the problem of torture so comprehensively, and he replied: 'What I was able to do I did for France, not for Algeria'.[27] On occasion, he ventured beyond the realm of publishing: he is known to have secretly given shelter to Rabah Bitat, one of the nine historic chiefs of the FLN, at Jeanson's request.[28] Maspero and Oswald, both associated with the French Communist Party, published texts clearly linked with the action of the FLN that reflected their own anti-militarism and unconditional support of Algerian independence. The dangers they shared led to long-lasting solidarities: long after the Algerian war ended, Lindon acted as advisor for the Editions Maspero and occasionally provided some financial support.[29]

The manner in which French political cultures functioned around the Algerian war was distinctive, and, in the early 1960s, few among Beckett's contemporaries were able to display the kind of commitment that Arden championed from afar. In practice, Sartre proved to be the only writer who could express dissent alone; he was able to do so without incurring a prison sentence or a trial – 'one does not put Voltaire in prison', was President de Gaulle's response – although public demonstrations by war veterans and partisans of a French Algeria called for him to be shot.[30] By celebrating a political commitment located in social realism, Arden was merely asserting the validity of his own approach to political writing; his accusation against Beckett also brings to the fore common assumptions about the politics of dissent and protest which, in the context of the Algerian war, are simply not valid. During the war and thereafter, the representation of the conflict remained the preserve of testimony and historical drama, with photographic journalism remaining the primary mode of documentation

[25] Georges Arnaud, *Mon procès* (Paris: Minuit, 1961), 83.

[26] *Provocation à la désobéissance: Le procès du Déserteur* (Paris: Minuit, 1962), 21.

[27] Pierre Vidal-Naquet, *Face à la raison d'Etat: Un historien dans la guerre d'Algérie* (Paris: La Découverte, 1989), 59.

[28] Simonin, *Le droit*, 46.

[29] Christian Baudelot, 'Hommage fraternel d'un défenseur à tous crins', *François Maspero et les paysages humains*, 53; Julien Hage, 'Une brève histoire des librairies et des éditions Maspero', ibid., 133–5.

[30] Marie-Christine Granjon, 'Raymond Aron, Jean-Paul Sartre et le conflit algérien', in *La guerre d'Algérie et les intellectuels français*, ed. Jean-Pierre Rioux and Jean-François Sirinelli (Paris: Complexe, 1991), 135; François Maspero, *Le droit à l'insoumission: Le dossier des '121'* (Paris: Maspero, 1961), 41–2.

on the French side.[31] Official and unofficial censorship shaped the whole spectrum of dramatic writing, and the plays written by prominent French authors during the war often relied on distinctive forms of historical coding, transposition and omission. Notable examples include Sartre's play about Nazism, *Les séquestrés d'Altona* (first performed in 1959), which raised troubling questions about Nazi occupation, national guilt and torture, and Emmanuel Roblès's *Plaidoyer pour un rebelle* (written in 1959 and published in 1965), which transposed the events leading to the execution of Fernand Iveton, an Algiers Communist and FLN militant, to another historical context, that of the Indonesian War of Independence against the Dutch. Similar tensions are at work in Genet's *Les Paravents* (published in 1961, in the wake of a long process of composition and reworking), where prescient political problems are reimagined through the nineteenth-century conquest of Algeria. These models of displacement and political translation are in keeping with those explored by Beckett in his texts of the late 1950s and 1960s, where the Algerian war serves as an important symbolic referent but is never invoked directly, in a manoeuvre that refracts the powerful forms of oblivion that have shaped the memorialisation of the war at large.

Torture, Testimony and Euphemism

Numerous testimonies about the Algerian war deal with torture, and associate torture with the use of electricity – more precisely, with the device known as 'la gégène', the term for the electrical dynamos and generators commonly used to power radios and telephones. The method had been present in the conduct of French colonial affairs since the mid-1930s, particularly in Indochina. Electric torture was cheap and simple, and left few physical marks and no proof that might be exhibited in court; it subsequently became a staple in the French army's dealings with Algerian suspects and FLN militants. In the context of a declared situation of national emergency, which granted special executive and judiciary powers to the army, electric torture did not simply become a powerful tool of mass repression and silencing; it also generated a whole new vocabulary.[32] The officers who led the Battle of Algiers in 1957 resorted to careful euphemisms,

[31] Benjamin Stora and Laurent Gervereau, *Photographier la guerre d'Algérie* (Paris: Marval, 2004); Philip Dine, *Images of the Algerian War: French Fiction and Film, 1954–1992* (Oxford: Clarendon, 1994).

[32] Raphaëlle Branche, *La torture et l'armée pendant la guerre d'Algérie, 1954–1962* (Paris: Gallimard, 2002), 28–31, 325–31.

synecdoches and metonymies to justify their activities: 'interrogation' was the term used by Roger Trinquier; 'procédé' or process was the word used by Jacques Massu, his superior, who was known for his distinguished military career with the Free French forces and during the Indochina War and the Suez Crisis.[33] In the vernacular employed by the military and the police, 'rock n' roll' designated torture by electricity; 'breast stroke', immersion in a bathtub; 'sunbathing', the burning of flesh; the napalm bombs targeting the Algerian forests and countryside were called 'special delivery tins'; and police batons were known as 'bidules' or gizmos.[34]

This idiom was a symptom of wider developments in information-gathering and its institutionalisation, which Vidal-Naquet memorably described at the trial of the Jeanson network as the preserve of a new 'univers concentrationnaire', in reference to Rousset's study of the Nazi camp system.[35] In other quarters, the gradual development of 'transit centres' and 'sorting centres' in Algeria and the rise of this new taxonomy were registered in different terms. A document dated March 1955, authored by a senior administrator commissioned to report on the actions of the police and the army, listed the abuses ('sévices') routinely committed by means of 'installations' such as 'the bathtub', 'electricity' and 'the tube'.[36] A few months later, another report corroborated these facts, concluding that the *gendarmerie* and the police in Algeria had adopted the same methods of investigation as the Gestapo.[37] The parallel was reiterated when Paul Teitgen, an eminent Resistance veteran, resigned from his post as General Secretary at the Algiers Préfecture in 1957. His letter of resignation to President Guy Mollet stated that he could recognise on the bodies of Algerian men interned in the 'hosting centres' ('centres d'hébergement') of Paul-Cazelles and Beni-Messous marks of torture that were identical to those which the Gestapo had imprinted on his own body; Teitgen concluded that he could no longer serve an administration that looked upon this practice as a matter of routine.[38] His statement later played a key role in the contexts of the

[33] Laurent Schwartz, *Le Problème de la torture dans la France d'aujourd'hui, 1954–1961* (Paris: Cahiers de la République, 1961), 4.

[34] Jean-Charles Jauffret, 'The War Culture of French Combatants in the Algerian Conflict', *The Algerian War and the French Army*, 104; Jim House and Neil MacMaster, *Paris 1961: Algerians, State Terror, and Memory* (Oxford: Oxford University Press, 2006), 40.

[35] Péju, *Le procès du réseau Jeanson*, 123.

[36] 'Le rapport de M. Roger Wuillaume, inspecteur général de l'administration', in *La raison d'Etat: Textes publiés par le Comité Maurice Audin*, ed. Pierre Vidal-Naquet (Paris: La Découverte, 2002), 68–70 (first published by the Comité Maurice Audin and *Vérité-Liberté* in July 1961, and republished by the Editions de Minuit in 1962).

[37] M. Mairey, 'Rapport relatif au fonctionnement des forces de police en Algérie', *La raison d'Etat*, 82.

[38] Pierre Vidal-Naquet, *Torture: Cancer of Democracy, France and Algeria 1954–1962*, trans. Barry Richard (Baltimore: Penguin, 1963), 63.

Jeanson trial and the *Déserteur* trial, at which Lindon also testified. State-sanctioned torture re-awakened the ghosts of Nazi occupation, and there are many indications that the discursive registers used to summon the conflict or deny its existence were also attempts to exorcise the spectres of the Vichy regime and memories of collaboration.[39] For many other Resistance veterans, this state of affairs was intolerable, and those who joined the network of 'suitcase carriers' around Jeanson shared the same political past and motivations.[40]

Torture was connected, in less obvious ways, to the tensions between territorial and legal forms of assimilation and coexistence that shaped citizenship in colonial Algeria. Those categorised as 'Algerian Muslims' had long been confined to an inferior civic status by enshrined laws and forms of segregation that denied their political rights until 1919. Ultimately, in 1958, the Constitution of the Fifth Republic granted limited political rights, including the right to vote as part of a separate electoral college, to all 'Algerian Muslims', women as well as men.[41] But these enshrined inequities leave many traces in war testimonies. Numerous texts by soldiers, deserters, tortured civilians and FLN militants describe atrocities perpetrated in governmental buildings, municipal halls, schools and stadiums – in other words, within the very sites that pertained to give a moral legitimacy to French republican proclamations of liberty, equality and fraternity. The topography of torture and imprisonment was frequently connected to symbols of the French Republic, in a way that once again situated republican ideals of social equality beyond the reach of the Algerian population. The most striking example appears in the journal of a former paratrooper, Pierre Leulliette, published by the Editions de Minuit in 1961, and censored like other books about torture and desertion. Leulliette evoked a military camp established in a disused factory in the Algiers district, and described the routine use of grey, coffin-like wooden boxes turned against the wall. Algerian detainees who had not spoken under torture were forced to stand in one of these boxes even when their legs could no longer carry them. These, however, were not coffins but polling booths lent by the local council, which had been transformed into torture devices reminiscent of the medieval

[39] Jean-Pierre Rioux, 'La guerre d'Algérie dans l'histoire des intellectuels', *La guerre d'Algérie et les intellectuels français*, 43; Kristin Ross, *Fast Cars, Clean Bodies: Decolonization and the Reordering of French Culture* (Cambridge, MA: MIT Press, 1995), 71–122.

[40] Martin Evans, *The Memory of Resistance: French Opposition to the Algerian War, 1954–1962* (Oxford: Berg, 1997); Hervé Hamon and Patrick Rotman, *Les porteurs de valises: La résistance française à la guerre d'Algérie* (Paris: Albin Michel, 1979).

[41] Shepard, *The Invention of Decolonization*, 20–43.

torture cells known as *malconforts*.[42] This moment clearly marked a turning point for Leulliette, and he returned to it when he testified in support of Lindon at the *Déserteur* trial.

Many of the torture testimonies published by the Editions de Minuit exposed the jargon employed by soldiers, paratroopers and police officers, and the redeployment of seemingly benign phrases to new military ends. *Le désert à l'aube* by Noël Favrelière related the widespread use of the 'corvée de bois' (wood-fetching duty), or execution without trial.[43] *Les Egorgeurs* by Benoist Rey revealed that 'to smile from one ear to the other' ('faire un grand sourire d'une oreille à l'autre') meant to cut someone's throat, while 'to take a one-way ticket' ('prendre un aller simple') qualified another type of summary execution.[44] Lindon's war publications were aligned with a much larger mass of documents published from 1957 onwards in established and small-circulation reviews (notably *Esprit*, *Les Temps Modernes*, *Témoignages et Documents* and *Vérité-Liberté*), which dealt with the campaign of pacification, the new camp system in Algeria and the transformation of colonial farms, villas and governmental buildings into sites of torture and detention. This, for many of Beckett's contemporaries, was the age of appeals, petitions and letters; for Charlotte Delbo, letter-writing became the last resort for those who were deprived of the means to take action, trapped in a political climate in which all conventional channels for political activity and dissent were failing.[45]

The question of torture preoccupied many across the French Left, who feared the rise of a violent Far Right hostile to Algerian political claims, and perceived its resurgence as a by-product of French colonial politics and war methods. From the early days, analogies between the French army's use of torture in Algeria and the practices of the Gestapo were common. The first public denunciations of torture as a method of repression – for example, by Claude Bourdet in *France-Observateur* and François Mauriac in *L'Express* – attempted to define a historical referent for the horrors of repression, gesturing towards the Dreyfus affair and the Vichy regime to alert the French public to the collapse of republican values.[46] The same parallels, in turn, provided a moral compass within movements of dissent in Paris and in France, enabling supporters of Algerian independence and detractors of torture to summon the spirit of Resistance movements that had

[42] Pierre Leulliette, *St Michel et le dragon: Souvenirs d'un parachutiste* (Paris: Minuit, 1961), 310–11.
[43] Noël Favrelière, *Le désert à l'aube* (Paris: Minuit, 1960), 71.
[44] Benoist Rey, *Les Egorgeurs* (Paris: Minuit, 1961), 28, 73.
[45] Charlotte Delbo, *Les Belles Lettres* (Paris: Minuit, 1961), 9.
[46] On the dominating 'dreyfusard', 'bolshevik' and 'third-worldist' temperaments, see Vidal-Naquet, 'Une fidélité têtue', 11.

defeated Nazism. Notably, de Beauvoir denounced the creation of 'extermination camps' masquerading as 'relocation camps', echoing the correspondence that many testimonies of torture forged between Nazi war crimes and French colonial policies.[47] As Darius Rejali points out, these analogies also formed a fully fledged historical thesis, and obscured the fact that the two principal techniques of stealth torture used in Algeria – pumping stomachs with water and electric torture – are characteristic of American, French, and Japanese policing traditions, and of modern democracies more generally.[48]

What was distinctive about the war testimonies published by Lindon was their emphasis on historical transmission and repetition. In a memoir reporting his long detention and torture, Djamal Amrani, Ali Boumendjel's brother-in-law, recalled a sergeant advising him to give in: 'we have seen tougher than you, and don't forget we were in Indochina'.[49] The testimonies of Algerian students published in *La Gangrène* related the manner in which 'Gégène' was used by the Direction de la Surveillance du Territoire (DST), the French intelligence service dedicated to domestic affairs, and cited a French Tunisian police officer: 'I got to know torture through the Nazis; now, I am applying it'.[50] The book (published and censored in 1958, and republished in an uncensored expanded edition in 1959) revealed that the students' interrogations and torture had taken place at the headquarters of the DST on Rue des Saussaies, a few doors away from the Elysée Palace, in a building owned by the Ministry of the Interior that had formerly housed the Gestapo headquarters and served as a site of torture in the Nazi hunt against the French Resistance. In another censored testimony, Henri Alleg, the Communist editor-in-chief of *Alger républicain*, related that Captain Faulques, who oversaw proceedings at the Villa Sésini – a colonial villa in Algiers that served as internment camp and torture chamber – would introduce himself as 'the famous SS captain'.[51] Through such testimonies, Lindon's catalogue shed light on the many identities of those who practised torture as part of their military or police functions during the Algerian war. A wealth of historical evidence has subsequently ascertained that torture was, in different circumstances, utilised by French officers decorated for their actions in the French Resistance, Indochina war veterans, former members of the Vichy militia, former SS officers who had joined

[47] Simone de Beauvoir, Preface, in *Djamila Boupacha*, by de Beauvoir and Gisèle Halimi (Paris: Gallimard, 1962), 1.

[48] Darius Rejali, *Torture and Democracy* (Princeton: Princeton University Press, 2007), 540, 165.

[49] Djamal Amrani, *Le Témoin* (Paris: Minuit, 1960), 39.

[50] *La Gangrène* (Paris: Minuit, 1959), 77.

[51] Henri Alleg, *La Question* (Paris: Minuit, 1958), 98.

the French Foreign Legion, Algerian war veterans, Algerian loyalists who had enrolled in the French army (the *harkis*), Algerians working for the auxiliary police force and young conscripts. Raphaëlle Branche has demonstrated precisely how torture gave rise to a peculiar 'economy of conviction' nurtured by euphemistic discourses that also reconfigured the question of torture, to exonerate the French army for breaching legal procedures and human rights conventions.[52]

The year 1962 saw several turning points in the debates about the army's special powers, notably during the trial by military court of Lieutenant Daniel Godot. Godot, a leader of the OAS, had orchestrated spectacular actions on behalf of the OAS including an attack against an arms depot outside Paris and the burglary of a Paris bank.[53] At his trial in August 1962, one of the witnesses, Captain Joseph Estoup, highlighted the distinctive meanings that had accumulated in the word 'torture'. This was the first time that an officer admitted not simply that torture was widely practised but that it was a military order.[54] Estoup explained to the tribunal that, while military language has consecrated the phrase 'intelligence work' ('faire du renseignement') and polite society prefers to say 'asking questions' ('presser de questions'), in plain French the military operations in Algeria could be described by a simple verb: *torturer*, to torture.[55]

Beckett took interest in the Godot affair; the name, naturally, caught his attention. In April 1962, he sent a cutting from *Paris-Presse, L'Intransigeant* to Bray reporting Godot's arrest near the Saint-Sulpice church in Paris, within walking distance of his flat on Boulevard St Jacques. The headline quoted Godot as declaring: 'C'est la guerre' ('We're at war').[56] The OAS waged war on several fronts across Algeria and France, and street shootings and bomb attacks were particularly numerous between December 1961 and March 1962, when it became clear that negotiations between the French government and the provisional Algerian government were making critical progress. The OAS had enormous resources at its disposal; in the morning of 5 March 1962, for example, up to 137 explosions were reported across Algiers in the space of two hours.[57] In Paris, the OAS campaign of 'plasticages' targeted many academics, journalists and political figures who

[52] Branche, *La torture*, 311–24, 423, 227–9.
[53] See Yves-Frédéric Jaffré, *Les tribunaux d'exception, 1940–1962* (Paris: Nouvelles Editions Latines, 1962), 331–2.
[54] Pierre Vidal-Naquet, ed., Preface, *Les crimes de l'armée française: Algérie 1954–1962* (Paris: La Découverte, 2001), i–ii.
[55] Ibid., 157.
[56] This cutting is from the 11 April 1962 issue of *Paris-Presse, L'Intransigeant*, and is attached to TCD MS 10948/1/177.
[57] *L'Humanité*, 6 March 1962, 3.

had supported pacifist or anti-colonial positions, always using the same methods.[58] Lindon, who lived two streets away from Beckett on Boulevard Arago, was perceived as a particular threat, and the OAS targeted his flat with explosives on 7 December 1961, at the opening of the *Déserteur* trial. Four days later, a Molotov cocktail was thrown into the front window of the Editions de Minuit, on Rue Bernard-Palissy.[59] Dissent also came at a high price for others: in the early months of 1961, explosives were left and thrown into Maspero's bookshop on several occasions, and Maspero himself was gravely injured in a street shooting.[60]

Beckett's letters convey his deep concern; in December 1961, he reports to Aidan Higgins that Lindon 'has been having a bad time on account of his anti-torture Documents and was dragged before the courts the other day for his publication The Deserter. Same night at midnight he was "plasticated" – his private apartment. No one hurt but much damage to premises. Verdict day after tomorrow. Fine probably. And he goes in permanent personal danger'.[61] The accounts that Beckett sent to friends about the OAS attack against Jean-Jacques Mayoux in February 1962 differ, betraying a deep shock and surprise – an odd response, given that this particular attack came in the wake of so many others. He renamed the OAS as 'the dynamiters' in a letter to Hutchinson, and wrote to Mayoux – a steadfast supporter of his work since the UNESCO days – to commiserate about the damage caused by 'those bastards'.[62] Mayoux was then known as a prominent pacifist militant; he had been a leading voice in one of the first anti-war organisations, the short-lived Comité d'Action des Intellectuels contre la Poursuite de la Guerre en Afrique du Nord.[63] Many of Beckett's collaborators and acquaintances were members of anti-war groups: Adamov, Beaufret, Blin, Robbe-Grillet and Geneviève Serreau, for example, also became involved with this committee upon its formation in 1955.[64]

The Editions de Minuit at War

To understand Beckett's relation to these strands of French political culture, it is necessary to consider Lindon's work of documentation and the vital

[58] Laurent Schwartz, *Un mathématicien aux prises avec le siècle* (Paris: Odile Jacob, 1997), 404–8.

[59] Simonin, *Les Editions de Minuit*, 482.

[60] François Gabaut, *Partisans. Une revue militante, de la guerre d'Algérie aux années 68* (PhD diss., University Paris 7-Diderot, 2001), 128–9.

[61] *LSB3*, 452. [62] *LSB3*, 469, 462.

[63] On this organisation, dissolved after 1956, see Le Sueur, *Uncivil War*, 54; Schwartz, *Un mathématicien*, 374–5.

[64] Nicolas Hubert, *Editeurs et éditions pendant la guerre d'Algérie, 1954–1962* (Paris: Bouchène, 2012), 97–8.

part that the Editions de Minuit played in the movement of dissent. The catalogue of the Editions de Minuit gathered together different collections structured according to genre and thematic focus; during the Algerian war the two major sub-catalogues were the 'White Collection' ('La Collection Blanche'), managed by Robbe-Grillet from 1955 onwards and conceived as a home for fiction authors including Beckett, and 'Documents', a collection created in 1949, in the wake of Tillion's *L'Algérie en 1957*, and featuring many books on the Algerian war.[65] The 'Documents' series was supervised by Lindon and Vidal-Naquet, a historian and classicist with whom Lindon shared strong political and personal affinities.[66] The 'Documents' published after 1957 included historical surveys, political essays that denounced the abdication of French executive and judiciary powers, and testimonies of soldiers, deserters and FLN militants that exposed the problems posed by torture and summary execution. Vidal-Naquet wrote important studies as part of Maurice Audin's Defence Committee and under his own name, including *L'Affaire Audin* (1958), in which he investigated the disappearance of Audin, a mathematician and member of the Algerian Communist Party suspected of involvement with the FLN. After the war, Vidal-Naquet also published a detailed study of torture, tracing its development from a police method in colonial Algeria to a military procedure and a 'clandestine State institution'.[67]

Due to the nature of the censorship laws passed in 1955 and 1956, the 'Documents' have acquired an important historical status, and they constitute – with the publications of the Editions Maspero, founded in 1959 – the bulk of the publications banned during the Algerian war. Between 1958 and 1962, nine books published by the Editions de Minuit were seized, out of a catalogue of twenty-three titles dealing with the Algerian war, along with twelve of nineteen books about the Algerian war published by Maspero.[68] Censorship was only the tip of the iceberg, as Lindon explained to Seaver at the height of the seizures and banning orders in 1961, detailing the 'police interrogations, late-night threatening phone calls' and 'attempts to close [. . .] down' the Editions de Minuit that he had managed to

65 Simonin, *Les Editions de Minuit*, 363; Anne Simonin, 'La mise à l'épreuve du nouveau roman. Six cent cinquante fiches de lecture d'Alain Robbe-Grillet (1955–1959)', *Annales. Histoire, Sciences sociales* 55, no. 2 (2000): 415–37.

66 See Pierre Vidal-Naquet, 'Présentation d'un document: Le journal de Me Lucien Vidal-Naquet', *Annales. Economies, Sociétés, Civilisations* 48, no. 3 (1993): 504.

67 Vidal-Naquet, *Torture*, 15.

68 Benjamin Stora, 'Une censure de guerre qui ne dit pas son nom. Algérie, années 1960', in *Censures. De la Bible aux larmes d'Éros*, ed. Martine Poulain and Françoise Serre (Paris: BPI-Centre Pompidou, 1987), 49–50; Simonin, *Le droit*, 12, 31, 58–9; Vidal-Naquet, *Face à la raison d'Etat*, 24 n50, 25.

withstand.[69] Lindon and some of his authors were charged for various offences, but this rarely led to formal prosecution. Before the war ended, Lindon bore eighteen inculpations for offenses including damage to the army's morale; defamation against the police and the DST; inciting the military to insubordination and desertion; provocation to desertion and complicity; and putting the security of the State at risk.[70] Some of his wranglings with the justice system were less visible: after republishing *La Gangrène* in July 1959, he was summoned to a confrontation with the former directors of the Sûreté Nationale, who had previously headed the police services, and after republishing Alleg's *La Question* in October 1959, he was asked to testify before a military judge.[71] Both Lindon and Maspero became so accustomed to book seizures that they would prepare small parcels for the police to take away.[72] Nevertheless, these seizures were extremely costly and placed a considerable strain on the day-to-day running of the Editions de Minuit. Lindon later stated that his small publishing house would not have survived the Algerian war if it hadn't been for Beckett, who lent him the money necessary to avoid bankruptcy.[73]

It seems that the professional relationships that Lindon had formed with other publishers around Beckett's work played a role in the translation and dissemination of the 'Documents' abroad. Calder, who always kept abreast of the new work published by Lindon, translated and published Alleg's *La Question*, and wrote an account of Vidal-Naquet's book about Audin's disappearance for the *New Statesman*. After some hesitation, Calder also published a translation of *La Gangrène*.[74] Seaver, then working at Grove Press, became involved with the American edition of Alleg's testimony.[75] Giulio Einaudi, Beckett's Italian publisher, issued translations of *La Gangrène* and *La Question*.

For Lindon, the 'White Collection' and the 'Documents' were intimately related; he frequently associated Alleg with Beckett when describing his distinctive catalogue, and stated that the decisions to publish *La Question* and

[69] Richard Seaver, *The Tender Hour of Twilight: Paris in the '50s, New York in the '60s: A Memoir of Publishing's Golden Age* (New York: Farrar, Straus & Giroux, 2011), 310–11.

[70] See Simonin, *Le droit*, 58–60; Simonin, *Les Editions de Minuit*, 481; Jérôme Lindon, 'Littérature dégagée', *New Morality* 2, no. 2–3 (1962): 110; Fouché, 'Le militant', 8.

[71] Simonin, *Le droit*, 29, 31 n59.

[72] David Macey, *Frantz Fanon* [2000] (London: Verso, 2012), 396; Julien Hage, 'Produire un écrit politique face à l'évènement: L'exemple des éditions François Maspero durant la guerre d'Algérie', in *Ecrire et publier la guerre d'Algérie: De l'urgence aux résurgences*, ed. Thomas Augais, Mireille Hilsum and Chantal Michel (Paris: Kimé, 2011), 23–36.

[73] Assouline, 'Enquête sur un écrivain secret', 27.

[74] Calder, *Pursuit*, 143–4.

[75] Seaver, *The Tender Hour of Twilight*, 244, 310.

Molloy had been self-evident in exactly the same way.[76] At another point, he commented on the affinities that he perceived between his political campaigns and the literary remit of his publishing house: 'I am Samuel Beckett's publisher: to have this chance and this honour is to benefit from an extraordinary freedom in a free country, and the least that can be done is to defend the conditions of this freedom when they are under threat'.[77] Beckett manifested his esteem in other ways; in June 1962, he wrote a tribute to Lindon for a Cologne radio station and emphasised Lindon's 'purity', 'nobility of character' and 'courage'. In this homage, Beckett states, 'I owe him everything', evoking 'what we all owe' to Lindon, this 'great publisher' and 'great man'.[78]

To evoke this collective debt is also to pay tribute to Lindon's work on the 'Documents' series, which went far beyond any call of duty. Lindon made important editorial interventions and reshaped some testimonies in ways that conceptualised the problem of torture in relation to past controversies embedded in the French political imagination. Alleg's original testimony, *Interrogatoire sous la torture*, was retitled *La Question*, in a manoeuvre that emphasised the archaic nature of torture, drew attention to the urgency of coming to terms with the 'Algerian question', and invoked the position taken by Zola, the archetype of the public intellectual, during the Dreyfus affair.[79] Lindon's touch is evident elsewhere, in a series of hard-hitting prefaces signed 'Les Editions de Minuit' and 'The Editors', which presented the methods of the French army in Algeria and the policies of the government as reflective of a mindset which had been integral to Nazi practice in the recent past. To *La Gangrène*, he added an epigraph: a citation by Minister of Justice Edmond Michelet, once an eminent member of the French Resistance, which associated the spread of torture with the sequels of Nazi totalitarianism. To Amrani's *Le Témoin*, he added a preface associating the techniques of French paratroopers in Algeria with those of the Gestapo, in which he warned French readers that, if the rise of French military power was left unchecked, the day would come when the young men undergoing electric torture and the young women submitted to rape would be their own children, rather than remote names in newspaper headlines. Ultimately, Lindon had such a crucial input in the conception and writing of some Algerian 'Documents' that, in a 1989 re-edition of *L'Affaire Audin*,

[76] Alexis Berchadsky, *La Question d'Henri Alleg: Un 'livre-événement' dans la France en guerre d'Algérie* (Paris: Découvrir, 1994), 77; Lindon, 'Littérature dégagée', 113; Simonin, *Les Editions de Minuit*, 430.

[77] Ibid., 309. [78] *LSB3*, 488–90.

[79] Berchadsky, *La Question*, 78–9; Simonin, *Les Editions de Minuit*, 429.

Vidal-Naquet noted that the cover should have borne Lindon's name alongside his own.[80] Elsewhere, he wrote that Lindon had played a vital part in the book's execution and had 'taught him how to write'.[81] The book jackets were inflected by the same editorial line: the back covers of Rey's *Les Egorgeurs* and Alleg's *La Question*, like many others, bore the phrase, 'The Editions de Minuit, founded clandestinely in 1942'. It is precisely because the Editions de Minuit were so intimately associated with an illustrious past of underground activism that Jeanson offered *Notre Guerre* (1960) to Lindon for publication – a book that was seized like many others.[82] There were other, less likely candidates: for example, Roger Trinquier, the hero of the Battle of Algiers, who once offered a book for publication to the Editions de Minuit.[83] Trinquier's visit put an end to a long-running practical joke involving Vergès, who, prior to this unforeseen twist, had often asked to be announced as Colonel Trinquier, in the hope that he might give Lindon a friendly jolt.

Beckett's epistolary accounts convey a sense that his publisher was working on the brink of disaster. In December 1959, he reports to Pinget that Lindon is absorbed in 'ses histoires de juge d'instruction' (his business with the examining magistrate): 'He has been charged, and is preparing his brief. He seems unworried by it all'.[84] In October 1960, he alludes to the trial of the Jeanson network and the uproar generated by the 'Manifeste des 121', announcing to Hutchinson that the Editions de Minuit may not be able to continue long enough to see the publication of *Comment c'est* in December.[85] To Bray, he writes that same month, 'Manivelle-Old Tune due out next week, if the Editions don't go sky high before'.[86] Eventually, in April 1962, he informs Higgins that the *Déserteur* trial is coming to an end, and that Lindon's legal battle will soon be resolved.[87]

Archive records indicate that Beckett purchased some of the polemical books published by Lindon. In September 1959, with a copy of Wiesel's Auschwitz testimony, he bought Alleg's *La Question* (this was, necessarily, a copy left over from previous seizures and 1958 reprints).[88] In May 1960, he acquired four copies of Maurienne's *Le Déserteur* and a copy of *Le droit et la colère*, by Jacques Vergès, Michel Zavrian and Maurice Courrégé (both

[80] Pierre Vidal-Naquet, *L'Affaire Audin 1957–1978* (Paris: Minuit, 1989), 7.
[81] Vidal-Naquet, *Face à la raison d'Etat*, 24. [82] Maspero, *Le droit à l'insoumission*, 8–9.
[83] Pierre Vidal-Naquet, *Mémoires, vol. 2: Le trouble et la lumière, 1955–1998* (Paris: Seuil, 1998), 123.
[84] *LSB3*, 264, 265.
[85] SB to Hutchinson, 7 October 1960, Mary Hutchinson Collection, HRHRC.
[86] *LSB3*, 360. [87] SB to Higgins, 17 April 1962, Beckett Collection, HRHRC.
[88] Published, respectively, in February and June 1958. 'Correspondence 1958–1959, Droits étrangers', Fonds Beckett, IMEC. On reprints of *La Question*, see Berchadsky, *La Question*, 181.

books were published in April 1960).[89] None of these volumes features in the inventory of his library, but this is unsurprising, since it is clear that his belongings underwent serious pruning over the years and that he gave away much of what he read. Other notable absents include his many crime paperbacks and detective novels, his copy of *Negro*, and the books on modern political thought and political history mentioned in correspondence and descriptions of his study on Boulevard Saint-Jacques.

Le droit et la colère – the second book that Vergès published with the Editions de Minuit after *Pour Djamila Bouhired* – is particularly interesting. It is a specialised publication on legal history and the exercise of justice during the Algerian war, co-authored by the three lawyers who represented the FLN, which deals with the legal framework through which 'special powers' were granted to the French government, the police and the army from 1956 onwards to take 'exceptional measures' to control the Algerian conflict. The book also responds to the decree of 12 February 1960 that bolstered the legal provisions made for the army and assigned all matters related to the Algerian war to military tribunals operating under military orders; Vergès, Zavrian and Courrégé protest against the abdication of civil justice and expose the decree as yet another breach of international human rights legislation, citing at various points the 1948 Universal Declaration of Human Rights and the Geneva Conventions. Torture, the authors emphasise, has become ubiquitous, and Djamila Bouhired, Alleg, Audin and Boumendjel are not isolated cases: the 'revelations' obtained through torture have become the main element in legal proceedings generally.[90] This account is faithful to the line adopted by Vergès as lawyer: at the trial of the Jeanson network during that same year, he also challenged the legality of legal proceedings by pointing to the military takeover of executive and judiciary powers. Many other publications from the 'Documents' series followed this line, presenting the army's violations of human rights conventions as invalidating the very foundations of French democracy.

The interest that Beckett manifested in Alleg's testimony is important, because it chimes with the controversy ignited by the book's publication and immediate ban in 1958. Knowlson's account of the Algerian war years suggests that Beckett drew on his experience of underground action: Knowlson explains that Beckett asked Marthe Gautier, Suzanne's close friend, to hide copies of *La Question* in her Paris flat, at an undetermined moment.[91] More recently, Gautier gave a different account, explaining that

[89] 'Correspondance personnelle. Droits étrangers. 1960–1961', Fonds Beckett, IMEC.
[90] Jacques Vergès, Michel Zavrian and Maurice Courrégé, *Le droit et la colère* (Paris: Minuit, 1960), 125.
[91] *DF*, 494.

it was Suzanne who had asked her to store copies of the book.[92] Suzanne probably thought that she and Beckett were too directly associated with Lindon to be able to hide anything themselves; she would have been aware that, by virtue of her specialism, Gautier – an illustrious researcher in genetics who discovered the cause of Down's syndrome[93] – had no obvious link to Lindon or to the academic circles involved in public dissent, who mostly gathered mathematicians, classicists and historians. These details matter, because the publication of *La Question* marked a turning point in political debate and dramatically expanded the remit of Lindon's editorial strategy.

Like Audin and Boumendjel, Alleg had been taken by French paratroopers to a 'sorting centre' in El-Biar, a suburb of Algiers, where he was tortured. The testimony, written in precarious circumstances at the Barberousse prison in Algiers, had been transmitted to Lindon by Alleg's wife and his lawyer.[94] What Alleg related was not simply how torture was used, but how administrative and military structures had been created to extract information by any available means. *La Question* was published on 18 February 1958, and was seized by the police five days later under the charge of 'participation to an attempt to demoralise the army, with the aim of compromising national defence'.[95] Within five weeks, 65,000 copies were sold, an unprecedented number for Minuit's traditionally small print-runs. Many readers bought multiple copies for safe-keeping or for further dissemination. In practice, police seizures did not normally lead to the pulping of whole print runs; banned books could still circulate clandestinely, were discreetly republished or were reprinted abroad. This was the case with *La Question*: after the ban, 90,000 unofficial copies were disseminated. The day after the seizure, the Centre d'Information et de Coordination pour la Défense des Libertés et de la Paix, known as the Centre du Landy, published an unofficial version of the book, made to fit on eight sheets of newspaper, which was then republished by another newspaper, *La Volonté populaire*. *L'Humanité* and *L'Express* encouraged their readers to buy the book, and parts of Alleg's testimony were published in *France-Observateur* and *Libération* (the daily founded by Emmanuel d'Astier de la Vigerie). The satirical newspaper *Le Canard Enchaîné* published Sartre's

92 Marthe Gautier, interview with the author, 7 November 2012.

93 See Marthe Gautier, 'La découvreuse oubliée de la trisomie 21', *La Recherche* 434 (2009): 54, www.larecherche.fr/savoirs/temoignage/decouvreuse-oubliee-trisomie-21-01-10-2009-79706.

94 Simonin, *Les Editions de Minuit*, 427; Didier Monciaud, 'Une vie d'engagements communiste et anticolonialiste. Repères sur la trajectoire et la contribution d'Henri Alleg (1921–2013)', *Cahiers d'histoire. Revue d'histoire critique* 122 (2014): 145–56.

95 My account below draws upon Berchadsky, *La Question*, 88–9, 95, 97–8, 123, 131–2; Simonin, *Les Editions de Minuit*, 418, 429; Hubert, *Editeurs et éditions*, 183.

review of *La Question*, also censored, in a small-print version readable with a magnifying glass. In March 1958, posters reproducing the book's blank cover, accompanied by a photograph of Alleg and a quotation from Sartre's review, were placarded across Paris. The following month, Lindon issued an appeal to President René Coty protesting against the seizure of Alleg's book, calling for an enquiry into the facts related by Alleg, and asking the government to condemn the use of torture in the name of the 1789 Declaration of the Rights of Man and the Citizen. The appeal was signed by André Malraux, Roger Martin du Gard, François Mauriac and Sartre.[96] In light of Lindon's struggles, Beckett's wranglings with British and Irish censorship during this period take on a rather different dimension.

Beckett's Algerian War Chronicles

In his letters to Bray, Hutchinson and others who had an interest in French politics, Beckett reported regularly on the political climate in Paris, sketching out major developments. The press cuttings enclosed in his letters to Bray, to whom he had grown very close, reveal his taste for centre and centre-left publications that were engaged in reporting contentious facets of the conflict, such as *Le Monde*, *Combat* and *France-Observateur*, all of which covered war events in minute detail. At the start of 1961, Beckett also read *Paris-Presse, L'Intransigeant* and *L'Express*, and listened regularly to news bulletins on the radio. Bray, then a BBC correspondent, was involved in the war's international coverage and was an ideal interlocutor; in May 1961, following the Generals' Putsch, a failed *coup d'état* that had sought to overthrow President de Gaulle and institute a military junta, the BBC asked her to translate articles from the French press for a Home Service broadcast on 'France and de Gaulle'.[97]

Beckett's letters to English-speaking friends begin to evoke the Algerian war in March 1956, the month during which Morocco and Tunisia proclaimed their independence and the French National Assembly voted a law giving 'special powers' to the government to quell the Algerian conflict. From April 1956 onwards, large numbers of conscripts were transferred to Algeria. These momentous changes resound in Beckett's correspondence: in March, to Susan Manning, he describes a joyless France where sinister political manoeuvres shape everything; in July, he explains to Cunard that the mail is no longer delivered because his postman has 'gone

[96] Simonin, *Les Editions de Minuit*, 429–30, 436. Albert Camus refused to sign.
[97] 'Copyright, Barbara Bray, 1955–1962', BBC Written Archives, Caversham.

to Algeria to do battle' with the streams of conscripts.[98] In September, he reports that the sky of Ussy-sur-Marne, where he frequently sought refuge, is lined with noisy jet fighters.[99] From 1958 onwards, his correspondence frequently alludes to political instabilities that caused successive governments to resign; clearly, attending to his daily routine against a backdrop of police controls, round-ups and violent repression targeting others proved immensely difficult to bear. This was a time marked by large-scale demonstrations, strikes and uprisings in Algiers, and by the continuation of guerrilla war elsewhere; Paris was home to a merciless conflict between the FLN and the police, and the construction of an organised FLN 'counter-state' in the French capital posed formidable challenges to the counter-intelligence services as well.[100] Under the command of Maurice Papon (who was later convicted for crimes against humanity for his actions in the Vichy regime), the Paris police resorted to savage methods to curb the advances of the FLN and to further the cause of the OAS, with which many were sympathetic. To Mary Manning Howe, in January 1959, Beckett describes a state wallowing in its own pomp and glory, such that living elsewhere beckons.[101] By September 1960, little has changed, and he confides to Bray that Paris is a city increasingly characterised by fear and oppression.[102] Others found war by stealth intolerable: Beckett's friends, the painter Bram van Velde and Marthe Kuntz, moved away from Paris in 1958 for this very reason.[103] It is clear on which side of the fence they stood; Kuntz was a former missionary who had published in 1938, as Marthe Arnaud, an anti-colonialist account of her years in Zambia, *Manière de blanc*, which was republished in serial form in 1939 in *L'Humanité* and seemingly led her to be interrogated by the police.[104]

The war anecdotes that feature in Beckett's letters were clearly added to keep his correspondents abroad loosely informed of crucial events, and rarely take on the form of full commentaries. Nevertheless, it is clear that the country portrayed by Beckett is in the throes of a full-blown and militarised conflict that is in no way confined to the other side of the

98 SB to Susan Manning, 15 March 1956, Beckett Collection, HRHRC; *LSB2*, 631.

99 SB to Cunard, 23 September 1956, Nancy Cunard Collection, HRHRC.

100 House and MacMaster, *Paris 1961*, 60–87.

101 SB to Manning Howe, 23 January 1959, Beckett Collection, HRHRC.

102 SB to Bray, 27 September 1960, TCD MS 10948/1/112.

103 Claire Stoullig, *Bram van Velde: Musée National d'Art Moderne, Centre Georges Pompidou* (Paris: Centre Pompidou, 1989), 190.

104 See Marthe Arnaud, *Manière de blanc: La colline aux grandes antilopes*, with a preface by Marcel Griaule (Paris: Éditions sociales internationales, 1938); Barrie Hastings's catalogue note for a 1981 Bram Van Velde exhibition, www.derives.tv/Barrie-Hastings-Bram-van-Velde; the fictionalised biography of Kuntz by Marie Cosnay, *Villa Chagrin* (Lagrasse: Verdier, 2006).

Mediterranean. His letters, notably, register the impact of the 'second front' opened by the FLN in metropolitan France: in September 1958, a month that saw numerous sabotages and strategic attacks, he reports that Alexis Péron (Mania and Alfred's son, then fulfilling his military service) is stationed with his army division near Paris, in anticipation of possible FLN attacks. Commenting on the referendum due to take place the next day on the constitution of the Fifth French Republic, which also applied to Algeria, he confides his fear that sinister political consequences are to be expected if the new constitution is not passed by popular vote.[105] Here and elsewhere, his observations do not convey the feeling of estrangement that other foreign residents without voting rights might have experienced.

Generally, beyond isolated references to Lindon's editorial work, the letters make no direct mention of the debates about torture, but it is clear that Beckett developed an interest in legal scandals and trials around this time. In the mid-1960s, he was immersed in Rupert Furneaux's *Courtroom USA*, a history of great courtroom battles in the United States in the first half of the twentieth century.[106] His correspondence refers not only to the prominent trials of the Algerian war years but also to the widely publicised trial of Adolf Eichmann.[107] It is likely that reports of torture, for Beckett, revived painful memories, and were reminders of what might have happened to him, had events taken a different turn in 1942. The Algerian war was close to home for other reasons: Suzanne Beckett had spent part of her youth in Tunisia, and her sister had subsequently made her life in Tunis (the date of her return to France is unclear: Deirdre Bair's biography, which erroneously mentions a sister living in Algeria at war,[108] suggests that she was still in North Africa in the late 1950s). It is likely that, for Suzanne, as was the case for many French settlers, the Algerian war and Tunisian independence were imbricated with a sense of personal loss and memories of a golden life in the colonies. Tunisia was unofficially implicated in the Algerian war and provided a safe haven to FLN leaders, who launched and coordinated attacks from its borders; the French government strongly resented the Tunisian position and attempted to curb its support to the FLN through various means, including implanting counter-intelligence agents in Tunis and bombing the Tunisian border village of Sakiet Sidi Youssef in 1958.[109]

[105] SB to Ethna McCarthy, 27 September 1958, A. J. Leventhal Collection, HRHRC.
[106] *LSB3*, 654–5. [107] *LSB3*, 440. [108] *SB*, 543.
[109] Macey, *Frantz Fanon*, 305; Sorum, *Intellectuals and Decolonization*, 120; Connelly, *A Diplomatic Revolution*, 86, 160–70, 180–3.

In January 1960, the tone and nature of Beckett's reports shift once again. At the time of the insurrection of the *pieds-noirs* in Algiers in January 1960 – the 'week of the barricades', in protest against de Gaulle's evident commitment to Algerian self-determination – he writes that he and Suzanne have remained 'glued' for eight days to the hourly news broadcasts on Europe 1.[110] In a letter to Bray dated 28 October 1960, he comments on the previous night, which had seen the first large-scale demonstration calling for an end to the war, organised by the largest students' union (the UNEF), professional trade unions, the SFIO and anti-war organisations. Nadeau, Blanchot, Mascolo and Antelme were among the demonstrators, and the march was met by a type of police brutality that anticipated later developments in May 1968, as Blanchot discovered.[111] Beckett's account conveys his alarm, and this is the first of several letters commenting on the brutality of Papon's police services. 'I was very worried about Lindon last evening after hearing the reportage on the students' manifestation by Europe I at 7.30. I rang him up and his wife said he had not come in. Then an hour later and he had – unscathed. He said the police were unprecedentedly brutal, batoning the women as readily as the men'.[112]

Letters from 1961 and 1962 reflect the pressures of a conflict edging ever closer. On 7 January 1961, the day prior to the referendum on Algerian self-determination, and the day after the publication of *Comment c'est*, Beckett writes to Bray that the clement seasonal weather is conducive at once to voting – for others – and to recommencing work on *Happy Days* – for him.[113] In April, in the wake of the Generals' Putsch, he describes everyday life under the new and strengthened state of emergency: 'Here apparently all quiet again. Tanks etc. gone. Great sigh of relief on coming back late from Odéon last night and hearing news on radio'.[114] In August, he reports his difficulties when driving through Paris: he describes a city ruled by fear and threat, where the commemoration of the 1944 liberation is celebrated under the watch of large numbers of police officers deployed in the eventuality of a terrorist attack.[115] In December, he writes to Alan Schneider: 'Things more and more sinister here politically, manifestations, [. . .] *plastiquages* day & night and town crawling with bestial cops'.[116] A month prior to the signing of the Evian Accords, he evokes a Paris prey to the OAS, where violence is ubiquitous and unrelenting.[117] In April 1962, he notes that Edmond Jouhaud, a leader of the OAS involved in the Generals'

[110] *LSB3*, 290, 292. [111] Bident, *Maurice Blanchot*, 401–2. [112] *LSB3*, 368.
[113] SB to Bray, 7 January 1961, TCD MS 10948/1/131. [114] *LSB3*, 408.
[115] SB to Bray, 24 August 1961, TCD MS 10948/1/160. [116] *NABS*, 116.
[117] SB to Jean Reavey, 17 February 1962, George Reavey Collection, HRHRC.

Putsch and detained at the neighbouring Santé prison, 'must be just leaving [the prison] now for the last day of this trial'.[118] In May, on the day that saw the arrest of another prominent OAS leader, André Canal, he describes an oppressive city crawling with police and reverberating with incessant police sirens.[119]

The years 1961 and 1962 correspond not simply to Lindon's increasing difficulties and to the OAS bombing campaign, but also to the height of the police repression against the FLN in Paris, the imposition of a curfew upon all Algerians, and the ruthless repression of demonstrations organised by the FLN and anti-war organisations. In September and October 1961, large numbers of bodies of North African origin, whose identity remains to this day unknown, were found drowned in the Seine, the canals and nearby rivers, and hanged in woods and orchards in the Paris suburbs; these deaths were not investigated but were attributed to the bloody conflict between the FLN and its rival organisation, the MNA (Mouvement National Algérien or Algerian National Movement), although it was clear that beating, strangling, drowning and shooting had become part of the methods employed by the police.[120] On 17, 18 and 20 October, a series of pacific demonstrations and strikes organised by the FLN to protest against discriminatory measures, and against the police curfew formalised a few weeks previously, were met by savage repression. More beatings, mass deaths by shooting and drowning, and the internment of Algerian demonstrators in the Palais des Sports, the Stade de Coubertin, the Beaujon stadium and the Parc des Expositions were seen on 17 October.[121] The number of casualties remains disputed but has been estimated as exceeding 120 deaths for September and October 1961; 17 October saw, as Jim House and Neil MacMaster emphasise, 'the bloodiest act of state repression of street protest in Western Europe in modern history'.[122] The full force of censorship kicked in; the reports by Paulette Péju published by Maspero soon after were seized, and *Octobre à Paris*, the documentary film shot by Jacques Panijel, with the support of the FLN, Audin's Defence Committee and the review *Vérité-Liberté*, remained censored until 1973. The ubiquitous violence that Beckett evoked in February 1962 applies not simply to the OAS, but to the aftermath of the October demonstrations. From November 1961 to February 1962, protests against the OAS organised by anti-fascist groups saw further displays of police violence. At a pacific demonstration on 8 February 1962, large numbers of demonstrators were injured at the Charonne metro station,

[118] *LSB3*, 475. [119] SB to Bray, 4 May 1962, TCD MS 10948/1/180.
[120] House and MacMaster, *Paris 1961*, 106–11. [121] Ibid., 113–36. [122] Ibid., 167, 1.

and nine died from beatings and suffocation. The Charonne demonstration became the focus of close public scrutiny, not least because, on this occasion, the victims were associated with the French workers' movement.[123] Beckett's missives allude, directly and subliminally, to such events.

Throughout January and February 1962, mass demonstrations, strikes and committees were formed against the 'fascist peril'; in all circumstances, the protest against the OAS was articulated as a resistance against fascism, and the parallels with Nazi occupation resurfaced with even greater immediacy.[124] On 26 October 1961, *France-Observateur* published a photograph of Algerian detainees waiting in the Palais des Sports, with a caption that read, 'Does this remind you of something?' alongside another image of Algerian men standing by a train, aligned in rows of three, and held at gunpoint by a French soldier.[125] In November, in response to an appeal issued by the FLN's French Federation in protest against the round-ups, beatings and murders of Algerians in Paris, *Les Temps Modernes* published a petition that called the French public, political parties and trade unions to campaign for an end to the curfew and the repression. 'If they remain passive, French people will become complicit with the racist fury currently unleashed in Paris, which takes us back to the darkest hours of Nazi occupation. We refuse to differentiate between the Algerians crammed in the Palais des Sports, waiting to be "turned away", and the Jews held in Drancy before their deportation'.[126] The appeal was signed by Aragon, de Beauvoir, Blin, Boulez, Breton, Lindon, Nadeau, Sartre, Seyrig, Simon, Duras, Vidal-Naquet as well as Jean Amrouche, Aimé Césaire, Claude Lanzmann and Elsa Triolet. Memories of Algerian demonstrators held in Paris sports stadia may have been on Beckett's mind when he recalled the Vichy regime in a conversation with Knowlson decades later; he mentioned that the Parc des Princes stadium had been used to imprison Jewish families before their transfer to Nazi camps.[127] This is an odd declaration: indeed, little is known about the function of the Parc des Princes in the 1942 round-ups; very few texts refer to it, since the stadium was rarely divested of its primary function of hosting sporting events during the Second World War.[128] Did Beckett have in mind the Vel d'Hiv? His misidentification of mass round-ups with

[123] Ibid., 242–52. [124] See 'Ils ont dit: Non au Fascisme', *L'Humanité*, 9 February 1962, 9.
[125] 'Aucun Français ne peut plus ignorer ça!', *France-Observateur*, 26 October 1961, 15–17.
[126] 'Appel', *Les Temps Modernes* 186 (1961): 624–8; 'Appel au peuple français', ibid., 623.
[127] *BR/RB*, 79.
[128] The only similar reference that I have found features in Jacques Maritain, *Le mystère d'Israel et autres essais* (Paris: Desclée de Brouwer, 1965), 179.

the Parc des Princes is certainly troubling and suggests that the Algerian war and the repression of 1961 had a bearing upon his memories.

The war was also part of Beckett's quotidian experience on a more mundane level. In October 1960, he and Suzanne began to move out of their small flat on Rue des Favorites, located in what Peggy Guggenheim contemptuously called a 'workmen's building'.[129] Their new home, a more spacious flat on Boulevard Saint-Jacques, was to remain Beckett's main residence for the rest of his life. The flat looked directly onto the Santé prison, and there are many accounts of Beckett's continued fascination for this dark and sinister building.[130] His study was 'à une portée de hurlement' or within screamshot, as Jack Thieuloy, a former inmate, put it in a book expressing gratitude to Beckett.[131] Maps of the prison show that the Becketts' flat looked onto blocks A, B and C and the two adjacent exercise yards, in the area situated along Rue Jean-Dolent – the street that, incidentally, housed the headquarters of the French Human Rights League.[132] Blocks A, B and C were the designated quarters of the political prisoners and the prisoners condemned to capital punishment.

The Santé prison was a strategic political prison with a specific segregated architecture, and it was commonly used for the detention of nationalist militants prior to and during the Algerian war. The figures are eloquent: the number of Muslim detainees grew from 15 per cent of the overall number in January 1956 to 35 per cent in January 1959 and 41 per cent in January 1960.[133] The prison housed many illustrious political prisoners, from the leader of the North African Star, Messali Hadj, to the historic chiefs of the FLN, Ahmed Ben Bella, Hocine Ait-Ahmed, Mohamed Boudiaf, Mohamed Khider and Mostefa Lacheraf. It was also used for leaders of the OAS and supporters of a French Algeria, the latter in lesser numbers. Living conditions at the Santé prison were harsh for Algerian prisoners, who were allocated cells in the most insalubrious parts of the building until a hunger strike was called in June 1959. The strike was long, and cells were

[129] Guggenheim, *Out of This Century*, 184.

[130] *DF*, 472, 642; Bernold, *L'Amitié de Beckett*, 78; John Montague, *The Figure in the Cave and Other Essays* (New York: Syracuse University Press, 1989), 107; Jean Demélier, 'La première fois', in *Objet Beckett*, ed. Marianne Alphant and Nathalie Léger (Paris: Centre Pompidou and IMEC, 2007), 102; Patrick Starnes, 'Samuel Beckett: An Interview', *Antigonish Review* 10 (1972): 51–2; John Calder, *The Philosophy of Samuel Beckett* (London: Calder, 2001), 12; Raymond Federman, *The Sam Book* (Ullapool: Two Ravens Press, 2008), 88–9.

[131] Jack Thieuloy, *Loi de Dieu* (Paris: L'Athanor, 1977), 8.

[132] Michel Fize, *Une prison dans la ville ... Histoire de la 'prison-modèle' de la Santé, 2ème époque: 1914–1983*, vol. 2 (Paris: Centre National d'Etudes et de Recherches Pénitentiaires, Ministère de la Justice, 1983), 14, 16, 29–35.

[133] Ibid., 25. Detainees were separated according to religious and ethnic background.

deprived of access to water and sanitation in reprisal.[134] But the protest yielded the desired results: after August 1959 all prisoners incarcerated for deeds related to the Algerian war were reclassified as political prisoners, under 'category A', and were granted dramatic improvements in their living conditions (the measure was enforced until April 1962, when all those imprisoned for homicide, intentional assault and battery, arrest and kidnapping, destructions, damages or plunder were excluded from this category and reclassified as 'category B').[135] Other hunger strikes took place in June 1960 and November 1961, and were coordinated across French prisons in which FLN militants were detained.

Beckett is said to have known the panoptic layout of the Santé prison inside out, particularly the position of the guillotine, situated in the courtyard at the corner of Boulevard Arago and Rue de la Santé. The guillotine remained in exactly the same place from its installation in 1899, after the demolition of La Grande Roquette, until the last execution in 1972.[136] Throughout the Algerian war years, the Santé prison continued to be used for capital punishment, and saw the executions of numerous FLN militants condemned under common law, for murder and other crimes considered as violations of common law. The exact number of executions remains unknown, but several sources allude to the many Algerian men who were guillotined in this courtyard, mentioning the executions that took place in December 1960, which acquired a particular political significance.[137] What Beckett could see from his window is anyone's guess, but it is certain that living next to a major prison entailed a concrete and terrifying proximity to hunger strikes and executions. Over time, he became familiar with the modes of communication used by the inmates, although he could never crack their special code, and he would occasionally communicate with them using a mirror and hand gestures. He frequently commented that he was able to hear 'howling' from the prison across the rooftops, and liked to remind his interlocutors that his window also looked on to the Panthéon, which houses the graves of illustrious architects of the nation.[138]

[134] Pierre Montagnon, *42 rue de la Santé: Une prison politique, 1867–1968* (Paris: Pygmalion and Gérard Watelet, 1996), 306–7.

[135] Fize, *Une prison*, 36; Robert Schmelck and Georges Picca, *Pénologie et droit pénitentiaire* (Paris: Cujas, 1967), 266.

[136] Eric Hazan, *The Invention of Paris: A History in Footsteps*, trans. David Fernbach (London: Verso, 2010), 162–3. *En attendant Godot* refers to La Petite Roquette, a prison for minors.

[137] Vidal-Naquet, *Torture*, 17; Patrick Kessel and Giovanni Pirelli, eds., *Le peuple algérien et la guerre: Lettres et témoignages d'Algériens, 1954–1962*, revised ed. (Paris: L'Harmattan, 2003), 517 n17.

[138] Arikha, *Major/Minor*, 125; Montague, *The Figure in the Cave*, 107; *LSB3*, 686.

Beckett and the Politics of Parisian Petitions

Beckett's relation to the waves of dissent that grew in France during the war was distinctive because, although he worked within circles that were extremely politicised, he had little direct involvement with the Parisian culture of petitions that formed around the Algerian war. The writing and dissemination of petitions has played an important role in French politics throughout the twentieth century; in the context of the Algerian war, however, this kind of activity proved crucial, not least because it developed in opposition to a prevailing mood of fear, indifference and incomprehension.[139] In many respects, the culture of petitions remained deeply normative: it largely excluded women, revolved around a limited array of professions and names, and was shaped by men who had a strong sense of their moral authority and social position.[140] It is unsurprising that Beckett should have felt that he had no place within it.

In a letter to Bray dated 1 October 1960, Beckett described his nationality – and hence his distinctive legal situation – as the only obstacle to signing the 'Manifeste des 121', the most controversial petition of the period to emerge from Paris circles. The text of the petition was and remains immensely powerful. It is a call to insubordination, which presents as a moral duty the refusal to enter into combat against the Algerian people and (in covert terms) pays homage to the work of Jeanson and his group, while drawing attention to the irresistible rise of a resistance movement growing from acts of insubordination and desertion. Proclaiming the right to insubordination along these lines was serious provocation: the legislation granting special powers to the government defined desertion to join Algerian forces as a crime to be sanctioned by military degradation and capital punishment if the deserter had taken weapons and ammunition.[141] The manifesto also denounces a censorious government that routinely resorts to torture, recalling that 'fifteen years after the destruction of the Hitlerian order, French militarism, as a result of the exigencies of this war, has managed to reinstate torture and to make it an institution in Europe once again'.[142]

139 See Charles-Robert Ageron, 'L'opinion française devant la guerre d'Algérie', *Revue française d'histoire d'outre-mer* 113 (1976): 231, 256; Michel Winock and Jean-Pierre Azéma, 'Pacifisme et attentisme', *La Guerre d'Algérie et les Français*, 15–24.

140 Dominique-Pierre Larger, *Les manifestes et déclaration de personnalités sous la Cinquième République (1958–1969)* (DES diss., University of Paris, 1971), 26–52.

141 'Décret no. 56–270 du 17 mars 1956 relatif aux peines applicables en Algérie aux individus coupables de désertion à une bande armée', *JORF*, 19 March 1956, 2656.

142 'Declaration of the Right to Insubordination in the Algerian War', in *Political Writings, 1953–1993*, by Maurice Blanchot, trans. and ed. Zakir Paul (New York: Fordham University Press, 2010), 16.

These declarations have a specific political context: the manifesto was published on the second day of the trial of the Jeanson network, on 6 September 1960, in *Vérité-Liberté* and two near-clandestine publications.[143] The 'suitcase-carriers' who were tried included six Algerian and eighteen French people; most of them (including Jeanson and three others, tried *in absentia*) were ultimately condemned to ten years of imprisonment and a heavy fine. The venue for the trial was the Cherche-Midi prison on Boulevard Raspail, a disaffected military prison close to the Montparnasse quarter where Beckett lived. He knew Jeanson, but in another capacity – as managing editor of *Les Temps Modernes*, where Jeanson had published an excerpt from *Malone meurt*.[144]

Beckett's comments to Bray are brief and certainly do not convey the extraordinary turmoil that raged throughout September and October, as the number of signatories swelled from the original 121 to 246, and further petitions and counter-petitions were issued. He wrote, simply: 'No talk of anything here but the Jeanson trial and the Manifesto of the 121. If I weren't a foreigner I suppose I'd be in it'.[145] Signing such a petition calling for insubordination and desertion could have led to the withdrawal of his residence permit, the document which granted to Beckett, an Irish citizen, the right to remain on French territory.[146] Legal texts were stringent: the law regulating residency emphasised that foreign residents posing a threat to the public order would be expelled from the French territory, and opened the possibility that residency permits would not be renewed.[147] For Beckett, anti-war petitioning also corresponded to a specific configuration of the French nation over which he, as a foreigner, had no ownership, although he was well aware of the common associations between the legacy of the Resistance and the growing movement of support for Algerian self-determination. When Alan Simpson enquired about his views on the manifesto, Beckett explained that 'not being a French citizen morally [forbade] him from expressing any public or even private opinions on these matters'; to Simpson's parallel with the days of the Resistance, he objected: 'That was different [. . .]. I was fighting against the Germans, who were making life

143 Bident, *Maurice Blanchot*, 399 n1, 605–6.

144 See Marie-Pierre Ulloa, *Francis Jeanson: A Dissident Intellectual from the French Resistance to the Algerian War*, trans. Jane Marie Todd (Palo Alto, CA: Stanford University Press, 2007), 68.

145 *LSB3*, 360.

146 See also *DF*, 495. Knowlson's account of Beckett's experience of the Algerian war years fuses two different petitions and debates associated with the trial of the Jeanson network in September 1960 and the *Déserteur* trial in December 1961.

147 'Ordonnance no. 45–2658 du 2 novembre 1945 relative à l'entrée et au séjour des étrangers en France', *JORF*, 4 November 1945, 7226.

hell for my friends, and not for the French nation.[148] That Beckett should evoke a moral obstacle in this context is significant: signatories of petitions such as the 'Manifeste des 121' had an unassailable sense of the legitimacy of their position, with many perceiving their campaign as the continuation of a past struggle against Nazism. For his part, Beckett understood the long history of colonialism all too well.

Much is crystallised in Beckett's absent signature, and there are numerous connections between his professional activities and the political group constituted by the manifesto. The signatories included many of his close friends and collaborators (Lindon, Blin, Martin); artists, philosophers and critics Beckett knew well, personally or through their work (Adamov, de Beauvoir, Blanchot, Breton, Michel Butor, Duras, Michel Leiris, Mayoux, Nadeau, Resnais, Robbe-Grillet, Nathalie Sarraute, Sartre, Geneviève Serreau, Claude Simon, Tzara); artists whose work he had discussed in his critical essays (André Masson, whose son Diego had joined the Jeanson network and other movements linked to the FLN). The text was written collaboratively by some of the initial signatories. Lindon was involved in its writing, dissemination and printing, and made the decision to publish the text with 121 signatures.[149] Blanchot, now recognised as one of the principal authors with Dionys Mascolo and Jean Schuster, made his anti-Gaullist sentiment very clear in other tracts and essays he wrote about the necessity of insubordination during the late 1950s and early 1960s. The 'Manifeste des 121' is clearly aligned with the position taken by *Le 14 juillet*, the short-lived review founded by Mascolo and Schuster in 1958: the essays that Blanchot wrote for the review denounce the instrumentalisation of the state of emergency and describe de Gaulle's unelected return to power with the backing of the military leaders of the Battle of Algiers as ushering institutionalised fascism.

The 'Manifeste des 121' and its signatories, for Anne Simonin, illustrate the specificities of a form of resistance that was cemented by personal friendships, finding a political articulation and realisation by means of, as well as within, personal solidarities.[150] This diagnosis aptly qualifies Beckett's politics during this period as well. On occasion, his work provided a platform for anti-war dissenters and enabled them to appear together publicly: for example, a list of guests to an April 1961 performance of *En attendant Godot* at the Odéon-Théâtre de France, put together by Lindon, included Duras, Maspero, Robbe-Grillet, Sarraute, Simon, Siné,

[148] Simpson, *Beckett and Behan*, 64–5. [149] Bident, *Maurice Blanchot*, 396–7, 396 n3.
[150] Simonin, *Le droit*, 10.

Vidal-Naquet and their respective spouses; all of them were among the '121' and had been earmarked for their political activity.[151] Beckett's personal ties to this circle endured, and he expressed solidarity with their endeavours in other ways, long after this episode. Throughout the 1960s and 1970s, he supported the literary activities of Geneviève Serreau and Nadeau, who edited *Les Lettres nouvelles*, a review that sought to advance the controversy around the 'Manifeste des 121' in 1960 and published several of Beckett's plays in the 1950s. The issue in which Nadeau reproduced the manifesto was banned, but he presented another platform to its signatories, subsequently dedicating an issue to them. Nadeau – also a historian of Surrealism – recalls being particularly touched when, in 1975, Beckett donated original editions of his first English texts to an auction destined to raise funds for his review *La Quinzaine littéraire*.[152]

The process of soliciting signatures for the 'Manifeste des 121' was delicate, and Beckett's peripheral position was far from unique. The publisher René Julliard, for example, who supported other anti-colonial movements, felt unable to sign and dissuaded Christian Bourgois, then his deputy, from doing so.[153] Genet wrote to his translator Bernard Frechtman that he could not sign it either, for moral reasons and by virtue of his criminal record, even though he fully supported Jeanson and the manifesto.[154] The political identities of the signatories were scrutinised carefully prior to the publication of the first 121 endorsements, and the number of contributors connected with Surrealism was kept to the minimum: as Schuster later explained, it was vital to ensure that the appeal would not come across as driven by Surrealist political activity.[155] Lindon was aware of the dangers inherent in signing the document, and it was decided that only French nationals would be invited to sign. Adamov, whose name comes first in the list of signatories, had obtained French citizenship a few years previously.[156] Pinget, a Swiss citizen, and Beckett were the only prominent representatives of Minuit's *nouveau roman* who did not feature in the manifesto. Lindon, who was keen to see his leading fiction writers represented, asked Robbe-Grillet to replace Beckett and endorse the manifesto, and Robbe-Grillet agreed to do so, although he never signed petitions, precisely because Beckett was unable to sign.[157]

[151] 'Représentations *En Attendant Godot*', Fonds Beckett, IMEC.

[152] Nadeau, *Grâces leur soient rendues*, 367.

[153] Hubert, *Editeurs et éditions*, 323.

[154] *La bataille des Paravents: Théâtre de l'Odéon, 1966*, ed. Lynda Bellity Peskine and Albert Dichy (Paris: IMEC, 1991), 26.

[155] Reynaud Paligot, *Parcours politique des Surréalistes*, 266–7.

[156] Pierre Mélèse, *Arthur Adamov* (Paris: Seghers, 1973), 175.

[157] Simonin, *Les Editions de Minuit*, 437.

This was no small gesture: the '121' were immediately put under great pressure and received home visits from the police encouraging them to retract their signature.[158] Shortly after, a series of governmental decrees were passed to bring about immediate sanctions. On 29 September, the Conseil des Ministres passed a decree stating that the signatories could no longer appear on radio or television, that they would be banned from working in public theatres and institutions in receipt of public subsidies, and that the films to which they contributed would no longer benefit from public funding. A later decree stated that the signatories could not be mentioned by name on the airwaves, an unfortunate decision that led to the cancellation of some literary broadcasts.[159] Some of the signatories (Lindon, Blanchot and others) were charged with 'provocation to insubordination', 'provocation to desertion' and 'inciting militaries to disobedience'.[160] Other sanctions included suspension from academic posts and the civil service, home searches, fines, prosecutions and imprisonment.

By early 1961, sanctions and legal pursuits were, in most cases, dropped; however, Blin and Martin were among the few who were acutely and lastingly sanctioned.[161] Blin's career in cinema and television came close to a halt until 1963. He wrote in his memoirs that, although nothing was ever said to him, he was unable to obtain work in radio and television for a year after the publication of the manifesto and found it extremely difficult to make a living.[162] Beckett's own decisions manifest an acute awareness of their predicament – including when, in December 1962, he wrote to Blin to offer him *Oh les beaux jours*, freshly translated:[163] he was also trying to facilitate his return to directing. Like Martin, Blin was offered occasional work in private theatres in Paris and abroad, and Beckett's correspondence suggests that he attempted to assist by mediating dialogue with trusted playwrights such as Pinter, and with theatres where his own work was held in high regard. Notably, the Paris premiere of Pinter's *Le Gardien* (*The Caretaker*), which opened at the Théâtre de Lutèce in January 1961, was directed by Martin, featured both Blin and Martin, and was part of a double bill with Pinget's *La Manivelle*, also directed by Martin. Blin's other contracts during these difficult times included directing Genet's *Les Nègres* in 1961 at London's Royal Court Theatre and *Fin de partie* in 1962 at the Théâtre de Carouge in Switzerland, as well as shreds of work beyond the theatre: he played a minor uncredited role in Martin Ritt's *Paris Blues* (1961), a

[158] Péju, *Le procès du réseau Jeanson*, 26. [159] Maspero, *Le droit à l'insoumission*, 38, 50.
[160] 'Nouvelles inculpations', *Combat*, 6 October 1960, 9; Bident, *Maurice Blanchot*, 400–1.
[161] See Reynaud Paligot, *Parcours politique des Surréalistes*, 267–8.
[162] Blin, *Souvenirs*, 179; *DF*, 495. [163] *LSB4*, 753.

jazz film starring Paul Newman, Sidney Poitier and Louis Armstrong.[164] As for Martin, he saw his contract with the Théâtre National Populaire annulled; unable to work for radio or television, he moved to Helsinki, where he directed a production of Boris Vian's *Les Bâtisseurs d'empire ou le Schmürtz*.[165] His career regained momentum a few years later, when he was cast as Colonel Mathieu, a high-ranking military strategist, in Gillo Pontecorvo's 1966 film *The Battle of Algiers*. Clearly, the construction of Mathieu as character owed much to what was known about the leaders of the Battle of Algiers, Jean Massu, Roger Trinquier and Paul Aussaresses, and about their distinguished careers marked by feats of bravery in the French Resistance and in Indochina. The first scene featuring Martin in Pontecorvo's film is reminiscent of the power dynamics explored in *En attendant Godot*, with which Martin as a theatre actor had famously experimented. The film begins with a confrontation involving a FLN militant who, under torture, has accepted to reveal Ali la Pointe's hiding place to the officers under Mathieu's command. The tortured man is shaking so much that he has to be held upright, while Mathieu exhorts him to make a further effort.

The 'Manifeste des 121' also marked a turning point for Lindon. Public support from political parties was scant, and Lindon left the PSU, then perceived as a rising political force against the continuation of the Algerian war, in protest against the party's condemnation of the petition.[166] With Adamov, Maspero, Sarraute, Vercors, Vidal-Naquet and many others, he testified as a witness at the trial of the Jeanson network on 20 September. In response to questions from Vergès, appointed to defend the Algerian 'suitcase carriers', Lindon invoked the longer underground history of the Editions de Minuit, stating that the 'Documents' belonged to the same combat as the clandestine texts from the early 1940s. He differentiated between the political efficiency of the FLN and his own publications, which had had little impact given that the facts denounced in his books had taken on greater magnitude. If these denunciations of torture had failed to curb its spread, he explained regretfully, this was perhaps because the work of the Editions de Minuit had remained strictly within the realm of legality under his watch.[167] Beckett followed these events at a remove. On 4 October 1960, he writes to Bray: 'Lindon as you will have seen was not detained

[164] Odette Aslan, *Roger Blin, Qui êtes-vous?* (Paris: La Manufacture, 1990), 345, 348, 353.
[165] *DF*, 495; *LSB3*, 373 n10.
[166] Simonin, *Le droit*, 41; Simonin, *Les Editions de Minuit*, 134; Vidal-Naquet, 'Une fidélité têtue', 6–7. Claude Bourdet, Pierre Vidal-Naquet and Laurent Schwartz were also members of the party.
[167] Péju, *Le procès du réseau Jeanson*, 125–7.

very long, but if the cat jumps the wrong way it's the end of Minuit'.[168] And on 22 October, less sympathetically, he describes a Lindon besieged by the very trouble and turmoil that his campaign created.[169]

The argument Lindon advanced at the Jeanson trial was the line to which he adhered again in December 1961, when he was prosecuted by the French government for publishing a novel whose main character advocates desertion. This was Maurienne's *Le Déserteur*, which presented in a fictional form the experience of its author, Jean-Louis Hurst, who had deserted the French army in 1958 and joined the Jeanson network. *Le Déserteur* focused on a Communist narrator inspired from Hurst's own experiences and two would-be deserters: an apolitical and atheist soldier representing the average reader and a Catholic soldier. The novel was seized upon its publication in April 1960, like two explicitly autobiographical accounts of desertion also published that year: Maurice Maschino's *Le refus* (published by the Editions Maspero) and Noël Favrelière's *Le désert à l'aube* (published by the Editions de Minuit). Proceedings against *Le Déserteur* – a text that seemed structured as a *roman à clef* – went much further, however.

This was the only time that Lindon was formally prosecuted in court and in the professional capacity of editor. Ironically, *Le Déserteur* was also the only war testimony that Lindon had chosen to present as fiction: the text had been published in Minuit's collection of historical novels, 'Les Jours et les Nuits'.[170] Lindon was found guilty of public provocation to military disobedience, while Hurst was found guilty of complicity with Lindon.[171] Both were fined. Lindon's plea at the trial crystallised around the issue of torture, its origins in military orders and hierarchies, and its illegality. Against the accusation of provocation to insubordination, he invoked the French republican tradition of dissent and freedom of speech, and the history of torture and massacres in occupied France. His witnesses included civilians who had confronted torture in Algeria and former soldiers who had published testimonies with the Editions de Minuit. Julliard and Claude Gallimard, acting as representatives of the profession, presented Lindon as the publisher of the greatest contemporary writers, naming Beckett, Butor, Pinget, Robbe-Grillet and Simon. The trial became part of the history of the Editions de Minuit in other ways: Lindon immediately published the minutes as a stand-alone volume, adding excerpts from press articles and letters of support. Many international publishers – including Calder and Rosset, seemingly encouraged by Beckett – wrote letters presenting

[168] *LSB3*, 362. [169] SB to Bray, 22 October 1960, TCD MS 10948/1/117.
[170] Simonin, *Le droit*, 31. [171] *Provocation à la désobéissance*, 21–2, 30, 35, 96, 132.

Lindon's fight as a defence of free expression against censorship. *Les Lettres françaises*, the magazine on literature and the arts supported by the French Communist Party and edited by Aragon, published letters of protest that Lindon also reproduced in the volume. Butor and Elsa Triolet described the trial as a matter of utmost seriousness and a tragic misapprehension of the role of literature. Others questioned the political principles at work in the trial; Simon noted his surprise that representatives of the justice system could issue verdicts on literature, a domain alien to their function.

The *Déserteur* trial marked the only moment at which Beckett added his signature to the stream of public documents and protests against the Algerian war, and probably the only moment at which he was invited to do so. In December 1961, he signed a petition launched by Simon that expressed solidarity with Lindon's editorial strategy. The text emphasised the necessity of acknowledging Maurienne's *Le Déserteur* as a work of fiction, and denounced the attempt of the OAS to intimidate Lindon for no better reason than wanting to manifest disapproval of the opinions emitted by a character in a novel.[172] The signatories highlighted the contribution of the Editions de Minuit to the international renown of French culture and, in a pointed gesture towards de Gaulle's handling of the war, deplored the government's inability to tolerate dissent. The text was published twice: first in *Le Monde*, then in an expanded version in *Les Lettres françaises*. The petition published in *Le Monde* was entitled '120 writers, artists, and editors express their "entire solidarity" to Mr Jérôme Lindon', suggesting an analogy with the 'Manifeste des 121', with Lindon standing, of necessity, as the missing signatory. Support grew quickly: the petition published in *Les Lettres françaises* a few days later signalled that '230 intellectuals convey their solidarity to Jérôme Lindon'.[173] The petition was endorsed by many of the signatories of the 'Manifeste des 121'; Beckett and Avigdor Arikha were among the few who had not signed previous documents. Arikha signed the second petition, in all likelihood at Beckett's invitation. Beckett's signature remained unnoticed by all except Peter Lennon, who noted in the *Irish Times* that Butor, de Beauvoir, Robbe-Grillet and Beckett had participated in the protest.[174]

Ultimately, this petition was a mere drop in a sea of appeals and protests. Its political significance lies elsewhere, in the longer associations that it

[172] '120 écrivains, artistes et éditeurs expriment à M. Jérôme Lindon "leur entière solidarité"', *Le Monde*, 19 December 1961, 8.

[173] 'Deux cent trente intellectuels assurent Jérôme Lindon de leur solidarité', *Les Lettres françaises*, 21–27 December 1961, 6.

[174] Peter Lennon, 'The Case of M. Lindon', *IT*, 31 January 1962, 8.

bolstered between individuals who already shared the same professional, political and artistic coordinates. When Beckett was awarded the Nobel Prize, he pushed the spotlight away from himself and firmly towards Lindon: his editor spoke on French television and to the press, and travelled to Stockholm to receive the prize. This moment comes across as a tribute to Lindon's political activities, rather than a gesture of friendship or an attempt to withdraw from an undesirable commitment (Nobel laureates were normally expected to send their national ambassador if they were unable to attend).[175] The Nobel Prize had, by then, generated numerous controversies. Denouncing the role played by the prize in Cold War dynamics, Sartre had famously refused it in 1964 (a decision that Beckett deemed perfectly understandable),[176] and Malraux had proposed in 1958, at the beginning of his term of office as Minister of Information and when debates about torture were gaining prominence, to send three Nobel prizewinners to Algeria – Roger Martin du Gard, Albert Camus and François Mauriac – to ascertain that torture was no longer in use.[177]

Torture, Political Scandals and Beckett's Rough Sketches

Beckett's texts of the 1950s and 1960s enter into dialogue not simply with these political developments, but with broader issues around guerrilla war, military action, torture, desertion and the remit of testimony articulated within and around the catalogue of the Editions de Minuit. Two little-known texts are directly indexed to debates about torture and repression: these are the radio play *Pochade radiophonique* or *Rough for Radio II*, and the stage play *Fragment de théâtre II* or *Rough for Theatre II*. Both texts borrow heavily from the conventions of the detective enquiry, and both examine the figure of the torturer and its common recasting as investigator. Such fondness for the detective plot was not uncommon: Ionesco's 1953 play *Victimes du devoir*, for example, features a character who argues that a play, no matter which, merely consists of an investigation taken to its ultimate resolution, and concludes that all the plays written since Antiquity are detective thrillers.[178] The ORTF, the French broadcasting service, clearly believed in such principle: its most popular entertainment programmes in the late 1950s included a radiophonic series called 'The Masters of Mystery',

[175] See also *DF*, 572.
[176] Jay A. Levy, 'Conversations with Samuel Beckett', in *The Critical Response to Samuel Beckett*, ed. Cathleen Culotta Andonian (New York: Greenwood Press, 1998), 200.
[177] Vidal-Naquet, *Torture*, 110.
[178] Eugène Ionesco, *Théâtre I* (Paris: Gallimard, 1954), 165.

featuring adaptations of novels by Georges Simenon, Agatha Christie and Arthur Conan Doyle, as well as new commissions.

In *Pochade radiophonique*, three characters are involved in extracting information from their victim: an Animator called A, a Stenographer called S (or D in the French text) and their silent aide, called Dick, who is heard handling a 'nerf de boeuf' or bull's pizzle. A has another potential weapon at hand, a ruler shaped as a cylinder that he bangs on his desk in rhythm. Their victim, called Fox, comes to them wearing a hood, a blind, a gag and earplugs. The French dialogues continually play with the limits of radiophonic form and the inherent invisibility of the characters: Dick's role is designated as 'donner', giving, and the word is used in an intransitive manner.[179] The process of obtaining a confession is embedded in the language of literary inspiration: A hopes that Fox will be 'better inspired today than heretofore' and appreciates the sibilance of Fox's declarations (275). The tone remains farcical: the title forbids neat associations, since a *pochade* designates a rushed sketch showing promising qualities as well as imperfections. Nonetheless, it is clear that targets have been set and 'recommendations' have been made, to obtain 'results' of quality and guarantee Fox's silence, or 'parfaite neutralisation', outside of the 'heures de séance' or session times (68). The characters are aware of the need to scrutinise their report before submission to their superiors; as A remarks, 'nous avons déjà assez d'ennuis comme ça' (71) (we're in trouble enough already (277)). Many actions are underlined by a partially articulated process of euphemisation, including when, in an attempt to elicit new revelations, S kisses Fox, who faints under the shock. The expression used in the French text, 'embrasser [. . .] [a]u sang' (to kiss to bleeding point) recalls the euphemistic rhetoric otherwise employed to designate torture and execution without trial (72). Despite some clear exaggerations, the techniques employed by Beckett's characters are anchored in the realm of historical experience: this is a torture scene that echoes the explanations given in testimonies such as Alleg's *La Question* concerning the practice of varying interrogation methods to obtain a confession. Much in Fox's declarations recalls the confused statements obtained from Alleg himself after a chemical injection designed to inhibit willpower.

Beckett's radio play, like *Fragment de théâtre II*, is dated from 'années 60?' in the published text; the date of its composition remains uncertain,

[179] SB, *Pas, suivi de Fragment de théâtre I et II, Pochade radiophonique, Esquisse radiophonique* (Paris: Minuit, 1978), 70 (hereafter cited parenthetically). In the English text, Dick is asked to 'function' (*CDW*, 277).

but late 1958 seems likely.[180] The play first appeared in 1975 in the Editions de Minuit's review, *Minuit*, but was not broadcast on French radio until 2006; a version of its English counterpart, *Rough for Radio II*, was broadcast by the BBC in 1976, and the text was published that same year by Grove Press. It is no coincidence that the play remained an unpublished manuscript for so many years. Even as a farce it had a peculiar political immediacy: the early 1960s saw the transformation of the leaders of the Battle of Algiers into national icons upholding the values of the French Republic – a transformation with which Beckett's *Pochade* would have sat uncomfortably. There is but a short step between Beckett's erudite Animator – who remains as fond of Dante, the 'divine Florentine' (278), as he is of experimenting with torture techniques – and Paul Aussaresses, who was handsomely rewarded for his services during the Battle of Algiers and subsequently pursued another successful career as counter-insurgency advisor to the American government, as he related in his memoirs. Indeed, Aussaresses had trained as a classical scholar with expertise on Virgil and the supernatural before embarking on a military career marked by the exercise of torture.[181]

Beckett was familiar with the role of torture in the longer history of colonisation: Casement's *Black Diaries*, which he read upon their publication by Grove Press in May 1959, describe techniques later emulated in Algeria, and evoke the Putumayo Indians of Peru submitted to torture 'by a chain fastened around the neck to one of the beams of the house or store', '[s]ometimes with the feet scarcely touching the ground the chain hauled taut', until the body is 'left almost extinct'.[182] His awareness of the bull's pizzle as a staple of torture long predates the play, and can be traced in his preparatory notes for *Dream of Fair to Middling Women* and 'Trueborn Jackeen'.[183] By the early 1960s, however, torture by flogging had become part of a rather different history. The Gestapo favoured the bull's pizzle – also known as 'la schlague' – in its dealings with the French Resistance, and it was one of the weapons infamously used by the SS in the Nazi camps.

[180] Pim Verhulst, '"Just Howls from Time to Time": Dating *Pochade radiophonique*', *SBTA* 27 (2015): 143–58.

[181] Paul Aussaresses, *The Battle of the Casbah* (New York: Enigma, 2002), 8, 164.

[182] Peter Singleton-Gates and Maurice Girodias, *The Black Diaries: An Account of Roger Casement's Life and Times, with a Collection of his Diaries and Public Writings* (New York: Grove, 1959), 268. On Beckett and Casement, see *Chronology*, 146; Patrick Bixby, 'The Ethico-Politics of Homo-ness: Beckett's *How It Is* and Casement's *Black Diaries*', *Irish Studies Review* 20, no. 3 (2012): 243–61.

[183] Pilling, *Beckett's Dream Notebook*, 46–57; Frost and Maxwell, 'TCD MS 10971/2: Irish History', 125.

The 1950s saw the rebirth of this practice in Algeria, where the bull's pizzle became a staple in 'interrogation centres' such as the Ferme Améziane, a former colonial farm placed under the command of an officer renowned for his cruelty.[184] Several documents pointed to these sinister continuities. In its May-June 1958 issue, for example, *Les Temps Modernes* published an account of pacification describing the common use of 'funnels, bellows, bull's pizzle, bathtubs, and all kinds of pulleys and presses' when 'tormenting' Algerian detainees in improvised rural prisons.[185]

There are other historical registers at work in *Pochade radiophonique*. The dirty work is given to a subaltern figure called Dick, who obeys orders from all parties. The name harbours a connection to military idiom: *bleu-bite* or 'blue dick' was the common designation for a newly arrived conscript, and *sous-bite* or 'second dick' could designate a second lieutenant freshly out of training school and recently stationed in Algeria.[186] The register of underground fighting also permeates Fox's delirium: he talks about his journeys through tunnels, about a 'mole' or 'taupe' submitted to 'soaping' before the 'embers', a woman called Maud, and a twin brother 'inside him' who has much to do with a brother-in-arms (277, 279). The French text draws on a distinctive lexicon: a 'taupe' qualified the German soldiers fighting in the trenches during the First World War; 'taupe' also designates a spy or an intelligence officer, as mole does in English.[187] 'Savonner' (to soap) has multiple meanings including to chastise, to flatter and to corrupt; 'braise' (embers) can also designate money. Beckett's redeployment of war memory has precedents in the catalogue of the Editions de Minuit: Fox's confession recalls Georges Bataille's *L'Abbé C.*, a novel from 1950 about a priest enrolled in the French Resistance and called Robert C., who, under torture, denounces his twin brother and his mistress, who are not members of a network.[188] The text is presented as a testimony written by the priest's twin brother and recovered by the editor. Its form aroused indignation; the book was depicted in *Les Lettres françaises* as an apology for wartime denunciation, and as a stain on the reputation of the Editions de Minuit as the

[184] Jean-Luc Einaudi, *La Ferme Améziane* (Paris: L'Harmattan, 1991), 17; Branche, *La torture*, 268–77; *La raison d'Etat*, 293–5.

[185] Jean-Luc Tahon, 'En "pacifiant" l'Algérie. 1955', *Les Temps Modernes* 147–8 (1958): 2096.

[186] Jauffret, 'The War Culture of French Combatants in the Algerian Conflict', 103.

[187] Lazare Sainéan, *L'Argot des tranchées d'après les lettres des poilus et les journaux du front* (Geneva: Slatkine, 1973), 53.

[188] The title is humorous and presents the novel as an ABC of testimony and underground action. The priest invented by Bataille recalls Robert Alesch; see Jean-Louis Cornille, *Les récits de Georges Bataille: Empreinte de Raymond Roussel* (Paris: L'Harmattan, 2012), 59.

publisher of the Resistance.[189] The dispute led Lindon into another court case, which he ultimately won.

Beckett's depictions of torture, in their fanciful and literal forms, here and elsewhere, also resonate with wider shifts around the idea of 'modern warfare'. In 1961, the year during which Beckett began to translate *Comment c'est* into English, Roger Trinquier published a counter-insurgency manual entitled *La guerre moderne*, which detailed the procedures deployed in Algeria and was later used as a training manual for American officers going to Vietnam.[190] The book proposes a model of productivity inspired from Taylorism: to divide the work of interrogation into small tasks and to implement the rules of shift work when collecting information. For Trinquier, all inhabitants of a territory to be conquered are potential terrorists, and to capture one suspect is potentially to get hold of another two, by virtue of the ways in which guerrilla war functions. His protocol invokes the primary unit of clandestine warfare, the 'half-cell' made up of three individuals with only one point of contact to other half-cells. This configuration, in which every member only knows three others from the network and no one beyond, was widely used by the FLN and had precedents in the French Resistance, where pseudonyms were also used to limit possible denunciations to the Gestapo under torture. The euphemisms born out of the new warfare championed by Trinquier find new articulations in Beckett's *pochade* and in texts featuring other 'half-cells' in connection with torture and denunciation.

Fragment de théâtre II or *Rough for Theatre II* engages the same political euphemisms and also imagines protective hierarchies and administrations keen to legitimate their practices. The setting is determined to an unusual degree for a Beckett play: the play is set in an office, on the sixth floor of a high-rise building, on a clear night, on the 24th of an unspecified month. The two speaking characters, A and B, appear to be involved in undercover intelligence work. A third character remains in the shadow: C, who stands motionless and silent by the window, apparently ready to jump. A and B rummage through reports of the failures C has previously experienced in the hope of encouraging defenestration, since they know that C is 'morbidly sensitive to the opinion of others' (242). They read out

[189] Denis Hollier, 'Georges Bataille devant la critique communiste', in *Georges Bataille: Actes du colloque international d'Amsterdam, 21 et 22 juin 1985*, ed. Jan Versteeg (Amsterdam: Rodopi, 1987), 65–6; Michel Surya, *Georges Bataille*, trans. Krzysztof Fijalkowski and Michael Richardson (London: Verso, 2002), 390–4.

[190] *La guerre moderne* (Table Ronde, 1961) also appeared as *Modern Warfare: A French View of Counterinsurgency* (Praeger, 1964).

testimonies from witnesses who were 'questioned' (239). They are, as B points out, ready: 'We have been to the best sources. All weighed and weighed again, checked and verified. Not a word here [*brandishing sheaf of papers*] that is not cast iron. Tied together like a cathedral' (238). Ultimately, C's mindset matters less than A and B's attempt to conceal involvement in his death. The reports they have gathered feature precisely the kind of declaration that might be cited in a press report describing an inexplicable suicide.

The shadow of torture looms over the proceedings: both investigators are knowledgeable about the 'mysterious' power of electricity and its remit (243). A yearns, 'violently', for modes of continuous surveillance; for means of 'staring' at his target without reprieve (245) – or for means of 'fixer les gens [. . .] vingt-quatre heures sur vingt-quatre' (53). Yet A and B struggle with the basics of intelligence-gathering. They are particularly uncertain about the architecture of the building – 'I could have sworn we were only on the sixth [floor]', A remarks (238) – and they need to calculate on the spot the height necessary to cause C's death based on his body weight. The possibility that A, B and C may be serving a political cause is ridiculed repeatedly; the '[t]estimony of Mr Peaberry, market gardener in the Deeping Fens and lifelong friend' describes C's cynicism towards established narratives about 'our national epos' and its 'calamities' (240). B, either reading from another testimony or expressing his own views, concurs and describes 'third fatherland', 'heart and conscience' and 'housing conditions' as 'so many disasters' (238).

The play had a long and uneasy genesis. Early drafts date from August 1958, and the play remained unpublished until 1976. Pinget noted the considerable difficulties that Beckett encountered in his journal, relating Beckett's aspiration to 'do something of high seriousness, something Racinian', and his frustration: 'Can't manage it. Says that everything he comes up with is appallingly comical'.[191] His doubts must have been compounded by the fact that the play's subject matter was intimately related to ongoing debates about the practices of the French counter-intelligence and police services, exposed in *La Gangrène* and elsewhere, and about the 'disappearances' of suspected FLN militants. A document published by Vergès, Courrégé and Zavrian in 1959 recorded the names, professions and addresses of 175 missing persons and the circumstances in which they had disappeared; two years previously, at the time of his resignation, Teitgen had offered an alarming estimate for the city of Algiers, evoking more than three thousand

[191] *LSB3*, 167 n2.

disappearances.[192] Some prominent figures were reported dead or missing months before Beckett started work on the play; 1957 saw the execution, disguised as a suicide, of the FLN leader Larbi Ben M'hidi, the murder of Marcel Audin under torture, masqueraded as an evasion, and the assassination of the lawyer and pacifist Ali Boumendjel, portrayed as a suicide. Boumendjel's death – widely discussed in the French press and related in Alleg's *La Question* and in Amrani's *Le Témoin* – holds particular significance for *Fragment de théâtre II*.

In an issue of 24–25 March 1957, *L'Echo d'Alger* reported that Boumendjel had jumped from the sixth floor of a building in the Algiers suburb of El-Biar, under the watch of paratroopers. Denouncing another example of 'Para-Pacification', Jeanson commented on Boumendjel's long interrogation, torture and forced sojourn in a psychiatric hospital. For Jeanson, the official explanation for Boumendjel's 'suicide', dated from 23 March, relies on 'buffooneries' that fail to dissimulate the real cause of death – murder. Jeanson highlights the importance of *mise-en-scène*, concluding: 'Ali Boumendjel could not appear in front of anyone, and certainly not in front of an investigating judge'.[193] Jeanson was not alone in denouncing a political conspiracy: numerous intellectuals, academics and respected figures of the French Resistance, including Vercors, wrote open letters and press articles protesting against the obfuscation of the facts.[194]

The uncharacteristically realist referent deployed in *Fragment de théâtre II* has many connections to this affair and to the catalogue of the Editions de Minuit. It is particularly significant that A and B – who are clearly competent in linguistic analysis – should be involved, in equal measure, in a process of investigation and in murder, and the names that they eventually use to address one another in the French and the English dialogues – 'Bertrand' and 'Morvan' – carry a distinctive weight. Morvan, the name of a French region that had housed a powerful *maquis* during the Second World War, also relates to established cultural codes to signify a proximity between writing and resistance. In the early years of clandestinity, the authors published by the Editions de Minuit were renamed after French regions, as Argonne, Minervois, Auxois, Thimerais, Vaucluse, Margeride, Vivarais or Mortagne.[195] The most illustrious wartime texts were by Vercors (Jean Bruller, *Le silence de la mer*), Cévennes (Jean Guéhenno, *Dans la*

[192] Jacques Vergès, Michel Zavrian and Maurice Courrégé, *Les disparus: Le Cahier Vert* (Lausanne: La Cité, 1959); Vidal-Naquet, *Torture*, 52.

[193] Francis Jeanson, 'Para-Pacification', *Esprit* 5 (1957): 815–16.

[194] Malika Rahal, *Ali Boumendjel: Une affaire française, une histoire algérienne* (Paris: Belles Lettres, 2010), 226–40.

[195] Thiesse, *Ecrire la France*, 286.

prison), Hainaut (Georges Adam, *A l'appel de la liberté*) and Forez (François Mauriac, *Le Cahier noir*).[196] This coding system proved remarkably effective: the real authors could not be identified. Lindon revived this tradition when he published Hurst's *Le Déserteur* under the pseudonym Maurienne. In the late 1950s, Morvan was one of the few place names that was not yet utilised as a pseudonym in the catalogue of the Editions de Minuit.

Other facets of Beckett's short comedy intersect with a history of espionage and counter-espionage that spans several decades. Bertrand, for example, was the surname of the chief French expert in cryptography during the Second World War; he played a critical role in the French Resistance and in Allied intelligence services, having procured the cipher device utilised by the Wehrmacht. Subsequently, Bertrand's wartime achievements led him to become Deputy Director of the French counter-espionage service dedicated to foreign affairs, the Service de Documentation Extérieure et de Contre-Espionnage (SDECE).[197] A Colonel Morvan, whose real name was Guy Marienne, had a similar itinerary: chief of the 'Darius' network in the French Resistance, Morvan founded a special service at the SDECE after the war, which actively sought to employ linguists, who could not be found in other services, and recruited members from all social and professional backgrounds, including journalists. Morvan's expertise lay in getting hold of military and diplomatic documents, personal correspondence and secret financial information, which few other agents had the skill to handle. His career was embedded in colonial politics: the SDECE was intimately involved in collecting intelligence and organising secret operations during the Algerian war and thereafter, in Algeria, France and its former colonies. Morvan, in particular, was involved in the kidnapping and disappearance of Mehdi Ben Barka, the Moroccan politician and leader of the Tricontinental, in Paris in 1965.[198]

Beckett and the Political Economy of Torture

Beckett's awareness of the political uses of torture was by no means limited to the Algerian war or its immediate aftermath. He seems to have maintained an interest in torture as political weapon in numerous other

[196] Simonin, *Les Editions de Minuit*, 486.

[197] Roger Faligot and Pascal Krop, *La piscine: Les services secrets français 1944–1984* (Paris: Seuil, 1985), 68–71, 193. Bertrand's memoirs – *Enigma: ou, La plus grande énigme de la guerre, 1939–1945* – were published in 1973.

[198] Philip M. Williams, *Wars, Plots and Scandals in Post-War France* (Cambridge: Cambridge University Press, 1970), 95.

contexts, visiting torture chambers in Nuremberg castle in 1931 and, forty years later, in Malta. He began to write about torture when he turned to the theatre: the third and final act of *Eleutheria*, his first full-length play, revolves around the attempts of the Glazier and the Spectator to elicit a revelation from Victor through all means at their disposal. The text alludes to Gestapo practices, but seems invested in pursuing these shadows in a different direction, since the torturer enrolled for the task is identified as Chinese. The proceedings are led by the Spectator, who refuses to second the Glazier's claim that torture is 'not done': 'Since when?'[199] The Spectator is familiar with methods of persuasion by escalation; he begins by informing Victor that '[t]his farce has gone on long enough', before complaining that the Glazier is 'going about it like a half-wit' (132, 137). In the French text, the Spectator employs the common historical euphemism for torture, *question*: 'Qu'il réponde à la question, sinon j'emploie les grands moyens' (145) 'He'd better answer the question, or I shall take drastic steps' (146)). His ultimatum invokes the long history of *la question* as the medieval term for torture, and its Latin root *quaestio*, torture and inquiry.

Torture, its associated rhetoric of utility and its intimacy with euphemism, are questions that also haunt Beckett's late plays. *What Where* – which he described as 'a story that I've been dragging with me for a long time [and] that I don't understand'[200] – presents an infernal process 'switch[ed] on' time and again, in response to the demands of a form of torture that does not leave physical marks, is closely allied to the use of electricity, and dictates that the torturer become the tortured. The question central to the play – the relation between the practice of torture and the possibility of reciprocity – finds an interesting parallel in the war memoir that Jacques Massu published in 1971, which ignited a public scandal: Massu used the occasion to issue an apology of torture, explaining that he had previously experimented with electrodes on his own body and ascertained that 'la gégène' was bearable.[201] It is certain that the French text, *Quoi où*, carries considerable weight; the process evoked is not 'giv[ing] the works' but 'bien travailler', a term whose meaning is indebted to its Latin etymology and meaning in Old French: to torture.[202] The obsolete meaning of the term was restored to standard usage in colonial Indochina and Algeria; the word 'travailler' recurs in Alleg's account of torture in the hands of French paratroopers, and in a prior report detailing the use of electric

199 SB, *Eleutheria*, trans. Wright, 141.
200 Bernold, *L'Amitié de Beckett*, 35.
201 Jacques Massu, *La vraie bataille d'Alger* (Paris: Plon, 1971), 165.
202 SB, *Catastrophe et autres dramaticules: Cette fois, Solo, Berçeuse, Impromptu d'Ohio, Quoi où* (Paris: Minuit, 1986), 90.

torture in Indochina, where the practice originated. In 1949, the journalist Jacques Chégaray related the presence of a 'machine to make people talk' in the quarters of French officers stationed in Indochina. His account showed that the dynamos used to power telephones and radios, a standard part of office equipment alongside the typewriters and army maps, had been put to new use to make locals 'spit'. As Chégaray's interlocutor, a military officer, made clear, all that was required was to connect the dynamo to the prisoner's body and turn the handle. This simple operation had made it possible for him to 'work' for three days on a silent woman who refused to speak.[203]

The shadow of colonial warfare bears upon Beckett's preparatory notes towards the 1985 television version of *Was wo* for the Stuttgart Süddeutscher Rundfunk, which temporarily evoke the possibility of characters wearing tarboosh, fez or turban.[204] Peculiar displacements are at work in this reimagining of the play for German television: the twist that Beckett temporarily envisaged and abandoned would have disrupted the neat alignments with Nazi torture that the German play may have invited. If these additions had been kept, the new headdress would have introduced a speculative nod to the French reliance on colonial battalions and the colonial police, possibly evoking the role played by the *harkis* in the practice of torture. It would also have invited associations with the historical practice of torture in the Ottoman Empire and in Turkey, an issue of concern to many in Germany and beyond, including Pinter, who visited Turkey with Miller that same year to investigate torture claims. The previous year, Pinter – one of Beckett's regular correspondents – had sent him his own play about torture, *One for the Road*, a few months before its publication.[205]

There is, of course, more to Beckett's plans than an indirect dialogue with Pinter. Much in Beckett's approach recalls Kafka's *The Trial* and 'In the Penal Colony', where interrogation and torture are integral to a process that finds its own justification within the procedures that enable their administration. What Beckett seems to have appreciated most about Kafka was his approach to form, and his remarks convey the gravity of his own reflection on the limited capacity of literature to represent suffering and horror. Israel Shenker relates that, in 1956, Beckett contrasted Kafka's work, where 'the consternation is in the form', with his own writing, where 'there

[203] Jacques Chégaray, 'Les tortures en Indochine', *Les crimes*, 17–18.
[204] See SB, *The Theatrical Notebooks of Samuel Beckett*, vol. 4: *The Shorter Plays*, ed. S. E. Gontarski (New York: Grove, 2001), 425.
[205] Harold Pinter Archive, British Library MS 88880; *LSB4*, 634.

is consternation behind the form, not in the form'.[206] He referred to Kafka's approach again many years later, when reading Genet's 'Quatre heures à Chatila', a text written in the wake of the Sabra and Shatila massacres and first published in 1983 by the Editions de Minuit in its *Revue d'études palestiniennes*.[207] André Bernold reports that, for Beckett, Genet's testimony utilises the 'same paradox' as Kafka – 'horror of content, serenity of form'.[208]

Other political forces bear upon Beckett's representations of torture, and they belong to an elusive colonial imaginary that the work both refracts and internalises. Beckett's manner of writing about the Algerian war through displacement and obfuscation is not specific to him, but remains aligned with the manner in which the conflict was represented by French writers through omission, substitution and displacement on a much larger scale. He was familiar with these representations: he read the controversial political plays of the period and was invited to performances that dealt with the history of the French Empire in direct and indirect ways. Furthermore, there are many connections between productions of Beckett's work and the political theatre of the 1950s and 1960s, primarily shaped by Blin, who was close to Genet and radical theatre groups. In 1957, the year he directed *Fin de partie* at London's Royal Court and at the Studio des Champs Elysées, Blin also worked with the Troupe des Griots, a black theatre company, and their collaboration extended from stage to screen, with the 1959 film *Les Tripes au soleil*.[209] With these actors, Blin also mounted his celebrated production of Genet's *Les Nègres* in 1959. Beckett was invited to a rehearsal but was dissatisfied by it; he was much more appreciative of the full performance he saw at the Théâtre de Lutèce, and noted the play's success with pleasure.[210]

This episode is part of a longer, fragmentary dialogue between Beckett and Genet, mediated by Blin, which involves a half-worded reflection on the Algerian war and emerges in shadowy form in Beckett's letters. Genet sent Beckett a copy of *Les Paravents* upon its publication in February 1961, for example; Beckett noted, in a letter to Bray, 'Not for me I fear', a remark that may apply to the play's exuberant form and flourish, rather than its content.[211] The play's explosive subject matter meant that performance was

[206] Israel Shenker, 'Moody Man of Letters', *NYT*, 6 May 1956, 129.

[207] Jean Genet, 'Quatre heures à Chatila', *Revue d'études palestiniennes* 6 (1983): 3–19.

[208] Bernold, *L'Amitié de Beckett*, 81.

[209] Aslan, *Roger Blin and Twentieth-Century Playwrights*, 59; Mark Taylor-Batty, *Roger Blin: Collaborations and Methodologies* (Bern: Peter Lang, 2007), 138–45; White, *Genet*, 495–504.

[210] *LSB3*, 250, 264. [211] *LSB3*, 397.

durably postponed; when Blin eventually directed *Les Paravents* in 1966 for the Odéon-Théâtre de France, the production proved deeply controversial, still, and was greeted by demonstrations outside and inside the theatre, marches by far-right groups and associations of war veterans, debates in the French National Assembly, and financial sanctions for the theatre.[212] Genet's perspective shifted: he perceived *Les Paravents* as a didactic play dealing with Algeria 'as a problem to be exposed to the French public', then as 'a mere masquerade'.[213] Identifying the details that would enable the production to evoke the 1950s took time and effort, as his letters to Blin reveal. To resolve this problem, the soldiers' costumes (which, for Genet, should evoke the colonial armies of the Duke of Aumale and General Bugeaud) were of a light apple green colour, quite unlike any army uniform.[214] Beckett may have had this production and the protests it generated in mind when, in December 1969, he wrote to Blin that for his next performance as Hamm he might wear a chechia.[215]

It is clear from other strands in Beckett's correspondence that, when it came to Algerian war plays, he preferred those that toyed with the conventions of political allegory.[216] He had a particular admiration for Roland Dubillard's *La Maison d'os*, a play set in a large house ruled by a fanciful owner, whose cave is littered with corpses, and he showed appreciation for Boris Vian's *Les Bâtisseurs d'empire ou le Schmürtz*, another variation on the drawing-room play in which the Schmürtz, savagely beaten by a family with various domestic objects, becomes a transparent representation of the colonial Algerian subject. These allegories are clearly indebted to the theatre of the absurd and its approach to political memory: to Beckett's early plays certainly – Vian's approach to dialogue owes much to *En attendant Godot* – as well as Ionesco's *Les Chaises* and Adamov's *L'Invasion*, both of which are permeated by half-elided allusions to deportation, the spoliation of the Jews and the memory of the Nazi camps.

In a manner that anticipates techniques later used by Dubillard, Genet and Vian to represent the Algerian war, French colonial politics appear as a concealed referent in *Fin de partie*. Beckett began drafting the play in early 1954 – a year marked by French capitulation in Indochina, bloody colonial uprisings across North Africa, a move towards autonomy in Morocco and Tunisia, and the emergence of new forms of political organisation in Algeria. *Fin de partie* refracts pervasive colonial anxieties: the distinctive power

[212] Bellity Peskine and Dichy, *La bataille des Paravents*, 28–32, 85–9.

[213] Jean Genet, *L'Ennemi déclaré* (Paris: Gallimard, 2010), 23; Genet, *Œuvres complètes*, vol. 4 (Paris: Gallimard, 1968), 222, 227.

[214] Blin, *Souvenirs*, 199. [215] Fonds Blin, IMEC. [216] *LSB3*, 457, 520, 529, 304.

relationship that ties Clov to Hamm remains inscribed in a colonial topography manifested through allusions to living habits and colonial trade. The dialogues deploy signifiers that summon the Maghreb and the lost empire in the French imagination: Nagg hankers for a piece of 'rahat loukoum', and Hamm notes that Clov normally wears 'babouches' but has, for once, swapped them for 'brodequins' or brogues, because the baboosh hurt his feet.[217] The numerous manuscript drafts reveal that the choice of footware was a matter that Beckett pondered carefully. In the published text, Hamm's evocation of Clov's missing baboosh becomes associated with his self-asserted right to authority, and with the maintenance of an enshrined hierarchy that is also reflected in Clov's ongoing struggles with French syntax and semantics. The missing baboosh also become an indicator that Clov's revolt against Hamm has begun to find articulation through nonverbal means: Hamm finds his replacement brogues immensely irritating, on the grounds that they are as noisy as 'un régiment de dragons' (77) – the section of the French cavalry associated with the long history of colonial conquest and the massacres of the Huguenots. In the English text, these references to military conquest are toned down or disappear, and no mention is made of a ghostly regiment of dragoons. At the same time, the play speaks powerfully to the political legacy of Nazism, as Adorno's celebrated essay argues. Such troubled and shifting referent is specific to the play's political context and echoes the historical concerns buttressing the Editions de Minuit's catalogue: *Fin de partie* was published in 1957, alongside testimonies correlating French colonial politics with the legacy of Nazism and other totalitarianisms. Its immediate bedfellows in the catalogue of the Editions de Minuit are Micheline Maurel's *Un camp très ordinaire* (1957), a book about the Neubrandebourg labour camp near Ravensbrück, Jacqueline Mesnil-Amar's *Ceux qui ne dormaient pas 1944–1946* (1957), a diary that raises the question of historical responsibility for the deportation of Jewish families and resistants, and Wiesel's *La Nuit*, Alleg's *La Question* and Vidal-Naquet's *L'Affaire Audin* (1958).

In the texts Beckett wrote or published in 1960 and 1961, at the height of the anti-war campaign, representations of torture carry explicit political resonances, not least because particular objects related to conservation, sanitation and hygiene – hence to the modernity and progress upheld as central to France's 'civilising mission' – are transformed into instruments of torture. These texts include *Comment c'est* (*How It Is*), the genesis of which was particularly trying and absorbed much of Beckett's time between

[217] SB, *Fin de partie* (Paris: Minuit, 1957), 74, 77.

December 1958 and late 1960. The text owes much to contemporaneous testimonies of conscription, pacification, torture and desertion, and to reports documenting Algerian methods of guerrilla war: it presents a simulacrum of military training and traces the movements of a figure crawling in mud, pulling along an old jute bag full of rotting tinned food reminiscent of army rations. This figure undergoes constant torment and torture – nails forced into the armpits, the engraving of letters into the flesh, thumps on the head and kidneys, the forcing of a tin-opener into the buttocks. The narrative tentatively gestures towards colonial ventures, evoking a turbaned head and white dhotis. Some names recur, particularly Krim, Kram, Bim and Bom (Bim and Bom, the Russian clowns who rose to fame during the late tsarist era, appear again in *What Where*). 'Krim' stands out in the published French text, not least because it accords with the name of one of the leaders of the Provisional Algerian Government, Krim Belkacem, renowned for his extensive experience of guerrilla warfare, and commonly called Krim. The only temporal landmark evoked in Part Two of *Comment c'est*, 'huit mai fête de la victoire' ('eighth of May Victory Day')[218] has a dual dimension: it recalls both the commemoration of V-Day and the date of the Sétif and Guelma massacres, the latter driven by the illusion that Algerian political aspirations could be crushed.

These textual elements are residues of a larger array of references to military manoeuvres and practices excised from earlier drafts – from the first and second parts of *Comment c'est* in particular, where military terminology featured prominently. The genetic edition compiled by Edouard Magessa O'Reilly reveals the dedication with which Beckett rethought and reshaped *Comment c'est*. In early drafts, many deleted paragraphs revolve around food rations, marches, corpses and the birth and death of empires. In discarded lines, the narrator describes in some detail his 'secteur' or sector and the manner in which it must be swept; he evokes a landscape shaped by ravines into which one may fall without warning, and an 'observateur' or observer in the process of conducting a survey.[219] Suspecting that he may have an interlocutor, his first response is to wonder whether he needs to spell out his name and position outright.[220] Everything that French usage and custom have borrowed from Arabic civilisations is marked off as such, from words such as 'azimuts' and 'zénith' to the 'système decimal arabe' or Arabic numeral system.[221]

[218] SB, *Comment c'est* (Paris: Minuit, 1961), 128–9; SB, *How It Is* [1964] (London: Faber, 2009), 71.

[219] SB, *Comment c'est/How It Is and/et L'Image: A Critical-Genetic Edition*, ed. and trans. Edouard Magessa O'Reilly (New York: Routledge, 2001), 255, 260, 50, 372, 285.

[220] Ibid., 254. [221] Ibid., 362, 357, 256.

Of particular significance is the word 'Aman', which appears in a paragraph evoking voluntary conscription, salvation and death on the battlefield, which was subsequently deleted.[222] Aman has a long history in Islamic law and designates a pledge between Muslims and non-Muslims to guarantee protection or clemency during battle, or an agreement to either end hostilities or issue pardon. Many accounts of the conquest of Algeria after 1840 relate the changing political procedures around the aman. To ask for the aman is to ask for mercy; to give it is to grant pardon.[223] The letters of Marshal Saint-Arnaud, who led some of the military conquest and became the great architect of pacification in Algeria, show that the request for the aman sometimes came with a gift to the French military. The gift might, in the early days of the conquest, consist of a horse to solicit good will,[224] but obtaining the aman later took more: the trading of hostages for example, or the payment of a heavy fine.[225] Saint-Arnaud observed these developments with satisfaction; never averse to the use of a pun, he related in 1847 that a group of rebels who had come to plead for the aman were, instead, given an 'amende' or fine.[226] His later letters associate the aman with the burning of villages, with mass killings orchestrated so that resistant tribes would ask for mercy, and, eventually, with a punishment or 'châtiment' without escape.[227] The memory of Saint-Arnaud was very much alive at the time of the Algerian war among those advocating the indivisibility of a France encompassing Algeria, who celebrated his legacy in the new forms of pacification of the 1950s.[228]

One could speculate endlessly about Beckett's motives for redrafting *Comment c'est*: did he fear that he might create more difficulties for Lindon by writing about torture, desertion and colonial warfare? His approach certainly sheds precious light on a technique tried and tested in other texts: the elision of such historical baggage is not confined to early drafts of *Comment c'est*, but is part of a practice of careful redrafting that Beckett honed across decades, in the wake of 'Trueborn Jackeen'. At the time of the Indochina War, between December 1951 and June 1952, for example, he wrote a series

[222] Ibid., 316.
[223] See Pierre de Castellane, 'Une campagne d'hiver: Souvenirs de la vie militaire en Afrique', *Revue des deux mondes* 19, no. 3 (1849): 815 n1.
[224] See Achille Leroy de Saint-Arnaud to Adolphe Leroy de Saint-Arnaud, 20 June 1842, *Lettres du Maréchal de Saint-Arnaud*, vol. 1 (Paris: Michel Lévy Frères, 1855), 393.
[225] Leroy de Saint-Arnaud to his brother, 8 August 1946, *Lettres du Maréchal de Saint-Arnaud*, vol. 2 (Paris: Michel Lévy Frères, 1855), 104.
[226] Ibid., 31 March 1847, 140.
[227] Ibid., 27 December 1845, 67; 31 March 1847, 140; 15 January 1847, 128.
[228] See Jacques Dinfreville, *L'effervescent Maréchal de Saint-Arnaud: Algérie 1840, Algérie 1960* (Paris: Scorpion, 1960), 179–200.

of short prose and dramatic texts dealing with colonial history and fantasies of colonial conquest.[229] One of these abandoned fragments – 'On le tortura bien' (we tortured him well) – deploys a dark, farcical register anticipating the later 'rough' plays: summoning the memory of the Irish Famine and the potato blight, the text relates the manner in which two characters torture a third, to uncertain ends. The procedures employed to obtain the telling of a story involve the insertion of a metal wire into the urethra or the rectum, as circumstances allow.[230] Once again, the technique relayed by Beckett draws upon historical circumstance: in the 1930s, in her widely debated diaries from a trip to Indochina, the journalist Andrée Viollis discussed the techniques employed by the French police in Cholon to obtain 'spontaneous confessions', describing their fondness for inserting wires shaped as a corkscrew into the urethra of their victim.[231]

As a historical subject to be addressed directly, then, torture largely remains the preserve of marginal, disowned or abandoned texts in Beckett's corpus. Yet he never ceased to return to the same colonial register and to explore the taxonomy of torture, including during the 1970s, when he eventually decided to publish *Pochade radiophonique* and *Fragment de théâtre II*. 'As the Story was Told', a short fragment written in English in 1973 and published two years later, is of particular interest in this regard. Imagining the failing and fractured memory of an administration dedicated to torture, the text revolves around a 'story' eventually revealed as an account of torture and death; it presents a narrator who eventually comes to recall his own involvement in this process, and attempts to respond to what an interlocutor tells him about half-forgotten 'sessions' that once took place in a canvas tent. 'Proceedings' was, temporarily, a variant that Beckett, alert to the difficulties posed by taxonomy, pondered in manuscript drafts.[232] In the published text, the 'object, duration, frequency and harrowing nature' of the sessions become more precise after each interjection from the narrator, and his own role is gradually remembered: he would wait nearby, in a hut located in a grove, at 'a distance so great even the loudest cry could not carry, but must die on the way'.[233] As he attempts to ask questions and comes to terms with the 'story', his thoughts temporarily drift away, towards

[229] For summaries, see Mark Nixon, 'Beckett's Unpublished Canon', *The Edinburgh Companion to Samuel Beckett and the Arts*, 282–91.

[230] 'On le tortura bien' is held at the Beckett International Foundation, University of Reading, under UoR MS 1656/3.

[231] Andrée Viollis, *Indochine S.O.S.* (Paris: Gallimard, 1935), 39.

[232] Mary Bryden, Julian Garforth and Peter Mills, eds., *Beckett at Reading: Catalogue of the Beckett Manuscript Collection at the University of Reading* (Reading: Whiteknights Press, 1998), 107.

[233] SB, 'As the Story was Told', *Samuel Beckett: The Complete Short Prose*, 255.

memories of a summer-house where he once contemplated the passing of time as a child. This association triggers a clear vision: he remembers a hand delivering a 'sheet of writing' to him through the canvas door, in the 'orange light' of late afternoon and after the end of 'sessions' (256). Eventually, it is revealed that an elderly man who was once required to 'say' during these sessions also 'succumbed in the end to his ill-treatment' (256). The fragment concludes with the reassurance that no one remembers anything at all, and that none of the evidence that would have enabled 'the poor man' to be pardoned was provided anyway (256).

Beckett's description of an improvised torture chamber, however elliptic, shares affinities with the testimonies published by the Editions de Minuit in the 1950s and 1960s. Some volumes included reports of a torture chamber in the Algerian countryside renamed 'Au bon accueil' (the welcome inn) and a torture chamber known as 'the hairdresser's shop'.[234] Others contained detailed information about the Paul-Cazelles camp in Algeria, which had begun as a small military base and was soon transformed into a large-scale regroupment camp to deal with mass arrests and interrogations. The camp itself primarily consisted of rows of canvas tents. The detainees – for the most part, Algerian men who were deemed 'irrecuperable' after their passage in the 'sorting centres' of Algiers – were submitted to forced labour and interrogations under torture, receiving rations of food and water that kept them at the threshold of survival.[235] The workings of the camp were described in detail in *Vérité-Liberté* in 1961, in a report reprinted by the Editions de Minuit the following year alongside other documents collected by Audin's Defence Committee. The circumstances related in 'As the Story was Told' certainly develop an imaginative proximity to these accounts.

It is in this diffuse, yet deeply evocative engagement that Beckett's writing resonates with the controversies that marked the 1950s and 1960s, and interrogates the cultural logic that prefers to envisage torture as an isolated response to crisis, rather than a political system in its own right. It is certain that Beckett's many representations of torture, in their published, 'rough' and unpublished forms, owe much to denunciations of the Algerian war such as those proffered by Lindon and others invoking the French memory of Nazism. Ultimately, however, Beckett's densely allusive texts cannot be assimilated to a coherent historical thesis, not least because their representations of torture and warfare cannot be indexed to a stable context by virtue of their bilingual form and fusion of different cultural referents. Nevertheless, acknowledging that, between 1954 and 1962, Beckett

[234] Rey, *Les Egorgeurs*, 31; *Provocation à la désobéissance*, 53.
[235] *La raison d'Etat*, 132–3, 259; Branche, *La torture*, 118–37.

was living in a country at war brings a significant corrective to received ideas about his work and its assumed generic humanism. A case in point is Beckett's oft-cited declaration that his work deals 'with distress' in an interview published in 1961. To Tom Driver, who enquired whether his plays deal 'with the same facets of experience religion must also deal with', Beckett answered that the kind of distress portrayed in his work was not personal, and was not the kind of distress that one had to 'look for'. This was the distress that is 'screaming at you even in the taxis of London', he said, in signs asking for help for 'the blind', 'orphans' and 'for relief for the war refugees'.[236] The distress and dispossession that Beckett located at the heart of modern life are indexed to specific circumstances: the only British campaign that benefited from such level of public exposure at this precise moment was a campaign to raise funds for Algerian war refugees living in camps in the border areas of Tunisia and Morocco. The appeal was led by the Oxford Committee for Famine Relief, now Oxfam, which founded a special UK Committee for Algerian Refugees.[237] The press advertisements carried in the British press featured striking images of starving Algerian children and described the conflict as a full-blown war, rather than as a series of 'events', as had become customary in France.[238] The context of Beckett's interview made such political referents prone to misunderstanding: it is unlikely that Driver and the readers of the small American magazine that published the interview in the summer of 1961 were attuned to the controversies surrounding the Algerian war. Yet the tension between the visibility and invisibility of distress that Beckett evoked in this interview arises from a distinctive political reality, both tangible and intangible. The troubled resurgence of a visceral political consciousness in Beckett's writing also brings important nuances to his declarations about the limits he ascribed to his imagination: in conversations with Arikha in particular, Beckett reportedly 'expressed regret that, because of his essentially non-didactic approach to writing, he was unable (and had certainly been unwilling) to write anything that dealt overtly with politics'.[239] The texts he wrote during the 1950s and 1960s suggest otherwise and are marked by a continued attempt to tackle immensely controversial subjects and craft new political nuances.

[236] *Samuel Beckett: The Critical Heritage*, 244–5.
[237] Maggie Black, *A Cause for Our Times: Oxfam, The First 50 Years* (Oxford: Oxfam and Oxford University Press, 1992), 54–5.
[238] 'Algerian Refugee Appeal', *Listener*, 5 June 1958, 960; 'Generals' Revolt', *Listener*, 11 May 1961, 856; Advertisement, *Financial Times*, 15 December 1960, 22; 'Appeal for Algerian Refugees', *Times*, 13 December 1957, 8.
[239] *DF*, 678.

Conclusion

The last decade of Beckett's life is marked by his militant stance in the face of discerned threats to his profession and, more broadly, to freedom of expression. This turn occurred in the 1970s, precisely as his support of international human rights campaigns also became more pronounced. The days spent pondering a new life in Moscow were long since past, and Beckett watched the working conditions of artists beyond the Iron Curtain with the same concern as many left-leaning liberals in France and in Western Europe. There remained no political posturing on his part, just action and characteristically few words: he signed petitions against human rights violations in the Soviet Union, in Chile under Pinochet and elsewhere across the world, and, when directly solicited by Oxfam and Amnesty International, he donated rare editions and manuscripts from his personal archive.[1] On occasion, such as when *Fin de partie* was performed at the Théâtre de l'Est Parisien as part of an Amnesty International event against the censoring and imprisonment of artists, he waived performance rights.[2] Censorship remained a preoccupation as always, but the movements of protest that Beckett latterly joined were more clearly framed by post-war human rights legislation: the last petition that he signed in 1989, a text in support of Salman Rushdie submitted to him by Pinter and English PEN, is a case in point. The petition attracted more than a thousand signatures from writers and intellectuals and was endorsed by numerous international organisations. It emphasised the need to defend the freedoms of opinion and expression outlined in the UN's Universal Declaration of Human Rights, asking political leaders and editors to do their utmost to ensure that the

[1] He donated drafts of 'Pour finir encore' and 'One Evening', for instance. My thanks to Justine Sundaram for information about 'Pour finir encore'. See also *Artists for Amnesty* (Dublin: Amnesty International, 1982); *LSB4*, 691.

[2] This was a 1980 production directed by Guy Rétoré, featuring Gisèle Casadesus and Pierre Dux, that was also staged in major Paris theatres. Folder 'Correspondence 1980–1981', Fonds Beckett, IMEC.

threats against Rushdie would be withdrawn.[3] The interrelated domains of political activity to which Beckett contributed in his late career were, once again, sharply gendered: women's rights and causes defended by female artists and intellectuals rarely entered the picture, and their near-absence from the political world in which Beckett operated poses important questions about the limits of his liberal politics and about implicit and explicit dynamics within literary networks, corroborating what is long known of prominent petitioning cultures more generally.[4]

World Politics and the End of the Cold War

Among all of Beckett's political gestures, *Catastrophe* has received closest attention. The circumstances are familiar: the French text was written in 1982, in response to a campaign calling for the liberation of Václav Havel, who was then, to the West, the visible face of anti-communism. Havel was serving a prison sentence for his involvement in VONS, Czechoslovakia's Committee for the Defence of Unjustly Persecuted Persons, and Charter 77, a human rights group defending free speech rights in Czechoslovakia. In the last decade of the Cold War, much crystallised around Havel: he became, as Michelle Woods has shown, 'a poster boy for free speech' in the West, commonly represented as the last bulwark against the ever-rising tide of Soviet cultural hegemony, although his plays and satires of Communism attracted little attention.[5] For many, *Catastrophe* marks the point at which Beckett left his characteristic discretion aside, and Havel is often perceived as the figure who ushered Beckett into his political coming of age. The circumstances call for greater nuance: Havel's imprisonment was one of many events that Beckett followed with attention, and Beckett's affinities with political theatre are, ultimately, unrelated to Havel's perspectives on playwriting and politics. Rather, *Catastrophe* followed from a long association with international human rights campaigns commencing under different auspices, with the anti-apartheid movements of the 1960s. By the early 1980s, Beckett had long been aware of the conditions in which actors, directors and playwrights worked in Poland, Yugoslavia and Czechoslovakia, albeit to varying degrees, as revealed in the generic reports he sent to

[3] 'Plus de sept cents écrivains pour la liberté d'expression', *Le Monde*, 3 March 1989, 4; Carol Coulter, 'Literary World in Rushdie Campaign', *IT*, 2 March 1989, 13.

[4] See Sirinelli, *Intellectuels et passions françaises*, 263–7.

[5] Michelle Woods, *Censoring Translation: Censorship, Theatre, and the Politics of Translation* (London: Continuum, 2012), xiii.

friends about his trip to Yugoslavia in 1958 and in later correspondence.[6] He found ingenious ways of helping Antoni Libera and Adam Tarn, editor of the Polish review *Dialog*, as well as artists such as Vadim Sidur – the avant-garde Soviet sculptor who faced enormous difficulties with the Moscow authorities. In Sidur's work, haunted by war, violence and the memorialisation of suffering, Beckett discerned a powerful anger and compassion.[7] At other points, he expressed concern about the treatment of artists under Stalin, but long after the facts like the majority of his contemporaries, and he expressed admiration for Nadezhda Mandelstam's memoir *Hope Against Hope*.[8] On occasion, his views on Cold War politics were aligned with the responses offered by established militants of the Left who harboured few illusions about Soviet repression.

Although he refused, in November 1958, to join a broader movement supporting Boris Pasternak following the Soviet writer's award of a Nobel Prize, Beckett later endorsed several campaigns denouncing violations of freedom of expression and movement in the Soviet Union and the Eastern Bloc. Pasternak, for Beckett, belonged to a different political landscape: to Reavey, who was canvassing support to allow Pasternak to travel to Sweden and receive his prize, Beckett sent a scathing response suggesting that this was the wrong political battle, fought too late. 'Is it because of the mighty word "Nobel" that we are suddenly to cry out against that ancient ignominy? And be sorry for the "artist" who condones it with his stipend? [. . .] I simply can't work up a squeak of indignation'.[9] Others shared Beckett's position: that month, in the Surrealist review *Bief: Jonction surréaliste*, Péret described as simply nauseating the 'concert of indignation' played in the West in response to Pasternak's conflict with the Soviet authorities.[10] For Péret, Pasternak's Nobel award was merely an attempt to reignite familiar Cold War tensions and, once again, obfuscate the silence that had previously greeted political assassinations and purges in the Soviet Union.

The petitions denouncing threats to civil liberties that Beckett signed some years later posed different political questions: these documents, thus far overlooked, reveal that he was alert to the vulnerability of Soviet political prisoners and refuseniks, and that he was particularly sensitive to the

[6] *DF*, 454–5; Predrag Todorovic, 'Beckett in Belgrade', *The Edinburgh Companion to Samuel Beckett and the Arts*, 453–64. Beckett's correspondence with Tarn is held at the Bibliothèque Polonaise de Paris (AKC 4526/01, 02).

[7] Dimitri Tokarev, 'Samuel Beckett et la Russie', *SBTA* 17 (2006): 17: 87; Musya Glants, 'The Challenger: Vadim Sidur and His Art', *Experiment: A Journal of Russian Culture* 18 (2012): 243, 249; *LSB4*, 409.

[8] On *Hope Against Hope*, see *LSB4*, 310.

[9] *LSB3*, 172.

[10] Benjamin Péret, *Œuvres Complètes*, vol. 5 (Paris: José Corti, 1989), 327.

situation of Jewish dissenters, scientists and intellectuals. In 1976, alongside fifty Nobel prizewinners, Beckett signed a petition initiated by Sartre and de Beauvoir asking for the release of the Jewish endocrinologist Mikhail Stern (who was freed the following year). The petition emphasised that '[e]ach one of us, each one of you can one day become the victim of State machination', concluding: 'We will never tire of reminding state apparatuses that their almighty power has humankind's justice for limit'.[11] Stern was serving a sentence in a Ukrainian labour camp after a trial for bribery and malpractice that Andrei Sakharov, the Soviet physicist and human rights campaigner, denounced as anti-Semitic provocation.[12] Others demonstrated that the trial had been orchestrated in retaliation for Stern's refusal to oppose the emigration of his sons to Israel, as the KGB had demanded.[13] His ordeal spurred a new awareness: the situation of dissidents in the Eastern bloc became a cause for concern to many in France – Foucault in particular, for whom Stern's trial marked the beginning of a new political commitment.[14] The following year, Beckett signed a similar appeal, published in the London *Times*, for the release of the human rights activist Anatoly Sharansky, who had been imprisoned after attempting to leave the Soviet Union to join his wife in Israel.[15] The petition arose from a campaign led by the British MPs Millie Miller (Labour) and John Gorst (Conservative), which had in turn originated in an open letter jointly signed by British MPs protesting the severe intimidation, mass arrests and accusations of treason to which Jews were being subjected in the Soviet Union. A counterpart letter in the *New York Times*, addressed to Leonid Brezhnev and bearing Beckett's name among the signatories, demanded Sharansky's immediate liberation.[16] In 1980, through Lindon, Beckett lent his support to a French committee defending Semyon Glouzman, who had denounced the use of psychiatry as a tool of repression against Soviet dissidents.[17] Glouzman, a psychiatrist, was serving a long labour camp sentence in Perm, and his situation was common knowledge: five years

[11] 'Cinquante Prix Nobel lancent un appel pour la libération du docteur Mikhael Stern', *Le Monde*, 25 March 1976, 6; 'Writer Freed', *IT*, 15 April 1977, 6.
[12] 'Detained Jewish Doctor Defended by Sakharov', *Guardian*, 5 December 1974, 4.
[13] 'Shtern's Trial Begins', *Guardian*, 12 December 1974, 4.
[14] David Macey, *The Lives of Michel Foucault* [1993] (London: Vintage, 1994), 378–81.
[15] 'October 6th. A Day to Think about Human Rights. And Anatoly Sharansky', *Times*, 6 October 1977, 3; 'Anatoly Sharansky', *Times*, 7 May 1977, 15.
[16] 'Free Anatoly Sharansky Now!', *NYT*, 8 November 1977, 24.
[17] 'Correspondence 1980–1981', Fonds Beckett, IMEC; Laurent Schwartz, *Un mathématicien aux prises avec le siècle* (Paris: Odile Jacob, 1997), 462–3; *Pour la libération de Vladimir Boukovski et Semion Glouzman* (Montereau: Comité des Mathématiciens and Comité contre les Hôpitaux Psychiatriques Spéciaux en URSS, 1976).

previously, *Esprit* had published a report by Glouzman and Vladimir Boukovski which explained how the psychiatric diagnosis and psychiatric asylums were used as tools against Soviet dissidents.[18] In 1984, as part of a small group including Ionesco, Soupault and Emmanuel Levinas, Beckett signed another petition launched by Sartre and de Beauvoir in support of Mark Markish, grandson of Peretz Markish, the Soviet Jewish poet executed during the Stalinist purges and posthumously rehabilitated. The latter's widow and sons had been allowed to emigrate to Israel, but Mark Markish and his family were denied permission to leave. The initial petition was addressed to Konstantin Chernenko, and a subsequent document invited letters of protest to be sent to Mikhail Gorbachev.[19]

Catastrophe, dedicated to Havel, has remained the most visible landmark in this overlooked history and gained greater prominence as Havel led Czechoslovakia's transition from peaceful revolution to democracy. The text was written for a special event baptised 'Une nuit pour Václav Havel', conceived for the Avignon theatre festival by AIDA (Association Internationale de Défense des Artistes victimes de la répression dans le monde), an organisation campaigning for the liberation of artists imprisoned for their political opinions. Since its foundation by Ariane Mnouchkine and Patrice Chéreau in 1979, AIDA had built a strong public profile, furthered by interviews broadcast on French television. Havel was one of the most prominent dissidents defended, alongside the Argentinian pianist Miguel Angel Estrella, the Estonian actor Ene Rammeld, and imprisoned and persecuted artists from Uruguay, Colombia, South Africa, Chile and China. From the beginning, the Havel campaign had encompassed political and artistic activity, and 'Une nuit pour Václav Havel' had precedents: after two AIDA delegations were expelled from Czechoslovakia, Mnouchkine's Théâtre du Soleil staged *Procès de Prague*, a reconstitution of the trial of VONS and Charter 77 members including Havel.[20] *Procès de Prague*, instigated by AIDA and Amnesty International, was based on trial notes that attendees had collected to give to the family and friends of the accused. It was performed in several venues across France, while another version was broadcast on German and Austrian television channels available in Czechoslovakia.[21] For those involved, *Procès de Prague* was not simply a

[18] V. Boukovsky and S. Glouzmann, 'Guide de psychiatrie pour les dissidents soviétiques', trans. Tania Mathon, *Esprit* 449, no. 9 (1975): 307–32.

[19] *The Jewish Frontier* 52, no. 2 (1985): 11.

[20] Patrice Chéreau, Antenne 2 Midi, 10 January 1980, Institut National de l'Audiovisuel online archive, www.ina.fr/.

[21] Georges Bonnaud, 'Chronique de l'illusion efficace (1968–1980)', in *Le théâtre d'intervention depuis 1968*, vol. 1, ed. Jonny Ebstein and Philippe Ivernel (Lausanne: L'Age d'Homme, 1983), 39.

political intervention, but a collective defence of the theatre professions that necessitated contributions from actors and theatre companies that seldom worked together.[22] The same principle shaped AIDA's intervention at the Avignon festival. Plans for a Havel Night spurred Beckett into thinking about collective action: he wrote *Catastrophe*, first and foremost, as a 'group gesture toward Václav Havel', and was 'appalled', as Knowlson reports, to hear of the restrictions imposed upon a fellow playwright.[23] In prison, Havel was only allowed to write one letter to his wife once a week on four sheets of paper; note-taking and drafting were strictly forbidden, and every word was scrutinised by the authorities.[24]

Catastrophe exposes what little becomes of theatre when those who write and enact are silenced: the voice that has taken over is that of a self-important director-bureaucrat, primarily concerned about making a punctual appearance at his next caucus. The text is, uncharacteristically, framed as a realist play staging the semblance of a rehearsal – the '[f]inal touches to the last scene'.[25] Beckett's parallel between brutal oppression and playacting has been widely recognised, but the play's political dimension evades consensus: it has been read as a solipsistic reflection upon the dispossessed body; as a rumination on the mechanics of theatrical spectacle; as an exposition of the tyranny practised by Soviet Communism; as an examination of the enduring power of dissent in the face of oppression. The dialogues expose hierarchies prevalent in the theatre on both sides of the Iron Curtain: the assistant, called A, is necessarily female and primed to respond to the Director's vision with '[p]encil on ear'.[26] The unseen lighting technician, named Luke, resents the imposition of the Director's whim and places him under pressure to provide clear indications, in 'technical terms'.[27] The position of the silent Protagonist, who remains in character beyond the limits of necessity, remains uncertain, calling into question the threshold between acting and obeying orders under coercion.

On another level, *Catastrophe* also acts as a meditation on what becomes of solidarity under the imperative to transform suffering into spectacle. The play offers a rebuke to the expectations of an imagined audience attending a charity event, awaiting a predicted performance of hardship in exchange for its donation. The callous Director is exclusively concerned with honing a stage aesthetic that will 'have them on their feet'.[28] The Protagonist that he and his Assistant have devised is a caricature of a political prisoner,

[22] Pierre Voltz, 'La région: Du côté du grand delta', ibid., 71–2. [23] *NABS*, 425; *DF*, 678.

[24] Edá Kriseová, *Václav Havel: The Authorized Biography*, trans. Caleb Crain (New York: St Martin's Press, 1993), 184.

[25] *CDW*, 457. [26] Ibid. [27] *CDW*, 460. [28] *CDW*, 461.

cynically made up to represent every and any detainee, and prematurely aged by detainment and hardship. Through the Protagonist and his ultimate refusal to bow down, it is possible to trace Beckett's reflection on a late Cold War rhetoric that, depending on circumstances, rendered Havel either as one case among many or as a romanticised political martyr. If the dedication identifies *Catastrophe* as a tribute to Havel, the Protagonist also brings to mind the many political prisoners who remained anonymous and beyond the reach of the spotlight: as such, *Catastrophe* suggests that Beckett was sensitive to the manner in which Western artists and politicians could harness human rights campaigns to bolster their own position and public interventions. The campaigns with which he had been associated prior to writing the play had exposed him to the new rhetoric of solidarity, but had not been germane to a reflection on militant action or the theatrical illusion itself. At the AIDA's Havel Night, *Catastrophe*'s ambiguity did not stand out: several pieces interrogated the meaning of writing for another from a position of privilege. Miller contributed a short monologue, *I Think about You a Great Deal*, featuring a Writer speaking to an Imprisoned One who does not face him directly and exits prematurely. The Writer complains about the volume of correspondence asking for his support ('save, save, save, save. [. . .] Things just can't be this bad. [. . .] Your situation seems worse than all the others, though – I'm not sure why'); eventually, he ventures a guess that '[i]n some indescribable way we are each other's continuation . . . '[29] Alfred Simon remarked that none of the invited authors – Beckett, Miller, Elie Wiesel, Jean-Pierre Faye, Andrée Chedid, Victor Haim and himself – had chosen to evoke Havel, Czechoslovakia or the Communist regime directly.[30] For Beckett, who watched a short feature on the AIDA's Havel Night on television, this experience proved mixed. Clearly, he resented the attempt made by Stephan Meldegg, the event's lead organiser and director, to introduce an explicit connection to Havel's imprisonment by presenting a 'Protagonist all trussed up with screaming white bonds to facilitate comprehension'.[31]

After his release, Havel wrote a warm letter to Beckett expressing gratitude.[32] 'It is I who stand in your debt', Beckett replied, explaining that he had read Havel's plays in French translation.[33] *Catastrophe*, to Havel,

[29] Arthur Miller, *I Think about You a Great Deal (An Expression of Solidarity with Václav Havel), Cross Currents: A Yearbook of Central European Culture* 2 (1983): 23, 24.

[30] Alfred Simon, 'Václav Havel en Avignon', *Esprit* 10 (1982): 114–16.

[31] *NABS*, 432.

[32] Václav Havel, 'Ein Gott im Paradies des Geistes', *Theater Heute* 31, no. 2 (1990): 1.

[33] *LSB4*, 614. Havel's theatre has been available in French translation since 1969, and in English translation since 1967. Grove Press, Beckett's American publisher, republished Vera Blackwell's English translation of *The Memorandum* in 1980.

also acted as a belated response from a figure with whom he had long engaged in imaginary dialogue: many years previously, in the aftermath of the Prague Spring, in 1968, Havel had issued an appeal to Western writers known for their pacifist and leftist opinions, naming Beckett, Sartre, Ionesco, Miller, Arnold Wesker, Friedrich Dürenmatt and Max Frisch. In this statement, broadcast on Western airwaves, Havel asked writers to condemn the Soviet occupation of Czechoslovakia, which he described as 'an unprecedented attempt at using violence in order to change the way of life of a country against the will of its legally instituted authorities and of all its people'.[34] Czech and Slovak writers, he explained, would be 'among the first again to suffer persecution and incarceration by the occupying powers', and needed urgent support. There are many indications in Havel's letters and diaries that Beckett's work held an enduring appeal and prompted him to reflect on the tensions in his relationship to communism. The letters he wrote from prison in the early 1980s mention Beckett regularly and celebrate the spiritual 'eddy' that Beckett's work has brought to theatre and to the world.[35] This sentiment was not uncommon: since the 1950s, Beckett's plays had been perceived as important and subversive political statements across the Eastern bloc.

A different context has taken precedence in discussions of *Catastrophe*: the work of *Index on Censorship*, which had expressed concern about Havel's situation since its first issues, and formalised the dialogue between Beckett and Havel by publishing Havel's *Mistake* alongside the English version of *Catastrophe* in 1984, shortly after Havel's release, in an issue recalling the plays' joint performance at the Stockholm Stadsteater as part of a 'Night of Solidarity' with Havel and Charter 77 the previous December. The translation of Havel's play – subtitled 'A Sketch by Czechoslovakia's Top Banned Playwright' – was firmly identified as a response to *Catastrophe*. However, a postface reproducing Havel's message for the premiere of *Mistake* indicated something else: that the play was written 'specially for the Swedish theatre evening organised to express solidarity with our Czechoslovak unofficial culture', in recognition of the longstanding Swedish support to the human rights movement in Czechoslovakia.[36] But no matter: for *Index on Censorship*, the association with Beckett was a golden opportunity. When the review initiated a new advertising campaign two years later, a portrait of Beckett wearing a gag was disseminated in British publications alongside the statement, 'If Samuel Beckett had been born in Czechoslovakia

[34] Henry Raymont, 'Radio Appeal by Czech Dramatist Received Here', *NYT*, 4 September 1968, 4.
[35] Václav Havel, *Letters to Olga*, trans. Paul Wilson (London: Faber, 1990).
[36] Václav Havel, 'Many Thanks to Our Swedish Friends', *Index on Censorship* 13, no. 1 (1984): 15.

we'd still be waiting for Godot'. The gag, a gesture towards *Catastrophe*, also invoked other campaigns: in 1980 already, the programme for the British Writers' Guild's 'Havel Afternoon' had showed Havel behind a row of pens disguised as prison bars.[37] *Waiting for Godot*, the text emphasised, was banned in Czechoslovakia like other texts expressing views that the government did not support. This was smart copy: 'Luckily, Beckett does not live in Czechoslovakia, but what of those writers who do? Fortunately, some of their work can be read in *Index on Censorship*, a magazine which fights censorship by publishing the work of censored poets, authors, playwrights, journalists and publishers'.[38] The campaign, coordinated by Tom Stoppard, had proceeded with Beckett's approval. Originally, Beckett had agreed to provide a photograph for a campaign against repression led by *Index on Censorship*, but Stoppard had not anticipated that the advertising company Saatchi and Saatchi would doctor the portrait, placing a gag over Beckett's mouth. Beckett's reply to Stoppard's embarrassed apology was characteristically brief: 'nothing against it'.[39]

Numerous commentaries present *Catastrophe* as a punctual intervention into the political sphere, and as the text in which Beckett's political voice was heard clearly for the first time. This alignment between Beckett and Western human rights campaigns owes much to the associations between *Catastrophe* and *Index on Censorship* in Britain; it is also indexed to more elusive shifts taking place around human rights movements on the international stage. The emergence of the Western artist as human rights defender is inscribed in broader political mutations: Samuel Moyn, for example, has traced the relation between the rise of neoliberalism in the West and the transformation of human rights into 'the last utopia' during the 1970s, arguing that human rights are tied to deep-seated historical myths about international dialogue, and to a new depoliticised politics that 'has sapped the energy from old ideological contests of left and right'.[40] Moyn's argument resonates with the type of appeal and political gesture that Beckett endorsed in the last decade of his life. Many of the petitions he signed attracted support from a motley crew of writers, artists, thinkers and politicians of different persuasions, and took on public forms that frequently obscured their initial motivations, ties to radical politics, or origins in political compromise. A good example is Manifesto-Appeal of the

[37] Woods, *Censoring Translation*, xiii.

[38] The advertisement appeared between 1986 and 1989 in publications including *East European Reporter*, *Fortnight*, *Granta*, *Private Eye*, *Punch*, *The Fiction Magazine* and *Third World Quarterly*, for example. See *Third World Quarterly* 11, no. 4 (1989): x.

[39] Ira Nadel, *Double Act: A Life of Tom Stoppard* (London: Methuen, 2002), 355.

[40] Samuel Moyn, *The Last Utopia: Human Rights in History* (Cambridge, MA: Belknap, 2011), 227.

Nobel Prizewinners from June 1981, widely perceived as a landmark statement against hunger and underdevelopment. Beckett features among the signatories alongside an impressive gallery of scientists, writers and political figures including Saul Bellow, Willy Brandt, Joseph Brodsky, Mairéad Corrigan, Seán McBride, Anwar El Sadat, Sakharov, Desmond Tutu, Lech Walesa, Elie Wiesel and Betty Williams. The document was presented to the UN's Geneva headquarters; it garnered support from representatives of the UN Conference on Trade and Development and numerous heads of state; it focused debate on world hunger at the Brussels EU Parliament and elsewhere, and contributed to a drive to increase spending on humanitarian aid. The manifesto, however, had specific origins: it was created by the MEP Marco Pannella, leader of the Italian Radical Party since the 1960s, and it was supported by Food and Disarmament International, a Brussels group of which Pannella was a member. The wording of the appeal reflected its ties to international campaigns for disarmament, solidarity and social justice that presented deprivation as a systemic political issue. In terms that some UN representatives found unsettling, the text defined world hunger in times of plenty as a 'new holocaust', called for coordinated civic disobedience and non-violence according to the precedent set by Gandhi, and denounced the lack of political will to address the problems generated by humanitarian aid – 'a cheap way to buy a good conscience', without 'sav[ing] those who rely on it'.[41]

Political Worlds

Ultimately, it is in a professional capacity, and in the fields of writing, publishing and theatre-making, that Beckett most frequently took action on political grounds. Helping writers working in less favourable circumstances was something he viewed as a duty. On occasion, he supported artists with whom he was not personally acquainted, particularly theatre artists who expressed strong political opinions. In 1971, he signed a collective letter to the Brazilian ambassador in Paris enquiring about members of the Living Theatre, a company renowned for its radical work and revolutionary aspirations. Members of the collective who had travelled to Brazil to perform in the *favelas* were arrested and were said to have suffered ill-treatment in the Belo Horizonte prison, where the police was known for torturing dissenters

[41] 'Manifesto-Appeal of the Nobel Prizewinners', website of the Italian Radical Party, www.radicalparty.org/content/manifesto-appeal-nobel-prizewinners; 'Laureates Call for Gandhian Stir', *Times of India*, 25 June 1981, 9; 'Starvation', *Guardian*, 5 August 1981, 7; Brian Donaghy, 'MEPs Debate World Hunger Options', *IT*, 17 June 1982, 8.

and political prisoners.[42] The plea for their liberation was supported by a hundred American, British and Italian artists.[43] Beckett's name also features on an international petition issued the same year protesting against the dismissal of Otomar Krejča from the directorship of Prague's Theatre Behind the Gate, and calling into question the interdiction to travel that had prevented Krejča from touring a production in Italy and France.[44] In other circumstances, Beckett expressed solidarity with the London theatres that had supported his work, and signed petitions against Margaret Thatcher's campaign of cuts to public expenditure on the arts in the United Kingdom. In 1982, with Peter Brook, Joan Miró and Dario Fo, he endorsed a letter to the London *Times*, asking Hammersmith Council to continue funding the Riverside Studios and objecting to its decision to divest funds to the Lyric Theatre.[45] In 1984, with John Osborne, Pinter and other British playwrights, actors and directors, he signed a similar petition protesting against cuts to the Royal Court's annual grant.[46]

These are just a handful of the many moments in which Beckett used his reputation to solicit publishers, governments and organisations on behalf of other artists. He offered assistance to many others informally, and retained particular sympathy for iconoclasts and radicals. Those who benefited from his help included, for example, Patrick Straram, member of the Internationale Lettriste and future Situationnist, or the little-known writer Jack Thieuloy.[47] In the 1970s, Beckett joined Thieuloy's Comité de Soutien, a committee formed to cover legal fees when Thieuloy was incarcerated in the Santé prison after attacking members of the Goncourt Prize jury. Thieuloy was an Algerian war veteran whose anti-militarism had led to his dismissal from the army; ten years after the episode, he published a memoir about his years as a paratrooper, describing the routine use of violence and torture.[48] B. S. Johnson was another of the many for whom Beckett wrote letters of recommendation and cheques; Johnson's biographer suggests that there was more to their friendship than a simple courtesy and

[42] John Tytell, *The Living Theatre: Art, Exile and Outrage* (London: Methuen, 1997), xii, 278–80, 297–304.

[43] 'Inquiétudes sur le sort du Living', *Le Monde*, 4 August 1971, 12.

[44] Krejča had an interest in Beckett's work and later directed *En attendant Godot* for the Avignon Festival. 'Theatre People Make Plea for Czech Director', *Times*, 1 May 1971, 4; Kenneth Rea, 'En attendant Godot', *Guardian*, 8 August 1978, 8.

[45] Bryan Appleyard, 'Riverside Studios Fighting for a Stay of Execution', *Times*, 29 July 1982, 9.

[46] R. W. Apple, 'Cut in British Art Grants Is Less than Feared', *NYT*, 31 March 1984, 14.

[47] Patrick Straram and Boris Donné, *La veuve blanche et noire un peu détournée* (Paris: Sens and Tonka, 2006), 81–2; *LSB2*, 424; Jean-Baptiste Mauroux, 'Jack Thieuloy', *Quinzaine littéraire*, 1–5 November 1976, 11; *DF*, 641.

[48] Jack Thieuloy, *Voltigeur de la lune: Récit* (Paris: Ramsay, 1984).

that Beckett was sympathetic to Johnson's politics.[49] This seems likely: the figures to whom Beckett paid formal tributes – notably, O'Casey and Herbert Marcuse – were known for their political profiles and long-standing commitment to socialism. Beckett's tribute to O'Casey – published in the *Irish Times*, a newspaper that had discussed O'Casey's political orientation in ample detail previously – celebrated a life marked by political commitment and exile ('To my great compatriot, Sean O'Casey, from France where he is honoured, I send my enduring gratitude and homage').[50] In contrast, the *mirlitonnade* he dedicated to Marcuse on the occasion of his eightieth birthday in 1978 comes across as a coded tribute to political activity. Beckett knew Marcuse solely as political thinker and figurehead of the student movements: his correspondence with Adorno from 1969 reflects on the 'Marcusejugend' or Marcusian youth, and its capacity for political conspiracy.[51] In the wake of this dedication, a warm exchange of letters ensued, in which Marcuse pointed to deep affinities between their respective endeavours: 'I have always felt that in the hopeless suffering of your men and women, the point of no return has been reached. The world has been recognized as what it is, called by its true name. Hope is beyond our power to express it'.[52] Like Marcuse, Beckett was well-attuned to the post-1968 thesis that everything carries a political charge. Ultimately, there were few facets of life, art or writing that he understood to be severed from politics. Even unlikely sources give a sense of this position: in her memoir, Antonia Fraser recalls an evening with Beckett and Bray in 1979, during which Bray defended the slogan 'everything is political', which rallied the student and labour movements long after 1968. To this Pinter objected, 'Nothing I have written, Barbara, nothing ever, is political'. And Beckett offered the reply familiar to any supporter of the 1968 movement: 'This very absence of politics is in itself a political statement'.[53]

There is abundant evidence of the energy and integrity with which Beckett expressed his concerns for justice, solidarity and the conditions in which freedom is lost and regained. He envisaged humanist philosophical traditions as part of a political system to be treated with scepticism: from his perspective, the very category of 'the human' remained a fraught

[49] Jonathan Coe, *Like a Fiery Elephant: The Story of B. S. Johnson* (London: Picador, 2004), 227, 328, 344.

[50] SB, 'Gratitude and Homage', *IT*, 30 March 1960, 8.

[51] Adorno, *Notes sur Beckett*, 22.

[52] 'Samuel Beckett's Poem for Marcuse and an Exchange of Letters', in *Art and Liberation: Collected Papers of Herbert Marcuse*, vol. 4, ed. Douglas Kellner (Abingdon: Routledge, 2007), 200–2.

[53] Antonia Fraser, *'Must You Go?': My Life with Harold Pinter* (London: Weidenfeld and Nicolson, 2010), 105, 74, 145.

concept reserved for times of mass deaths and massacres. In 1945, he described humanism as the philosophy that rears its head only when ruthless oppression and disaster strike; the Holocaust, unnamed, weighs heavily over his evocations of religious 'butcheries' and the massacre of Lisbon Jews in 1506.[54] The sense of being trapped in dark times pervades many reported conversations with friends: in his gloomiest moments, he ventured that life in the eighteenth century would have been far preferable.[55] Coffey remembered his fondness for Baudelaire's 'Une charogne', a poem relating an encounter with a rotting carcass that Beckett read as a historical allegory and greeted with a cryptic diagnosis: 'It will take a long time, centuries'.[56] With Bowles, Beckett discussed a 'contemporary malaise' in the human spirit, commenting on the 'black-out' of history and the importance of 'the *extreme*': 'Only at the *extreme* can you get to grips with the real problem'.[57] Montague recalled a writer who saw 'naked pain and suffering everywhere' and a 'human spirit [. . .] on its knees', concluding: 'Everything is on fire'.[58]

The foundation of modern politics, for Max Weber, is crystallised in the relation between violence and the state as 'that human community which (successfully) lays claim to the *monopoly of legitimate physical violence*'.[59] Few authors shed as revealing a light on the hard face of politics as Beckett, a writer whose work persistently represents raw power and domination, as well as those elusive zones where memory and oblivion, violence and peace, life and death are brought together. Today, the visionary political streak of his writing is as difficult to ignore as its distinctive interrogation of what goes on when long-established certainties crumble and when stalemate threatens to persist, and it is no wonder that *Endgame* and *Waiting for Godot* should have become so attractive to political journalists and speech writers wishing to shed light on unpredictable situations. Nonetheless, it has become extremely difficult to disentangle the work's political legacies from the cultural economics spawned by neoliberal capitalism. The political Beckett, with his unconventional knowledge and experience, does not stand much of a chance when pitted against the high priest of failure, resignation and acceptance that proves so seductive in many different cultural and economic spheres at present. His witty lines on trying again, failing again and failing better have been fetishised in strikingly different contexts,

[54] SB, *Le monde et le pantalon, suivi de Peintres de l'empêchement* (Paris: Minuit, 1990), 43–4.
[55] *BR/RB*, 216. [56] Coffey, 'Memory's Murphy Maker', 34. [57] Bowles, 'How to Fail', 28.
[58] John Montague, 'An Appreciation of Samuel Beckett', *Guardian*, 27 December 1989, 13.
[59] Max Weber, *Political Writings*, ed. Peter Lassman and Ronald Speirs (Cambridge: Cambridge University Press, 1994), 310–11.

from the tattooed forearm of tennis player Stan Wavrinka to contemporary marketing and management manuals, in which the concept of 'failing better' is frequently presented as the way forward. Many of those who have reclaimed Beckett as their moral guide have done so at a time when they have secured every success and seek confirmation: recent examples include the actor Daniel Radcliffe, who also pondered a tattoo of the celebrated aphorism, and Nick Clegg, former leader of the UK's Liberal Democrats and former Deputy Prime Minister, who praised Beckett's capacity to ask dangerous questions in the run-up to the 2010 General Election.[60]

Another Beckett persists elsewhere, in a world that all too often *is* on fire; in this other world, we can trace the lineaments of a very different political legacy. His plays continue to be performed in devastated cities where hope is a scarce commodity: in the aftermath of Hurricane Katrina, for example, a New Orleans performance of *Waiting for Godot* offered a powerful reflection on the tragic situation of the city's inhabitants. Many continue to find solace in the calls for courage and fortitude that remain central to Beckett's work, and the humour with which it presents 'going on' as the only possibility: indeed, these are the qualities that spurred the Freedom Theatre in the Jenin refugee camp on the West Bank to stage a performance inspired from *Waiting for Godot* to mark their return after the assassination of their founder and mentor, Juliano Mer Khamis.[61] Recent news stories refract a wider feeling that no other writer portrays hardship with quite the same accuracy and gravity.[62] A BBC news report states that, in Syria, a man who has lost everything found fleeting consolation in memories of Beckett's humour, perceiving the absurd wait of his dispossessed characters as a reflection of Syria's political situation. Another depicts an actor from Damascus, granted asylum in Sweden and pondering a performance of *What Where* as a way of explaining what torture might be to those around him. Yet another report describes conversations with two destitute Syrian children living on the streets of Beirut, who have heard about *Waiting for Godot*. They have no doubt that the play reflects their own lives, and the game

[60] Lewis Smith, 'Kids Would Be Magic, Says Daniel Radcliffe', *Independent*, 26 May 2013, www.independent.co.uk/news/people/news/kids-would-be-magic-says-daniel-radcliffe-and-he-d-like-to-play-potter-senior-8632916.html; Nick Clegg, 'My Hero Samuel Beckett', *Guardian*, 30 April 2010, www.theguardian.com/books/2010/apr/30/nick-clegg-my-hero-samuel-beckett.

[61] See the Freedom Theatre website, www.thefreedomtheatre.org/while-waiting/.

[62] Ian Pannell, 'How *Waiting for Godot* Offers Syrians Hope', BBC News, 29 April 2012, www.bbc.co.uk/news/magazine-17857241; Matilde Gattoni and Matteo Fagotto, 'Stranded in Sweden', *Newsweek*, 26 March 2014, http://europe.newsweek.com/photo-essay-stranded-sweden-238408?rm=eu; Emily Jane O'Dell, '"My Boys": The Syrian Street Kids Who Found Me', *Salon*, 20 September 2014, www.salon.com/2014/09/21/my_boys_the_syrian_street_kids_who_found_me/.

they have coined – 'I am Samuel Beckett!' 'No, *I* am Samuel Beckett!' – is perhaps the simplest and most moving tribute to the vitality of Beckett's political imagination. When death, violence and forced displacement are immediate political realities, Beckett's writing becomes much more than literature.

Select Bibliography

Adorno, Theodor W. 'Commitment'. Translated by Francis McDonagh. *New Left Review* I, 87–88 (1974): 75–89.

Notes sur Beckett. Translated by Christophe David. Caen: Nous, 2008.

'Trying to Understand *Endgame*'. Translated by Michael T. Jones. *New German Critique* 26 (1982): 119–50.

Walter Boehlich, Martin Esslin, Hans-Geert Falkenberg and Ernst Fischer. '"Optimistisch zu denken ist kriminell": Eine Fernsehdiskussion über Samuel Beckett'. *Frankfurter Adorno Blätter* 3 (1994): 78–122.

Badiou, Alain. *On Beckett*, edited by Nina Power and Alberto Toscano. Manchester: Clinamen, 2003.

Bair, Deirdre. *Samuel Beckett: A Biography.* London: Jonathan Cape, 1978.

Barry, Elizabeth. 'Beckett, Bourdieu and the Resistance to Consumption'. *Modernist Cultures* 2, no. 1 (2010): 31–41.

'Translating Nationalism: Ireland, France and Military History in Beckett's *Mercier et Camier*'. *Irish Studies Review* 13, no. 4 (2005): 505–15.

Bixby, Patrick. 'The Ethico-Politics of Homo-ness: Beckett's *How It Is* and Casement's *Black Diaries*'. *Irish Studies Review* 20, no. 3 (2012): 243–61.

Samuel Beckett and the Postcolonial Novel. Cambridge: Cambridge University Press, 2009.

Blackman, Jackie. 'Beckett Judaizing Beckett: A "Jew from Greenland" in Paris'. *Samuel Beckett Today/Aujourd'hui* 18 (2007): 325–40.

Boxall, Peter. 'Samuel Beckett: Towards a Political Reading'. *Irish Studies Review* 10, no. 2 (2002): 159–70.

Since Beckett: Contemporary Writing in the Wake of Modernism. London: Continuum, 2009.

ed. *Beckett/Aesthetics/Politics.* Special section of *Samuel Beckett Today/Aujourd'hui* 9 (2000): 207–94.

Bradby, David. *Beckett: Waiting for Godot.* Cambridge: Cambridge University Press, 2001.

Casanova, Pascale. *Samuel Beckett: Anatomy of a Literary Revolution.* Translated by Gregory Elliott. London: Verso, 2006.

The World Republic of Letters. Translated by M. B. DeBevoise. Cambridge, MA: Harvard University Press, 2004.

Craig, George, Martha Dow Fehsenfeld, Dan Gunn and Lois More Overbeck, eds. *The Letters of Samuel Beckett, vol. 2: 1941–1956*. Cambridge: Cambridge University Press, 2011.

The Letters of Samuel Beckett, vol. 3: 1957–1965. Cambridge: Cambridge University Press, 2014.

The Letters of Samuel Beckett, vol. 4: 1966–1989. Cambridge: Cambridge University Press, 2016.

Cronin, Anthony. *Samuel Beckett: The Last Modernist*. 1996. London: Flamingo, 1997.

Dow Fehsenfeld, Martha, and Lois More Overbeck, eds. *The Letters of Samuel Beckett, vol. 1: 1929–1940*. Cambridge: Cambridge University Press, 2009.

Duerfahrd, Lance. *The Work of Poverty: Samuel Beckett's Vagabonds and the Theater of Crisis*. Columbus: Ohio State University Press, 2013.

Eagleton, Terry. *Heathcliff and the Great Hunger: Studies in Irish Culture*. London: Verso, 1995.

'Political Beckett?' *New Left Review* 40 (2006): 67–74.

Elam, Keir. 'Catastrophic Mistakes: Beckett, Havel, the End'. *Samuel Beckett Today/Aujourd'hui* 3 (1994): 1–28.

Engelberts, Matthijs. 'Théâtre et oppression dans *Catastrophe* de Samuel Beckett: Réflexivité moderniste et référence politique'. *Revue d'histoire du théâtre* 50 (1998): 169–90.

Feldman, Matthew. *Beckett's Books: A Cultural History of Samuel Beckett's 'Interwar Notes'*. London: Continuum, 2006.

Fischer, Ernst. *Art against Ideology*. Translated by Anna Bostock. London: Allen Lane, Penguin Press, 1969.

Fox, Michael David. '"There's Our Catastrophe": Empathy, Sacrifice, and the Stageing of Suffering in Beckett's Theatre'. *New Theatre Quarterly* 17, no. 4 (2001): 357–72.

Friedman, Alan Warren, ed. *Beckett in Black and Red: The Translations for Nancy Cunard's Negro (1934)*. Lexington: University Press of Kentucky, 2000.

Füger, Wilhelm. 'The First Berlin *Godot*: Beckett's Debut on the German Stage'. *Samuel Beckett Today/Aujourd'hui* 11 (2001): 57–63.

Gaffney, Phyllis. 'Dante, Manzoni, De Valera, Beckett . . . ? Circumlocutions of a Storekeeper: Beckett and Saint-Lô'. *Irish University Review* 29, no. 2 (1999): 256–80.

'Neither Here nor There: Ireland, Saint-Lô, and Beckett's First Novel in French'. *Journal of Beckett Studies* 9, no. 1 (1999): 1–26.

Gibson, Andrew. 'Beckett, de Gaulle and the Fourth Republic 1944–49: *L'Innommable* and *En attendant Godot*'. *Limit(e) Beckett* 1 (2010). http://www.limitebeckett.paris-sorbonne.fr/.

'Beckett, Vichy, Maurras, and the Body: *Premier amour* and *Nouvelles*'. *Irish University Review* 45, no. 2 (2015): 281–301.

'Franco-Irish Beckett: *Mercier et Camier* in 1945–6'. In *Samuel Beckett: Debts and Legacies*, edited by Peter Fifield and David Addyman, 19–38. London: Bloomsbury, 2013.

Samuel Beckett. London: Reaktion, 2009.

Golden, Sean. 'Familiars in a Ruinstrewn Land: *Endgame* as Political Allegory'. *Contemporary Literature* 22, no. 4 (1981): 425–55.
Gontarski, S. E., ed. *The Edinburgh Companion to Samuel Beckett and the Arts*. Edinburgh: Edinburgh University Press, 2014.
Gordon, Lois. *The World of Samuel Beckett, 1906–1946*. New Haven: Yale University Press, 1996.
Hansen, Jim. 'Samuel Beckett's *Catastrophe* and the Theater of Pure Means'. *Contemporary Literature* 49, no. 4 (2008): 660–82.
Terror and Irish Modernism: The Gothic Tradition from Burke to Beckett. Albany: SUNY Press, 2009.
Harmon, Maurice, ed. *No Author Better Served: The Correspondence of Samuel Beckett and Alan Schneider*. Cambridge, MA: Harvard University Press, 1998.
Harrington, John. *The Irish Beckett*. Syracuse, NY: Syracuse University Press, 1991.
Hill, Leslie. '"Up the Republic!": Beckett, Writing, Politics'. *MLN* 112, no. 5 (1997): 909–28.
Houston Jones, David. *Samuel Beckett and Testimony*. Basingstoke: Palgrave Macmillan, 2011.
Huber, Werner. 'Godot, Gorba, and Glasnost: Beckett in East Germany'. *Samuel Beckett Today/Aujourd'hui* 2 (1993): 49–58.
Katz, Daniel. 'What Remains of Beckett: Evasion and History'. In *Beckett and Phenomenology*, edited by Ulrika Maude and Matthew Feldman, 144–57. London: Continuum, 2009.
Kennedy, Seán, ed. *Beckett and Ireland*. Cambridge: Cambridge University Press, 2010.
ed. *Historicising Beckett*. Special section of *Samuel Beckett Today/Aujourd'hui* (2015): 21–131.
and Katherine Weiss, eds. *Samuel Beckett: History, Memory, Archive*. New York: Palgrave Macmillan, 2009.
Kiberd, Declan. *Inventing Ireland: The Literature of the Modern Nation*. London: Vintage, 1996.
Knowlson, James. *Damned to Fame: The Life of Samuel Beckett*. London: Bloomsbury, 1996.
and John Haynes. *Images of Beckett*. Cambridge: Cambridge University Press, 2003.
and Elizabeth Knowlson, eds. *Beckett Remembering/Remembering Beckett*. New York: Arcade Publishing, 2006.
Kubiak, Anthony. *Stages of Terror: Terrorism, Ideology, and Coercion as Theatre History*. Bloomington: Indiana University Press, 1991.
Lamont, Rosette C. 'Crossing the Iron Curtain: Political Parables'. In *Beckett Translating/Translating Beckett*, edited by Alan Warren Friedman, Charles Rossman and Dina Sherzer, 77–84. University Park: Pennsylvania State University Press, 1987.
'Samuel Beckett's Wandering Jew'. In *Reflections of the Holocaust in Literature*, edited by Randolph L. Braham, 35–53. Boulder, CO: Social Science Monographs, 1990.
Libera, Antoni. 'Beckett's *Catastrophe*'. *Modern Drama* 28, no. 3 (1985): 341–7.

Lloyd, David. *Anomalous States: Irish Writing and the Postcolonial Moment*. Dublin: Lilliput Press, 1993.

Irish Culture and Colonial Modernity 1800–2000: The Transformation of Oral Space. Cambridge: Cambridge University Press, 2011.

McCormack, W. J. 'Samuel Beckett and the *Negro Anthology*'. *Hermathena* (1992): 73–92.

McMullan, Anna. 'Irish/Postcolonial Beckett'. In *Palgrave Advances in Samuel Beckett Studies*, edited by Lois Oppenheim, 89–109. Basingstoke: Palgrave Macmillan, 2004.

McNaughton, James. 'Samuel Beckett's "Echo's Bones": Politics and Entailment in the Irish Free State'. *Modern Fiction Studies* 60, no. 2 (2014): 320–44.

Miller, Tyrus. 'Beckett's Political Technology: Expression, Confession, and Torture in the Later Drama'. *Samuel Beckett Today/Aujourd'hui* 9 (2000): 255–78.

'Dismantling Authenticity: Beckett, Adorno, and the "Post-War"'. *Textual Practice* 8, no. 1 (1994): 43–57.

Mooney, Sinéad. *A Tongue Not Mine: Beckett and Translation*. Oxford: Oxford University Press, 2011.

Moorjani, Angela. 'Beckett's *Molloy* in the French Context'. *Samuel Beckett Today/Aujourd'hui* 25 (2013): 93–108.

Morin, Emilie. 'Beckett, Samuel Johnson and the "Vacuity of Life"'. *Beckett/Philosophy*, edited by Matthew Feldman and Karim Mamdani, spec. issue, *Sofia Philosophical Review* 5, no. 1 (2011): 228–50.

Samuel Beckett and the Problem of Irishness. Basingstoke: Palgrave Macmillan, 2009.

'Samuel Beckett, the Wordless Song and the Pitfalls of Memorialisation'. *Irish Studies Review* 19, no. 2 (2011): 185–205.

Morresi, Renata. *Nancy Cunard: America, modernismo, negritudine*. Urbino: Edizione QuattroVenti, 2007.

Murphy, David. '"I Was Terribly Frightened at Times": Irish Men and Women in the French Resistance and F Section of SOE, 1940–5'. In *Franco-Irish Military Connections, 1590–1945*, edited by Nathalie Genet-Rouffiac and David Murphy, 269–94. Dublin: Four Courts, 2009.

'Paddy fait de la résistance. Les Irlandais dans la Résistance française et la section F du SOE, 1940–1945'. *Revue historique des armées* 253 (2008), http://rha.revues.org/.

Nixon, Mark. 'Chronology of Beckett's Journey to Germany 1936–1937 (Based on the German Diaries)'. *Journal of Beckett Studies* 19, no. 2 (2010): 245–72.

Samuel Beckett's German Diaries, 1936–1937. London: Continuum, 2011.

ed. *Publishing Samuel Beckett*. London: British Library, 2011.

and Matthew Feldman, eds. *The International Reception of Samuel Beckett*. London: Continuum, 2009.

O'Reilly, Edouard Magessa, ed. *Comment c'est/How It Is and/et L'Image: A Critical-Genetic Edition*. By Samuel Beckett. New York: Routledge, 2001.

Oppenheim, Lois. 'Playing with Beckett's Plays: On Sontag in Sarajevo and Other Directorial Infidelities'. *Journal of Beckett Studies* 4, no. 2 (1995): 35–46.

Pearson, Nels C. '"Outside of Here It's Death": Co-Dependency and the Ghosts of Decolonization in Beckett's *Endgame*'. *ELH* 68, no. 1 (2001): 215–39.
Perloff, Marjorie. '"In Love with Hiding": Samuel Beckett's War'. *Iowa Review* 35, no. 1 (2005): 76–103.
Piette, Adam. 'Torture, Text, Human Rights: Beckett's *Comment c'est/How It Is* and the Algerian War'. In *Around 1945: Literature, Citizenship, Rights*, ed. Allan Hepburn, 151–74. Montreal: McGill-Queen's University Press, 2016.
Pilling, John. *Beckett's Dream Notebook*. Reading: Beckett International Foundation, 1999.
A Samuel Beckett Chronology. Basingstoke: Palgrave Macmillan, 2006.
Quigley, Mark. *Empire's Wake: Postcolonial Irish Writing and the Politics of Modern Literary Form*. New York: Fordham University Press, 2013.
Rabillard, Sheila. 'The Body in Beckett: *Dénégation* and the Critique of a Depoliticised Theatre'. *Criticism* 34, no. 1 (1992): 99–118.
Roach, Joseph. '"All the Dead Voices": The Landscape of Famine in *Waiting for Godot*'. In *Land/Scape/Theater*, edited by Elinor Fuchs and Una Chaudhuri, 84–93. Ann Arbor: University of Michigan Press, 2002.
Ronen, Ilan. '*Waiting for Godot* as Political Theater'. In *Directing Beckett*, edited by Lois Oppenheim, 239–49. Ann Arbor: University of Michigan Press, 1994.
Roof, Judith A. 'Staging the Ideology behind the Power: Pinter's *One for the Road* and Beckett's *Catastrophe*'. *Pinter Review* 2, no 1 (1988): 8–18.
Sandarg, Robert. 'A Political Perspective on Catastrophe'. In *Make Sense Who May: Essays on Samuel Beckett's Later Works*, edited by Robin J. Davis and Lance St John Butler, 137–44. Gerrards Cross: Colin Smythe, 1988.
Schonmann, Shifra. 'Between Text and Counter-Text: Theatre in Search of Political Meaning'. *Contemporary Theatre Review* 3, no. 2 (1995): 171–80.
Sheehan, Paul. 'Waiting for Nothing: Commitment, Resistance, and Godot's Underground Ancestry'. In *In Dialogue with Godot: Waiting and Other Thoughts*, edited by Ranjan Ghosh, 99–112. Lanham, MD: Lexington, 2013.
Simonin, Anne. *Les Editions de Minuit, 1942–1955: Le devoir d'insoumission*. Paris: IMEC, 2008.
Smith, Russell, ed. *Beckett and Ethics*. London: Continuum, 2008.
Stacey, Sarah Alyn. '*Patria non immemor*: Ireland and the Liberation of France'. In *Southern Ireland and the Liberation of France: New Perspectives*, edited by Gerald Morgan and Gavin Hughes, 1–22. Bern: Peter Lang, 2011.
Stonebridge, Lyndsey. *Placeless People: Rights, Writing and Refugees*. Oxford: Oxford University Press, 2018.
Sussman, Henry, and Christopher Devenney, eds. *Engagement and Indifference: Beckett and the Political*. Albany: SUNY Press, 2001.
Tophoven, Erika. *Becketts Berlin*. Berlin: Nicolaische Verlagsbuchhandlung, 2005.
Uhlmann, Anthony. *Beckett and Poststructuralism*. Cambridge: Cambridge University Press, 1999.
Weisberg, David. *Chronicles of Disorder: Samuel Beckett and the Cultural Politics of the Modern Novel*. Albany: SUNY Press, 2000.

Ulin, Julieann. '"Buried! Who would have buried her?": Famine "Ghost Graves" in Samuel Beckett's Endgame'. In *Hungry Words: Images of Famine in the Irish Canon*, edited by George Cusack and Sarah Gross, 197–222. Dublin: Irish Academic Press, 2006.

Wills, Clair. *That Neutral Island: A Cultural History of Ireland during the Second World War*. London: Faber, 2007.

Index